Men in Charge?

Men in Charge?

Rethinking Authority in Muslim Legal Tradition

Edited by Ziba Mir-Hosseini,
Mulki Al-Sharmani and Jana Rumminger

ONEWORLD

A Oneworld Book

First published by Oneworld Publications, 2015

Copyright © Ziba Mir-Hosseini, Mulki Al-Sharmani and Jana Rumminger 2015

ISBN 978-1-78074-716-3
ISBN 978-1-78074-717-0 (eBook)

Typeset by Siliconchips Services Ltd, UK
Printed and bound in Great Britain by TJ International Ltd,
Padstow, Cornwall

Oneworld Publications
10 Bloomsbury Street
London WC1B 3SR
England

Contents

Foreword

This book grew out of a project initiated by Musawah, the global movement for equality and justice in Muslim families. Musawah, which means 'Equality' in Arabic, is led by Muslim women who seek to publicly reclaim and redefine Islam's spirit of justice for all. Initiated in 2007 by Sisters in Islam, the Malaysian women's rights group, Musawah was launched in February 2009 in Kuala Lumpur at a gathering that brought together over 250 women and men, activists, scholars and policymakers from 47 countries, including 32 countries that are members of the Organisation of Islamic Cooperation.

Musawah links scholarship with activism to bring new perspectives on Islamic teachings, with the objective of inserting women's voices and concerns into the production of religious knowledge and legal reform in Muslim contexts. As a knowledge-building movement, Musawah's first project was to rethink the two concepts *qiwamah* and *wilayah*, which are commonly understood in Muslim legal tradition as mandating men's authority over women. These legal concepts shape the ways in which the Muslim family is understood and gender relations are structured, and continue to underpin the discriminatory legal framework that governs family life and women's rights in Muslim law and practice.

The decision to prioritize the issue of *qiwamah* and *wilayah* as Musawah's first feminist knowledge-building project was driven by the urgent need to rethink these discriminatory legal postulates in light of the changing realities of women's lives today. This five-year Knowledge Building Initiative on *Qiwamah* and *Wilayah* brought together scholars trained in different academic fields with Musawah activists and researchers to engage with Muslim legal tradition in a serious, rigorous and critical fashion. These participants offered a range of knowledge and skills related to Muslim legal tradition, feminist methodologies, women's lived realities, and diverse legal systems, which led to rich discussions that explored the possibility and necessity of reform.

The primary objective of the project was to produce new feminist knowledge through rethinking the ideals and realities of the two key legal concepts *qiwamah* and *wilayah* in the context of twenty-first-century understandings of equality and justice. The initiative consisted of three main elements. The first entailed collaboration with scholars to conduct theological, sociological and legal studies of the two concepts within Muslim legal tradition. The second was a participatory Global Life Stories Project with teams of academics and activists in ten countries (Bangladesh, Canada, Egypt, Gambia, Indonesia, Iran, Malaysia, Nigeria, Philippines and the United Kingdom) which undertook documentation and analysis of women's life stories in order to shed light on how *qiwamah-* and *wilayah*-based norms and practices have shaped their experiences. The final element involved opening spaces – such as in-person and electronic discussions and communications – where scholars and activists from different regions could work together to develop new understandings of the two concepts.

This team of scholars and activists met several times to build evidence-based knowledge and progress towards meaningful change in Muslim gender norms. Five main workshops and seminars were held in various places as part of the project: Cairo, Egypt (January 2010); Jakarta, Indonesia (July 2011); Amman, Jordan (November 2011); Bali, Indonesia (April 2012); and Kuala Lumpur, Malaysia (December 2012). These meetings were organized to exchange knowledge, provide critical feedback to the draft scholarly papers, develop the methodology used in the life stories documentation process, and build new understandings and analysis of the life stories. Local scholars and women's rights groups joined the Musawah team in discussions and reflective debates in the cities where the meetings were held.

As founding director of Musawah, I am proud that this initiative, in key aspects of its design and research processes, reflects the Musawah belief that the production and sharing of knowledge must be participatory and interdisciplinary, recognize non-traditional forms of expertise and begin from contexts rather than texts. We believe that in this way the knowledge produced will be grounded in the lived realities of women and men, such realities then informing the approach to the text and the questions to be asked.

Since its launch in 2009, Musawah has gained an international reputation for its groundbreaking holistic approach to knowledge production, public education and law reform to advance the rights of women living in Muslim contexts. It is contributing critically to the new feminist voices in Islam that appeal to the higher objectives of the faith in order to challenge patriarchal interpretations of the *Shari'ah* from within Islamic tradition. Using a holistic framework that integrates Islamic teachings, universal human rights standards, contemporary state constitutions and laws and the lived realities of women and men, it seeks to apply feminist and rights-based approaches to the understanding of equality and justice in Muslim legal tradition. Such approaches help reveal the tension between the egalitarian and hierarchical voices in the tradition and uncover women's voices that have been silenced in the production of religious knowledge so that their concerns can be heard and their interests can be promoted.

We in Musawah would like to record our deepest gratitude to the three coeditors of this book, who were closely involved in all aspects of our Knowledge Building Initiative on *Qiwamah* and *Wilayah*. Ziba Mir-Hosseini, as the convener of the Knowledge Building Working Group, tirelessly and passionately led the conceptualization of the initiative, worked closely with the contributors to this book and nursed it through every stage in order to maintain clarity of mission and concept. Mulki Al-Sharmani and Jana Rumminger, as members of the Knowledge Building Working Group, took responsibility for organizing and implementing the various activities undertaken in this initiative, particularly the process of producing and editing this book. In addition, Mulki Al-Sharmani, as the coordinator of the Global Life Stories Project, led the process of implementing the project in the ten participating countries, guiding and nurturing the teams of researchers based in these countries as they gathered data on women's realities and analysed their findings. Jana Rumminger, as the coordinator of the initiative, held various parts of the work together with her usual meticulousness and dedication, ensuring consistency and precision. In the Musawah Secretariat in Kuala Lumpur, we call them our dream team.

This book, which offers new understandings of *qiwamah* and *wilayah*, will be followed by other outputs from this knowledge-building initiative. They will be made available on the Musawah website (http://www.musawah.org). It is hoped that the new knowledge produced through this project will contribute to reform towards equality and justice for women living in Muslim contexts and build a new Muslim legal framework that regards marriage as a partnership of equals.

Zainah Anwar
Director, Musawah

Acknowledgements

This book arose out of the five-year Musawah Knowledge Building Initiative on *Qiwamah* and *Wilayah*. It would be impossible to bring together an initiative of this scope and nature without assistance and support from all corners of the globe.

Several individuals contributed immensely to the initiative. The late Cassandra Balchin helped us carefully think through its structure and objectives and also developed a legal mapping tool that helps reveal how *qiwamah* is embedded in contemporary laws and practices. Kamala Chandrakirana helped shape the work with her unwavering insistence on starting from lived realities, recognizing multiple forms of expertise and valuing long-term efforts at movement building. Muhammad Khalid Masud has been a steadfast presence in all of Musawah's knowledge-building activities.

Besides writing their chapters and engaging in multiple rounds of feedback, the authors were fully invested in the process; most participated in multiple workshops and discussions that advanced the initiative. Kari Vogt, Christian Moe and Lena Larsen from the Norwegian Centre for Human Rights generously collaborated on workshops and shared scholarship and insights from the programme entitled 'New Directions in Islamic Thought'. Amira El-Azhary Sonbol, Anver Emon, Zahia Jouirou, Adis Duderija and the late Dr Abdul Moty Bayoumi contributed papers and expertise at two early workshops. Numerous Musawah Advocates from different parts of the Muslim world, including Asha Elkarib, Aminetou Mint El Mokhtar, Ratna Osman, Roya Rahmani, Nadia Shamroukh, Azza Soliman and Faeeza Vaid, also contributed ideas and experience at these workshops.

Deena Hurwitz and students in the University of Virginia International Human Rights Law Clinic conducted several research projects on international human rights and *qiwamah*. Cecilia Ng, Marina Durano, Shanthi Thambiah, Wafa Awni Al-Khadra and Hania Sholkamy helped us consider how to include socioeconomic data in the research.

The Global Life Stories Project, which provided a foundation for our understanding of how *qiwamah* and *wilayah* operate in practice, was a major undertaking in itself. We wish to thank Alimat, an Indonesian coalition working to advance gender equality and justice, and its five members who made up the Indonesian pilot project team. In particular, we are thankful to Nur Rofiah, who took the lead in articulating *qiwamah* and *wilayah* as simple, understandable elements, which helped with capacity building throughout the project. We also extend our thanks to the organizations and institutions that took part in the Global Life Stories Project in the ten participating countries. The names of those involved are mentioned in the chapter that reports on the project.

We express our gratitude to a number of organizations and individuals that helped plan the five workshops in Egypt, Jordan, Indonesia and Malaysia: Center for Egyptian Women's Legal Assistance, Jordanian Women's Union, Alimat, Semarak Cernang Nusa, Komnas Perempuan, and Sisters in Islam, and particularly Azza Soliman, Noha Ali, Nur Rofiah, Azida Khalid, Nadia Shamroukh, Reem Abu Hassan, Sawsan Ishaq, Yanti Nurhayati and Adila Aziz.

We also wish to thank Oxfam Novib, the Norwegian Ministry of Foreign Affairs and the Ford Foundation for their generous financial support, and UN Women for early support for the Life Stories pilot project.

We are very indebted to Sisters in Islam, including its members, staff and Board of Directors, who have often taken risks to support Musawah's vision and goals and have consequently facilitated the initiative and outcomes such as this volume. Most of all, we wish to thank Rozana Isa, Adila Aziz, Natasha Dar, Meghana Bahar and Layali Eshqaidef of the Musawah Secretariat and the members of the Musawah International Advisory Group for their continuous feedback and support.

The work of pulling together the manuscript could not have been completed without the sharp editing skills and candid opinions of Richard Tapper and Jason Woodard.

Finally, our thanks to Zainah Anwar, Director of Musawah and founding Executive Director of Sisters in Islam, who has inspired and encouraged us throughout the Musawah journey.

Ziba Mir-Hosseini, Mulki Al-Sharmani and Jana Rumminger
June 2014

Note on Translation and Transliteration

Translation and transliteration are always thorny issues. Most of the authors provided their own translations of Arabic texts; this has been noted in each chapter. For the sake of consistency, the translation of Qur'anic verses and terms follows Abdullah Yusuf Ali, *The Meaning of the Holy Qur'an* (1989), unless otherwise noted.

For transliteration, we have tried to standardize the contributors' varied usages by adapting the *International Journal of Middle Eastern Studies* system, with few diacritical marks. Inconsistencies undoubtedly remain, but readers who are familiar with Arabic should have no trouble recognizing the terms.

Introduction

Ziba Mir-Hosseini, Mulki Al-Sharmani
and Jana Rumminger

M uslim legal tradition does not treat men and women equally. At the root of this discrimination lies the assumption that men are and should be in charge of women, expressed in the concepts of *qiwamah* and *wilayah* that place women under men's guardianship. *Qiwamah* generally denotes a husband's authority over his wife and his financial responsibility towards her. *Wilayah* generally denotes the right and duty of male family members to exercise guardianship over female members (e.g. fathers over daughters when entering into marriage contracts) and grants fathers priority over mothers in guardianship of their children. These two concepts underlie the logic of most contemporary Muslim family laws and are manifested in legal provisions that regulate spousal and parental duties and rights. In some Muslim contexts, the two concepts have also been the basis for placing legal and/or social restrictions on women's participation in the public sphere and their undertaking leadership positions.

As constructed in classical *fiqh* (Islamic jurisprudence) and reflected in present-day laws and practices, these two concepts played and continue to play a central role in institutionalizing, justifying and sustaining gender inequality in Muslim contexts. Behind these laws and practices lies an ancient idea: men are strong, they protect and provide; women are weak, they obey and must be protected.

Qur'anic verse 4:34[1] is often invoked as the textual basis for the assumed normativity of male authority and hierarchical gender relations. The concept of *qiwamah* – the term itself does not appear in the Qur'an – is derived from the term *qawwamun* (translated as 'protectors and maintainers') in the above-mentioned verse (see Abou-Bakr in this volume). The root *qama* can have many meanings in Arabic, such as 'stand up', 'comply', 'proceed', 'provide for', 'revolt', 'endure', 'lift up'. Terms based on the root *qama* occur in the Qur'an only two other times, in verses 4:135 and 5:8, where *kunu qawwamin* is commonly understood to mean 'stand out firmly' (see Lamrabet in this volume).

The second term, *wilayah*, does occur in the Qur'an, but not in a sense that endorses men's authority over women.[2] Yet this is the interpretation of the term enshrined in juristic rulings on marriage.

In relation to marriage and relations between spouses, however, other terms appear several times: *ma'ruf* (common good) and *mawaddah wa rahmah* (love and compassion). Why did the classical jurists not choose to translate these two terms into legal rulings? Why and how did verse 4:34, and not other relevant Qur'anic verses, become the foundation for the legal construction of marriage? How, and through what juristic processes, was men's authority over women legitimated and translated into laws? What does male guardianship, as translated in the concepts *qiwamah* and *wilayah*, entail in practice? Why are these two concepts still the basis of gender relations in the imagination of those modern-day jurists and Muslims who resist and denounce the notion of equality in marriage as alien to Islam? How can we rethink and reconstruct them in ways that can accommodate gender equality? In other words, how can

---

[1] The verse reads, 'Men are the protectors and maintainers of women, because Allah has given the one more [strength] than the other, and because they support them from their means. Therefore the righteous women are devoutly obedient, and guard in [the husband's] absence what Allah would have them guard. As to those women on whose part ye fear disloyalty and ill-conduct, admonish them [first], [Next], refuse to share their beds, [And last] beat them [lightly]; but if they return to obedience, seek not against them means [of annoyance]: For Allah is Most High, great [above you all].'

[2] The word *wilayah* itself appears in verse 18:44, where it refers to God's protection of humans, and in verse 8:72, where it refers to the parameters of protection that early Muslims in Mecca and Medina owed one another in their pursuit of safety from persecution and the right to worship. Words related to *wilayah* such as *wali* and its plural *awliya'* appear in many verses as an attribute of God or to describe human beings in particular contexts and stories in the Qur'an. But none of the verses on which the jurists based the doctrine of *wilayah* in regard to marriage guardianship (2:221, 2:232, 2:234, 2:237, 4:2, 4:3, 4:6, 4:25, 24:32, 60:10, 65:4) uses the term *wali* or *wilayah*. For more on *wilayah*, see Masud (2013, pp. 132–3).

we argue for an egalitarian construction of family laws from within Muslim legal tradition?

These questions are central to the ongoing struggle for equality and justice in Muslim families. This book is a contribution to that struggle and suggests answers to some of the questions, telling us why and how male dominance came to be entangled within Muslim legal tradition, showing how it is produced and sustained in contemporary times and indicating paths to gender equality and justice from within the tradition.

The book's main thesis is that the concepts of *qiwamah* and *wilayah* have mistakenly been understood as placing women under men's authority, with the result that they have become the building blocks of patriarchy within Muslim legal tradition. Those who seek to establish an egalitarian construction of gender rights in Muslim contexts must rethink and reconstruct these concepts and the readings of Islam's sacred texts on which they are based.

NEW KNOWLEDGE AND ENGAGEMENT WITH TRADITION

Patriarchy and gender inequality are not unique to Muslim contexts (Lerner, 1986). Nor are Muslim women a homogeneous group with uniform challenges. Extensive literature documents the complex and multi-layered inequalities that women in different Muslim contexts confront, and which are not reducible to religion (e.g. Kandiyoti, 1991; Joseph, 1996; Bodman and Tohidi, 1998). But it remains true and relevant that legal discrimination against women in many Muslim societies is traceable to state codes that draw on Islamic jurisprudence such as family laws (Mir-Hosseini, 1993; Sonbol, 1996; Welchman, 2004; Tucker, 2008). The power of juristic doctrines in shaping Muslim gender norms is not limited to codified family laws, but is also reflected in systems of uncodified religious rulings and interpretations that Muslim communities throughout the world, whether in majority or minority contexts, live by and use to organize their family life and relations (Quraishi and Syeed-Miller, 2004; Fournier, 2010; Menski, 2011; Hammer, 2013).

The most pervasive gender-based legal inequalities that confront Muslim women relate to spousal and parental roles and rights. In many Muslim family codes, men can unilaterally repudiate their wives, take four wives, have legal claim to their wives' obedience (translated as wives' residence in and sometimes confinement to the matrimonial home and consent to sexual relations with husbands) and have sole guardianship over children. Women's access to divorce is usually restricted; they often cannot have guardianship of their children; and their claim to spousal maintenance is often contingent on their 'obedience' to their husbands.

In the last few decades, numerous scholars have specifically tackled patriarchal interpretations and text-based sources of gender inequalities in Muslim legal tradition.[3] This emerging field of knowledge has often been termed and contested as 'Islamic feminism'.[4] In particular, many have focused on verse 4:34.[5] Most of this literature, however, has dealt with the second part of the verse and the notion of *nushuz* (disobedience) and whether husbands are allowed to beat their wives as a form of spousal disciplining.

In recent years, critics have attempted to identify epistemological and methodological gaps in Islamic feminism as a field of knowledge (Rhouni, 2010; Seedat, 2013b; Hidayatullah, 2014). Others have developed and built on this area of knowledge, particularly in its methodology and epistemological insights (Mir-Hosseini et al., 2013; Abou-Bakr, 2013; Aslan et al., 2013). In the spirit of the latter, this book seeks to develop feminist knowledge that is grounded in Muslim tradition while engaging critically with it.

The contributors, scholars from different disciplines and backgrounds, came together in a Musawah research initiative to address a lacuna in the debates over family law reforms and approaches to women's rights in Muslim contexts. On the one hand, a large majority of Muslim religious scholars are gender blind; they are unaware of feminist theories and the importance of gender as a category of thought. On the other hand, many women's rights activists and campaigners in Muslim contexts, in line with mainstream feminism, have long considered engagement with religious ideas and practitioners to be counter-productive; they want to work only within a human rights framework and avoid any religion-based arguments. But the epistemological heritage of feminism, alongside its denotation as a consciousness, can enable

---

[3] See, for example, al-Hibri (1982), Hassan (1987), Mernissi (1991), Wadud (1999; 2006), Webb (2000), Barlas (2002), Mir-Hosseini (2003), Shaikh (2004), Abou-Bakr (2004), Ali (2006; 2010) and Lamrabet (2007; 2012).

[4] See, for example, Abou-Bakr (2001), Mir-Hosseini (2006; 2011), Tohidi (2007), Barlas (2008), Badran (2009; 2011), Moll (2009), Vanzan (2010), Sholkamy (2010), Ali (2012) and Seedat (2013a).

[5] A representative, but not comprehensive, list of such works includes Shaikh (1997), al-Faruqi (2000), Abou El Fadl (2001), Mubarak (2004), Bauer (2006), Ali (2006), Mahmoud (2006), Silvers (2006), Scott (2009) and Chaudhry (2013).

us to understand what we know about women and gender in all branches of knowledge, including religious thought.

The contributors use their expert knowledge and skills to challenge, rethink and redefine the main concepts that sustain the patriarchal assumptions and biases that are institutionalized in Muslim legal tradition. Different contributors trace how the concepts *qiwamah* and *wilayah* originated and have been used in the tradition and in contemporary laws; shed light on the ways in which these two concepts lie at the root of legal discrimination against Muslim women; and unpack the underlying premises of the concepts and the discourse and doctrines that they have produced.

Our aim is to demystify these concepts and reinterpret them through feminist knowledge that is grounded in Muslim legal tradition and its core theological and ethical principles. We seek to facilitate a systematic and reflective conversation between this tradition and Muslim feminism – a conversation that can inform general awareness, change policy and reform laws in the quest for Muslim gender justice. We believe this conversation so far has been haphazard. Through the multidisciplinary studies of *qiwamah* and *wilayah* that are presented in this volume, the contributors bring to this conversation their insights about interlinked aspects of the textual and legal bases of Muslim gender inequality, and what reflects and sustains this inequality in public discourses and social practices. We provide alternative understandings of the two concepts, drawing on Qur'anic ethics and principles, Sufi concepts that are central to the theological principles guiding God–human relations, and a holistic feminist approach that links Muslim tradition to modern forms of knowledge, such as theories of knowledge, justice and equality, as well as feminist methodologies. Above all, we ground these understandings in lived realities and women's experiences.

OVERVIEW OF CHAPTERS

The book comprises ten chapters that build on and communicate with one another. In the first chapter, 'Muslim Legal Tradition and the Challenge of Gender Equality', Ziba Mir-Hosseini sets the stage by discussing why this multi-dimensional new knowledge about *qiwamah* and *wilayah* is a necessary political and epistemological project for Muslim feminists who engage with religion in their quest for gender equality and justice. She frames the project in the context of the twentieth-century shifts, both global and local, in the politics of religion and relations between Muslim legal tradition, the state and social practice. She maps out how the idea of gender equality emerged as a challenge to Muslim legal tradition, and then sheds light on the efforts that have been underway since the early twentieth century to produce new knowledge about the notions of gender equality and justice in Islamic legal thought. She details the methodologies of three important reform thinkers (Tahir al-Haddad, Fazlur Rahman and Nasr Abu Zayd) whose texts appeared at significant moments in the century: codification, the rise of political Islam and the rise of Islamic feminism. Her chapter shows links between the democratization of the production of knowledge, and ways in which the struggle for egalitarian family laws in Muslim contexts is embedded in the larger struggle for social justice and democracy.

The next set of chapters examines how particular passages in Islam's sacred texts have become the basis for gender inequality in Muslim legal tradition. In 'The Interpretive Legacy of *Qiwamah* as an Exegetical Construct', Omaima Abou-Bakr traces the development of ideas of male authority and superiority through the treatment of the concept of *qiwamah* in exegetical literature (*tafsir*). Applying a genealogical reading to interpretations of verse 4:34, she shows how *qiwamah* became constructed as a juristic concept that in turn shapes hierarchal gender rights in the family domain and affirms male authority and superiority versus female dependence and inferiority. She documents the significant changes in understandings of verse 4:34, from the classical exegete al-Tabari in the tenth century to modernists such as Muhammad 'Abduh. She also reviews some of the main interpretive approaches adopted by a number of contemporary reformist scholars to provide alternative readings of the verse and the notion of male authority.

In 'An Egalitarian Reading of the Concepts of *Khilafah*, *Wilayah* and *Qiwamah*', Asma Lamrabet sets out to unearth the core ethical values that underlie the Qur'anic message and to recover the Qur'anic meaning of *qiwamah*. She draws a sharp distinction between, on the one hand, the positive and empowering meanings of the terms *qiwamah* and *wilayah* in the Qur'an and, on the other, the gendered hierarchical meanings with which the two concepts have become imbued in Islamic jurisprudence (*fiqh*) and in exegesis (*tafsir*). By returning to their original meanings and linking them to another key Qur'anic concept, *istikhlaf* (equality in building human civilization), she frees both concepts from their patriarchal baggage. Her analysis of the three concepts and their relation to one another shows that, rather than denoting male authority and superiority, *qiwamah* and *wilayah* are part of the Qur'an's core message to all human beings, regardless of gender, race or class, to assume the responsibility of building human civilization, doing good and forbidding evil, and realizing justice in both public and private spheres.

In 'Producing Gender Egalitarian Islamic Law: A Case Study of Guardianship (*Wilayah*) in Prophetic Practice', Ayesha Chaudhry builds on Lamrabet's quest for the alternatives in the tradition by shedding light on new readings of *ahadith* (prophetic reports) concerned with marriage and consent that provide trajectories for egalitarian gender rights. She examines selected *ahadith* on *wilayah* in regard to women's consent and marriage. She considers both the challenges and the opportunities presented by each *hadith* to Muslim feminists who are committed to recovering the Prophet Muhammad's example in establishing an egalitarian vision of marriage. Chaudhry sheds light on prophetic messages and acts that interrupt patriarchy and reflect concern for women as full human beings.

In the final chapter of this section, 'Islamic Law, Sufism and Gender: Rethinking the Terms of the Debate', Sa'diyya Shaikh explores how Sufi thought, and in particular a number of core concepts related to the God–human relationship and human beings' spiritual calling on this earth, can provide a corrective to juristic constructions of gender relations and rights. She examines two Sufi concepts and shows how they can provide a basis for rethinking Muslim juristic tradition on gender. The first concept is the notion that 'every human being has the ability and responsibility to strive towards and realize the same ultimate goals, and gender is irrelevant to the realization of such existential goals'. She explains that this Sufi concept can provide us with a theological and ethical basis for resisting patriarchy. She draws on the work of the thirteenth-century Sufi thinker Ibn al-Arabi for the second concept, the Sufi notion of the relationship between human nature and God and the human state of complete spiritual realization (*al-Insan al-Kamil*) as a reflection of refined divine attributes. She shows that commitment to spiritual advancement as part of seeking the path of a closer God–human relationship, which is incumbent on men and women, can be the basis for egalitarian gender relations and roles. By bringing Sufi perspectives to debates on gender in Islamic law, she draws attention to how Muslim feminists can create spaces from which they can rethink the formulation of the *fiqh* canon in light of the 'deepest existential and religious priorities in Islam'.

The next four chapters are case studies that show how male authority is manifested, negotiated and bypassed in contemporary laws and practices. In '*Qiwamah* and *Wilayah* as Legal Postulates in Muslim Family Laws', Lynn

Welchman examines how current Muslim family laws have included or discarded the concepts of *qiwamah* and *wilayah* as legal postulates that shape the ways in which the concept of the Muslim family is understood and family relations are structured. Focusing on Arab Muslim family laws, she shows how countries have taken varying steps in reforming areas of family laws that are most shaped by the two concepts, namely spousal maintenance, wifely obedience, divorce, parental guardianship and custody of children. She pays special attention to the Moroccan and United Arab Emirates (UAE) state codes as two case studies that present opposite ends of a continuum of approaches to reform. She concludes that the scope and nature of reforms in family laws depend on multiple factors such as political will, effective and sustained advocacy and an enabling societal environment.

In 'Islamic Law Meets Human Rights: Reformulating *Qiwamah* and *Wilayah* for Personal Status Law Reform Advocacy in Egypt', Marwa Sharafeldin takes the reader through a case study of how Egyptian activists have grappled with Islamic law and human rights norms as they have sought to reform the country's personal status laws in light of problems arising from the lived realities of women. She investigates the complexities involved when non-governmental organizations (NGOs) attempt to develop and promote new understandings of *qiwamah* and *wilayah* in contemporary Muslim family laws. Through analysis of extensive field data on the advocacy efforts of a network of Egyptian NGOs that mobilized to reform the personal status law in the period 2007–10, she examines how the activists understood and navigated Islamic law and human rights norms and formulated propositions and arguments that cannot be neatly classified as egalitarian or as patriarchal and discriminatory. She also probes the multiple factors that shaped the interpretive process undertaken by the activists as they developed their understandings of *qiwamah* and *wilayah*. The most significant of these factors are the problems women face in their lives, as well as the personal beliefs, relationships and engagements that individual activists have with their own religious tradition.

In '"Men are the Protectors and Maintainers of Women...": Three Fatwas on Spousal Roles and Rights', Lena Larsen explores how practising European Muslims and religious actors, namely muftis, deal with the shifting realities of spousal roles in Muslim families, in which wives are increasingly shouldering the responsibility of providing for their families. Larsen examines selected fatwas issued by the renowned mufti Syed ad-Darsh and the European Council for Fatwa and Research that tackle the issues of spousal maintenance, *qiwamah* and women's new economic roles in the family. She shows how muftis, in light of the new realities of Muslim families, arrive at nuanced understandings of *qiwamah* that still maintain the husband's obligation to provide if he is able to, but also leave room to reinterpret the husband's role as encompassing a diverse range of care responsibilities, and to encourage (though not obligate) working women to help provide for their families. These fatwas reflect the complex process through which muftis try to strike a balance between a number of challenges: to issue fatwas that are responsive to the new realities of Muslim families; to balance the interests of the petitioners and the need to maintain the harmony of familial relations; and not to go beyond the boundaries of mainstream transnational Islamic religious discourse, which still maintains hierarchical gender norms.

In 'Understanding *Qiwamah* and *Wilayah* through Life Stories', Mulki Al-Sharmani and Jana Rumminger report on Musawah's Global Life Stories Project and seek to show why it is methodologically important to revisit *qiwamah* and *wilayah* in terms of how women experience the two concepts as they are manifested in laws, policies and gender norms. The Global Life Stories Project, part of the Musawah Knowledge Building Initiative on *Qiwamah* and *Wilayah*, documented and analysed the life stories of fifty-eight Muslim women in ten countries (Bangladesh, Canada, Egypt, Gambia, Indonesia, Iran, Malaysia, Nigeria, Philippines and the United Kingdom). The authors describe the methodology that was developed and used in the project and explain how this process was guided by Islamic ethics and feminist research principles. They discuss some of the initial key findings, focusing on the striking disconnect between the juristic and legal construction of gender roles and the lived realities of many Muslim women. Many women play active economic roles in their families and do not receive the protection and sustenance they are promised by the legal postulates of *qiwamah* and *wilayah*. Yet women's economic contributions to their households do not necessarily lead to egalitarian gender relations. The findings also highlight the shifts and developments that have taken place in women's self-knowledge and relations vis-à-vis normative systems and Muslim legal tradition. Finally, the authors reflect on the layered significance of the project as well as the challenges encountered.

'The Ethics of *Tawhid* over the Ethics of *Qiwamah*', which serves as a conclusion, is a first-person account by the prominent theologian Amina Wadud of her personal and intellectual trajectory of grappling with the concept of male authority and gender inequality as articulated in dominant classical and contemporary readings of verse 4:34 and the legal and social norms that have been based on these interpretations. Her analysis draws on her understandings and perspectives on these issues and certain events that she has witnessed in her life journey. She also reflects on how her thinking about these issues has developed. She then proposes and explains the 'tawhidic paradigm' as 'a way to reach the goal of a society that is built on Islamic ethics' and to overcome 'the injustice that *qiwamah* entails in our time and in many Muslim contexts'.

The chapters in this volume engage critically with *qiwamah* and *wilayah*, two core concepts around which the edifice of gender inequality in Muslim legal tradition is constructed. They problematize dominant exegetical and juristic understandings of *qiwamah* and *wilayah*; unearth alternative and empowering interpretations of the two concepts in the Qur'an and *Sunnah*; propose ethical and just alternatives to traditional juristic constructions of gender relations and rights; map ways in which contemporary Muslim family codes are premised on the two concepts or have been reformed to align more closely with conceptions of justice in which gender equality is inherent; and shed light on how Muslim women in selected countries experience and negotiate religious interpretations, social norms and laws that are informed by *qiwamah* and *wilayah*. Read as a whole, this volume presents new knowledge and ideas that make a compelling case for gender equality and justice from an Islamic perspective.

REFERENCES

Abou-Bakr, Omaima. 2001. 'Islamic Feminism? What's in a Name? Preliminary Reflections'. *Middle East Women's Studies Review* 15–16: pp. 1–2.

Abou-Bakr, Omaima. 2004. 'Surat al-Rajul fi al-Kitabat al-Islamiyah: Bayn al-Tafasir al-Qadima wa al-Haditha'. In *A'isha Taymur: Tahaddiyat al-Thabit wa-al-Mutaghayyir fi al-Qarn al-Tasi' 'Ashar*, edited by Hoda Elsadda, pp. 144–68. Cairo: Women & Memory Forum.

Abou-Bakr, Omaima (ed.). 2013. *Feminist and Islamic Perspectives; New Horizons of Knowledge and Reform*. Cairo: Women and Memory Forum with the Danish–Egyptian Dialogue Institute and the Danish Center for Research on Women and Gender.

Abou El Fadl, Khaled. 2001. *The Search for Beauty in Islam: A Conference of the Books*. Oxford: Rowman & Littlefield.

Al-Faruqi, Maysam. 2000. 'Women's Self-Identity in the Qur'an and Islamic Law'. In *Windows of Faith: Muslim Women Scholar Activists in North America*, edited by Gisela Webb, pp. 72–101. Syracuse, NY: Syracuse University Press.

Al-Hibri, Azizah. 1982. 'A Study of Islamic Herstory: Or How Did We Ever Get into This Mess'. *Women's Studies International Forum* 5 (2): pp. 207–19.

Ali, Kecia. 2006. *Sexual Ethics and Islam: Feminist Reflections on Qur'an, Hadith, and Jurisprudence*. Oxford: Oneworld.

Ali, Kecia. 2010. *Marriage and Slavery in Early Islam*. Cambridge: Harvard University Press.

Ali, Zahra. 2012. *Féminismes Islamiques*. Paris: La Fabrique.

Aslan, Ednan, Marcia Hermansen and Elif Medeni (eds). 2013. *Muslima Theology: The Voices of Muslim Women Theologians*. Frankfurt: Peter Lang.

Badran, Margot. 2009. *Feminism in Islam: Secular and Religious Convergences*. Oxford: Oneworld.

Badran, Margot. 2011. 'From Islamic Feminism to a Muslim Holistic Feminism'. *Institute of Development Studies Bulletin* 42 (1): pp. 78–87.

Barlas, Asma. 2002. *Believing Women in Islam: Unreading Patriarchal Interpretations of the Qur'an*. Austin: University of Texas Press.

Barlas, Asma. 2008. 'Engaging Islamic Feminism: Provincializing Feminism as Master Narrative'. In *Islamic Feminism: Current Perspectives*, edited by Anitta Kynsilehto, pp. 15–24. Tampere: Tampere Peace Research Institute.

Bauer, Karen. 2006. '"Traditional" Exegesis of Q 4:34'. *Comparative Islamic Studies* 2 (2): pp. 129–42.

Bodman, Herbert and Nayereh Tohidi (eds). 1998. *Women in Muslim Societies: Diversity within Unity*. Boulder, CO: Lynne Rienner.

Chaudhry, Ayesha S. 2013. *Domestic Violence and the Islamic Tradition: Ethics, Law, and the Muslim Discourse on Gender*. Oxford: Oxford University Press.

Fournier, Pascal. 2010. *Muslim Marriages in Western Courts*. Williston, VT: Ashgate.

Hammer, Juliane. 2013. '"Men are the Protectors of Women": Negotiating Marriage, Feminism, and (Islamic) Law in American Muslim Efforts against Domestic Violence'. In *Feminism, Law, and Religion*, edited by Marie A. Failinger, Elizabeth R. Schiltz and Susan J. Stabile, pp. 237–56. Farnham, UK: Ashgate.

Hassan, Riffat. 1987. 'Equal Before Allah? Woman–Man Equality in the Islamic Tradition'. *Harvard Divinity Bulletin* 7 (2): pp. 26–9.

Hidayatullah, Aysha A. 2014. *Feminist Edges of the Qur'an*. Oxford: Oxford University Press.

Joseph, Suad. 1996. 'Patriarchy and Development in the Arab World'. *Gender and Development* 4 (6): pp. 14–19.

Kandiyoti, Deniz (ed.). 1991. *Women, Islam, and the State*. London: Macmillan.

Lamrabet, Asma. 2007. *Le Coran et les Femmes. Une Lecture de Libération*. Lyons: Tawhid.

Lamrabet, Asma. 2012. *Femmes et Hommes dans le Coran: Quelle Égalité?* Paris: Albourag.

Lerner, Gerda. 1986. *The Creation of Patriarchy*. Oxford: Oxford University Press.

Mahmoud, Mohamed. 2006. 'To Beat or Not to Beat: On the Exegetical Dilemmas over Qur'an, 4:34'. *Journal of the American Oriental Society* 126 (4): pp. 537–50.

Masud, Muhammad Khalid. 2013. 'Gender Equality and the Doctrine of Wilaya'. In *Gender and Equality in Muslim Family Law: Justice and Ethics in the Islamic Legal Tradition*, edited by Ziba Mir-Hosseini, Kari Vogt, Lena Larsen and Christian Moe, pp. 127–54. London: I.B. Tauris.

Menski, Werner. 2011. 'Islamic Law in British Courts: Do We Not Know or Do We Not Want to Know?' In *The Place of Religion in Family Law: A Comparative Search*, edited by Jane Mair and Esin Örücü, pp. 15–36. Mortsel, Belgium: Intersentia.

Mernissi, Fatima. 1991. *The Veil and the Male Elite: A Feminist Interpretation of Women's Rights in Islam*. New York: Basic Books.

Mir-Hosseini, Ziba. 1993. *Marriage on Trial: A Study of Islamic Family Law, Iran and Morocco Compared*. London: I.B. Tauris.

Mir-Hosseini, Ziba. 2003. 'The Construction of Gender in Islamic Legal Thought and Strategies for Reform'. *Hawwa* 1 (1): pp. 1–28.

Mir-Hosseini, Ziba. 2006. 'Muslim Women's Quest for Equality: Between Islamic Law and Feminism'. *Critical Inquiry* 32 (4): pp. 629–45.

Mir-Hosseini, Ziba. 2011. 'Beyond Islam vs. Feminism'. *Institute of Development Studies Bulletin* 42 (1): pp. 67–77.

Mir-Hosseini, Ziba, Kari Vogt, Lena Larsen and Christian Moe (eds). 2013. *Gender and Equality in Muslim Family Law: Justice and Ethics in the Islamic Legal Tradition*. London: I.B. Tauris.

Moll, Yasmin. 2009. '"People Like Us" in Pursuit of God and Rights: Islamic Feminist Discourse and Sisters in Islam in Malaysia'. *Journal of International Women's Studies* 11 (1): pp. 40–55.

Mubarak, Hadia. 2004. 'Breaking the Interpretative Monopoly: A Re-examination of Verse 4:34'. *Hawwa* 2 (3): pp. 261–89.

Quraishi, Asifa and Najeeba Syeed-Miller. 2004. 'No Altars: A Survey of Islamic Family Law in the United States'. In *Women's Rights and Islamic Law*, edited by Lynn Welchman, pp. 179–219. New York: Zed Books.

Rhouni, Raja. 2010. *Secular and Islamic Feminist Critique in the Work of Fatima Mernissi*. Boston: Brill.

Scott, Rachel M. 2009. 'A Contextual Women's Rights in the Qur'an: Readings of 4:34'. *Muslim World* 99 (1): pp. 60–85.

Seedat, Fatima. 2013a. 'When Islam and Feminism Converge'. *Muslim World* 103 (3): pp. 404–20.

Seedat, Fatima. 2013b. 'Islam, Feminism, and Islamic Feminism: Between Inadequacy and Inevitability'. *Journal of Feminist Studies in Religion* 29 (2): pp. 25–45.

Shaikh, Sa'diyya. 1997. 'Exegetical Violence: Nushuz in Qur'anic Gender Ideology'. *Journal for Islamic Studies* 17: pp. 49–73.

Shaikh, Sa'diyya. 2004. 'Knowledge, Women, and Gender in Hadith: A Feminist Interpretation'. *Islam and Christian–Muslim Relations* 15 (1): pp. 99–108.

Sholkamy, Hania (ed.). 2010. 'Islam and Feminism'. In *Contestations* 1: http://www.contestations.net/wp-content/uploads/2010/10/contestations1.pdf

Silvers, Laury. 2006. '"In the Book We Have Left out Nothing": The Ethical Problem of the Existence of Verse 4:34 in the Qur'an'. *Comparative Islamic Studies* 2 (2): pp. 171–80.

Sonbol, Amira El-Azhary (ed.). 1996. *Women, the Family and Divorce Laws in Islamic History*. Syracuse, NY: Syracuse University Press.

Tohidi, Nayereh. 2007. 'Muslim Feminism and Islamic Reformation: The Case of Iran'. In *Feminist Theologies: Legacy and Prospect*, edited by Rosemary Radford Ruether, pp. 93–116. Minneapolis: Fortress Press.

Tucker, Judith. 2008. *Women, Family, and Gender in Islamic Law*. Cambridge, UK: Cambridge University Press.

Vanzan, Anna. 2010. *Le Donne di Allah: Viggio Nei Feminismi Islamici*. Milan: Mondadori Bruno.

Wadud, Amina. 1999. *Qur'an and Woman: Rereading the Text from a Woman's Perspective*. Oxford: Oxford University Press.

Wadud, Amina. 2006. *Inside the Gender Jihad: Women's Reform in Islam*. Oxford: Oneworld.

Webb, Gisela (ed.). 2000. *Windows of Faith: Muslim Women Scholar-Activists in North America*. Syracuse, NY: Syracuse University Press.

Welchman, Lynn (ed.). 2004. *Women's Rights and Islamic Law*. London: Zed Books.

Muslim Legal Tradition and the Challenge of Gender Equality*

Ziba Mir-Hosseini

T he twentieth century saw a proliferation of debates among Muslims on the theme of 'the status of women in Islam'. Much of the argument was apologetic – a defence against modernists' criticisms of the discriminatory family laws and unequal gender relations that were understood to be justified by Islamic texts and Muslim legal tradition.[1] Muslim women advocates of equality between men and women in law, let alone in social or political life, were late to find a voice, though only marginally later than their counterparts among non-Muslims.

In this chapter, I trace the story of how the idea of gender equality emerged as a challenge to Muslim legal tradition during the twentieth century. The rise of nation states and of the modern concept of citizenship in Muslim contexts in the early part of the century brought the beginnings of developments, such as the growth of literacy among both men and women and the rapid growth of mass media, which radically, and at an accelerating speed, changed the way in which knowledge was produced and distributed. Major transformations in the politics of religion, law and gender in Muslim contexts accompanied a sharpening confrontation between two notions of justice and two modes

---

* This chapter develops the treatment of the subject in Mir-Hosseini (2013).
[1] For an overview of these arguments, see Stowasser (1993), Ali (2003), Mir-Hosseini (2007) and Duderija (2011).

of knowledge production. The pre-modern ideas that informed Muslim legal tradition encountered modern ideals of universal human rights, equality and personal freedom. Laws and practices that supported male authority over women, once considered natural and common sense, came to be seen as unjust and discriminatory. Established patriarchal interpretations of the *Shari'ah* have been strongly challenged, and the textual sources that supported them have been criticized as hypocritical, or at best contradictory.

I begin by outlining the notion of male authority as constructed by classical jurists, which continues to be reflected in contemporary Muslim family laws. I then explore the endeavour that has been underway since the early twentieth century to produce new and transformative knowledge about the notions of gender equality and justice in Islamic legal thought. I focus on three texts by reform thinkers that appeared at significant moments in the history of family law reforms, which together offer a framework and a methodology for reinterpreting Islam's sacred texts relating to family and gender relations. I do this against a background of the shifts in the politics of religion, law and gender in Muslim contexts since the early twentieth century that led, by the end of the century, to the emergence of feminist voices and scholarship in Islam. I end with the implications of these developments for the project of constructing egalitarian family laws from within an Islamic framework.

MALE AUTHORITY AS A LEGAL POSTULATE

At the heart of the unequal construction of gender rights in Muslim legal tradition is the idea that God has given men authority over women. Defenders of male authority frequently invoke, as their main textual justification, Qur'anic verse 4:34, from which classical jurists derived the concept of *qiwamah*, developing it into a guiding principle to define and regulate gender relations. Thus we should start with this verse and the ways in which it has been interpreted and translated into legal rulings. It reads,

Men are *qawwamun* [protectors/maintainers] in relation to women, according to what God has favored some over others and according to what they spend from their wealth. Righteous women are *qanitat* [obedient], guarding the unseen according to what God has guarded. Those [women] whose *nushuz* [rebellion] you fear, admonish them, and abandon them in bed, and *adribuhunna* [strike them]. If they obey you, do not pursue a strategy against them. Indeed, God is Exalted, Great.

Kecia Ali, from whom I have taken this translation, leaves the italicized words untranslated, pointing out that any translation of each of these key terms amounts to an interpretation (Ali, n.d.). I have inserted translations that approximate the consensus of classical Muslim jurists and are reflected in a set of rulings (*ahkam*) that they devised to define marriage and marital relations. These rulings rest on a single postulate: that God made men *qawwamun* over women and placed them under male authority. For these jurists, men's superiority and authority over women was a given, legally inviolable; it was in accordance with a conception of justice that accepted slavery and patriarchy, as long as slaves and women were treated fairly. They naturally understood the verse in this light; they used the four key terms in the verse to define relations between spouses, and notions of justice and equity.

This is what Lynn Welchman (2011, p. 7) refers to as the *qiwamah* postulate – using 'postulate' in the sense defined by Masaji Chiba (1986, p. 7): 'A value system that simply exists in its own right'. It operates in all areas of Muslim law relating to gender rights, but its impact is most evident in the laws that classical jurists devised for the regulation of marriage and divorce. Welchman's chapter in this volume illustrates how the postulate works in contemporary family laws.

I have discussed elsewhere the legal structure of marriage in classical *fiqh* or jurisprudence (Mir-Hosseini, 2003; 2007; 2012); here I merely outline its salient features. The jurists defined marriage as a contract of exchange and patterned it on the contract of sale (*bay'*), which served as a model for most contracts in *fiqh*. The contract, called '*aqd al-nikah* (the contract of coitus), has three essential elements: *ijab*, the offer made by the woman or her guardian; *qubul*, acceptance by the husband; and *mahr*, a gift from the husband to the person of the bride. The contract establishes a set of default rights and obligations for each party, some supported by legal force, others by moral sanction. Those with legal force revolve around the themes of sexual access and compensation, as expressed in two central legal concepts: *tamkin* (also *ta'a*) and *nafaqah*. *Tamkin*, obedience or submission, specifically sexual access, becomes the husband's right and thus the wife's duty; whereas *nafaqah*, maintenance, specifically shelter, food and clothing, becomes the wife's right and the husband's duty. But if a wife is in a state of *nushuz* (disobedience) she loses her claim to maintenance.[2] Whereas the husband has the unilateral and extra-judicial right to terminate the contract by *talaq* or repudiation, a wife can only terminate the contract with her husband's consent or the intervention of the court – if she produces a valid reason.[3]

There were, of course, differences between and within the classical schools over the meanings of these three interrelated concepts – *nafaqah*, *tamkin* and *nushuz* – but they all shared the same conception of marriage, and the large majority made a woman's right to maintenance dependent on her obedience to her husband. They disagreed, Ibn Rushd (1996) tells us, over 'whether maintenance is a counter-value for (sexual) utilization, or compensation for the fact that she is confined because of her husband, as in the case of one absent or sick' (p. 63). And it was within the parameters of this logic – men provide and women obey – that notions of gender rights and justice acquired their meanings.

This is not to deny that classical jurists were concerned with women's rights or their welfare; they did their best to protect women against a husband's potential abuse by narrowing the scope of his authority to the unrestricted right to sexual relations with his wife. This in turn limited a wife's duty of obedience to her sexual availability, and only when it did not interfere with her religious duties (for example, when fasting during Ramadan, or when bleeding during menses or after childbirth). Legally speaking, if we take the classical *fiqh* texts at face value, according to some of them a wife had no obligation to do housework or to care for the children, even to suckle her babies; if she did these, she could demand 'wages'. Likewise, a man's right to discipline a wife who was in a state of *nushuz* was severely restricted; he could discipline her, but not inflict harm. For this reason, some jurists recommended that he should 'strike' his wife only with a handkerchief or a *miswak*, a twig used for cleaning teeth (Mahmoud, 2006, footnote 35). But they made no attempt to limit a man's right to *talaq* (unilateral divorce), although there are numerous moral injunctions that could have enabled them to do so. For instance, there are sayings of the Prophet to the effect that *talaq* is among the most detested of permitted acts and that when a man pronounces it God's throne shakes. In its legal structure, *talaq*, unlike marriage, was defined as a unilateral act that needed neither grounds nor the consent of the wife.

---

[2] For a concise discussion of *nushuz* in Islamic discourses, see Ali (2007).
[3] For further discussions of how early jurists conceptualized marriage, see Rapoport (2005) and Ali (2010).

Whether these rulings reflect the Qur'anic conception of marriage or corresponded to actual practices of marriage and gender relations is another area of enquiry that recent scholarship in Islam has started to uncover. Studies on courtroom practices give us a much more complex picture of marital relations and court practices in pre-modern times (Rapoport, 2005; Sonbol, 1996; Tucker, 2000), while those which examined the Qur'anic concept of marriage show the theological error in the very idea that God has given men authority over women (Hassan, 1987; 1999; Wadud, 1999; 2006; Barlas, 2002; al-Hibri, 1982; 2003). Five chapters in this volume (Abou-Bakr, Chaudhry, Lamrabet, Shaikh and Wadud) give us very cogent arguments and convincing textual evidence to this effect and offer alternative egalitarian interpretations of Islam's sacred texts.

I suggest that the juristic construct of *qiwamah*, developed in the context of the marriage contract, provided the rationale for other legal disparities, such as men's rights to polygamy and to unilateral repudiation, women's lesser share in inheritance, and the ban on women being judges or political leaders. That is to say, women were not qualified to occupy positions that entailed the exercise of authority in society because they were under their husband's authority and not free agents and they would thus be unable to deliver impartial justice. Similarly, since men provided for women, women's lesser share of inheritance was just. These inequalities in rights were also rationalized and justified by other arguments, based on assumptions about innate, natural differences between the sexes, such as women being by nature weaker and more emotional, qualities inappropriate in a leader, and that they are created for childbearing, a function that confines them to the home, which means that men must protect and provide for them.[4]

MEETING THE CHALLENGE OF EQUALITY: REFORMIST APPROACHES

With the advent of modernity, the idea of male authority over women started to lose its hold. From the turn of the twentieth century, Muslim reformist thinkers have tried to reconcile what they understood to be fundamental

---

[4] For the ways in which these arguments shape legal rulings, see in particular Ali (2010), 'Abd Al'Ati (1997) and Mahmoud (2006).

principles in Muslim law and ethics with modernist conceptions of justice and gender relations.

In what follows I discuss and contextualize three reformist writings that appeared at key moments in the politics of Muslim family law reforms. The first is a 1930 book by the Tunisian Tahir al-Haddad, *Women in the Shari'a and in Our Society*,[5] written in the context of the early twentieth-century debates surrounding codification, when *fiqh* rulings were being grafted onto modern legal systems. The second is an article by the Pakistani Fazlur Rahman, 'The Status of Women in Islam: A Modernist Interpretation' (1982b); it was published when political Islam was at its zenith and Islamists, proclaiming the slogan 'Return to *Shari'ah*', were dismantling earlier reforms. The third is a paper by the Egyptian Nasr Abu Zayd, 'The Status of Women between the Qur'an and *Fiqh*' (2013), written when Muslim feminist voices had already emerged and were in conversation with reform thinkers like him.

I have chosen to focus on these three particular writings for several reasons. First, they offer a framework for rethinking the notions of justice and gender relations that underpin classical *fiqh* rulings. Each of these texts tells us about not only the state of the debate at the time, but also the forces against which Muslim reformists have had to struggle. Secondly, all three authors met a great deal of opposition in their own countries, where their ideas were declared heretical; all three paid a price for their ideas and for going against official dogma. Yet, thirdly, their writings proved instrumental in shaping later discourse and developments and inspired the feminist scholarship in Islam exemplified in this volume.

The first moment: codification

During the twentieth century, many Muslim-majority countries adopted new legal codes relating to marriage and family. The new codes were based on classical *fiqh* rulings, but incorporated reformed elements in order to accommodate some modern expectations and realities.[6] Reforms were introduced from the framework of Muslim legal tradition, by mixing principles and rulings from different *fiqh* schools and by procedural devices, without directly challenging

---

[5] A recent English translation by Husni and Newman (2007) is titled *Muslim Women in Law and Society: Annotated Translation of al-Tahir al-Haddad's Imra'tuna fi 'l-shari'a wa 'l-mujtama'*. Unless otherwise stated, quotations and references are from this translation.

[6] For codification, see Anderson (1976) and Mahmood (1972).

the patriarchal construction of marriage and marital relations.[7] They focused on increasing the age of marriage, expanding women's access to judicial divorce and restricting men's right to polygamy. This involved requiring the state registration of marriage and divorce, or the creation of new courts to deal with marital disputes. The state now had the power to deny legal support to those marriages and divorces that did not comply with official, state-sanctioned procedures (Mir-Hosseini, 2009).

While making some concessions to contemporary demands for improved rights for women, the effect of these reforms was not only to give the state an unprecedented authority to enforce its chosen prescriptions for marriage procedures and family practices, but also to entrench traditional patriarchal interpretations of the sacred texts and the legal and ethical assumptions behind them.[8]

The first of our texts appeared in this political context of the codification and superficial reform of Muslim family laws. Tahir al-Haddad (1899–1936) studied Islamic sciences at Zaytouna, the prestigious centre of religious studies in Tunisia, and qualified as a notary in 1920. He opted for journalism and became involved in the movement for independence from France. He developed a keen interest in workers' and women's conditions and became active in the trade union movement. His activism made him deeply concerned about the situation of workers and women and the injustices to which they were subjected. In 1927 he published a book on labour law and in 1930 a second book, *Our Women in the Shari'a and Society*, which contains his critique of the way in which women were treated in Tunisian society, which al-Haddad attributed to erroneous interpretations of Islam's sacred texts. This book caused an immediate uproar in Tunisia; he was denounced and his degree revoked by his seminary colleagues in Zaytouna, and he was declared an apostate.[9] Al-Haddad died in 1936 in poverty and isolation.

Our Women in the Shari'a and Society is part of a nationalist and reformist debate on the 'status of women in Islam' that was ignited by the encounter

---

[7] These were established *fiqh* devices: eclectic choice (*takhayyur*) and mixing (*talfiq*) of legal opinions and rulings from different schools; the exercise of *ijtihad* remained limited. For a discussion, see Rahman (1980).

[8] For discussion of how these reforms have had mixed benefits for women, see Abu-Odeh (2004), Mir-Hosseini (2007; 2009) and Sonbol (1996; 1998).

[9] For the political context, reactions to al-Haddad's book, and the politics of family law in Tunisia, see Salem (1984), Boulby (1988) and Charrad (2001).

with Western colonial powers.[10] Critical of *fiqh* rulings, reformists called for women's education, for their participation in society and for unveiling. One subtext in this debate was the repudiation of the colonial premise that 'Islam' was inherently a 'backward' religion and denied women their rights; another was the quest for modernization and the reform of laws and legal systems as part of the project of nation-building. Without women's education and their participation in society, the modern, independent and prosperous state for which they were struggling could not be achieved.[11] Al-Haddad's book was distinctive in one major respect: it went beyond mere criticism by providing a framework for rethinking *fiqh* legal concepts.

There are two related elements to al-Haddad's framework. First is the distinction between norms and prescriptions that are essential to Islam as a religion, thus eternal, and those which are contingent, thus time and context bound. In al-Haddad's words:

> We should take into consideration the great difference between what Islam brought and its aims, which will remain immortal in eternity, such as belief in monotheism, moral behaviour, and the establishment of justice, dignity and equality among people. Furthermore, we have to consider the social situation and the deep-rooted mind set that existed in Arab society in the pre-Islamic era when Islam first emerged. (Husni and Newman, 2007, p. 36)

The second element is what he termed *al-siyasa al-tadrijiyya*, the policy of gradualism, which he argued governed the process of legislation in the Qur'an and *Sunnah*. In Islam the 'highest aim is equality among all God's creatures', but it was not possible to achieve this aim in the seventh century and during the lifetime of the Prophet; 'the general conditions in the Arabian Peninsula forced the legal texts to be laid down gradually, especially those concerning women' (Husni and Newman, 2007, p. 104). 'Islam is the religion of freedom', but it tolerated 'the selling and buying of human beings as goods, and their exploitation as animals for the duration of their lives' (Husni and Newman, 2007, p. 48). This toleration was a concession to the socioeconomic imperatives of

---

[10] Qasim Amin's *The Liberation of Women* (1899) was the most influential of this literature; for a critical discussion, see Ahmed (1992, chapter 8).

[11] For the intellectual genealogy of al-Haddad's text, see Husni and Newman's introduction (2007, pp. 1–25); for accounts of the intellectual and social change that made women's issues central to politics, see Ahmed (1992, chapter 7); for the experience of different countries, see Keddie (2007, pp. 60–101).

the time. It was not then possible to do away with slavery altogether, but the Qur'an and the Prophet encouraged the freeing of slaves and made it crystal clear that the principle is freedom. For exactly the same reason, patriarchy was tolerated then, but again the Qur'an made it clear that the principle in Islam remains equality.

This framework enabled al-Haddad to offer different readings of verses 4:34 and 2:228 – the two verses that constitute the prime textual support for the institution of male authority over women.[12] He argues that both verses must be read in the context of the marriage and divorce practices of the time and the privileges that men enjoyed before Islam; the intent in both verses was to restrain these privileges and to protect women in the face of them. This becomes clear when we read these verses in their entirety and in conjunction with those which precede and follow them. In verse 4:34 a husband is required to provide for his wife, so that 'the continued growth of the world' can be ensured; he is given the right to 'correct' his wife's behaviour in order to prevent a greater ill, namely divorce. This verse is not speaking about the rights and duties of spouses, but is about the course of action to be taken when there is marital discord, and it offers ways to resolve such discord. This becomes clear in the verse that follows, which reads, 'If you have reason to fear that a breach might occur between a couple, appoint an arbiter from among his people and an arbiter from among her people; if they both want to set things right, God may bring their reconciliation' (4:35). Men are addressed because they are the ones who, then as now, have the power to terminate marriage, and the objective was to restrain this power and give the marriage a chance. Likewise, with respect to verse 2:228,[13] which the jurists read as evidence of men's superiority, al-Haddad maintains that it must be read in its entirety and in connection with the previous and following verses, which are all related to marital separation and the protection of women. The final part of the verse speaks of men's power to divorce, and this is what 'men having a degree over women' is about; divorce was in their hands.

---

[12] For how the link between these two verses was made through the exegesis, see Abou-Bakr in this volume.

[13] Verse 2:228 reads, 'Divorced women shall wait concerning themselves for three monthly periods. Nor is it lawful for them to hide what Allah Hath created in their wombs, if they have faith in Allah and the Last Day. And their husbands have the better rights to take them back in that period if they wish for reconciliation. And women shall have rights similar to the rights against them, according to what is equitable; but men have a degree [of advantage] [darajah] over them. And Allah is Exalted in Power, Wise.'

With respect to marriage and gender roles, there are again two important elements in al-Haddad's approach. First, he rejects the argument that women are unfit for certain activities and that their primary role is motherhood. 'Islam did not assign fixed roles to men and women…Nowhere in the Qur'an can one find any reference to any activity – no matter how elevated it may be, and whether in government or society – that is forbidden to woman' (Husni and Newman, 2007, p. 39). Yes, men and women are different; women give birth and are physically and emotionally suited to care for children, but this in no way means that Islam wanted them to be confined to the home and to domestic roles. The problem is not with Islam but with patriarchy, with reducing women to sex objects; it is 'primarily due to the fact that we [men] regard them [women] as vessels for our penises'.[14]

Secondly he breaks away from the transactional logic of marriage in *fiqh*, and places mutual affection and cooperation at the centre of the marital relationship:

> Marriage involves affection, duties, intercourse and procreation. Islam regards affection as the foundation of marriage since it is the driving force, as witnessed by the following verse:
>
> > And among His signs is this, that He created for you mates from among yourselves, that you may dwell in tranquillity with them, and He has love and mercy between your (hearts): Verily in that are signs for those who reflect. (verse 30:21)
>
> As for duty, this refers to the fact that husband and wife have to work together to build a life. In this sense, duty both preserves and enhances the emotional ties that exist between them and which enable them to carry out their duty wilfully. (Husni and Newman, 2007, p. 57)

By shifting the focus from verse 4:34 to verse 30:21, al-Haddad was able to break the link not only between maintenance and obedience as constructed in classical *fiqh* texts, but also between male authority over women (*qiwamah*), as derived from verse 4:34, and male superiority (*darajah*), derived from verse

---

[14] This phrase appears towards the end of al-Haddad's preface to the book; here I did not use Husni and Newman's translation, which renders the phrase as 'we regard them as an object to satisfy our desires' (Husni and Newman, 2007, p. 31).

2:228. By contextualizing these verses, he was able to offer an egalitarian interpretation of both. This also enabled him to make freedom of choice (*hurriyyat
al-ikhtiyar*) the starting point for regulating marriage. Love and compassion,
al-Haddad argues, cannot develop in a relationship that is imposed; women,
like men, must have the freedom to choose their spouses and must be able to
leave an unwanted marriage, and this is what Islam mandates.

Al-Haddad's ideas and proposals for reform were indeed radical for the
time, which to a large extent explains the harsh reaction of the clerical establishment to his book. He went much further than other twentieth-century
reformers, even arguing for equality in inheritance, an issue that became a
priority for Muslim women's movements only in the next century.[15] But in
1956, in a changed political context, when the nationalists/modernists had
prevailed and Tunisia was an independent nation state, many of al-Haddad's
proposals for reform were adopted. Under the leadership of Habib Bourghiba,
the modernists embarked on reform of the judiciary, and among their first acts
was the codification of family law. The new code made polygamy illegal and
gave women equal access to divorce and child custody, though the inheritance
laws remained unchanged. All these reforms were of course introduced from
above; when women were still not vocal participants in the debate.[16]

The second moment: the rise of political Islam

Following the Second World War, more Muslim-majority countries, including
newly founded states such as Pakistan, broke away from their colonial rulers
and, along with increasing modernization in various forms, came under the
control of monarchies or republics of different political hues. Political movements proliferated, in different shapes and combinations – Marxist, nationalist and, increasingly, Islamist.

The rise of Islam as both a spiritual and a political force in the 1970s
brought a reversal of the movement towards secularization of laws and legal
systems. Some of the reforms introduced earlier in the century by modernist
governments were dismantled, for example in Egypt, but particularly in
Iran, where political Islam had its greatest triumph in the 1979 popular

---

[15] A joint campaign by Moroccan and Tunisian women's organizations went public in 2006
with a two-volume publication (Association des Femmes Tunisiennes pour la Recherche et le
Développement [AFTURD], 2006).
[16] For an overview and analysis of these reforms, see Kelly (1996).

revolution that brought clerics into power. In the same year, Pakistan introduced the Hudood Ordinances that extended the ambit of *fiqh* to certain
aspects of criminal law. Yet 1979 was also the year when the United Nations
General Assembly adopted the Convention on the Elimination of All Forms
of Discrimination against Women (CEDAW), which gave gender equality
a clear international legal mandate.

Our second text, 'The Status of Women in Islam: A Modernist Interpretation', appeared in 1982, when political Islam was at its zenith and Islamists, proclaiming the slogan 'Return to *Shari'ah*', were busy reversing earlier
reforms. Fazlur Rahman (1919–88) was another reformer whose ideas met
a great deal of opposition in his own country, Pakistan. The formation of
his ideas belongs to the tail end of Western colonialism in Muslim contexts,
when processes of nation-building, modernization and reform of the judiciary, and codification of family law were well underway. Rahman was more of
a scholar than an activist; his intellectual genealogy is from reform thinkers
in the Indian subcontinent. He was instructed in traditional Islamic sciences
by his father, a renowned Islamic scholar, and went on to study Arabic and
Islamic studies at Punjab University in Lahore and Islamic philosophy at the
University of Oxford.

In 1961 he was invited by General Ayub Khan to help reform religious
education in Pakistan, and he became director of the Islamic Research Institute, an intellectual think tank tasked with steering the path of modernization
and reform in ways that would not offend the religious establishment (Saeed,
2004).[17] His reformist ideas and critical approach to Islamic tradition made
him a target for Ayub Khan's influential religious and political opponents.
The fiercest opposition came from religious conservatives and centred on the
question of women's rights and the reform of family law. Rahman began to
receive death threats and eventually decided to return to academic life in the
West. In 1968 he was appointed professor of Islamic thought at the University of Chicago, where he remained until his death in 1988, leaving behind
an impressive body of publications. His work in turn has been the subject of
study, and played an important role in the development of Islamic studies in
the US.[18] But his vast output, all in English, remains almost unknown in the

---

[17] Major family law reforms in the Indian subcontinent, namely the 1939 Dissolution of
Marriages Act and the 1961 Muslim Family Laws Ordinance, took place before Rahman's
directorship. Women's groups were instrumental in pushing for these reforms.
[18] For studies on Fazlur Rahman's work, see Sonn (1991), Moosa (2000) and Saeed (2004). For
his impact on American Islamic discourse, see Waugh and Denny (1998).

Arab world and in traditional religious circles, and his influence in his own country, Pakistan, has been limited.

Unlike al-Haddad, Rahman did not write a book about women's rights, nor did he offer specific proposals for reforming Muslim family law. He considered the reform of Muslim family laws to be on the whole moving in the right direction, and he saw the weight of conservatism in Muslim contexts as the main obstacle to bringing about radical reform (Rahman, 1980). But his writings are permeated by a critique of patriarchal readings of Islam's sacred texts, and his framework for interpreting the ethico-legal content of the Qur'an has been crucial to feminist scholarship in Islam.[19]

His last major work, *Islam and Modernity* (1982a), is a call for a fresh engagement with the Qur'an and a critical reassessment of the entire Islamic intellectual tradition: theology, ethics, philosophy and jurisprudence. The Qur'an, Rahman contends, is not a book of law; it 'is the divine response, through the Prophet's mind, to the moral-social situation of the Prophet's Arabia, particularly to the problems of commercial Meccan society of the day' (Rahman, 1982a, p. 5). Not all of these solutions are relevant or applicable to all times and all contexts; but the moral principles behind them are immutable and permanently valid. These moral principles show us the way, the *Shari'ah*, and how to establish a society on earth where all humans can be treated as equals, as they are equal in the eyes of God (Sonn, 1998, p. 128).

In the course of the historical development of Islam, the moral principles behind Qur'anic laws came to be distorted; and a body of law named *Shari'ah* (never mentioned in the Qur'an in the sense of a system of law) became the defining element of Islam. This distortion had its roots in political developments after the Prophet's death and in the subsequent decay and stagnation of Islamic intellectualism, which pre-date Islam's encounter with Western colonial powers. Muslims failed to create a viable system of Qur'an-based ethics. From the outset, jurisprudence in Islam overshadowed the science of ethics; Muslim scholars relied more on Persian and Greek sources to develop an Islamic ethics than on the Qur'an. Rahman suggests that the link between theology, ethics and law will remain tenuous as long as Muslims fail to make the crucial distinctions in the Qur'an and the Prophet's *Sunnah*: between essentials and accidentals, and between prescriptive and descriptive (Saeed, 2004, pp. 43–5).

---

[19] For his views on gender rights and his impact on the development of a new Islamic feminism, see Sonn (1998).

In 'The Status of Women in Islam: A Modernist Interpretation' (1982b), published in the same year as *Islam and Modernity* (1982a), Rahman contends that the legal passages in the Qur'an on the subject of women are part of an effort to strengthen the position of the weaker segments of the community, which in pre-Islamic Arabia were the poor, orphans, women, slaves and those chronically in debt. By reforming existing laws and practices and introducing new ones, the Qur'an aimed to put an end to their abuse and to open the way for their empowerment. What the reforms achieved was 'the removal of certain abuses to which women were subjected': they banned female infanticide and widow inheritance and reformed the laws of marriage, divorce and inheritance. As with slavery, however, these reforms did not go as far as abolishing patriarchy; they expanded women's rights and brought tangible improvements in their position – though not social equality. Women retained the rights they had to property and were no longer treated as property; they could not be forced into marriage against their will and they received a marriage gift (*mahr*); they also acquired better access to divorce and were allocated shares in inheritance (1982b, pp. 286–9).

The essential equality between the sexes is clearly implied in the Qur'an; both men and women are mentioned separately 'as being absolutely equal in virtue and piety with such unflinching regularity that it would be superfluous to give particular documentation' (1982b, p. 291). Rahman adds,

> The Qur'an speaks of the husband and wife relationship as that of 'love and mercy' adding that the wife is a moral support for the husband (30:21). It describes their support for each other by saying, 'they (i.e. your wives) are garments unto you and you are garments unto them' (2:187). The term 'garment' here means that which soothes and covers up one's weakness. (1982b, p. 293)

Those sayings attributed to the Prophet that speak of women's inferiority and require them to obey and worship their husbands, Rahman argues, are clearly 'a twisting of whatever the Qur'an has to say in matters of piety and religious merit' (1982b, p. 292) and marriage. Such sayings also contradict what we know of the Prophet's own conduct, thus must be rejected. The Qur'an does speak of inequality between sexes. But when it does, it gives the rationale, which has to do with socioeconomic factors. Verse 4:34 'gives two rationales for male superiority: (1) that man is "more excellent", and (2) that man is charged entirely with household expenditure' (1982b, p. 294).

What the Qur'an appears to say, therefore, is that since men are the primary socially operative factors and breadwinners, they have been wholly charged with the responsibility of defraying household expenditure and upkeep of their womenfolk. For this reason man, because by his struggle he has gained more life-experience and practical wisdom, has become entitled to 'manage women's affairs,' and, in case of their recalcitrance, admonish them, leave them alone in their beds and, lastly, to beat them without causing injury. (1982b, pp. 294–5)

Having given his interpretation of verse 4:34 and the rationale behind the gender inequality in the Qur'an, Rahman then poses two questions: Are these socioeconomic roles on which gender inequality is based immutable, even if women want to change them? If they are changeable, how far can they be changed? His answer to the first question is a definite no. These inequalities are not inherent in the nature of the sexes; they are the product of historical socioeconomic developments. Once women acquire education and participate in society and economy, the 'degree' that the Qur'an says men have over women also disappears. But the answer to the second question, Rahman contends, is not that simple, and he is hesitant whether 'women should ask or be allowed to do any and all jobs that men do' – although he admits that 'if women insist on and persist in this, they can and eventually will do so' (1982b, p. 295). He has no doubt that law reforms must give women equality in all other spheres; classical *fiqh* rulings in marriage, divorce and inheritance can and must be reformed because 'it is the most fundamental and urgent requirement of the Qur'an in the social sector that abuses and injustices be removed' (1982b, p. 295). These inequalities are now the cause of suffering and oppression and go against the Qur'anic spirit, which is that of the equality of all human beings.

He then goes on to discuss in detail the laws of polygamy, divorce, inheritance and hijab and reiterates the gist of his framework:

One must completely accept our general contention that the specific legal rules of the Qur'an are conditioned by the sociohistorical background of their enactment and what is eternal therein is the social objectives or moral principles explicitly stated or strongly implied in that legislation. This would, then, clear the way for further legislation in the light of those social objectives or moral principles. This argument remains only elliptically hinted at by the Modernist, who has used it in an *ad hoc* manner only for the issue of polygamy, and has not clearly formulated it as a general principle. (1982b, p. 301)

Rahman ends by stressing that legal reform can only be effective in changing the status of women in Muslim contexts when there is an adequate basis for social change. It is only then that the Qur'anic objective of social justice in general and for women in particular can be fulfilled; otherwise its success will be limited, transitory and confined to certain social groups (1982b, p. 308).

The third moment: the emergence of 'Islamic feminism'

Fazlur Rahman's article addressed a debate that had been going on for many decades among Muslim modernists – almost all of them men. Women were still largely absent from the debate, as they had been from the process of reform and codification of family law in the first part of the century. But the article appeared at the point when women's rights had just become part of human rights discourse, and human rights treaties and documents, in particular CEDAW, were giving women a new language in which to frame their demands.

The last two decades of the twentieth century saw the concomitant development, globally and locally, of two powerful but seemingly opposed frames of reference. On the one hand, with the encouragement of CEDAW, the international women's movement expanded and NGOs emerged with international funding and transnational links and gave women a voice in policymaking and public debate about the law. On the other hand, Islamist political movements – whether in power or in opposition – started to invoke *Shari'ah* in order to dismantle earlier efforts to reform and/or secularize laws and legal systems. Tapping into popular demands for social justice, they presented this dismantling as 'Islamization' and as the first step to bringing about their vision of a moral and just society.

These Islamist measures, however, had some unintended consequences. The most important was that they brought the classical *fiqh* texts out of the closet, exposing them to unprecedented critical scrutiny and public debate. A new wave of Muslim reform thinkers started to respond to the Islamist challenge and to take Islamic legal thought onto new ground. Using the conceptual tools and theories of other branches of knowledge, these thinkers have extended the work of previous reformers and developed further interpretive-epistemological theories. What distinguishes them from their predecessors is that instead of seeking an Islamic genealogy for modern concepts like equality, human rights and democracy, they focus on how religion is understood, how religious knowledge is produced and how rights are constructed in Muslim legal tradition.

Meanwhile, attempts to translate anachronistic patriarchal interpretations of the *Shariʿah* into policy provoked many women to increasing criticism and drove them to greater activism. Socioeconomic imperatives had already brought many more women than before into education and employment. These developments opened new spaces for activism and debate. Women were now finding ways to sustain a critique, from within, of patriarchal readings of the *Shariʿah* and of the gender biases of *fiqh* texts. A new discourse, a new way of thinking about gender, arose among Muslims, which has come to be labelled 'Islamic feminism' – a conjunction that was unsettling to many Islamists and some secular feminists (Mir-Hosseini, 2006). This discourse was further facilitated by the rapid spread of new technologies, notably the internet; and these new technologies have regularly shown their potential for the mobilization of campaigns for change. Uncovering a hidden history and rereading Islam textual sources, the new 'Islamic feminists' started to reclaim Islam's egalitarian message. Pioneers among them were Azizah Al-Hibri, Riffat Hassan, Amina Wadud and Fatima Mernissi, followed by others who are breaking new ground.[20] Their voices started to draw attention from media and academia, via public meetings and workshops that provided a platform for scholar-activists.

In the new century, in the aftermath of the 11 September 2001 attacks, the 'War on Terror' added another level of complexity to the politics of gender and Islam. The invasions of Afghanistan and Iraq – both partially justified as promoting 'freedom' and 'women's rights' – combined with the double standards employed in promoting UN sanctions, showed that both international human rights and feminist ideals are open to manipulation and that there is a huge gap between these ideals and the practices of their proponents. For some Muslim women this was also a turning point, as they felt caught between those trying to impose a patriarchal and violent vision of their faith and those trying to impose a neocolonial project in the name of human rights and feminism (Mir-Hosseini, 2012).

---

[20] For recent assessment of this body of work, see Abou-Bakr (2013), Seedat (2013) and Hermansen (2013).

This was the context in which our final text was produced. The author, Nasr Hamid Abu Zayd, was among the most prominent and radical of the new reformist thinkers. He presented 'The Status of Women between the Qur'an and *Fiqh*' to participants at a workshop in Cairo in January 2010, including conservatives, reformists and feminists.[21]

A notable scholar of the Qur'an, Nasr Hamid Abu Zayd (1943–2010) was born in a small village in Egypt, where he received a traditional religious education; he later studied literature in Cairo University and obtained his doctorate in Islamic studies. In a compelling account of his engagement with Qur'anic studies, Abu Zayd traced its evolution, starting from memorization of the entire Qur'an as a child, his early sympathies with the Muslim Brotherhood, his entering the academic world and his vocal criticism of the dominant Islamic discourse in Egypt, which led to his exile (Abu Zayd, 2011). His aim was 'to achieve a scientific understanding of the Qur'an, and... to brush aside layers of ideological interpretation, in order to unearth the historical reality of the text' (Kermani, 2004, p. 175). In 1990 he published a groundbreaking book, *The Concept of the Text* (*Mafhum al-Nass*), in which he brought to the traditional field of Qur'anic studies concepts and tools from other scholarly disciplines, namely modern linguistics and philosophical hermeneutics. His criticism of the instrumentalization of religion, and his challenge to the ulama's monopoly of sacred texts, made him the target of attacks by Islamists and religious leaders in Egypt, who denounced him as an apostate and tried to annul his marriage. Forced into exile in 1995, he resumed his academic career in the Netherlands as professor of Islamic studies at Leiden University, where he remained until his untimely death in June 2010. His critical approach to the Qur'an has enlivened the international scholarly debate on Islam and human rights.

A deeply religious man, Abu Zayd defined himself as 'one of the Arab and Muslim adherents of "rationalism", a "rationalism" which does not exclude or despise religion as mere psychological phantom' (2011, p. 55). Equally at ease with popular Islam and with his deep knowledge of classical religious sciences, Abu Zayd engaged in international scholarly debate on Islam and human rights. In two books (both in Arabic), he addressed the issue of women's rights. His latest thinking on the issue was presented at the Cairo workshop

---

[21] This workshop was organized under the auspices of the Norwegian Centre for Human Rights as part of their project New Directions in Islamic Thought (http://www.jus.uio.no/smr/english/about/programmes/oslocoalition/islam/). Musawah had recently been launched and Abu Zayd was an enthusiastic supporter.

in January 2010, in a paper that he had intended to expand and revise for publication.[22]

In this paper, 'The Status of Women between the Qur'an and *Fiqh*', Abu Zayd starts by quoting the Egyptian reformist Muhammad 'Abduh (1845–1905), who contrasts *fiqh* and Qur'anic conceptions of marital relations:

> Marriage, according to *fiqh*, is a contract which renders the female vagina the property of a male. The Qur'an's view, however, is that marriage is one of the Divine signs (*ayat*): 'Among His Signs is this, that He created for you mates from among yourselves, that you may dwell in tranquillity with them, and He has put love and mercy between you; verily in that are Signs for those who reflect' (verse 30:21). (2013, p. 153)

The vast chasm between Qur'anic and *fiqh* conceptions of marriage, Abu Zayd argues, has to do with how, early in the history of Islamic sciences,

> The worlds of the Qur'an, or its multi-dimensional worldview, were separated, in fact fragmented. Theology took over the world of divinity, i.e. the divine nature; philosophy took over the world of metaphysics, i.e. the cosmos, the grades of existence, nature, and so on; Sufism took over the ethical-spiritual world; and legal theory took over the legislative world. (2013, p. 154)

All reformists, from the onset, have been concerned with the consequences of this fragmentation, which have come to be felt more acutely in modern times. In the past few centuries, the gradual but steady marginalization of theology, philosophy and mysticism has left the legal domain as the only representative of Islam. This is particularly problematic, Abu Zayd reminds us, because what has now come to define Islam comprises a very limited portion of the Qur'an; out of 6,236 verses, at most only 500 contain legal material (2013, p. 157).

This has intensified the disconnect between the Qur'an's ethical/spiritual domains of meaning, in which human equality is affirmed, and social/legalistic domains of meaning, in which this equality is negotiated. 'To reconnect the

---

[22] The paper was not published until after his death in June of that year. I was a convenor of the workshop and an editor of the resultant book, *Gender and Equality in Muslim Family Law: Justice and Ethics in the Islamic Legal Tradition*, in which we decided to publish his paper in its original form (Abu Zayd, 2013).

worlds of the Qur'an', he argues, 'we need to approach the Qur'an differently', and it is here that the tools and theories of modern linguistics and hermeneutics can come to our aid.

> The Qur'an was communicated as a series of oral discourses during the last twenty years of the Prophet's life (612–632); each discourse has its occasion, audience, structure, type, mode and message. These discourses were later collected, arranged and written down in the *mushaf*.[23] The difference between the *mushaf* arrangement and the chronological order of these discourses is a well-known fact. The *mushaf* gave the Qur'an the form of a book, which in its turn redefined the Qur'an as a Text. (Abu Zayd, 2013, p. 154)

To reach and transmit his message, God adopted a human language; the first addressees of the Qur'an were the seventh-century Arabs, whose language, which was part of their social reality, became also the language of the Qur'an. Like any text, the language of the Qur'an is not self-explanatory, but is in need of interpretation, which is the raison d'être of the Qur'anic sciences ('ulum al-Qur'an), whose task has been to decipher and understand the language of the Qur'an. When we read classical Qur'anic scientific literature in the light of modern theories about textual analysis, we realize, in Abu Zayd's words,

> The Qur'an, although recognized as a holy text, is a historically and culturally determined text. This historical text is the subject of understanding and interpretation, whereas God's words exist in a sphere beyond any human knowledge. Therefore, sociohistorical analysis is needed for its understanding and a modern linguistic methodology should be applied for its interpretation. The Qur'an is a message revealed from God to man through the Prophet Muhammad, the Messenger of God and a human. The Qur'an is very clear about that. A message represents a communicative link between a sender and a recipient through a code or linguistic system. Because the sender in the case of the Qur'an cannot be the object of scientific study, the scientific introduction to the analysis of the text of the Qur'an can only take place

---

[23] In Qur'anic studies *mushaf*, literally 'collection of pages', denotes the 'compiled, written pages of the Qur'an' as distinct from the Qur'an, which denotes the specific 'revelation that was read to the Prophet Muhammad'.

through the study of the contextual reality and the cultural milieu of seventh-century Arabia. (2011, p. 82)

So, 'it will be always necessary to analyse and to interpret the Qur'an within the contextual background from which it originated'; but, 'being a unique text, the Qur'an employs a special linguistic encoding dynamics in order to convey its specific message' (2011, p. 83). To understand what seem to be 'contradictions' with respect to equality in general, and between genders in particular, Abu Zayd contends that, apart from removing the layers of ideological interpretation, which entails consciousness of the historical reality of the Qur'an, we need to realize that the Qur'an 'was originally a series of discourses', and to analyse it as such.

> For now, I propose dividing the worlds of the Qur'an – its multi-dimensional worldview – into five interdependent domains, each of which reflects one level that has been taken away and disconnected from the other levels in one of the Islamic disciplines, namely *fiqh*, theology, philosophy and mysticism. (2013, p. 155)

These domains are: 1) cosmology; 2) the divine–human relationship; 3) the ethical and moral dimension; 4) the societal level; and 5) punishment (*hudud*) (2013, pp. 155–6). To understand the Qur'anic view on gender relations, Abu Zayd maintains that, apart from removing the layers of ideological interpretation, which entails consciousness of the historical reality of the Qur'an, we need to reconnect the different domains of meanings – or different worlds – of the Qur'an.

> On the cosmological level, [human equality] is stated in the opening verse of the chapter 'Women' (*Al-Nisa*, 4:1), which addresses humans: 'O mankind! Reverence your Lord Who created you from a single soul from which He created its mate and from them He emanated countless men and women; reverence Allah through Whom you demand your mutual (rights) and (reverence) the wombs (that bore you): for Allah ever watches over you.' It is quite significant that the term 'soul', *nafs*, is a feminine word, and that the mate created from it is named *zawjaha*, which is a masculine word that could be translated as 'twin' or 'husband'. The second meaning is highlighted in 7:189: 'It is He who created you from a single soul and made out of it its mate that he might dwell

with her (in love).' As the chapter about women opens with absolute cosmological equality, the entire chapter, which contains most of the legal regulations concerning marriage, should always be connected to the principle of equality. Another point to support this proposition is the frequent reference to justice, 'adl. (2013, p. 161)

Likewise, 'On the ethical-spiritual level, equality is also sustained; both men and women receive the same reward for their righteous actions. In a cluster of verses [16:90, 16:97, 4:124, 40:40, 3:195] presenting a discourse of admonition, divine justice is put forward as the governing principle'. In verses 9:71–2 'the believers are presented as one unified community of males and females in mutual intimate guardianship' (p. 161).[24]

> On the societal level, however, differentiation is acknowledged. In the case of religious difference, there exists a discourse of discrimination. Gender differentiation, however, is free from any discrimination. Qur'anic gender differentiation developed into discrimination in the *fiqh* literature due to a certain cultural and socio-historical context. (p. 162)

The existence of passages in the Qur'an that treat men and women differently, Abu Zayd stresses, is not an obstacle to an egalitarian construction of gender rights in Islam. He concludes his paper by raising two questions:

> [W]hy should we demand of the Qur'an that it violate the established rules in the societal domain of meaning? It should be recognised that when the Qur'an sustains absolute equality in both the cosmological and the ethical–spiritual domain, this is the direction in which the Qur'an would like Muslims to upgrade the societal domain of inequality. Traditional law-makers failed to do so because there was no sociocultural development in this direction …

> The demand for gender equality is a product of our modern era of human rights. The challenging question is: are Muslims able to exert the same courage to upgrade the societal domain of meaning to the high level of the cosmological and the ethico-spiritual domains? (Abu Zayd, 2013, p. 164)

---

[24] See Lamrabet's chapter in this volume for an expansion of this theme.

*

The authors of all three texts considered here sacrificed a great deal personally to propose gender-egalitarian readings of key Qur'anic passages and offer radical approaches and methods for reforming discriminatory legal practices. They have all had great influence on the development of current reformist thinking – and not surprisingly have put proponents of traditionalist ideas and practices on the defensive. Their writings have become the backbone of feminist scholarship in Islam, which is taking reformist thought onto new ground by insisting on gender as a major framework of analysis.

EGALITARIAN FAMILY LAWS: PROSPECTS AND IMPLICATIONS

Against this background we can now turn, in conclusion, to the project of constructing egalitarian family laws within an Islamic framework, its prospects of success and the challenges that confront its advocates. It is clear from the arguments of the foregoing texts that current discriminatory laws regarding marriage and gender relations are neither divine nor immutable; rather, they are juristic constructions premised on a postulate that is no longer valid or acceptable: that God placed women under male authority. By establishing gender hierarchy and discrimination, the juristic concepts qiwamah and wilayah are in effect the 'DNA of patriarchy'[25] in Muslim legal tradition. Those who seek to establish an egalitarian construction of gender rights in Muslim contexts must address and redefine the understanding of these legal concepts in line with contemporary notions of justice, in which gender equality is inherent.

Because of the radical transformations, global and local, in the politics of religion, state and gender since the early twentieth century, Muslim legal tradition faces growing challenges that pose, in effect, an epistemological crisis.[26] But moments of crisis are also moments of opportunity and change.

---

[25] I take this from Gilligan, who calls the gender binary and hierarchy the 'DNA of Patriarchy' (2011, p. 18).

[26] I borrow this concept from the philosopher Alasdair MacIntyre (1988, pp. 350–2), who argues that every rational enquiry is embedded in a tradition of learning, and that tradition reaches an epistemological crisis when, by its own standards of rational justification, disagreements can no longer be resolved rationally. This, he goes on, gives rise to an internal critique that will eventually transform the tradition.

There are several dimensions to this crisis. One is the changed relationship between Muslim legal tradition, state and social practice. As we have seen, in the course of the twentieth century in many Muslim countries, the partial reform and codification of *fiqh* provisions led to the creation of a hybrid family law; codes and statute books replaced *fiqh* manuals, and family law became the concern of the legislative assembly of a nation state, which had neither the legitimacy nor the inclination to challenge patriarchal interpretations of the *Shari'ah*. With the rise of political Islam in the last part of the century, these *fiqh* manuals and their gender discourse became closely identified with Islamist political movements whose rallying cry was 'Return to *Shari'ah*'. At the same time, the expansion of international feminism and creation of women's NGOs brought women to centre stage, so that women themselves, rather than the abstract notion of 'gender equality', are now at the heart of family law reforms. Earlier in the century, women were merely the subject of these debates and were absent from the processes of reform and codification of family law; as the century came to a close, they were refusing to be merely objects of the law, but rather claiming the right to speak and to be active participants in the debates and in the process of law-making. These developments intensified the confrontation between Islamists and feminists, which by the end of the century led to the emergence of new forms of activism and a new gender discourse, now known as 'Islamic feminism', to separate patriarchy from the reading of Islam's sacred texts.

Another dimension of this crisis is that ideas of 'justice' have changed, posing challenges to traditionalist Muslim theology, law and society. Where patriarchal and authoritarian/discriminatory laws and practices have prevailed with regard to gender issues and family structures, they are justified in religious terms, notably with reference to concepts derived from the much-debated verse 4:34. Muslim legal thought traditionally operates with an Aristotelian, deserts-based notion of justice (Kadivar, 2013), as in the *fiqh* axiom, 'justice is maintaining everything in its proper place': men and women have their proper, essential places in family and society, and justice consists of keeping them in these places and giving them rights accordingly.[27] Such a notion of justice, which once dominated most legal systems, has been profoundly contested by the modern expansion of democratic and human rights discourses that have made equality inherent to generally accepted conceptions of social justice. Yet it continues to be reproduced, in a modified form, in contemporary Muslim

---

[27] For another critical discussion, see Eshkevari (2013, pp. 192–3).

family laws that adopt a 'protectionist' approach. This perpetuates outmoded gender stereotypes that keep hierarchical power relations intact, referring to the fundamental premise of *qiwamah*; that is to say, because the sexes are different, because women are weak and men are strong, because men protect and provide for women, justice mandates that men have authority and superior rights.

The dissonance between contemporary notions of justice and gender rights and those which underpin the established interpretations of the *Shari'ah* is one of the challenges that face those attempting to construct an egalitarian family law within an Islamic framework. Muslim reformist thinkers – like those in other major religious traditions – have devised a number of strategies for meeting the challenge.[28] Chief among these strategies have been differentiating the changeable from the unchangeable in the texts, referred to by some authors as the specific and the universal, mutable and immutable, accidental and essential, descriptive and prescriptive; discerning the Lawgiver's aims (*maqasid*) and the changes that these aims would have led to in the course of time; and locating both the sacred texts and the rulings that the classical *fuqaha* derived from them in their historical and political contexts.[29]

Armed with these strategies, some twentieth-century Muslim reformists, responding to the multiple and diverse legal and social dilemmas faced by Muslim families and societies, have argued, from within the tradition, for bringing *Shari'ah*-based family laws into conformity with contemporary expectations and realities. I have gone into some detail to show how three reformists deployed these strategies in texts that appeared at key moments of the debate. All three were pioneers of the new trend of Islamic reformist thought that is seeking a fresh engagement with Islam's sacred texts. What this new trend is making clear is that the textual sources of Islam are not inherently patriarchal, nor do they set out an exhaustive body of eternal laws. What they give us is ethical guidance and principles for the creation of just laws. The Qur'an upholds justice and exhorts Muslims to stand for justice; but it does not give us a definition of justice; rather it gives direction, the path to follow towards justice, which is always time and context bound. To understand the Qur'an's direction, they contend, we need a critical reassessment

---

[28] Silvio Ferrari (2006) discusses how religious legal systems adapt to change, drawing parallels between the Roman Catholic Church and Jewish and Islamic law.

[29] Kurzman (1998; 2002) introduces and gives samples of the works of Muslim thinkers; Abu Zayd (2006) provides a critical historical analysis.

of the entire Islamic intellectual tradition: theology, ethics, philosophy and jurisprudence.

But, as the accounts of al-Haddad, Rahman and Abu Zayd testify, this fresh approach faces a major obstacle: entrenched patriarchal and authoritarian structures and the way they conspire to silence voices of reform and change. The proponents of traditionalist ideas and practices will not easily relinquish established interpretations of the *Shari'ah*, as reflected in classical *fiqh* rulings that allowed discrimination on the basis of gender and faith. The struggle for gender equality in Muslim contexts is part of the wider struggle for political democracy, pluralism and freedom of expression; the democratization of the production of religious knowledge has an essential role in this struggle. The fate of women's rights, and in turn the transition to democracy, remained hostage to the fortunes of political forces and tendencies during the twentieth century. More recent political developments – notably, the emergence and suppression of the Green movement in Iran in the aftermath of the disputed 2009 presidential election, and subsequent uprisings in Egypt, Tunisia, Libya, Syria and Turkey – have once again revealed the extent to which women's rights in Muslim contexts are vulnerable to local and global power struggles between forces with other priorities. Islamist elements, which tend to win popular support in times of upheaval, are almost always motivated by traditionalist patriarchal assumptions and policies supported by established pre-modern interpretations of the *Shari'ah*. These interpretations provide Islamists with the theological and ideological justification to keep women under male authority and treat them as second-class citizens.

In other words, the problem is not with the text but with context and the ways in which the text is used to sustain patriarchal and authoritarian structures. The strategy must be not just logical argument and informed reinterpretations from within the tradition; there must also be challenges on the political front. What are the motives and interests of those who claim the authority to speak in the name of religion, who manipulate established interpretations of the texts for authoritarian purposes and who in effect appeal to concepts such as *qiwamah* not only to support male authority in the family but also to maintain authoritarian and absolutist approaches to religion?

Feminist voices and scholarship in Islam take up these challenges. They are opening the way for a meaningful and constructive conversation between feminism and Muslim legal tradition. This conversation has both epistemological and political implications. On the epistemological side, feminist critical theory enables us to see how unreflective assumptions and 'commonsense' arguments limit and deform our knowledge, and so gives us tools for analysing relations between the production of knowledge and the practices of power.[30] It also provides us with a research methodology for giving voice to women and inserting their concerns and interests in the process of law-making.[31] Above all, it enables us to ask new questions: What is the best way of approaching the tension between 'protection' and 'domination' that is inherent in the very concepts of *qiwamah* and *wilayah*, however we define them? What does 'protection' mean? Does it have to entail hierarchy and control? How do we achieve equality and justice in the family? What kind of laws and legal reforms are needed to promote them? Do they entail identical rights and duties for spouses? When does unequal treatment in law become discrimination? How can we deal justly with differences between men and women?

These questions have been at the centre of feminist legal theory, as evidenced in the shift from 'formal' to 'substantive' approaches to equality.[32] A formal model of equality, which often advocates gender-neutral laws, focuses on equal treatment in law but does not necessarily enable women to enjoy their rights on the same basis as men. This is so because it rests on a false premise; neither the starting point nor the playing field are the same for both sexes. Not only do women not have the same access as men to socioeconomic resources and political opportunities, but women are not a homogeneous group; class, age, race and socioeconomic situation are all important factors in the ways in which women have been disadvantaged. A substantive approach to equality, by contrast, takes these factors into account, by aiming 'at the elimination of individual, institutional and systemic discrimination against disadvantaged groups which effectively undermines their full and equal social, economic, political and cultural participation in society' (Kapur, 2012, p. 268). Instead of striving for gender-neutral laws, the emphasis here is on the kinds of laws and legal reforms that regulate power relations between genders in such a way that women are able to enjoy dignity, security and respect in the family and full participation in society.

On the political front, bringing current Islamic legal thought into conversation with feminism can pave the way for transcending ideological dichotomies such as 'secular' versus 'religious' feminism, or 'Islam' versus 'human rights', to which Muslim women's quest for equality and dignity has remained hostage

---

[30] This is a particular concern of feminist standpoint theory; for a discussion, see Harding (2004, pp. 11–15).

[31] For a discussion, see Ramazanoğlu (2002).

[32] For a concise discussion of these two different approaches, see Kapur (2012, pp. 266–72).

since the early twentieth century. These dichotomies have masked the real site of the battle, which is between patriarchal and authoritarian structures, on the one side, and egalitarian and democratic ideologies and forces, on the other. Unmasking this reality entails two linked processes: recovering and reclaiming the ethical and egalitarian ethos in Islam's sacred texts, and decoding and exposing the relation between the production of knowledge and the practices of power. It is only then that we can aspire to real and meaningful change that can transform the deep structures that have shaped our religious, cultural and political realities.

REFERENCES

'Abd Al'Ati, Hammudah. 1997. *The Family Structure in Islam*. Indianapolis: American Trust.

Abou-Bakr, Omaima (ed.). 2013. *Feminist and Islamic Perspectives: New Horizons of Knowledge and Reform*. Cairo: Women and Memory Forum with the Danish–Egyptian Dialogue Institute and the Danish Centre for Research on Women and Gender.

Abu-Odeh, Lama. 2004. 'Modernizing Islamic Law: The Case of Egypt'. *Vanderbilt Journal of Transnational Law* 37 (4): pp. 1043–146.

Abu Zayd, Nasr. 1990. *The Concept of the Text: A Study of the Qur'anic Sciences* (Mafhum al-Naṣṣ: Dirasah fi 'Ulum al-Qur'an). Cairo: al-Hayah al-Misriyah al-Ammah lil-Kitab.

Abu Zayd, Nasr. 2006. *Reformation of Islamic Thought: A Critical Historical Analysis*. Amsterdam: Amsterdam University Press.

Abu Zayd, Nasr. 2011. 'Towards Understanding the Qur'an's Worldview: An Autobiographical Reflection'. In *New Perspectives on the Qur'an: The Qur'an in its Historical Context*, edited by Gabriel Said Reynolds, pp. 47–87. London: Routledge.

Abu Zayd, Nasr. 2013. 'The Status of Women between the Qur'an and *Fiqh*'. In *Gender and Equality in Muslim Family Law: Justice and Ethics in the Islamic Legal Tradition*, edited by Ziba Mir-Hosseini, Kari Vogt, Lena Larsen and Christian Moe, pp. 153–68. London: I.B. Tauris.

AFTURD. 2006. *Egalité dans l'Héritage: Pour Une Citoyenneté Pleine et Entière*. Tunis.

Ahmed, Leila. 1992. *Women and Gender in Islam: Historical Roots of a Modern Debate*. New Haven: Yale University Press.

Al-Hibri, Azizah. 1982. 'A Study of Islamic Herstory: Or How Did We Ever Get into This Mess'. In *Women's Studies International Forum* 5 (2): pp. 207–19.

Al-Hibri, Azizah. 2003. 'An Islamic Perspective on Domestic Violence'. *Fordham International Law Journal* 27 (1): pp. 195–224.

Ali, Kecia. 2003. 'Progressive Muslims and Islamic Jurisprudence: The Necessity for Critical Engagement with Marriage and Divorce Law'. In *Progressive Muslims: On Justice, Gender, and Pluralism*, edited by Omid Safi, pp. 163–89. Oxford: Oneworld.

Ali, Kecia. 2007. 'Religious Practices: Obedience and Disobedience in Islamic Discourses'. In *Encyclopedia of Women in Islamic Cultures*, vol. 5, edited by Suad Joseph, pp. 309–13. Leiden: Brill.

Ali, Kecia. 2010. *Marriage and Slavery in Early Islam*. Cambridge, MA: Harvard University Press.

Ali, Kecia. n.d. 'Muslim Sexual Ethics: Understanding a Difficult Verse, Qur'an 4:34'. http://www.brandeis.edu/projects/fse/muslim/diff-verse.html, accessed 1 January 2014.

Anderson, James Norman. 1976. *Law Reforms in the Muslim World*. London: Athlone.

Barlas, Asma. 2002. *Believing Women in Islam: Unreading Patriarchal Interpretations of the Qur'an*. Austin: Texas University Press.

Boulby, Marion. 1988. 'The Islamic Challenge: Tunisia since Independence'. *Third World Quarterly* 10 (2): pp. 590–614.

Charrad, Mounira. 2001. *States and Women's Rights: The Making of Postcolonial Tunisia, Algeria and Morocco*. Berkeley: University of California Press.

Chiba, Masaji. 1986. 'Introduction'. In *Asian Indigenous Law in Interaction with Received Law*, edited by Masaji Chiba, pp. 1–9. London: Kegan Paul International.

Duderija, Adis. 2011. *Constructing a Religiously Ideal 'Believer' and 'Woman' in Islam: Neo-traditional Salafi and Progressive Muslims' Methods of Interpretation*. New York: Palgrave.

Eshkevari, Hassan Yousefi. 2013. 'Rethinking Men's Authority over Women: Qiwama, Wilaya and Their Underlying Assumptions'. In *Gender and Equality in Muslim Family Law: Justice and Ethics in the Islamic Legal Tradition*, edited by Ziba Mir-Hosseini, Kari Vogt, Lena Larsen and Christian Moe, pp. 191–212. London: I.B. Tauris.

Ferrari, Silvio. 2006. 'Adapting Divine Law to Change: The Experience of the Roman Catholic Church (with Some References to Jewish and Islamic Law)'. *Cardozo Law Review* 28 (1): pp. 53–65.

Gilligan, Carol. 2011. *Joining the Resistance*. Cambridge, UK: Polity Press.

Harding, Sandra (ed.). 2004. *The Feminist Standpoint Theory Reader: Intellectual and Political Controversies*. London: Routledge.

Hassan, Riffat. 1987. 'Equal before Allah? Woman–Man Equality in the Islamic Tradition'. *Harvard Divinity Bulletin* 17 (2): http://www.globalwebpost.com/farooqm/study_res/islam/gender/equal_riffat.html, accessed 1 January 2014.

Hassan, Riffat. 1999. 'Feminism in Islam'. In *Feminism and World Religions*, edited by Arvind Sharma and Kate Young, pp. 248–78. New York: State University of New York Press.

Hermansen, Marcia. 2013. 'New Voices of Women Theologians'. In *Muslima Theology: Voices of Muslim Women Theologians*, edited by Ednan Aslan, Elif Medeni and Marcia Hermansen, pp. 11–34. Frankfurt: Peter Lang.

Husni, Ronak, and Daniel Newman (eds). 2007. *Muslim Women in Law and Society: Annotated Translation of al-Tahir al-Haddad's Imra'tuna fi 'l-shari'a wa 'l-mujtama', with an Introduction*. London: Routledge.

Ibn Rushd. 1996. *The Distinguished Jurist's Primer*, vol. 2 (*Bidayat al-Mujtahid wa Nihayat al-Muqtasid*), translated by Imran Ahsan Khan Nyazee. Reading: Garnet.

Kadivar, Mohsen. 2013. 'Revisiting Women's Rights in Islam: "Egalitarian Justice" in Lieu of "Deserts-Based Justice"'. In *Gender and Equality in Muslim Family Law: Justice and Ethics in the Islamic Legal Tradition*, edited by Ziba Mir-Hosseini, Kari Vogt, Lena Larsen and Christian Moe, pp. 213–36. London: I.B. Tauris.

Kapur, Ratna. 2012. 'Unveiling Equality: Disciplining the "Other" Woman through the Human Rights Discourse'. In *Islamic Law and International Human Rights Law*, edited by Anver M. Emon, Mark S. Ellis and Benjamin Glahn, pp. 265–90. Oxford: Oxford University Press.

Keddie, Nikki. 2007. *Women in the Middle East: Past and Present*. Princeton, NJ: Princeton University Press.

Kelly, Patricia. 1996. 'Finding Common Ground: Islamic Values and Gender Equity in Tunisia's Reformed Personal Status Law'. In *Shifting Boundaries in Marriage and Divorce in Muslim Communities, Special Dossier*, edited by Homa Hoodfar, pp. 74–105. Grabels, France: Women Living under Muslim Laws.

Kermani, Navid. 2004. 'From Revelation to Interpretation: Nasr Hamid Abu Zayd and the Literary Study of the Qur'an'. In *Modern Muslim Intellectuals and the Qur'an*, edited by Suha Taji-Farouki, pp. 169–92. Oxford: Oxford University Press.

Kurzman, Charles (ed.). 1998. *Liberal Islam: A Sourcebook*. Oxford: Oxford University Press.

Kurzman, Charles (ed.). 2002. *Modernist Islam 1840–1940: A Sourcebook*. Oxford: Oxford University Press.

MacIntyre, Alasdair. 1988. *Whose Justice? Which Rationality?* Indiana: University of Notre Dame Press.

Mahmood, Tahir. 1972. *Family Law Reforms in the Muslim World*. Mumbai: N.M. Tripathi.

Mahmoud, Mohamed. 2006. 'To Beat or Not to Beat: On Exegetical Dilemmas over Qur'an 4:34'. *Journal of the American Oriental Society* 126 (4): pp. 537–50.

Mir-Hosseini, Ziba. 2003. 'The Construction of Gender in Islamic Legal Thought: Strategies for Reform'. *Hawwa* 1 (1): pp. 1–28.

Mir-Hosseini, Ziba. 2006. 'Muslim Women's Quest for Equality: Between Islamic Law and Feminism'. *Critical Inquiry* 32 (1): pp. 629–45.

Mir-Hosseini, Ziba. 2007. 'Islam and Gender Justice'. In *Voices of Islam*, vol. 5, *Voices of Diversity and Change*, edited by Vincent Cornell and Omid Safi, pp. 85–113. Westport, CT: Greenwood.

Mir-Hosseini, Ziba. 2009. 'Towards Gender Equality: Muslim Family Laws and the Shari'ah'. In *Wanted: Equality and Justice in the Muslim Family*, edited by Zainah Anwar, pp. 23–63. Petaling Jaya: Musawah.

Mir-Hosseini, Ziba. 2012. 'Sexuality and Inequality: The Marriage Contract and Muslim Legal Tradition'. In *Sexuality in Muslim Contexts: Restrictions and Resistance*, edited by Anissa Helie and Homa Hoodfar, pp. 124–48. London: Zed Books.

Mir-Hosseini, Ziba. 2013. 'Muslim Family Laws, Justice and Equality: New Ideas, New Prospects'. In *Gender and Equality in Muslim Family Law: Justice and Ethics in the Islamic Legal Tradition*, edited by Ziba Mir-Hosseini, Kari Vogt, Lena Larsen and Christian Moe, pp. 7–34. London: I.B. Tauris.

Moosa, Ibrahim. 2000. 'Introduction'. In *Revival and Reform in Islam*, by Fazlur Rahman. Oxford: Oneworld.

Rahman, Fazlur. 1980. 'A Survey of Modernization of Muslim Family Law'. *International Journal of Middle Eastern Studies* 11 (4): pp. 451–65.

Rahman, Fazlur. 1982a. *Islam and Modernity: Transformation of an Intellectual Tradition*. Chicago: University of Chicago Press.

Rahman, Fazlur. 1982b. 'The Status of Women in Islam: A Modernist Interpretation'. In *Separated Worlds: Studies of Purdah in South Asia*, edited by Hanna Papanek and Gail Minault, pp. 285–310. Delhi: Chanakya.

Ramazanoğlu, Caroline with Janet Holland. 2002. *Feminist Methodology: Challenges and Choice*. London: Sage.

Rapoport, Yossef. 2005. *Marriage, Money and Divorce in Medieval Islamic Society*. Cambridge, UK: Cambridge University Press.

Saeed, Abdullah. 2004. 'Fazlur Rahman: A Framework for Interpreting the Ethico-legal Content of the Qur'an'. In *Modern Muslim Intellectuals and the Qur'an*, edited by Suha Taji-Farouki, pp. 37–66. Oxford: Oxford University Press.

Salem, Norma. 1984. 'Islam and the Status of Women in Tunisia'. In *Muslim Women*, edited by Freda Hussain, pp. 141–68. London: Croom Helm.

Seedat, Fatima. 2013. 'When Islam and Feminism Converge'. *Muslim World* 103 (3): pp. 404–20.

Sonbol, Amira El-Azhary (ed.). 1996. *Women, Family and Divorce Laws in Islamic History*. Syracuse, NY: Syracuse University Press.

Sonbol, Amira El-Azhary. 1998. 'Ta'a and Modern Legal Reform: A Reading'. *Islam and Christian–Muslim Relations* 9 (3): pp. 285–94.

Sonn, Tamara. 1991. 'Fazlur Rahman's Islamic Methodology'. *Muslim World* 81 (3–4): pp. 212–30.

Sonn, Tamara. 1998. 'Fazlur Rahman and Islamic Feminism'. In *The Shaping of An American Islamic Discourse: A Memorial to Fazlur Rahman*, edited by Earle H. Waugh and Frederic M. Denny, pp. 123–45. Atlanta: Scholars Press.

Stowasser, Barbara. 1993. 'Women's Issues in Modern Islamic Thought'. In *Arab Women: Old Boundaries, New Frontiers*, edited by Judith E. Tucker, pp. 3–28. Bloomington: Indiana University Press.

Tucker, Judith. 2000. *In the House of Law: Gender and Islamic Law in Ottoman Syria and Palestine*. Berkeley: University of California Press.

Wadud, Amina. 1999. *Qur'an and Woman: Rereading the Sacred Text from a Woman's Perspective*. Oxford: Oxford University Press.

Wadud, Amina. 2006. *Inside the Gender Jihad: Women's Reform in Islam*. Oxford: Oneworld.

Waugh, Earle H. and Frederic M. Denny (eds). 1998. *The Shaping of an American Islamic Discourse: A Memorial to Fazlur Rahman*. Atlanta: Scholars Press.

Welchman, Lynn. 2011. 'A Husband's Authority: Emerging Formulations in Muslim Family Laws'. *International Journal of Law, Policy and the Family* 25 (1): pp. 1–23.

The Interpretive Legacy of *Qiwamah* as an Exegetical Construct

Omaima Abou-Bakr

T he objective of this survey is to trace the accumulation of interpretations and understanding of the Qur'anic term *qawwamun* in the genre of *tafasir* literature, noting significant evolutions, changes or shifts in meaning that have occurred along this chronological path. How exactly did the Qur'anic sentence *'al-rijal qawwamun 'ala al-nisa' bima faddala Allah ba'dahum 'ala ba'd wa bima anfaqu min amwalihim'*[1] – which is part of the larger verse 4:34, in its turn part of a larger passage, and part of a larger structure of governing principles – become an independent and separate (transcontextual) patriarchal construct? Perhaps if we understand this historical and cultural process, we will be able to refute certain meanings and reconstruct others.

In the last ten years, in particular, recent scholarship has proliferated in the specific area of scrutinizing *tafsir* literature with regard to certain terms

---

[1] Abdullah Yusuf Ali's (1989) translation of this sentence in verse 4:34 reads, 'Men are the protectors and maintainers of women, because Allah has given the one more [strength] than the other, and because they support them from their means.' The remainder of the verse is, 'Therefore the righteous women are devoutly obedient, and guard in [the husband's] absence what Allah would have them guard. As to those women on whose part ye fear disloyalty and ill-conduct, admonish them [first], [Next], refuse to share their beds, [And last] beat them [lightly]; but if they return to obedience, seek not against them Means [of annoyance]: For Allah is Most High, great [above you all].'

or phrases related to gender notions.[2] Needless to say, the foremost terms to attract the attention of scholars and researchers interested in rethinking and reinterpreting gender verses have been *darajah*, *faddala*, *qawwamun*, *qanitat*, *nushuz*, etc.[3] Producing research on verse 4:34 has turned into an obsession and an industry. It is indeed the verse that most often touches our lives as Muslim women and so deserves our attention and scholarly contestation. This increasing research also embodies the very idea of Muslim women's right to participate in *ijtihad* and the production of Islamic knowledge.

The traditional division and categorization of the exegetical corpus is usually made according to either methodological approaches or historical phases. The first set of classifications include: a) interpretation according to reported traditions (*bil-ma'thur*); b) interpretation according to individual opinion (*bil-ra'y*); c) symbolic Sufi interpretation (*al-ramzi* or *kashfi*); d) the thematic or topical approach (*al-mawdu'i*); e) rhetorical/literary analysis (*al-bayani*); and f) scientific interpretation (*'ilmi*). Historically, works of Qur'anic interpretation are divided into three phases. The first phase is the initial period of the Prophet Muhammad and his Companions; the second phase corresponds to the second generation of the Followers or disciples; and the third phase marks the beginning of formal documentation and the emergence of the 'science of exegesis' (*'ilm al-tafsir*) as a separate branch within the religious sciences.[4]

The commentaries this chapter examines belong to this latter formal phase and cover only the two initial classified methodological approaches of *ra'y* and *ma'thur*. In general, it appears that an individual exegete's hermeneutical stance or theological school (*madhhab*) has little bearing on particular gender notions and interpretations. Hence, this genealogical investigation of *qiwamah* demonstrates a powerful, traditional legacy of its own.

The first section of this chapter presents examples of exegetes' formulations and discourse relating to *qiwamah* over the course of ten centuries. The

---

[2] The following are selected samples of articles (not including discussions that appear in book chapters): al-Hibri (1982), Hassan (1999), Marin (2003), Mahmoud (2006), Ammar (2007), Bauer (2009), Shaikh (1997; 2007), Elsaidi (2011) and Chaudhry (2013).

[3] Abdullah Yusuf Ali (1989) translated *darajah* as 'degree (of advantage)'; *faddala* as 'favour'; *qawwamun* as 'protectors and maintainers'; *qanitat* as 'devoutly obedient'; and *nushuz* as 'disloyalty and ill-conduct'. Muhammad Asad (1980) translated *darajah* as 'precedence over'; *faddala* as 'bestowed more abundantly'; *qawwamun* as 'take full care of'; *qanitat* as 'devout'; and *nushuz* as 'ill-will'.

[4] See al-Dhahabi (1976) for the most authoritative scholarly work on the history and development of the science of *tafsir* and its schools.

second turns to a brief mapping of current proposed strategies by Muslim feminists and reformists towards reinterpreting the term and concept. I conclude with suggestions of further trajectories and nuances to explore in future research.

THE CHRONOLOGICAL PATH OF MEDIEVAL AND MODERN CONSTRUCTIONS

This evolution from *qawammun* to the patriarchal construct of *qiwamah* went through four discursive stages. The initial stage was turning the descriptive *qawwamun* into a normative or prescriptive conception, signalled by the transformation to a grammatical *masdar* (a verbal noun or infinitive), namely *qiyam*, which later developed into *qiwamah*. The second stage was consolidation through amassing reasons for the hierarchal concept of *qiwamah*. Third, jurists expanded the concept through linking it to *darajah* (degree) in Qur'anic verse 2:228 and selected *ahadith*. Finally, there was a modernist turn of linking it to the ideology of domesticity and women's *fitrah* (created nature).[5]

The first stage – turning the descriptive *qawwamun* into the normative prescriptive construction *qiyam* – began with Abu Ja'far Muhammad al-Tabari, a scholar and historian who was born in 839 CE at Amul in the province of Tabaristan and died in 923 CE in Baghdad. Al-Tabari created the first comprehensive commentary on the Qur'an, *Jami' al-Bayan fi Tafsir al-Quran*, by collecting and documenting the ample material of traditional understandings that survived until his time. This earliest *tafsir* became a standard work upon which later commentaries drew, and it contains valuable information for modern historical-critical research. Al-Tabari used a meticulous, systematic method to cite the diverse chain of authorities and reports used in understanding and interpreting each verse, then evaluated them, exercised his judgement and presented his own explanation and commentary.

The period in which al-Tabari lived, studied and travelled across Iraq, Syria and Egypt can be characterized politically as the breakdown of the traditional, centralized authority of the Abbasid caliphate, yet socially, culturally and intellectually as a formative age. Ira Lapidus (1988) calls these historically significant centuries – the ninth to thirteenth centuries CE – the 'post-imperial' period, when the diffusion of certain forms of social, educational and religious

---

[5] Unless otherwise noted, all translations from the original Arabic are my own.

organization across Muslim lands became the new determinants of a discernible identity for these societies:

> [This new formation] bequeathed a repertoire of cultural and religious ideas which remain operative in Islamic lands to the present day. From this era came the forms of Islamic orthopraxis contained in hadith and law, Sufi forms of ethical and spiritual self-cultivation, Shi'i concepts of religious leadership, ideals of mystical and Gnostic transcendence, popular saint worship and magical practices, and a socially active and reformist Islamic idea. This period also gave rise to the basic elements of Islamic social organization: states, schools of law, and Sufi tariqat. Finally this era set the precedent for a separation between state institutions and Muslim religious communities. (p. 237)

Hence, this period witnessed the solidification of Sunni schools of law and subsequent ulama communities or associations of scholars, teachers and students, organizing higher education and training teachers and judges. As Lapidus (1988) notes, the ulama were not so much involved in politics as in community affairs and the control of legal administration and educational and charitable activities: 'Their concern was to uphold public morality, to apply the Shari'a to family and commercial affairs, to educate, to heal, and to mediate local conflicts' (p. 233). In other words, in studying the ideas, notions and voices embedded in theological writings, we try to understand the mutuality of the reflection of sociocultural norms in these writings and, at the same time, the influence of these discourses on reconstructing social reality.

Al-Tabari's exegesis is identified as the masterwork that laid the foundation for this genre and set numerous concepts and trajectories in motion thereafter. In his explanation of *qawwamun*, he used the phrase *ahl qiyam 'ala nisa'ihim* (watching over or being in charge of their women) to establish men's collective task or responsibility of *qiyam* in disciplining women (al-Tabari, 1961, vol. 8, p. 290). He understood the second portion of the verse – 'because Allah has given the one more [strength] than the other, and because they support them from their means' – as the reason why men were designated to be 'people of this disciplining task'. The main basis for the right to discipline was that God privileged them to provide women with their dower and sustenance. Hence, not only did al-Tabari initiate and put into motion the hierarchal idea of moral superiority and the right to discipline (*ta'dibihinna*), but he also instituted the twisted logic of turning the divine assignment to provide economic support into a reason for privilege: 'they provide because they are better, or they are better because they provide'.

Thus, the original direct meaning of *qawwamun/bima faddala* (financial support by the means God gave them) developed this way: 1) from descriptive to normative/from responsibility to authority; 2) introducing the noun *qiyam* (which paved the way to the later *qiwamah*) as an essentialist notion of moral superiority;[6] 3) from the restricted meaning of providing financial support to a wider range of a generalized status of all men everywhere and at all times; and 4) from a relative, changing condition of material bounty on account of inheritance to an unconditional favouritism based on gender. As Amina Wadud (1999) puts it, what Allah has preferred is restricted to the material, and not absolute (p. 71).

The second stage – consolidation through amassing reasons for the hierarchical construction of *qiwamah* – can be identified with the Persian-Arab scholar Abu al-Qasim Mahmud ibn Umar al-Zamakhshari (d. 1144), who completed in 1134 his *Al-Kashshaf 'an Haqa'iq Ghawamid al-Tanzil*, which is rich in linguistic-rhetorical analysis and strongly revealed his Mu'tazilite ideas and doctrine. Modern researchers maintain that this 'pronounced dogmatization of the exegesis' made his commentary less influential and significant in the general history of Qur'anic commentaries (Gatje, 1976, p. 36). However, examined from the perspective of highlighting the interpretation of *qiwamah*, his text picked up the strand of hierarchy from al-Tabari and dropped the reference to economic provision. He concentrated on two points. First, he consolidated superiority and the right to discipline by introducing a metaphor that likened the relationship between men and women to the relationship between 'rulers' and 'subjects', in that they 'manage them by ordering and forbidding' (*amirin, nahin*). Second, he consolidated the notion of *tafdil* (favouring) as the God-given reason for the fact that they are in control (*musaytirin*) (al-Zamakhshari, 1948, vol. 1, p. 394). Again, notice the transformation of *bima faddala*, the verb, to a general conceptual noun.

---

[6] Amani Saleh (2002) has made the point that 'the term *qiwamah* in its verbal noun form did not occur in the Qur'an in the same manner as other notions that occurred textually thus [as a noun], and the Qur'an was careful to clarify accurately their connotations and elements, such as the terms of *iman, taqwa, kufr, fusuq*...etc.' (p. 49). She goes on to say, 'The term *qiwamah* seems to be more of a *fiqhi* concept coined by the *fuqaha'* to express their special reading of the issue of gender in the Qur'an, just like other *fiqhi* concepts that became *shar'i* later on, e.g. *al-hakimiyyah, al-imamah*...etc.'

Al-Zamakhshari provided a long list of justifications for this divinely ordained preference: men are better in 'reason, resoluteness, determination, strength, writing (in most cases), horsemanship, spear-throwing'; among them are 'the prophets and the ulama'; further, 'they perform the *imamah*, the *jihad*, the *adhan*, the *khutbah*, *'i'tikaf*, loud *takbirat*[7] (according to Abu Hanifah), bearing witness in *hudud* and *qasas*,[8] increase of inheritance shares and divisions, *wilayah* in marriage, the right to pronounce divorce and revoke it, the number of spouses, lineage, in addition to having beards and wearing turbans'. Notice the mixed bag of innate qualities, social customs and *fiqhi* deductions, a confusing and arbitrary mix that has stayed with us for centuries.

The famous Persian-Arab theologian and religious philosopher Fakhr al-Din al-Razi (d. 1209), a Shafi'i who also wrote on physics, medicine and astronomy, was opposed to Mu'tazilite doctrines. Throughout his works, he attempted to reconcile philosophy and religious traditions, hence he was accused at times of rationalism. His *Al-Tafsir al-Kabir* is considered an Ash'arite answer to Mu'tazilite Qur'anic exegesis, as represented by al-Zamakhshari, since he brought in a great deal of his own philosophical views. He began his interpretation by taking the verse back to its financial implications and linking it to inheritance. He attempted to explain the justification of the increase in men's inheritance shares: 'Although both men and women share their mutual enjoyment of one another, God ordered men to pay to them dower and sustenance; hence, the increase in one side is met by an increase in the other side, so as if no excess (*fadl*) whatsoever' (al-Razi, 1938, vol. 10, p. 87). Al-Razi meant that the monetary increase to men through inheritance was met by the increase in financial responsibility towards women; hence, no surplus, but rather equality in the distribution of financial resources. The interpretation would have been quite reasonable had it stopped there. Unfortunately, he proceeded to maintain the previous circular logic that men's responsibility of support arose from their privileged status.

Building on al-Tabari's idea of authority to discipline (*musallatun 'ala 'adabihin*) and al-Zamakhshari's idea of men as rulers ('as if God made the man *amir* upon her with executed rule concerning her'), al-Razi discussed the reasons why God instituted 'men's *saltanah* over women'. He stated two main reasons

---

[7] The translations of the respective terms are as follows: leading the prayer; fighting for the cause of God; calling for the prayer; giving the sermon in collective prayer; spending time of solitude and prayer in the mosque; calling *Allahu Akbar* (God is great) in a loud voice.

[8] *Hudud* are understood to be particular types of crimes for which the punishment has been specified in the Qur'an, such as stealing, fornication, etc. *Qasas* is retribution for the crime of murder.

matching the two portions of the verse. The first reason that men are better than women was a combination of intrinsic (*haqiqiyyah*) characteristics and in *shar'i* rules: knowledge, mental capacity, physical ability, resoluteness, horsemanship, spear-throwing, being prophets, ulama and imams, undertaking *jihad*, the *adhan*, the *khutbah*, bearing witness, more inheritance shares, being charged with blood-money, with *wilayah* in marriage, divorce, and number of wives, and lineage. Notice that he automatically repeated al-Zamakhshari's list of reasons, but also added a few more of his own. The second reason, according to al-Razi, was the portion in the verse 'wa *bima anfaqu min amwalihim*', which he took to mean 'a man is better than a woman because he gives her dower and sustenance'.

Another theologian and scholar from Persia in the time of the Atabek ruler Abu Bakr ibn Sa'd was Abd Allah ibn 'Umar al-Baidawi, who was educated in Baghdad, became a judge in Shiraz and died in Tabriz in 1286. In his *Anwar al-Tanzil wa-Asrar al-Ta'wil*, he summarized most of al-Zamakhshari's material, but also expanded and added from other sources, assimilating the commentary to mainstream Sunni theology. This work was highly regarded by Sunni scholars and used as a textbook in Islamic schools until the sixteenth century. Because of its condensed nature (two volumes), it was one of the first Qur'anic exegeses published in Europe (1846–8).

Al-Baidawi immediately began the commentary on verse 4:34 with what has become a standardized expression – the notion of men 'being their [women's] sovereign like rulers over subjects' (1968, vol. 1, p. 217). His contribution, however, lay in distinguishing between innate features or causes of divine preference (*wahbi*) and others that are acquired (*kasbi*), again matching the two portions of the verse. He reproduced the previous lists, adding a new expression in reference to divorce: *al-istibdad bi-l-furaq* (i.e. independently and autocratically taking the decision of parting). Notice how the assumption of 'rule' as the main indicator of the relationship between husbands and wives superseded the injunction of economic support.

The next commentator along this path was Abu Abdallah al-Qurtubi, a famous exegete, *muhaddith* and jurist scholar who was born in Cordoba, Spain, where he was first educated, went to Egypt to study *hadith* and *tafsir* after Cordoba's capture in 1236 and died there in 1273. His twenty-volume commentary, *al-Jami' li-Ahkam al-Qur'an*, was known to reflect his Maliki jurist point of view; however, this comprehensive work was not limited to legal issues, since all interpretive points were also thoroughly investigated and commented upon.

Al-Qurtubi's commentary on the verse recalls that of al-Razi, as he initially related qiwamah to men's spending from increased financial sources of inheritance shares, as referred to in verse 4:11. Al-Qurtubi explained that God showed the reason for this increased share in inheritance: it was because husbands paid dower and provided for women; hence, 'the benefit of this preference goes back to them [women]' (al-Qurtubi, 1967, vols 5–6, p. 168). However, he also resembled al-Razi in following this piece with a contradictory presentation of preference, not merely on account of material resources, but also based on innate gender characteristics expressed in that age's scientific terms:

It is said that men have the privilege of mind and better management… and it has been said that men have strong natures that women do not have because men's disposition is determined by heat and dryness which gives them strength and hardness, whereas women's disposition is determined by humidness and coldness, giving them the characteristics of leniency and weakness. (Al-Qurtubi, 1967, vols 5–6, p. 169, emphasis mine)

Al-Qurtubi here signalled the beginning of a new trajectory that attempts to use either contemporaneous cultural views or the time's known scientific 'facts' as evidence to corroborate an exegete's perception of gender differences. This strategy has gained even more dominance in modern commentaries, which have further consolidated and elaborated on linking the biological to the personal, translating differentiation into hierarchy.

In interpreting the rest of the verse, al-Qurtubi maintained the right to discipline, with a warning to men 'not to abuse their companionship', and added to the list of male rights or privileges that of 'enjoining the right and forbidding the wrong'. Then he referred to the juristic understanding and interpretation that if a husband was incapable of providing, then he would not be qawwam over his wife – meaning that he can be sovereign only when he provides. Notice the confusion, back and forth, between two notions of qiwamah. Contingent upon financial support or an absolute condition? An injunction to spend or a feature of divine preference?

The third stage of expansion, elaboration and accumulation of evidence of men's superiority on all levels began with Abu al-Fida 'Imad al-Din Isma'il ibn 'Umar Ibn Kathir (1301–73), the Syrian historian, muhaddith and exegete. Influenced by Ibn Taymiyyah (d. 1328), his approach was conservative and strongly dependent on past traditions. According to the modern scholar of the 'science of *tafsir*', al-Dhahabi (1976), Ibn Kathir is the most famous of exegetes – since the pioneer al-Tabari – to use in exaggeration the *ma'thur* method (reported traditions and *ahadith*).

In this discursive stage, Ibn Kathir expanded the notion of men's superiority through the use of Abu-Bakara's famous *hadith* about women's leadership (No people will prosper that has delegated a woman to lead their affairs), and he stipulated that women cannot be judges in the context of verse 4:34, thereby extending the scope of male supremacy and authority from the domestic to the public sphere. In addition, Ibn Kathir linked verse 4:34 to the notion of *darajah* in verse 2:228 and obsessively compiled all of the *ahadith* on wifely obedience and reverence to husbands that he could gather (Ibn Kathir, n.d., vol. 1, p. 491). Ironically, when a classical exegete escaped the 'atomistic methodology' described by Amina Wadud (1999), he did it to render a 'false' or forced connection that extracted Qur'anic terms out of context and turned them into building blocks of concept construction. It is also baffling that because of this method of digging up various *ahadith* and sayings by the Companions to explain most verses, this exegesis has become a classic in the Muslim world today – popular and widely cited in *khutbas* and religious classes.

The mid-thirteenth to mid-sixteenth century is roughly the period of the Mamluk regime that governed Egypt, Syria, southeastern Asia Minor and western Arabia. This regime was known for its military power and prosperity. Historians note in particular a flourishing in the area of higher religious education: Cairo, for example, saw the establishment of dozens of madrasas, through the pious foundations and endowments of sultans and emirs, in addition to generous funding to support teachers and students. This is also the period that witnessed the spread of dozens of women *muhaddithat* and *faqihat* (specialized religious scholars and teachers) across Muslim lands, who taught in their homes, lectured in major mosques and graduated male students (Abou-Bakr, 2003). In addition to the works that documented the learning, teaching activities and travels of these elite women scholars, other historical sources from the same period recorded details of the social and public lives of ordinary women in the urban centres of Mamluk states. A good example is *Al-Madkhal* by Abu Abdallah ibn al-Hajj al-'Abdari (d. 1336), a didactic treatise in which he vehemently criticized the manners, lifestyles and public activities of women, which were becoming very apparent during his times (Lutfi, 1991). Similar tracts concerned with public morals and order were meant to combat the *bid'a* (false innovations in religious practices) of popular culture of the times, such as visitation and veneration of graves, widespread visibility of women, and women's participation in street festivities and musical celebrations (singing, using tambourines and dancing). A number of Mamluk rulers went as far as banning certain activities, especially women's visitation to graves on Fridays and during the *'eid* (Shoshan, 1993, pp. 68–9).

This context may explain the concomitant rising tone of moralizing and bias against women in particular and religiously justifying restraint. We can view the *tafsir* by Jalal al-Din al-Suyuti (d. 1505) in this light. He was a prolific Egyptian scholar of all fields in religious learning and held teaching and legal positions in the Shafi'i school of law. His commentary, known as *Tafsir al-Jala-layn*, is still widely in use today because of its conciseness and practicality. Ironically, we may notice a departure from the general methodological characteristic of concise paraphrase of verses and vocabulary related to the *qiwamah* concept. His explanation instead is an excellent example of the interpretive strategy noted in Ibn Kathir, as well as its pinnacle, for the number of pages devoted to verse 4:34 alone reached six pages and the relevant *ahadith* or analogue citations reached twenty-seven. The majority of *ahadith* cited were weak (mainly from the less authoritative collections) and the excessive accumulation and repetition of negative pronouncements on women, ascribed to the Prophet or the Companions, recall typical medieval misogynistic literature found in European traditions.[9] Among the most famous troubling *ahadith* are the metaphoric wifely 'prostration' to husbands, the 'licking of ulcers and pus', and 'responding to a husband's desire even when on a camel's back' – all appearing for the first time in a *tafsir* work in the context of interpreting *qiwamah* in verse 4:34 with exaggerated insistence or obsession.

Two themes in particular are reiterated hysterically: a wife's absolute subservience and obedience to a husband's orders, and the prohibition of going outside the house without his approval. The question can be raised here about the need felt by this fifteenth-century exegete to stress these issues. In line with what has been mentioned before, Ruth Roded in her *Women in Islamic Biographies* (1994) observed that particularly during the thirteenth- and fourteenth-century Mamluk period, historical records showed the widespread appearance of Muslim women in the public arena in various fields and that

---

[9] See the chapter 'Faith-Based Assumptions and Determinations Demeaning to Women' in Abou El Fadl (2001) for a comprehensive and excellent refutation of these traditions.

official edicts were issued trying to stop or limit their presence and free circulation outdoors (p. 138).[10] Are these religious texts simply a conservative reaction to contemporaneous social reality and a growing desire to limit women's movements in the public arena? In other words, such exegetical, jurist and *fatawa* texts and the dominant religious discourse could indicate what some religious scholars envisioned and wished for gender relations and the place of women; they are not necessarily an authentic reflection of social reality in all its dimensions and practicalities.

The fourth stage came with the modernist development of adding the ideology of domesticity and the 'scientific' justification of biological essentialism through the use of the notion of women's *fitrah* – their 'inborn' nature. The first modern exegete to make extensive use of these ideas was the Egyptian reformist Muhammad 'Abduh (d. 1905) at the turn of the twentieth century. In *Tafsir al-Manar*, his seminal and influential early modern work, he introduced the notion of 'the *fitri* reason' of qiwamah ('Abduh, 1990, pp. 55–8). He also wrote about wives 'living under the *riyasah* [rule and leadership] of husbands' as a condition that followed the requirements of human nature. 'Abduh particularly elaborated on the compound notion of *riyasah–ra'is–mar'us* (i.e. rule/leadership–leader–ruled), constructing the marital relationship as a boss–subordinate relationship. He was also the first exegete to adapt a relevant biblical reference[11] when he stated that 'a man is like the head, and the woman is the body', and it is 'no shame for a human being to have his head better than his hand'. Huge emphasis was put on enumerating and explaining women's biological and domestic functions, beginning with pregnancy, childbirth, nursing and child-rearing, to being 'manager/keeper of the house', since 'the home is like a small kingdom'. This 'house/domestic life' (*al-hayah al-manziliyah*) was a woman's 'natural work' ('*amaluha al-tabi'i*) according to 'the system of innate natural disposition' (*nizam al-fitrah*). These are all terms incorporated for the first time in a *tafsir* work and strongly reflect the beginning of the modernist ideology of sanctifying domesticity and 'naturalizing' or 'essentializing' the division of gender roles. A serious consequence to this discourse is the conclusion that 'even if the *shar'* had allowed women to deliver the Friday *khutbah*, the *adhan*, and lead the prayers, this wouldn't have prevented that the *fitrah* requires for men to be sovereign *qawwamin* over

---

[10] For more on the Mamluk period, see Stilt (2011).
[11] '[T]he head of every man is Christ; and the head of the woman is the man; and the head of Christ is God' (1 Cor. 11:3).

women' ('Abduh, 1990, vols 5–6, p. 58). 'Abduh's pronouncements directly opposed those of the classical jurists, who did not include domestic service as incumbent upon women in marriage.

Subsequent twentieth-century exegetes continued using this composite of meanings and definitions, refining and developing medieval gender biases through the division of male and female psychological natures, one disposed to rational and abstract thinking, the other emotional, nurturing and fixated on details. This 'natural' organization of human nature led to a corresponding God-ordained division of private domesticity versus public work. Hence, the discourse here reshapes the old medieval hierarchy in modern, pseudo-scientific terms.

Among the most typical of this trend are Sayyid Qutb (d. 1966) and Shaykh Muhammad Mitwalli al-Sha'rawi (d. 1998). Qutb, an Egyptian critic and Islamist thinker and activist, called for the immediate and exact application of God's laws as part of his vision of a truly Islamic state, and so was known for his politically radical ideas and considered an icon of some factions of current political Islamism. He produced a full Qur'anic commentary, Fi Zilal al-Qur'an (1952), in which he explicated verse 4:34 and other verses related to gender in terms of biological and psychological essentialism, in addition to a strict division of gender roles according to a private/public divide. He argued this is a God-inscribed organization of human society.

Qutb was among the early twentieth-century writers to articulate in very clear terms the basically modern, conservative view of 'the human institution of the family' (Qutb, 1952, pp. 57–60). He reasoned that, like in any other formal organization, it is necessary that parties in the family perform their 'specialized functions' according to their 'capabilities and readiness'. Because men have the function of working and providing, God provided them with 'innate physical, neural, mental, and psychological characteristics' to aid them in performing this function. Since women are to concentrate on their function of bearing and raising children, they were also provided with the appropriate innate characteristics. Qutb continued in a long passage to detail women's special qualities of gentleness, kindness and quick emotional response (to children's needs), and men's attributes of toughness, slow response and the use of thinking and deliberation – on account of the primeval hunting and protective instincts.

The second proponent of this discourse, Shaykh Muhammad Mitwalli al-Sha'rawi, was a popular and loved Egyptian religious scholar and preacher, most famous for his early televised weekly sessions of Qur'anic interpretations, which are still occasionally aired on Egyptian and Arab television. Like Qutb, he consolidated further the conservative gender ideology, including the complementarity of the sexes and the paternalistic attitude towards wives and mothers (al-Sha'rawi, n.d.; 1982). The thrust of al-Sha'rawi's argument revolved around the unique biological functions of pregnancy, childbirth and nursing, which for him formed the basis of gender difference in essential life tasks and in human nature. Al-Sha'rawi felt that a woman's role as mother is what determines her very character, so she is ruled by nurturing drives and emotions; this is in contrast to the main masculine traits of reason and rationality. Although al-Sha'rawi stated that this division of functions does not mean men are better than women (or vice versa), this kind of superficial reasoning has always been used to justify female intellectual inferiority and unsuitability for any work other than motherhood.

Just as the Mamluk sociocultural context could help explain the gender views of contemporaneous exegetes, this 'Islamist' version of modernist gender norms can be explained as arising from intellectuals' reactions to colonial modernity and their defensive attitude of protecting and preserving cultural identity in the form of the status of women and traditional family relations.

The last example to consider in this journey is the current standard and officially sanctioned understanding of qiwamah, which can be read in the 1978 sixth edition of Al-Muntakhab fi Tafsir al-Qur'an al-Karim (Selected Interpretation of the Sublime Qur'an), the simplified and widely used commentary by al-Majlis al-'A'la lil-Shu'un al-Islamiyah (the Higher Council of Islamic Affairs of Egypt) (1978). I translate the passage literally:

> Men have *the right* of maintenance and care of women, as well as managing their affairs by what God gave them of attributes that qualify them to undertake this *right*. Further, because they are the ones who strive and work hard to earn the money that they spend on the family. (p. 114, emphasis mine)

In terms of discourse analysis, 'maintenance and care' are described as a 'right' belonging to men, not a divine injunction or a duty incumbent upon them, and financial providing occurs as a secondary issue, superseded by the idea of personal attributes. Furthermore, there is a clear assumption that only men work and earn money.

REFORMIST INTERPRETIVE STRATEGIES

An early precursor of the attempt to shake the 'absolute' essentialist under-standing of *qiwamah* and suggest an element of contingency or relative status is the Egyptian poetess and writer A'isha Taymur (1840–1902) in her treatise published in 1892, *Mir'at al-Ta'ammul fi al-Umur*. Taymur, who belonged to the upper elite class, expected men to fulfil the material needs of wives even if the latter were themselves affluent. She voiced a conservative, classist view, blaming husbands for abandoning their expected social and leadership roles. However, she presented a conditioned understanding of *qiwamah*. Her orig-inal intention was to reform the ways of negligent and wayward husbands of the upper class who were not performing their duties of 'fulfilling the needs of their wives' (Taymur, 2002, p. 29) and not assuming their marital responsibilities.[12]

The logic of her discussion was as follows: when men abandoned their duties, they forced women to assume the role of managers of their families and their lives, and so men lost their status when they stopped fulfilling its requirements. In the course of the argument, Taymur included a short alle-gorical narrative that used animal symbolism. A lion grew lax in his hunting duties and stopped bringing the kill; he let the lioness hunt instead. After some time, she began eating the best parts of the prey and giving him the leftovers. The lion got angry and demanded a priority share in keeping with his high status. The lioness replied, 'No, that's when you were you, and I was I; now, I became *you*, and you became *me*: you are entitled to get from me what I was entitled from you, and I am entitled to get from you what you were entitled from me.'

Even if the intended moral of this story was a warning to men and soci-ety at large of the danger of this 'unconventional' reversal of roles, Taymur's contribution was to shed light on a conditioned, shifting *qiwamah*, contin-gent on men fulfilling their material and moral responsibilities. She viewed financial support of women as a *condition of*, not a reason for, guardianship – which was a subtle but important distinction at this early historical stage. I would also describe this approach as gender sensitive or reflecting woman's

---

[12] The phenomenon of men marrying into rich families for greed and squandering their wives' fortune on gambling and alcohol was one of the social ills of the time. For a full biography of Taymur and an extensive analysis of the political, social and cultural context of Egypt at the end of the nineteenth century and the impact on middle-class gender relations, see Hatem (2011).

perspective in observing that temporary financial guardianship may be needed so as not to overburden mothers, especially when giving birth and nursing, with the responsibility of supporting themselves, and in shifting the discourse of blame and self-reform to men. Another interpretive possibility is that she was problematizing the notion that men have more rights than women because of the financial obligations assigned to men.

This view of the conditioned *qiwamah* appears as the cornerstone of several contemporary interpretations, including those of al-Hibri (1982) and Radwan (1988; 2005); Wadud's view of a 'flexible' and 'acquired' *qiwamah* (1999); Abou El Fadl hinging the status of maintainer on 'objective capacities' (2001, p. 210); Bayoumi's discussion of an 'extraneous and potentially changing' *qiwamah* (2009, p. 62); and Abu Zayd's understanding of *qiwamah* as descriptive of a social reality that we are urged to change (2007, p. 213). These articulations reject an inherent, permanent right of authority, suggesting a changeable state of affairs.

Another strategy of contemporary scholars is the textual contextualization used by Maysam al-Faruqi and Asma Barlas. Al-Faruqi (2000) relies on a method that privileges 'an interpretation corroborated by the verses of the Qur'an' themselves as 'stronger than an interpretation corroborated only by a source external to the Qur'an' (p. 88). This is done through a close textual reading that pays attention to the logical and linguistic coherence of the Qur'anic text and the context of its units and passages. Hence, she focuses on the meaning of *bima* in the first portion of verse 4:34 and connects this divine command to verses 4:11 and 4:32, which are concerned with the double inheritance share and the means of providing sustenance. Al-Faruqi's argument is that textual evidence does not warrant *qiwamah* as an endowed state of excellence because the term 'is used within an entire section that starts from the beginning of the same *surah* (chapter) with the issue of possessions in conjunction with marriage and inheritance' (p. 85). Through textual analysis of the context of the verses and entire passages in which they appear, she disproves unjustified favouritism or arbitrary preference.

Similarly, Barlas (2002) uses close scrutiny of the denotation of Qur'anic words to add more nuance and divest the concept of *qiwamah* of its patriarchal implications: 'Even though the Qur'an charges the husband with being the breadwinner, it does not designate him head of the household, especially as the term has been understood in Western feudal cultures' (p. 187). Such designation, she argues, 'was contingent on traditional patriarchal definitions of the father-as-husband and the husband-as-father'. The Qur'an does not adhere to this right of rule for the father figure or use the concept of 'head of household'.

A third interpretive strategy can be seen in the work of scholars such as Gamal al-Banna (d. 2013) and Khaled Abou El Fadl. Al-Banna was an independent, erudite Islamic scholar and prolific writer who, as part of his comprehensive intellectual and hermeneutical reformist project that he called *da'wat al-'ihya' al-islami* (the call of Islamic revival), espoused the governing principle that Qur'anic pronouncements and commands are encompassing and general enough to merit within them developing diverse interpretations that can evolve with changing times and contexts.[13] Criticizing Muslims' abandonment of the Qur'an itself in favour of the body of superfluous exegetical literature, al-Banna called for a return to a basic understanding of 'Qur'anic discourse' (*al-khitab al-qur'ani*), a dynamic guide for centuries to come as consecutive times allow more progressive applications (al-Banna, 1995, p. 92; 1999, p. 179). This approach was adopted by Abou El Fadl and has influenced his specific reflections on *qawwamun*, which he describes as ambiguous.

In approaching the issue of how exactly to interpret the words of God today, Abou El Fadl outlines a methodology centred on two elements: first, exhausting all possible theological proofs and implications through a thorough investigation of the totality of evidence; and, second, following the moral trajectory of the Qur'an in its entirety and its comprehensive guiding principles. The sophistication – and complexity – of this method stems from the fact that Abou El Fadl is not willing to completely forgo consideration of the classical traditions and rely only on timely and contemporary interpretations. He also insists on using textual hermeneutics in the light of ultimate divine intent, refusing to ascribe to God 'what is immoral and ugly'. In other words, he makes a connection between the value of beauty and moral pursuit: 'I argue that there is much beauty in the traditional Islamic methodologies of knowledge, but I also argue that even the traditional methodologies should be reoriented toward an unrelenting and persistent exploration of a core Islamic value – beauty'. He maintains that 'Shari'a is the search for the beautiful because it is the search for God'; hence, we may search 'the Divine Will through several avenues of evidence', yet it 'must also be searched through a moral and ethical inquiry' (Abou El Fadl, 2006, pp. 70–1).

---

[13] See al-Banna (2003), in which he critiques the foundations of both classical and modern exegesis and presents his own vision of an approach that restores to the Qur'an its revolutionary meanings and message.

This means that Abou El Fadl's interpretive method is neither totally literalist (relying only on intricate linguistic and stylistic analysis) nor solely focused on generalized and ultimate ethical values at the expense of marginalizing the Qur'anic text and its interpretative tradition (i.e. focusing on the purpose of the text, the spirit not the letter). His is a holistic method that combines and synchronizes textual analysis, overarching moral norms and the classical traditions. Thus, for Abou El Fadl, the word *qawwamun* in verse 4:34 does not have a fixed meaning. The textual reading suggests that guardianship means men being sustainers of women, including service and protection. However, the status of *qiwamah* is hinged on a particular operative cause (*'illah*), which is the ability to earn and spend. If a man is not supporting the family, if a wife is also contributing financially or has equal earning potential, then a man's *qiwamah* cannot exist. But, most of all, the legitimate possibility of constructing a meaning of *qiwamah* that fulfils the ultimate Qur'anic criteria of beauty and moral import is left open by the text and its underlying ethical principles.

The work of Kecia Ali and Amina Wadud, and particularly Wadud's recent work, represents a fourth interpretative philosophy. Their perspective towards hermeneutical strategies is marked by a tendency to transcend 'textual' interpretation altogether and to establish a different theoretical stance. This development is clearly articulated by Amina Wadud in her second book, *Inside the Gender Jihad* (2006), which records the change in her interpretive orientation. Describing her own previous project of 'Qur'anic hermeneutics from a gender perspective' in *Qur'an and Woman* as 'apologetics', she now states that this alternative interpretation has proven insufficient and there is a need to go beyond it. The inspiration of the Qur'anic worldview remains, but because particular articulations in the Qur'an as a text are problematic, there exists the 'possibility of refuting the text, to talk back, to even say "no"' (Wadud, 2006, p. 191). Wadud here tries to find a solution to the persisting problematic faced by Islamic feminist interpreters in dealing with difficult, explicit texts. Whereas previously such researchers have tried to resolve this difficulty by drawing attention to the general 'principles' of the Qur'an as a frame of reference, in the light of which specific texts and injunctions should be understood and interpreted, Wadud takes the issue to another level. The 'letter' of the divine text remains a problem, and it is time to stop grappling with it and direct our attention to its 'potential trajectory' – how and where it points humankind. As a divine guidance, the Qur'an should be looked upon as 'a window to look *through*', or a 'doorway with a threshold to pass *over* toward…infinite possibilities' (Wadud, 2006, p. 197). This new perspective would be a means to avoid literal application or implementation of a text when it opposes our current, more progressive human development and understandings. Hence, one can maintain that in this sense the Qur'an is a text 'in process', and it forces us to move to a stage of 'post-text in this post-revelation social, cultural, and philosophical context' (Wadud, 2006, p. 192).

Kecia Ali (2006) elaborates on this new approach of going beyond literalism – in both interpretive endeavours and application. She suggests that 'the Qur'anic text itself requires Muslims to sometimes depart from its literal provisions in order to establish justice' (p. 55). It is still a source of divine guidance to the direction of righteousness, but its sometimes-insufficient regulations must be viewed as only 'a starting point for the ethical development of human beings and the transformation of human society' (p. 150). Her final expression on the issue comes in Platonic terms: there will always be limitations to the Qur'anic text 'as manifested in the earthly realm', and so it can only be 'a pale shadow of the ultimate Reality' (p. 134). Concern about such articulations arises from the implication that the Qur'an has either failed to fulfil its role as an applied system of divine guidelines to wisdom and righteousness, or that it ought to be emptied of its content while maintaining merely the form and symbolism of its sacred ontological status.

CONCLUDING REMARKS

The above has been a discourse analysis of some representative *qiwamah* interpretations in the exegetical tradition, plus a presentation of recent hermeneutical considerations relevant to our efforts to explain verse 4:34 anew.

General strategies of constructing dominant patriarchal interpretations on *qiwamah* have revolved around the following: a) conceptualization, i.e. turning it into a notion; b) separating it from the context of previous verses (4:11, 4:12, 4:32, 4:33) and establishing it as an isolated, self-contained principle; c) generalizing from a limited and specific financial injunction to a pervasive rule and standard criterion that govern all aspects of the marital relationship; and d) creating unfounded meanings, turning the responsibility of spending into a cause of privilege, hierarchy and authority.

Hence, the main task of this chapter was unpacking this process by underlying and analysing additions, transformations and creations of meaning by consecutive interpreters, according to their own personal views stemming from their historical, sociocultural contexts. This unravelling has also demonstrated that the construction of *qiwamah* has been used to construct an 'Islamic model' of marriage and gender relations based on normative male leadership.

The contemporary reformists mentioned above have proposed the following alternative understandings of the concept: viewing *qiwamah* as conditioned and changeable; contextualizing it within either the totality of the Qur'an's non-patriarchal thrust or within whole verse units; situating it within the broader ethical paradigm of the Qur'an; or, finally, transcending the text. In these hermeneutical approaches, the following discursive counter-strategies can be noted: divesting *qiwamah* of meanings of power, domination or authority; decentring it within the general Islamic understanding of marriage and marital relations; and restricting or limiting it to the context of the relevant verse(s) (e.g. the Qur'an explaining the reason behind the double inheritance shares and that men's earnings or profit are meant to provide for women in their families, not for selfish enjoyment).

In the end, this analysis leads us to conclude that *qiwamah* is not hierarchy, not moral superiority or paternalism, not divine favouritism, not authority or sovereignty, not an absolute, unqualified right to rule and lead, not a fixed honorary status, not the privilege to spend, and not an exclusive right to earn money and be the sole breadwinner.

How then are we to read verse 4:34? A number of other interpretive possibilities are worth pursuing. Could it be, as it is commonly understood, an injunction to organize the distribution and expenditure of diverse earnings and inheritances? Could it be a gender-sensitive divine recommendation for men to be financially responsible for the women in their families, especially during times of pregnancy, childbirth and nursing, without this responsibility entailing something in return on the part of the wife (e.g. obedience or conjugal relations)? How do we break the link between this injunction and interpretations of privilege or exchange, while connecting it to a holistic Qur'anic paradigm that can produce an alternative meaning? The doors of *ijtihad* are to be reopened.

REFERENCES

'Abduh, Muhammad. 1990. *Tafsir al-Manar*, edited by Muhammad Rashid Rida. 12 vols. Cairo: Al-Hay'a al-Misriya al-'Amma.

Abou-Bakr, Omaima. 2003. 'Teaching the Words of the Prophet: Women Instructors of the Hadith: Fourteenth and Fifteenth Centuries'. *Hawwa* 1 (3): pp. 306–28.

Abou El Fadl, Khaled. 2001. *Speaking in God's Name*. Oxford: Oneworld.

Abou El Fadl, Khaled. 2006. *The Search for Beauty in Islam*. Lanham, MD: Rowman & Littlefield.

Abu Zayd, Nasr. 2007. *Dawi'r il Khof: Qi'rah fi Khitab al-Mara'ah*. Beirut: al-Markaz al-Thaqafi al-Arabi.

Al-Baidawi. 1968. *Anwar al-Tanzil wa-Asrar al-Ta'wil*. Cairo: Matba'at al-Babi al-Halabi.

Al-Banna, Gamal. 1995. *Nahwa Fiqh Gadid*, vol. 1. Cairo: Dar al-Fikr al-Islami.

Al-Banna, Gamal. 1999. *Al-mar'ah al-Muslimah bayna Tahrir al-Qur'an wa-Taqyid al-Fuqaha'*. Cairo: Dar al-Fikr al-Islami.

Al-Banna, Gamal. 2003. *Tafsir al-Qur'an al-Karim bayna al-Qudama wa al-Muhdathin*. Cairo: Dar al-Fikr al-Islami.

Al-Dhahabi, Muhammad Husayn. 1976. *Al-Tafsir wa-al-Mufassirun*. Cairo: Dar al-Kutub al-Hadithah.

Al-Faruqi, Maysam. 2000. 'Women's Self-Identity in the Qur'an and Islamic Law'. In *Windows of Faith: Muslim Women Scholar Activists in North America*, edited by Gisela Webb, pp. 72–101. Syracuse, NY: Syracuse University Press.

Al-Hibri, Azizah. 1982. 'A Study of Islamic Herstory: Or How Did We Ever Get into This Mess?' *Women's Studies International Forum* 5 (2): pp. 207–19.

Ali, Abdullah Yusuf. 1989. *The Meaning of the Holy Qur'an*. Beltsville, MD: Amana.

Ali, Kecia. 2006. *Sexual Ethics and Islam: Feminist Reflections on Qur'an, Hadith, and Jurisprudence*. Oxford: Oneworld.

Al-Majlis al-'A'la lil-Shu'un al-Islamiyah (Higher Council of Islamic Affairs of Egypt). 1978. *Al-Muntakhab fi Tafsir al-Qur'an al-Karim*. Cairo: Wizarat al-Awqaf, al-Majlis al-'A'la lil Shu'un al-Islamiyah (Ministry of Endowment, the Higher Council of Islamic Affairs).

Al-Qurtubi. 1967. *Al-Jami' li-Ahkam al-Qur'an*. 20 vols. Cairo: Dar al-Kutub al-Misriyah.

Al-Razi, Muhammad ibn 'Umar Fakbr al-Din. 1938. *Al-Tafsir al-Kabir*. 32 vols. Cairo: al-Matba'at al-Bahiyya al-Misriya.

Al-Sha'rawi, Muhammad Mitwalli. 1982. *Qadaya al-Mar'ah al-Muslimah*. Cairo: Dar al-Muslim.

Al-Sha'rawi, Muhammad Mitwalli. n.d. *Nazarat fi al-Qur'an*. 53 vols. Cairo: Akhbar al-Yawm.

Al-Tabari, Abu Ja'far ibn Jarir. 1961. *Jami' al-Bayan an Ta'wil ay al-Qur'an*, edited by Mahmud Muhammad Shakir and Ahmad Muhammad Shakir. 16 vols. Cairo: Dar al-Ma'arif.

Al-Zamakhshari, Mahmud ibn 'Umar. 1948. *Al-Kashshaf 'an Haqa'iq Ghawamid al-Tanzil*. 3 vols. Cairo: Matba'at al-Babi al-Halabi.

Ammar, Nawal. 2007. 'Wife Battery in Islam: A Comprehensive Understanding of Interpretations'. *Violence against Women* 13 (5): pp. 516–26.

Asad, Muhammad. 1980. *The Message of the Qur'an*. Gibraltar: Dar al-Andalus.

Barlas, Asma. 2002. *Believing Women in Islam: Unreading Patriarchal Interpretations of the Qur'an*. Austin: University of Texas Press.

Bauer, Karen. 2009. 'The Male Is Not Like the Female (Q 3:36): The Question of Gender Egalitarianism in the Qur'an'. *Religion Compass* 3 (4): pp. 637–54.

Bayoumi, Abd al-Mo'ati. 2009. *Min Qadaya al-Mar'a* (Women's Issues). Cairo: Center for Egyptian Women's Legal Assistance.

Chaudhry, Ayesha S. 2013. *Domestic Violence and the Islamic Tradition: Ethics, Law, and the Muslim Discourse on Gender*. Oxford: Oxford University Press.

Elsaidi, Murad H. 2011. 'Human Rights and Islamic Law: A Legal Analysis Challenging the Husband's Authority to Punish "Rebellious" Wives'. *Muslim World Journal of Human Rights* 7 (2): pp. 1–25.

Gatje, Helmut. 1976. *The Qur'an and Its Exegesis*. London: Routledge & Kegan Paul.

Hassan, Riffat. 1999. 'An Islamic Perspective'. In *Sexuality: A Reader*, edited by Karen Labacqz, pp. 337–72. Cleveland: Pilgrim Press.

Hatem, Mervat. 2011. *Literature, Gender, and Nation-Building in Nineteenth-Century Egypt: The Life and Works of A'isha Taymur*. New York: Palgrave Macmillan.

Ibn Kathir, Abu al-Fida 'Imad al-Din Isma'il ibn 'Umar. n.d. *Tafsir al-Qur'an al-Azim*. 4 vols. Cairo: Dar Ihya' al-Kutub al-'Arabiyah.

Lapidus, Ira. 1988. *A History of Islamic Societies*. Cambridge, UK: Cambridge University Press.

Lutfi, Huda. 1991. 'Manners and Customs of 14th Century Cairene Women: Female Anarchy vs. Order in Muslim Perspective Treatises'. In *Women in Middle Eastern History*, edited by Nikkie Keddie and Beth Baron, pp. 99–121. New Haven: Yale University Press.

Mahmoud, Mohamed. 2006. 'To Beat or Not to Beat: On the Exegetical Dilemmas over Qur'an, 4:34'. *Journal of the American Oriental Society* 126 (4): pp. 537–50.

Marin, Manuela. 2003. 'Disciplining Wives: A Historical Reading of Qur'an 4:34'. *Studia Islamica* 97: pp. 5–40.

Qutb, Sayyid. 1952. *Fi Zilal al-Qur'an*. 8 vols. Beirut: Dar Ihya al-Turath al-Arabi.

Radwan, Zeinab. 1988. *Al-Islam wa Qadaya al-Mar'ah*. Cairo: al-Hay'ah al-'Ammah lil-Kitab.

Radwan, Zeinab. 2005. *Al-Tafsirat al-Khati'ah lil-Din*. Cairo: al-Majlis al-Qawmi lil-Mar'ah.

Roded, Ruth. 1994. *Women in Islamic Biographical Collections*. Boulder, CO: Lynne Rienner.

Saleh, Amani. 2002. 'Pairing and Impairing: Re-conceptualizing Gender through the Qur'an'. *Women and Civilization* 3: pp. 17–53.

Shaikh, Sa'diyya. 1997. 'Exegetical Violence: Nushuz in Qur'anic Gender Ideology'. *Journal of Islamic Studies* 17: pp. 49–73.

Shaikh, Sa'diyya. 2007. 'A Tafsir of Praxis: Gender, Marital Violence, and Resistance in a South African Muslim Community'. In *Violence against Women in Contemporary World Religion: Roots and Cures*, edited by Dan Maguire and Sa'diyya Shaikh, pp. 66–89. Cleveland: Pilgrim Press.

Shoshan, Boaz. 1993. *Popular Culture in Medieval Cairo*. Cambridge, UK: Cambridge University Press.

Stilt, Kristen. 2011. *Islamic Law in Action: Authority, Discretion and Everyday Experiences in Mamluk Egypt*. Oxford: Oxford University Press.

Taymur, A'isha. 2002. *Mir'at al-Ta'ammul fi al-'Umur*. Cairo: Women & Memory.

Wadud, Amina. 1999. *Qur'an and Woman: Rereading the Sacred Text from a Woman's Perspective*. Oxford: Oxford University Press.

Wadud, Amina. 2006. *Inside the Gender Jihad: Women's Reform in Islam*. Oxford: Oneworld.

An Egalitarian Reading of the Concepts of *Khilafah*, *Wilayah* and *Qiwamah**

Asma Lamrabet

T he question of women and gender equality in Islam is undoubtedly one of the most controversial topics in contemporary debates.
It seems to embody all of the cultural, sociological and political
tensions of our time. Within the discussion, however, the voices, reflections and aspirations of women – the people most concerned with the topic
– have been suppressed by two forces: on the one side, by proponents of
Islamic traditionalism who cling to a rigid interpretation of Islam; and, on
the other side, by advocates of the empowerment of women who reject any
reference to Islam, because they believe it is the key factor in discrimination
against women.

To rethink this topic means leaving the beaten track of traditionalist
religious conformism, but it also implies forsaking the exclusivist vision of
an abstract modernity devoid of spiritual references. Between these two
camps, which remain forever locked in a fruitless confrontation, we need
to draw a fresh, contemporary, reformist vision, able not only to give a new

---

* This chapter was originally written in French. Translation from the original French to English
is by Amina Chibani and Richard Tapper. Translations of Qur'anic verses are by Abdullah
Yusuf Ali unless otherwise noted. Translations of other original Arabic sources are by the
author.

impetus to the empowerment of Muslim women but also to reclaim this topic from superficial and archaic analyses proposed by outdated conservative readings.

For this, we must first go beyond the *Nahda* type of reformism[1] in which the issue has been classified under the heading of 'status and rights of Muslim woman'. This has not only consolidated the idea of a masculine norm in Islam, but also relegated specific rights, generally of a subordinate nature, to women. Even worse, this idea has been given an aura of sanctity. The *Nahda* conception of reform, however useful it may have been in the context of its development, is no longer relevant in our current context of globalized modernity. It must be asserted and repeated, again and again, that in Islam women do not have specific rights, nor a particular status. They are neither 'pearls' nor 'flowers' – patronizing terms often used in Islamic discourse to infantilize women. Rather, women are human beings, with the duties, obligations, rights, hopes and aspirations that are inherent in all people.

We should reapproach the Qur'anic text by reading it through the interpretative framework of equal universal human rights, according to the standards of our time, just as the scholars who preceded us, centuries ago, took from the Qur'an what their own understanding and their historically and socioculturally conditioned ideas allowed them. By initiating this rereading of the Qur'an – as a sacred text, of course, but with a sacredness that leaves it wide open to time and its vagaries – we will be able to find key concepts of gender equality at the heart of the spiritual message that will allow Muslims, as both believers and human beings seeking transcendence, to claim equality as a universal human right as well as a fundamental spiritual value.

In this chapter, I look at the three Qur'anic concepts that embody the spiritual message of Islam but have long been misinterpreted to sustain unegalitarian principles. These are: *istikhlaf* (equality in building human civilization), *wilayah* (shared responsibility of men and women) and *qiwamah* (management of public and private space by men and women). By revisiting these concepts from a perspective that embraces central Qur'anic values, we will be able to

---

[1] *Nahda* ('Renaissance') refers to the period in Arab–Islamic thought between the end of the eighteenth century and the middle of the twentieth century, following centuries of decline. *Nahda* inaugurated emancipation that included women's claims, but entirely in colonial and postcolonial contexts.

understand how the spiritual message of Islam regarding men and women is one in which justice and equality are inseparable.

APPROACHING THE QUR'AN

The Qur'an is, first and foremost, a message addressed to humanity in all its glory – but with all its weaknesses too. In the Qur'anic concept of *insan* (human being), all human beings, regardless of gender, race or class, are created from one essence,[2] reflect the beauty and perfection of God,[3] carry human weakness[4] and are the ones whom the sacred text addresses with its message for spiritual advancement and liberation from all kinds of oppression.[5]

To fulfil this message, the Qur'an instructs that human life be guided by the ethical values that are at its heart. Our calling on this earth is to achieve *tawhid*, the unity of Allah;[6] this leads us to *istikhlaf*, our individual responsibility to fulfil our role as God's *khalifah* (vicegerent) on earth.[7] To fulfil this role, we need to obtain and embody *'ilm* (knowledge),[8] *'adl* (justice),[9] *'aql* (reason),[10] *hurriyyat al-mu'taqad* (freedom of belief),[11] *ikhtilaf* (diversity)[12] and *mahbah* (love).[13] It is through the lens of these Qur'anic ethical values that we should understand *qiwamah* and *wilayah* and gender relations and rights today.

Thus issues relating to women in the Qur'an should not be addressed by extracting isolated and fragmentary verses from the whole to construct interpretations that are sometimes far removed from the Qur'anic ethic. Rather, these issues and related verses need to be located within a normative framework that allows us to classify Qur'anic injunctions according to their aim and ultimate purpose.

---

[2] Verse 7:189: 'It is He who created you from a single soul' (author's translation).
[3] Verse 95:4: 'We created the human being in the best form' (author's translation).
[4] Verse 4:28: 'And God wants to lighten your difficulties. And He created the [human being] weak' (author's translation).
[5] Verses 109:6 and 18:29.
[6] Verses 51:56, 21:25 and 21:108.
[7] Verse 2:30.
[8] Verses 39:9, 16:43 and 96:1.
[9] Verses 40:17, 42:15 and 16:90.
[10] Verses 2:242, 12:2, 29:43 and 22:46.
[11] Verses 6:135, 10:99 and 18:29.
[12] Verses 11:118 and 5:48.
[13] Verses 2:165 and 5:54.

We must distinguish between three kinds of Qur'anic verses relating to the spiritual message of Islam:

Verses with universal aims. These verses advocate universal values such as justice, equality, fairness and respect for human dignity. They place the human (*al-insan*) at the centre of all spiritual philosophy. The majority of verses are universal, and these constitute the basis of the Qur'anic message.

Temporary verses that are confined in their application to the context of revelation. These verses are linked to a given historical period and place, namely that of seventh-century Arabia. They met the specific requirements of that context but can be considered obsolete today. Obvious examples are verses speaking of the distribution of war spoils, slavery or corporal punishment. The importance of these verses lies not in their literal meaning or their application but in their aims and in the spirit of justice that underlies them.

Verses that need reinterpretation in new social contexts. Examples of these verses are those which deal with women's issues in a manner consistent with the patriarchal expectations and structures of the 'time of revelation'. These verses, such as those dealing with marriage and family, sometimes endorse discriminatory attitudes and practices of the time or reform such practices without actually repealing them.

Most interpretations confound these three types of verses and prioritize those which are temporary or those concerned with specific social dimensions over the universal ones. As a result, the spiritual message of the Qur'an is undermined. Furthermore, culture-based and traditionalist readings of only a few verses have ended up becoming the dominant religious discourse on women's issues, whereas the rest of the divine message is assumed to be addressed to men only.

The spiritual message of Islam regarding men and women, in which justice and equality are inseparable, can only be understood by adopting and embodying Qur'anic ethical values as well as having a sound understanding of the relative level of universality of Qur'anic verses. With this framework, we can reread three major Qur'anic concepts (*istikhlaf*, *wilayah* and *qiwamah*) that have long been misunderstood.

ISTIKHLAF OR EQUALITY IN BUILDING HUMAN CIVILIZATION

At the heart of the Qur'an lies the concept of *istikhlaf*, which indicates the intimate relationship between men, women and their Creator. This concept symbolizes, in a general manner, one of the most exalted missions assigned to men and women: building human civilization on earth. *Istikhlaf* appears several times in the Qur'an in different formulations. Depending on the context of the verse, we can infer at least three meanings of the term:

The general sense of succession or *khilafah* (caliphate); the *khalifah* (caliph) is the successor, i.e. one who occupies the place of another in his domain (e.g. 6:165, 10:14, 10:73, 2:30, 38:26).

The plural form *khala'if*, denoting peoples, tribes and even generations that succeed one another (e.g. 7:69, 7:74, 7:150, 7:169)

A sense of succession related to the responsibilities of managing the world, as entrusted to humans by God. Verse 2:30 is central to understanding the aim behind the creation of human beings on earth: 'Behold, thy Lord said to the angels: "I will create a vicegerent on earth." They said: "Wilt Thou place therein one who will make mischief therein and shed blood? – whilst we do celebrate Thy praises and glorify Thy holy [name]?" He said: "I know what ye know not."'

The vast majority of exegetes agree that by 'vicegerent on earth' the Qur'an meant human beings (*bani adam*) or the human race in God's first initiative to populate the earth (Ibn Kathir, 2003, vol. 1, p. 80). God has honoured human beings by delegating to them this symbolic function of managing what God has entrusted them with: God's creation.

This 'vicegerency' is therefore a privilege granted to humans over other creatures, in the sense that they were given preference over angels, who despite their spiritual superiority were not considered as worthy of assuming this heavy responsibility. Human beings, men and women, were endowed with reason and therefore chosen by the Creator to undertake this supreme function of populating the earth and arranging the conditions of their existence in this world. In other words, humans are called upon to carry out responsible and conscious governance, for which they will be held accountable.

So *khilafah*, in the Qur'anic understanding, is conditioned above all by this responsibility incumbent upon every human being on earth. Human beings are *khalifah* (representatives), but not in a literal sense of actual representatives of God on earth. Rather, they are trustees of a mission: they are responsible for managing life on earth.

However, throughout the history of Islamic civilization the concept of *khilafah* has undergone religious appropriation by political powers, legitimated by the scholars at their service. The concept of caliph has passed from the spiritual sense of a responsibility delegated by God to all humans, to that of an elected political representative, to the supposed legal representative of God on earth. The political significance assigned to it by the early caliphs was moved from the political to the religious sphere, with scholars authorizing the use of the title 'Caliph of God' and thereby legitimizing the 'sacredness' of a ruler appointed by God. This helped establish a custom of the most servile submission; since caliphs held a divinely ordered authority, disobeying them became tantamount to disobeying God. It was no longer a matter of a contract between rulers and ruled, but a true theocratic power that demanded obedience to the ruler as a divine right. Furthermore, because of existing patriarchal social norms coupled with the promotion of weak *ahadith* and supposedly 'inherent' characteristics of men and women (see Abou-Bakr in this volume), it became natural that only men could be rulers and fulfil this divine responsibility.

The concept underwent several manipulations throughout the course of history and the political tragedies that played out in Islamic lands. From a spiritual conception that highlighted the accountability of all humans, then a spiritual and political conception used by the first four 'rightly guided caliphs' (*khulafa al-rashidin*) in the sense of political succession and collective responsibility, it was transformed, in the hands of subsequent caliphs, into a formidable tool of oppression used by only a few powerful men.

Taking into account the Qur'anic concept of *insan* and the aforementioned core ethical values of the sacred text leads us to rediscover the initial spiritual inspiration and original meaning of *khilafah*, which is the sense of responsibility of all humans – both men and women – in this terrestrial life. Together with this responsibility, humans are offered another attribute, that of 'liberty'.[14]

---

[14] Diagne (2008) speaks about this liberty that is bestowed on humans: 'The Qur'anic account of the creation of humans seems to acknowledge that they have been trusted with a treasure that they alone can manifest: liberty' (p. 20).

Responsibility and liberty go together, two concepts linked by a common ethic that makes them inseparable.

This central notion of bearing responsibility for and managing the world, as described in the Qur'an, is important to consider when we debate equality between men and women and their sociopolitical involvement in public space. Equality for men and women should be read to mean equality in the responsibility and corresponding liberty to choose, to work, to manage and to participate in the progress of society and the world in which they live. That is the prime meaning of *khilafah*, inscribed in the spiritual message as one of the foundations of an egalitarian conception of both men and women as responsible and free to manage the world and report back to the One who entrusted them with this mission.

WILAYAH OR SHARED RESPONSIBILITY OF MEN AND WOMEN

One crucial, unequivocal verse in the Qur'an lays the ground for the concept of equality between men and women:

> The believers, men and women, are *awliya'* [allies] of one another. They enjoin *al-ma'ruf* [the good] and forbid *al-munkar* [the bad],[15] they observe *salat* [prayers] and give *zakat* [charitable alms] and obey God and His Prophet. (9:71)

Some very explicit universal verses such as this, which exhort equality between men and women, have been marginalized in Islamic thought. They are rarely cited and are even at times completely overlooked in favour of other verses that are more difficult to interpret or whose application was contingent on the time of revelation.

In this verse, the term *awliya'*, which is the plural of *wali*, refers to alliance, mutual assistance and mutual reinforcement. *Al-wali* is one of God's attributes, meaning the one who strengthens, protects and supports. In common use, a *wali* is also the one who manages, who possesses the ability to represent

---

[15] *Al-munkar* refers to all that is rejected by all members of a given society – a set of morally unacceptable practices. In Qur'anic etymology it is considered the antonym of *al-ma'ruf* or the common good.

a minor; in other words, one who serves as a guardian over someone or something or one who can manage, govern and be entrusted, among other things, with affairs of state. There are other derivatives of the same root such as *al-wala'*, which can mean closeness, friendship, loyalty and fidelity. There is also *al-wilayah*, mostly known in legal parlance as denoting the highest positions in political governance, which Muslim jurists referred to as *wilayah 'ammah* or general governance. In this category there are several types of *wilayah* such as that of the caliph, the judge (*al-qadi*) and the treasurer (*al-muhtasib*).[16]

Verse 9:71 begins with a major command that calls men and women to remain mutually supportive through a spiritual, emotional and companionate alliance based on common belief in God and his Prophet. It is a benevolent association that is portrayed in words like *awliya'* – allies of one another – where one perceives this subliminal closeness between men and women whereby one is part of the other in communion and harmony. This *wilayah* that unites hearts and actions enables gender equality. This equality translates, in everyday life, into concrete actions and acts of human solidarity, where the only criterion for evaluating each other is integrity and moral rectitude.

These notions, obvious as they are, cannot be found in most traditional exegesis, where this verse has been interpreted rather loosely. Indeed, this clear, even undeniable exhortation to equality between men and women, especially in the management of the public or sociopolitical sphere, is virtually absent from the classical commentaries.

It is true that, overall, classical exegesis does acknowledge a spiritual equality between men and women as a foundation of Islam. This spiritual equality is based essentially on the practice of worship and on rewards and punishments in the hereafter. But this is the only equality that is recognized, since most commentators try to find a religious compromise between gender equality in worship practices and traditional gender hierarchy and complementarity as the norm in most other cases. This complementarity has always been understood as a manifestation of the classical division of roles in the family, but also in public life, where women have been confined to secondary, subordinate roles compared with those assigned to men. Thus most scholars have interpreted this verse as yet another one about spiritual equality, especially in worship (*'ibadat*), not least because the second part of the verse mentions prayer and almsgiving.

---

[16] For more on the semantic field of the terms *wilayah* and *wali*, including references in the Qur'an, see Masud (2013).

Yet this verse contains a prescription of paramount importance that constitutes its core: the injunction to enjoin the common good and discourage bad actions, which, we can clearly see, is an independent provision that precedes the prescription related to acts of worship. In other words, the Qur'an describes ideal male and female believers as being, first of all, people who help each other, on equal terms, in enjoining the common good and forbidding bad deeds, presumably in society generally, *and then* people who perform their religious rituals, *salat* and *zakat*, always in unity and mutual solidarity.

Ibn Kathir (1301–73) was one of the few commentators to draw attention to two important elements in this verse. First, he noted that the *wilayah* described in this verse as the alliance between men and women among themselves is identical to one that the Prophet of Islam described in one of his famous *ahadith*, where he affirms, 'All believers are united, generous and forgiving to each other, just like the human body; as soon as one of its organs suffers from any disease, the whole body reacts with fever and pain' (Ibn Kathir, 2003, vol. 2, p. 350). This *hadith sahih* (authentic *hadith*) alone sums up, through the metaphor of the human body, an essential aspect of human relations: each and every person's continuous awareness of the other. The Prophet, in this *hadith*, tried to instruct believing men and women in the inestimable human value of empathy, without which it is difficult to speak of living together.

Ibn Kathir's second and no less important observation is that the injunction here to the common good is identical to that referred to in verse 3:104, which states, 'Let there arise out of you a band of people inviting to all that is good, enjoining what is right [*al-ma'ruf*] and forbidding what is wrong [*al-munkar*]; They are the ones to attain felicity.' Most scholars consider that this verse conveys one of the essential Qur'anic principles and affirms one of the fundamental goals of Islam: to establish justice and common well-being (*maslaha*) in the society or community where one lives.

We find this command to enjoin the common good several other times in the Qur'an (for example, 3:110 and 3:114). In addition, whenever the Prophet was asked which Muslim was best, he responded, 'The one who enjoins good and forbids evil' (al-Zamakhshari, n.d., vol. 2, p. 315). It has consequently been the subject of prolific interpretations by commentators.

It is interesting to see how this Qur'anic principle – enjoining the common good (*al-ma'ruf*) and forbidding the bad (*al-munkar*), which is identical to what one finds in the *wilayah* verse – has been differently analysed and interpreted in the different commentaries. Most commentaries have considered this Qur'anic injunction to be of major importance, since we can measure the degree of each individual's commitment to building a just and morally equitable society in its practical application to social realities on the ground. The commentators are nearly unanimous that this injunction is part of an overall political and social agenda that exhorts Muslims to promote ethical values and respect for others, to be open to the world, to be on a permanent quest for knowledge, to act in the common interest, to be intelligent and denounce injustice in any form, and never to be silent in the face of social and political oppression and discrimination. Consequently, the majority of classical hermeneutical texts understood the command as an obligation to sociopolitical action, incumbent upon the whole of the community or an elite part of it, to guarantee the minimal conditions for social justice and prosperity inside that community.

But it is surprising to find that this same command, when found in verse 9:71 about *wilayah* and the alliance between men and women, does not lead to the same commentaries, except by Ibn Kathir when he refers cautiously to other possible interpretations. The verse explicitly talks about men and women as being spiritually equal and emphasizes that men and women are both obligated to sociopolitical action towards social justice. Yet, in interpreting this verse, commentators generally focus only on spiritual equality between men and women and not on men and women's equal responsibility to 'enjoin the common good and forbid the bad'. When the exact same injunction is addressed to people or believers in general in other verses (such as 3:104, 3:110 or 3:114), exegetes have interpreted it as a prescription towards social justice concerning men only, even though there is agreement among the scholars that the term 'the believers' or 'people' refers to men and women and that these exhortations concern women just as much as men.[17]

Yet verse 9:71 is clear and unambiguous: 'The believers, men and women, are allies of one another. They enjoin the common good and forbid the bad, they observe prayers and give charitable alms and obey God and his Prophet.' The Qur'an stresses emphatically this close cooperation or *wilayah* between men and women in sociopolitical action, before generalizing it to acts of religious ritual.

Some reformist thinkers have harkened back to this original meaning and confirmed the idea that joint sociopolitical participation by men and

---

[17] For instance, Yusuf al-Qaradawi (1998) has written, 'When God says "O you people!" or "O you believers", women are definitely concerned' (p. 171).

women is unequivocally advocated in the Qur'an. For example, Rashid Rida (1865–1935), the Egyptian reformist, commented on verse 9:71 as follows: 'This verse makes a point of inviting women as well as men to enjoin good and forbid evil actions. This includes speech and writing but also criticism of political leaders, caliphs, kings, princes and other persons. Women, at the time of revelation, knew that and put it into practice' (Aboû Chouqqa, 2007, vol. 2, p. 646). The Syrian scholar Ahmed Kuftaro (1912–2004) said, 'Allah deliberately mentioned women in this verse in order to insist on their effective participation, knowing that the term "mu'minin", believers, conventionally includes women' (Kuftaro, 2002). The Lebanese scholar Dr Sayed Muhammed Hussein Fadlallah (1935–2010), in his interpretation of this verse, stated, 'Once we understand that justice embraces everything positive in life, and that evil comprises everything negative in it, we will then realize that men and women are partners in building up life. And just like men are responsible of the society, women also are equally responsible of the society they live in. So...men and women have vast areas to conquer, building life shoulder to shoulder as human beings, equal in humanity' (Fadlallah, n.d.a).

Through a contextualized reading, we can also integrate this concept of *wilayah* into a framework for equal citizenship. The call of the Qur'an to this shared responsibility of women and men in the political management of society is the equivalent of a key democratic principle requiring equal responsibility of all citizens. Thus, the concept of *wilayah* could be understood as a corollary of equal citizenship in Muslim societies.

This sense of *wilayah* as promoting sociopolitical participation has diminished through the history of Islamic civilization because of various despotic or authoritarian regimes that have governed Muslim societies and countries for long periods of their history. From its universal political and intellectual dimensions, it was downgraded to a strictly delimited area of religious ritual, *al-wilayah al-diniyah* (religious guardianship) (Laroui, 2008, p. 158). Many Muslims are unaware that they have a say, granted by Islam, in the management of their own religious and political affairs. Rather, they have been instructed to live and understand religion and their relationships with government authorities in terms of fear and blind obedience.[18]

---

[18] See the relevant discussion by Fatima Mernissi (2010): 'Islam is probably the only monotheistic religion the scientific investigation of which is discouraged if not forbidden, because a rationally analysed Islam is difficult for despots to subjugate...it is fear of the Imam' (p. 73).

In verse 9:71, however, we can use the Qur'anic concept of *insan* and an understanding of the universality of the verse to read the concept of *wilayah* in its broadest sense, requiring all humans to perform equally all the actions that can bring about positive change in societies. It is as much a matter of political citizenship as of day-to-day citizenship. Most importantly here, men and women are called on equally to be the agents of change in their respective societies.

Like other principles constantly upheld by the Qur'an, this verse and all the egalitarian ideas it affirms – like *wilayah*, political partnership, citizenship, and political action in support of the common good – have never been properly valued in Islamic thought, especially compared with other principles and concepts that are secondary in the Qur'an but have over time become priorities for a large number of Muslims because of ideological and literalist propaganda.[19] Thus, this verse has long been overlooked, being understood by most erudite Muslims as only one more verse about gender equality in the matter of worship. But in present-day democracies in a globalized world, it is essential to reread this verse and reformulate the principles it reveals, especially given its relevance and significance for modern Muslim societies.

It is also vital for the concept of *wilayah* to regain its importance and centrality to gender relations. All other Qur'anic concepts regarding women should be reread and redefined in light of the concept of *wilayah* in order to rediscover and restore the egalitarian spirit that motivates the spiritual message of Islam. It is only on this condition that all the other questions about women and men, many of which are inherently time bound, can be analysed and properly understood in our contemporary context.

QIWAMAH OR MANAGEMENT OF PUBLIC AND PRIVATE SPACE BY MEN AND WOMEN

The one point most often raised to 'prove' the absolute superiority of men over women is undoubtedly the Qur'anic concept of *qiwamah*. In the mind of scholars and lay Muslims alike, it has come to signify male authority. This is

---

[19] An example of these secondary Qur'anic concepts is the matter of the dress code (addressed to both men and women), which has been reduced to the single issue of women's hijab. This is of minor importance compared with so many other Qur'anic principles like *wilayah*.

one of the most flagrant misconceptions to have shaped the Muslim mind over the centuries. It assumes that the Qur'an has definitively decreed the absolute authority of the husband over his wife and, for some, the authority of all men over all women.

Qiwamah comes from the Qur'anic term *qawwamun* or *qawwamin*, both being plural forms of the noun *qawwam*. This comes from the root *qama*, which in Arabic may have as many as thirty meanings: 'stand up', 'comply', 'carry', 'take on', 'proceed', 'rise up', 'provide for', 'revolt', 'endure', 'lift up', etc. The word *qawwamun/qawwamin*, referring to the successful performance of the act *qama*, is found in three Qur'anic passages.

The best known and most often cited verse that supposedly justifies the superiority of men is the following:

Men are *qawwamun* over women according to what God *faddala ba'dahum 'ala ba'd* [has favoured some over others] and according to what they spend from their wealth. Righteous women are *qanitat* [obedient] guarding the unseen according to what God has guarded. Those [women] whose *nushuz* [rebellion] you fear, admonish them, and abandon them in bed, and *adribuhunna* [strike them]. If they obey you, do not pursue a strategy against them. Indeed God is exalted. (4:34)

The other two verses that mention this term are:

O ye who believe! *Kunu qawwamin* [stand out firmly] *bilqisti* [for justice], as witnesses to Allah, even as against yourselves, or your parents, or your kin, and whether it be [against] rich or poor: for Allah can best protect both. Follow not the lusts [of your hearts], lest you swerve, and if you distort [justice] or decline to do justice, verily Allah is well acquainted with all that ye do. (4:135)

O ye who believe! *Kunu qawwamin* [stand out firmly] *lillahi shuhada' bilqisti* [for Allah, as witnesses to fair dealing], and let not the hatred of others to you make you swerve to wrong and depart from justice. Be just: that is next to piety: and fear Allah. For Allah is well acquainted with all that ye do. (5:8)

There are two dimensions to *qiwamah*: public (*qiwamah 'ammah*) and private (*qiwamah khassah*) (Ezzat, 2000). The first verse uses *qawwamun* with regard to men and women's relations in what has generally been considered the 'private' sphere. The second two verses use the term *qawwamin* for all believers, in what can be considered the 'public' sphere. Before looking closer at the first verse that invokes so-called male authority in the private sphere, I shall analyse *qiwamah* as it appears in the other two verses that address both men and women in the public sphere. In examining all three verses, it is important to use the approach that respects the Qur'anic concept of *insan* and the internal cohesion and context of verses in the Qur'an.

Qiwamah in the public sphere, or qiwamah 'ammah

Most commentators agree that verses 4:135 and 5:8 exhort believing men and women to respect core values such as justice, fairness and impartiality in all their actions and judgements. In both verses we find the same injunction: in the first verse, '*kunu qawwamin bilqisti*' (be firm and rigorous in your implementation of justice) and, in the second, '*kunu qawwamin lilahi shuhada*' (be determined and precise in your testimonies).

Both verses command unconditional respect for the values of fairness and justice, even – and especially – in the matter of a judgement against oneself or one's relatives, the rich or the poor, or even an enemy whom we resent or dislike for one reason or another. The Qur'an's insistence on this value of justice (*qist*) demonstrates the necessity for a morality that respects the equality and humanity of all beings.

Qiwamah in both verses could then be translated as a formidable need for justice that should animate the hearts and consciences of all believing women and men. This *qiwamah*, this self-imposed obligation of fairness, justice and careful judgement, is a major exhortation in the Qur'an's message. This is the true meaning of the term *qawwamun*, which stipulates an impartial moral consciousness and a perfect rigour in fairness and testimony.

Justice and fairness are the hallmark of Islam. This entire spiritual message is a reminder, a *dhikr*, of the values that should constitute a primordial dimension of the religious consciousness of every man and woman. These values promoted by the Qur'an, of a *qiwamah* for justice, should be taught in Islamic curricula and in Muslim men and women's moral education. We pray to God five times a day, we observe the fast of Ramadan, we learn the Qur'an by heart, yet this *qiwamah* for justice is virtually absent from our daily life and our moral practice. This has led to the formation of an abysmal gap between religious practice and the wider Islamic ethics, which seems to grow deeper by the day throughout the Muslim world and to be reducing the grandeur of the final monotheistic revelation to a simple religious tradition that is excessively formal and ritualistic.

A *marfu'* (elevated) *hadith* of the Prophet affirms that 'An hour of justice equates to sixty years of devotional practices ['*ibadat*]' (Abi Ennaim, n.d., p. 117). Verses 4:135 and 5:8 correspond to a vision of a general *qiwamah* that men and women are required to apply during their lives on earth, which is a basic spiritual dimension of the Qur'anic ethic.

Qiwamah in the private sphere, or *qiwamah khassah*

Most translations of verse 4:34 render the word *qawwamun* as 'authority' or 'management': 'Men have authority over women' or 'Men are in charge of managing women's affairs'. This is found in virtually all classical as well as contemporary exegesis. All of the classical commentaries (*tafasir*) explain it as a privilege granted to the husband, a divine favour bestowed on the man, indeed on all men. The majority of commentators interpreted this concept *qawwamun* as the natural predisposition of man to be the 'master' of the woman (*ra'isaha*), her superior (*kabiraha*), her ruler (*al-hakimu 'alayha*), the one who has the right to 'discipline' her if she strays from the straight path (*mu'adibuha idha 'awajat*).[20]

Other commentators such as Ibn Abbas spoke of the control or hegemony of men over the moral life of women (*musalatun 'ala adab al-nisa*).[21] Al-Zamakhshari (n.d., vol. 1, pp. 441–2) stated that men have the right to dominate women (*musaytirin 'alayhin*) in all spheres of social life. Some such as Ibn al-Qayyim al-Jawziyyah (1991, vol. 2, p. 67) went as far as comparing the wife to a captive or a slave who should remain under the authority of a husband with absolute power.

They all agreed in favouring men, beyond their roles as husbands, with this preference (*bima faddala*) bestowed by the Creator. The second phrase in the verse – 'because Allah has made one of them to excel the other' or 'by right of the advantage God has given one [men] over the other [women]' – was

---

[20] See the commentary by Ibn Kathir (2003, vol. 1, p. 605) on verse 4:34: '*al-rajul qaymun 'ala el-mar'aa, ay huwa ra'isaha wa kabiraha wa al-hakim 'alayha wa mu'adibuha*' (The man is *qayyim* over the woman, that is he is her master, her superior, her ruler, her disciplinarian).

[21] See Ibn Abbas's commentary on the same verse in al-Razi (2004).

generally understood as God favouring men over women or confirmation of all men's superiority over all women.

In the same *tafsir* and according to the large majority of commentators, the pre-eminence of men was justified by a set of faculties that predestine men to be naturally superior to women. Here are some examples of the plethora of such arguments, found in most classical commentaries:

> Men are naturally endowed with more reason than women. Women are deficient in reason because of their excessive emotionality and their tendency to resolve problems by emotion rather than rationality.

> Only men hold positions of great political and juridical responsibility, such as high command, governance and magistracy. Only men are qualified to lead prayers, give Friday sermons, act as witness or give the call to prayer.

> Prophethood is only for men, never for women. Men make war and have a right to the spoils. Man's share in inheritance is double that of women.

> Men give dowers to their wives. Men are endowed with greater physical strength than women. Men can be women's guardians but never the other way around. Polygamy is one of men's rights and proof of their superiority. Unilateral divorce is men's exclusive right.

> Men are better equipped for erudition, wisdom and science than women. Women's inherent weakness is a natural attribute due to their physical and biological makeup.[22]

These are some examples of the reasons or the proofs on which the exegetes based their essential argument about the natural superiority of men over women. This is how classical commentators inferred that women are structurally

---

[22] These statements are found in the works of commentators such as al-Tabari (2002, vol. 4, p. 79), Ibn Kathir (2003, vol. 1, p. 605) and al-Qurtubi (2007, vol. 3, p. 152). I pass in silence over ridiculous claims such as 'men are superior to women because of their beards and turbans'. See Abou-Bakr in this volume.

inferior and that men's *qiwamah* over women can only be the Qur'anic confirmation of all their assumptions.

Verse 4:34 was unquestionably the verse on which the whole model of the family in Islam was shaped. All of the other Qur'anic verses, at least all of the texts referring to women, were read in the light of this concept, understood as men's right over women.

The verse was seen as a commandment bestowing on men the right to be women's 'absolute rulers' by conferring on men virtually absolute moral and material authority. In return for maintenance by their husbands, wives are expected to be obedient to this masculine authority. This ties in with the logic of the marriage contract, which affirms that the husband has all rights over his wife, who belongs to him body and soul just like any other merchandise, as long as he ensures the *nafaqah* or financial maintenance of her (see Mir-Hosseini in this volume). *Qiwamah* and its corollary obedience (*ta'a*) have facilitated the proliferation of a whole religious literature that devalues women and has hindered the judicial and social implementation of the liberating spirit of the Qur'anic message regarding women and their status in marriage and the family.

Consequently, it has become common to read in certain religious writings that the way to heaven for women is obedience to their husbands. This contradicts one of the founding principles of Islam, namely that obedience and submission are due only to God. It questions the unity of God (*tawhid*), a major notion on which the whole spiritual dimension of Islam rests (Wadud, 2009, and in this volume).

This interpretation of the concept of *qiwamah* was imagined and developed in the context of political developments whose objectives were completely removed from the emancipatory spirit conveyed by the message of the Qur'an. For instance, although verses such as 2:177, 90:30 and 9:60 encouraged believers to free slaves, especially female ones, and made it a profound act of piety to do so, not long after the Prophet's death, during the Islamic conquests, the taking of *jariyat* (female slaves) became a sign of rulers' wealth. It was in this new social context, with *jariyat* cloistered in the palaces and political consultation (*shura*) replaced by autocracy, that jurists (*fuqaha*) developed their interpretations of concepts like *qiwamah*. Shaped by patriarchal social pressures on one side and by political autocracy on the other, *qiwamah* was construed according to the reading of *hakimiya* (political governance), since the husband's authority was explicitly likened to that of the *hakim* (head of state).

As political governance at the time was autocratic and despotic, *qiwamah*, by extrapolation, became synonymous with familial despotism (*tasalut*), a term we find in classical explanations of *qiwamah*. The dynamic of domination that applied at the highest political level began in the family unit. A wife subjected to her husband's authority instilled in her progeny an unquestioning acceptance of this authority and by extension that of the political rulers. They were seen as two sides of the same coin and considered, moreover, as emanating from a sacred order.

However, the word *qawwamun*, which was erroneously translated as 'authority', actually means provider or supporter in the context of the verse. The rest of the verse says, 'because according to what they spend from their wealth' – meaning that men are *qawwamun* because they use their resources to support and provide for their spouses' and families' needs.

This is one of the core Qur'anic concepts that must be made perfectly clear for better understanding of all the principles that flow from it. It is about a concession granted to women regarding the financial expenses of the family. The verse is situated in the general cultural context of the time: financial responsibility for the family generally fell on the shoulders of the husband, who was consequently considered to be its head in practically all cultures.

The rest of the verse, '*bima faddala ba'dahum 'ala ba'd*', is often interpreted as 'because of the favours that Allah has given to one [men] over the others [women]'. However, a literal translation would be, 'because of the favours Allah has given to one over the other' (without a gender specification) – favours granted to some men or women over some other men or women. If there had been a gender specification, the verse would have been '*bima faddala lahu ba'dahum 'ala ba'dihina*'. As Muhammad 'Abduh has explained, this verse stipulates that some men are favoured over some women, and some women are favoured over some men. This means a mutual preference in accordance with the Qur'an's spirit of fairness and with the reality of human societies (Reda, 1999, vol. 5, p. 55).[23]

When we put the verse in context, and reread it in the light of other verses and concepts relating to marriage as described in the Qur'an, we see that *qiwamah* is in fact not a privilege given to men by God, but rather a duty, in that the husband is assigned the moral and material responsibility of providing

---

[23] For a critique of 'Abduh's interpretation of this verse, see Abou-Bakr in this volume, who argues that the modernists also continued to perpetuate a non-egalitarian conception of *qiwamah*.

for the needs of his wife and family. *Qiwamah* is not an honour (*tashrif*) but a responsibility (*taklif*), unlike what patriarchal interpretations claim when they deduce the innate superiority of men.

Sayed Qutb (2008) located this concept strictly within the institution of marriage, which supports the notion of private (*khassah*) *qiwamah*.[24] He said that the verse should be read in the light of this conjugal institution, and affirms that the favour (*fadl*) accorded to the husband is because of the financial responsibility incumbent on him, while stressing that, in return, it is not a matter of the wife's obedience but rather of mutual respect between the two marital partners. Therefore, he said, 'in order to organize the institution of marriage and clarify the functions of its members, the qiwamah is conferred in this text upon man' (Qutb, 2008, p. 649).

Other contemporary commentators such as 'Abduh and Mohammed Shaltut explain this concept as an additional obligation for men. *Qiwamah* was given to the husband not because of his gender but only in his capacity as manager and financial maintainer of the household. This means that if this maintenance function were to fall on the wife – as is often the case in modern societies – she should exercise this *qiwamah*; thus no male exclusivity is involved.

In order to deconstruct the semantic confusion surrounding men's *qiwamah*, we must first limit it to the conjugal household. The material responsibility incumbent on men is about household management and is specific to this particular part of marital life. Private *qiwamah* operates inside the nuclear family and in no way concerns the public, sociopolitical sphere, which, according to the Qur'an, must be managed by both men and women according to the criteria of the *qiwamah* of fairness and justice.

Secondly, we should analyse and interpret private *qiwamah* within the normative framework of conjugal relations, as already described, and according to the Qur'anic ethic of marriage. It is impossible to reach an objective explanation of the verse about *qiwamah* if we do not take into account the whole Qur'anic text and all of the verses concerning women which stipulate equality and establish a dynamic of female autonomy that was unthinkable in the social context of the Prophet's time.

Qiwamah should therefore be read in reference to gender relations alongside notions such as *ma'ruf* (common good). *Ma'ruf* appears in different injunctions addressed to men, such as those regulating conjugal life, divorce,

---

[24] Sayed Muhammed Hussein Fadlallah (n.d.b) makes the same point in his interpretation of this verse in *Min Wahy al-Qur'an Surat an-Nisa* (pp. 34–5).

nursing, and social coexistence, always with the aim of altering male social behaviour towards women by introducing this ethical principle of common good (what is just) as the fundamental principle of gender relations.

The term *ma'ruf* occurs numerous times in the Qur'an,[25] while the term *qiwamah* is not mentioned at all, and the term *qawammun* from which *qiwamah* is derived is mentioned only once in regard to marital relations. Yet *qiwamah* has taken a disproportionate importance in Arab–Muslim thinking compared with *ma'ruf*, which often seems to be absent.

We should also read private *qiwamah* together with other verses that concern family life, such as those enjoining husbands and wives to shared responsibilities, to mutual help (*ba'duhum awliya' ba'din*) (9:71), to love and tenderness (*mawaddah wa rahmah*) (30:21) and particularly to harmony and reciprocal consultation (*taradi wa tashawur*) (2:233). Another key Qur'anic obligation to consider is justice (*'adl*), which is extolled throughout the revelation as an indispensable precondition for all human relations.

If we restore the concept of *qiwamah* to its context within marriage according to these Qur'anic principles, how can we accept arguments for the absolute authority of the husband and the blind submission of the wife? How can we tolerate justifications based on women's inferiority and natural weakness, or accept theories – still fashionable in contemporary Islamic thought – that portray all women as creatures devoid of reason whose sole vocation is to 'satisfy' a husband? How can we assess these discriminatory claims in the light of the Qur'anic demand for justice, the obligation of marital cooperation, of mutual responsibility, of love, generosity and mutual self-giving?

Qiwamah is not authority conferred on the husband. It is the responsibility, obligation or duty of men – husbands, fathers or otherwise – to maintain the conjugal household, a family structure that is common to most cultures, from time immemorial, and provide for the needs of their family and all relatives who are in need. The involvement of men in household management is a way of balancing certain tasks between the couple. It enables women, particularly those of childbearing age, to raise their children without constraint. This is relevant today, since despite developments in women's participation in public life the question of sharing family duties is far from resolved.

It is worth noting that no Qur'anic verse allocates specific household tasks or functions to either of the sexes, despite what many Muslims believe. Not

---

[25] See 2:178, 2:180, 2:228, 2:232, 2:233, 2:234, 2:236, 2:241, 3:104, 3:110, 3:114, 4:6, 4:19, 7:157, 9:67, 9:71, 9:112, 22:41 and 31:17.

a single verse mentions domestic work as solely a task for women. In a *hadith* reported by al-Bukhari (1987, vol. 1, p. 159), when 'Aisha, the Prophet's wife, was asked what the Prophet would do in his house, she answered that he would serve his family and when it was time for prayer he would get up and pray. In similar *ahadith* reported by Imam Ahmad and Ibn Hibban, 'Aisha said he would do simple, everyday tasks such as sewing clothes, mending vessels, milking animals and serving his family (Kodir, 2012). Such was the behaviour of the one who practised *qiwamah* in his own family while being the Messenger of the Creator. The Prophet's *qiwamah* was to be at his family's service; it was not authoritarianism, let alone despotism. He tried to practise in his daily life what he had learned from the spiritual message – among other things, that equality before God necessarily implies equality between his creatures, men and women, in everyday life.

Through the concept of *qiwamah*, the Qur'an insists on men's financial responsibility in conjugal life, especially during periods when women are physiologically vulnerable – such as during pregnancy, confinement and nursing – and need to be assured of moral and material support and help. The spirit of the Qur'an is encapsulated in the importance of securing the conditions for protection of the most vulnerable, including women in certain circumstances, as well as children and the elderly.

In some ways this ties in with certain current feminist and human rights demands for substantive equality between men and women. Substantive equality requires that women have equality of opportunities and results in all spheres of social life, which includes extra provisions or support for special needs, such as maternity and reproductive health, to ensure de facto equality (International Women's Rights Action Watch [IWRAW] Asia Pacific, 2009, p. 4). *Qiwamah* can be considered an extra provision that assures the wife moral and material security in her conjugal life because of her specific responsibilities.

CONCLUDING REMARKS: 'STANDING FOR JUSTICE'

Istikhlaf, wilayah and *qiwamah* in the Qur'an must be read together as standing for justice. These three key concepts embody the spiritual message of Islam and encapsulate the shared responsibilities on earth of women and men: managing the affairs of the world; enjoining good and forbidding evil; and doing justice. Through our role as Allah's *khalifah*, every human being is trusted with a mission and responsibility for managing life on earth; this lays the foundation for our equality as women and men. *Wilayah* refers to the public responsibility that falls on both women and men to do good and stop harm. *Qiwamah* dictates moral responsibility and a commitment to fairness and justice in one's actions. It follows that we cannot understand or lay out absolute doctrines for the notion of private *qiwamah* or *wilayah* or any other context-specific concepts mentioned in the Qur'an without taking them back to these three broader comprehensive central principles.

To reduce *wilayah* to male guardianship over dependent wards or *qiwamah* to an assumed authority of the husband amounts to violating the spiritual principles of the Qur'anic message regarding the ethics of marriage and family life. We must not forget that the meaning of Qur'anic concepts will evolve over time, especially since the Qur'an never set out to determine specific social roles for men and women. In today's social context, it is time to reclaim the Qur'anic concept of *wilayah* as a principle that dictates responsible and constructive membership and participation of women and men in society and to understand *qiwamah* as part of the general shared responsibility spoken about in the Qur'an in its conception of marriage.[26]

Juristic concepts and principles that regulate gender relations and rights in present-day Muslim societies and laws, such as *qiwamah* and *wilayah*, must be reformed to attain Qur'anic core ethical principles. This necessarily entails ending patriarchy and gender hierarchy so as to experience fully the unity of God and human submission to the divine and to do God's will on this earth. The Qur'anic concept of *insan* and its vision for human existence demand equality and justice for all men and women.

REFERENCES

Abi Ennaim. n.d. *Fadilatu al-Adilin Mina el Wulat al-'Adilin*. Riyadh: Dar Alwatan.

Aboû Chouqqa, Abd al-Halim. 2007. *Encyclopédie de la Femme en Islam*. Paris: Editions al Qalam.

Al-Bukhari, Imam Abu 'Abdullah Muhammad bin Isma'il. 1987. *Mukhtasir Sahih al-Bukhari* (Translation of the Meanings of the Summarized Sahih al-Bukhari). Medina: Dar-al-Islam.

Al-Jawziyyah, Ibn al-Qayyim. 1991. *I'lam al-Muwaqqi'in 'an Rabb al-'Alamin*. Beirut: Dar al-Kotob al-Ilymiyah.

---

[26] This explains how in 2004 the new Moroccan Law of the Family (*Mudawwana*) replaced the old notion of 'the husband as head of the family' with co-responsibility and placed the family under the joint supervision of both spouses.

Al-Qaradawi, Yusuf. 1998. *Min Fiqh al-Dawla fi al Islam*. Cairo: Dar al-Shorouk.

Al-Qurtubi. 2007. *Al Jami' li-Ahkam al-Qur'an*. Cairo: Dar al-Hadith.

Al-Razi, Muhammad ibn 'Umar Fakhr al-Din. 2004. *Al-Tafsir al-Kabir*. 32 vols. Beirut: Dar al-Kutub al-Ilmya.

Al-Tabari, Abu Ja'far ibn Jarir. 2002. *Jami' al-Bayan fi Ta'wil ay al-Qur'an*. Beirut: Dar Ibn Hazm.

Al-Zamakhshari, Mahmud ibn 'Umar. n.d. *Tafsir al-Kashaf*. Cairo: Maktabat Misr.

Diagne, Souleymane Bachir. 2008. *Comment philosopher en Islam?* Paris: Editions du Panama.

Ezzat, Heba Raof. 2000. 'Al-Qiwamah bayna al-Sulta al-Abaweya wa al-I'idara al-Shureya'.

Fadlallah, Muhammad Hussein. n.d.a. 'The Role of a Woman I'. http://english.bayynat.org/WomenFamily/woman1.htm

Fadlallah, Muhammed Hussein. n.d.b. 'Min Wahy al-Qur'an, Surat an-Nisa 34–35'. http://arabic.bayynat.org/HtmlSecondary.aspx?id=5770

Ibn Kathir, Abu al-Fida 'Imad al-Din Isma'il ibn 'Umar. 2003. *Tafsir al-Qur'an al-'Azim*. Cairo: Dar al-Hadith.

IWRAW Asia Pacific. 2009. 'IWRAW Asia Pacific Knowledge Portal: Convention on the Elimination of All Forms of Discrimination against Women (CEDAW)'. http://www.iwraw-ap.org/convention/doc/cedaw.pdf

Kodir, Faqihuddin Abdul. 2012. 'Straightening the Culture of Interpreting Hadith about Women: Hadith Dirasah 24th Edition'. http://www.rahima.or.id/index.php?option=com_content&view=article&id=945

Kuftaro, Ahmed. 2002. 'Interpretation of *Surat at-Tawbah* 71–73'. http://www.kuftaro.net/arabic/activity1.php?activity_no=4%20&%20act_no=%204

Laroui, Abdellah. 2008. *Al Islah wa lal-Sunna*. Casablanca: Al-Markaz al-Arabi al-Thaqafi.

Masud, Muhammad Khalid. 2013. 'Gender Equality and the Doctrine of *Wilaya*'. In *Gender and Equality in Muslim Family Law: Justice and Ethics in the Islamic Legal Tradition*, edited by Ziba Mir-Hosseini, Kari Vogt, Lena Larsen and Christian Moe, pp. 127–54. London: I.B. Tauris.

Mernissi, Fatima. 2010. *Islam and Democracy*. Paris: Editions Albin Michel.

Qutb, Sayyid. 2008. *Fi Zilal al-Qur'an*, vol. 2. Cairo: Dar al-Shorouk.

Reda, Imam Mohammed Rachid. 1999. *Tafsir al-Qur'an al-Hakim, Tafsir 'il Manar'*, vol. 5. Beirut: Dar al-Kutub al-Ilmya.

Wadud, Amina. 2009. 'Islam Beyond Patriarchy through Gender Inclusive Qur'anic Analysis'. In *Wanted: Equality and Justice in the Muslim Family*, edited by Zainah Anwar, pp. 95–110. Petaling Jaya: Musawah.

Producing Gender-Egalitarian Islamic Law

A Case Study of Guardianship (*Wilayah*) in Prophetic Practice

Ayesha S. Chaudhry

Mining historical, pre-modern, precolonial religious texts for redemptive sources that confirm and affirm contemporary, modern, postcolonial ethical values and norms is fraught with unique challenges. All contemporary believers who simultaneously hold gender egalitarianism and gender justice to be inviolable truths and are also members of religious traditions that are deeply rooted in patriarchal social and historical backgrounds must engage in a variety of creative hermeneutical strategies to make historical religious texts map onto their own contemporary contexts. The Muslim feminist movement, then, is no different from Christian and Jewish feminist movements in its central aim: to make a patriarchal tradition speak and be relevant to modern egalitarian values, so that those committed to gender justice are not forced to choose between their ethics and their religious identity. Muslim feminists, like other religious feminists, seek to find ways in which they can belong to and critically engage with their own histories as believers. In this sense, the religious feminist movement may be compared to various nationalist projects in which citizens express patriotism and a commitment to the nation state while also critically engaging the history of oppression upon which the nation state was founded.

In the Islamic tradition, Muslim feminists have focused almost exclusively on the Qur'anic text, seeking to uncover latent or apparent gender-egalitarian impulses that can frame a vision of Islam in line with new conceptions of justice.[1] There is good reason for this: the Qur'an is considered to be the literal word of God by mainstream Muslims today. Since it is considered to be universally applicable, it makes sense to root a gender-egalitarian vision of Islam in the Qur'anic text.

However, there is another authoritative source in Islam that has not been systematically tackled by Muslim feminist scholars. In the Muslim belief system, the Qur'an was revealed to Prophet Muhammad, a man who lived in seventh-century Arabia. Not only was he the receptacle of divine revelation as captured in the Qur'anic text, but he was – and still is – considered to be a perfect human being, often referred to as the 'embodied Qur'an'. As a result, prophetic practice (*Sunnah*), which encompasses both the Prophet's actions and words, is a central source of authority in Islam alongside the Qur'an.[2]

There are many reasons why prophetic reports may have been largely ignored in progressive and reformist feminist Islamic movements. First, when framing an egalitarian vision of Islam, it makes sense to anchor such a vision in the sacred and authoritative scripture of Islam. If God can be shown to advocate for a gender-egalitarian vision of Islam, then feminist scholars have a strong foundation from which to proceed to other authority-granting sources.

Second, while the Qur'an has a manageable, finite and agreed-upon text, which according to Muslims represents the revelation from God to Prophet Muhammad, prophetic practice (*Sunnah*) is far more amorphous and nebulous. Although prophetic practice is captured in at least two bodies of literature – prophetic biographies (*sira*) and prophetic reports (sing. *hadith*, pl. *ahadith*) – and applied en masse in exegetical and juridical literature, *Sunnah* is primarily accessed through prophetic reports.[3] Whereas the Qur'an is only

---

[1] Scholars who have already noted this trend include Ali (2004), Clarke (2003), Mir-Hosseini (2013) and Shaikh (2004).

[2] Jonathan Brown (2009) writes, 'The normative legacy of the Prophet is known as the Sunna, and, although it stands second to the Quran in terms of reverence, it is the lens through which the holy book is interpreted and understood. In this sense, in Islamic civilization the Sunna has ruled over the Quran, shaping, specifying, and adding to the revealed book' (p. 3). For more about the role of *Sunnah* in deriving law, see Weiss (1992, chapter 4).

[3] Brown (2009) acknowledges that, although *Sunnah* is 'not fully synonymous with "hadith"', the 'concerned study of ḥadiths…[became] the essential route for learning and implementing the Sunna of the Prophet' (p. 150). Given this, I use the terms *Sunnah* and 'prophetic practice' interchangeably, since Prophet Muhammad's practice is commonly accessed and understood in Muslim rhetoric through *ahadith*.

one volume and can be physically held in one's hand, prophetic reports figure in the hundreds of thousands, span many volumes and have multiple authors.

Furthermore, the very structure of *hadith* reports testifies to their potentially dubious nature: each *hadith* is made up of a chain of transmission (*isnad*) and a text (*matn*). The chain of transmission comes first and establishes the lineage of each story about Prophet Muhammad, and the text is the actual report or story. As a result, the reader/scholar is immediately confronted with questions of the authenticity of a particular report. Who reported this text? What sort of character did each person in the chain of transmission have? Did they have any reason to lie? How do we know a given report truly reflects the words or actions of Prophet Muhammad? In Islamic scholarship, there is a sharp divide regarding how prophetic reports ought to be viewed: should they be seen as a highly reliable canon that captures Prophet Muhammad's actual practice and words, or do they merely represent the early communities' beliefs and aspirations about Prophet Muhammad's practice given that they were collected decades and even centuries after his death?[4] Muslim communities for whom prophetic practice is authoritative regard *hadith* literature as reflecting actual prophetic practice. Since this chapter addresses the reader who views Prophet Muhammad's practice as authoritative, I shall accept the *hadith* literature at face value, as representing Prophet Muhammad's actual behaviour and words.

A third reason why Muslim feminists may have avoided prophetic reports in fashioning a gender-egalitarian vision of Islam is simply the circumstances of Prophet Muhammad's life. The Qur'an, as the literal, eternal word of God but revealed in a patriarchal social and historical context, might be liberated from its patriarchal contextual and linguistic constraints. However, Prophet Muhammad cannot be liberated from his context; his words and actions are always directly connected to historical events that sometimes reflect and sometimes subvert his context. The resulting image is of a Prophet who is fully a product of his environment, and yet transcended its strictures. This has led to two conceptions of the Prophet that are difficult to reconcile. On the one hand, Prophet Muhammad can be read as an essentially radical, egalitarian man, whose gender-egalitarian vision – like the Qur'anic text – was constrained by the seventh-century Arabian social and historical context in which he lived. Given his context, Prophet Muhammad did the most he

---

[4] For contrasting approaches to the study of *hadith*, compare Goldziher and Lewis (1981) and Brown (2009).

could to create conditions for gender egalitarianism, without actually fulfilling this vision in his lifetime. To this end, he effected numerous legal changes, such as outlawing female infanticide, replacing the bride price traditionally paid by a bride's family to her husband with a dower (*mahr*) that was paid by bridegrooms to brides upon marriage, granting women a share in inheritance, and more.

On the other hand, Prophet Muhammad can also be read as a fully seventh-century Arabian man who embodied the social milieu and historical context of his time. In this view, Prophet Muhammad was a patriarchal man who was nevertheless divinely guided to institute gender-egalitarian reforms. Prophet Muhammad's personal participation in a patriarchal society was unavoidable and was demonstrated time and again. He married between ten and twelve women in his lifetime, most of whom he was married to at the same time. It is believed that he married his youngest wife when she was between six and nine years old. He did not promote the leadership of women in his community in Medina. In this second view of Prophet Muhammad, it is much more difficult to disentangle the man himself from his social and historical context, especially in contrast with the Qur'an, the patriarchy of which may be ignored, explained away or understood simply as a necessary constraint when a universal text is revealed into an historical moment. The Prophet is considered to be a perfect human, the best of men, the embodied Qur'an. And yet he was a man who belonged and was comfortable in seventh-century Arabia.

In both visions of Prophet Muhammad, as a fundamentally egalitarian or patriarchal man, he is seen as engaging in actions that confirm and challenge patriarchy. For example, though he had multiple wives in the later part of his life after his first wife passed away, thus affirming patriarchal norms, his first marriage with Khadijah was entirely monogamous, thereby representing a more egalitarian impulse. Or, although he promoted the spiritual equality of men and women, which was a move towards gender egalitarianism, he linked women's spiritual ascendance to their level of submission to male authority figures such as their husbands, which exemplifies a patriarchal valuation of gender. It is the patriarchal nature of Prophet Muhammad's character and choices as captured in *hadith* reports that pose a challenge for a Muslim feminist reading of Islam.

So what redemptive value might Prophet Muhammad's example offer the Muslim feminist project? In what way might Muslim feminists use Prophet Muhammad's example to champion gender egalitarianism? It is tempting to simply ignore prophetic practice, citing the unstable nature of *hadith*

transmissions and sources. However, any gender-egalitarian vision of Islam
will be ineffective both theoretically and practically if it ignores prophetic practice. For one thing, a complex gender-egalitarian interpretation of Qur'anic
texts can be discounted by citing prophetic practice to the contrary. Furthermore, since prophetic practice is considered a foundational source of Islamic
law, any serious and comprehensive feminist engagement with the Islamic
tradition must address this source.

Given that prophetic practice cannot be ignored, Muslim feminists have
two options. The first is to portray Prophet Muhammad as a feminist; as
someone who championed women's equality and challenged patriarchy.
However, this is anachronistic, since it projects modern values back onto
seventh-century Arabia. It is not fair to expect Prophet Muhammad to have
been a feminist when feminism, as a social movement, did not exist. The other
option is to accept Prophet Muhammad in the patriarchal context in which he
lived, all the while looking for indications of his resisting patriarchy in even the
smallest ways possible. Doing so allows Muslim feminists to highlight under-
emphasized prophetic practice and also makes Prophet Muhammad's practice
relevant to believers in the twenty-first century. Where does Prophet Muhammad's practice illustrate his concern for women as full human beings? When
does his practice interrupt patriarchal expectations in order to limit men's
rights? These small acts of resistance are significant because they represent a
break in patriarchal expectations, leading one to ask where this resistance comes
from. Why is patriarchy interrupted at all in Prophet Muhammad's practice?
It is precisely in these moments that the gender-egalitarian interpretations
of the Qur'an by Muslim feminists are most fully supported, because these
moments can be read as the counter-patriarchal influence of Prophet Muhammad's interaction with the divine in prophetic practice.

This methodology of searching *hadith* for counter-patriarchal influences
might be criticized as agenda driven and not a genuine search for the 'true'
prophetic impulse. However, this methodology may surprisingly be in line
with the way prophetic reports were used in the Islamic scholarly tradition in
the precolonial period. For example, when Qur'an commentators and jurists
cited prophetic reports to support their particular interpretations of the
Qur'anic text, they often drew only on the texts of prophetic reports, regardless of whether the chain of transmission was weak or strong.[5] The chain of

---

[5] Brown (2009) writes, 'Scholars of the Late Sunni Tradition made large numbers of hadiths
admissible in religious discourse by exploiting the tremendous range of questionable hadiths

transmission of a prophetic report usually came into play only when a scholar wanted to debunk another scholar's position or interpretation.

Furthermore, Qur'an commentators and jurists drew on prophetic practice selectively to argue for a particular legal position or Qur'anic interpretation, making prophetic practice fit into their own framework rather than portraying Prophet Muhammad as a complex person. For instance, in the case of the husbandly privilege to discipline wives in verse 4:34 of the Qur'an, exegetes and jurists supported the right of husbands to hit their wives for disciplinary purposes by citing prophetic reports that emphasized the magnitude of the rights of husbands over their wives, rather than prophetic reports that might challenge such disciplinary rights (Chaudhry, 2013, chapter 5). They regularly cited prophetic reports in which Prophet Muhammad described a husband's rights over his wife as so grand that if he had to command one human to prostrate to another, it would be a wife to her husband; or that a wife's salvation lay in her husband's pleasure/displeasure; or that Prophet Muhammad did not like a woman who complained against her husband; or that a husband ought not to be questioned about how he treated his wife, particularly with regard to hitting his wife. In contrast, no scholar cited the prophetic report in which Prophet Muhammad's youngest wife 'Aisha reported that Prophet Muhammad never hit anyone – not a child, woman, or slave – in his life, except when fighting in war; or the report in which Prophet Muhammad cursed a man who repeatedly hit his wife; or when he divorced a man from his wife because the man had hit her excessively (Chaudhry, 2013, chapter 5; 2011). In employing Prophet Muhammad's prophetic practice selectively to support a gender-egalitarian vision of Islam, Muslim feminists would be doing exactly what Muslim scholars did when using prophetic practice to support patriarchal perspectives of Islam. The malleability of prophetic practice is not new, nor is the methodology of selective reading; it is the gender-egalitarian principles guiding the reading, as well as the self-conscious and forthright nature of this reading, that is modern and creative.

---

found in the late musnad collections of the tenth to twelfth centuries as well as the principle that weak hadiths were acceptable as proof on non-legal issues. Basing their argument on the above-mentioned stance of early masters like Ibn Hanbal, leading late Sunni scholars like al-Nawawi and al-Suyuti all agreed that as long as a hadith was not forged it could be used in any discussion not concerning the prohibition and permissibility of an act. In order to raise a hadith to the level of admissibility in such cases, all a scholar had to do was prove that it was not forged – proving that it was merely "weak" sufficed' (p. 108).

ROOTING GENDER-EGALITARIAN LAWS IN PROPHETIC PRACTICE (*SUNNAH*)

A few Islamic studies scholars have already begun to illustrate ways in which prophetic practice can be brought to bear on a gender-egalitarian vision of Islam. Kecia Ali (2004) has suggested that when approaching prophetic practice it is helpful to think of Prophet Muhammad's words and actions as divided into two broad categories: 'exemplary' and 'exceptional'. This permits contemporary believers to engage with prophetic practice in a constructive way, emulating Prophet Muhammad when his practice conforms to contemporary standards of ethical excellence and withholding emulation – and repudiation – when his practice seems ethically problematic (Ali, 2004). This is a useful tool for thinking about prophetic practice such as his marriage to 'Aisha when she was still a minor. Although some Muslim scholars have based their objections to instituting a minimum marriage age for girls in Yemen on the grounds of the example of Prophet Muhammad's marriage to 'Aisha, others have advocated a minimum marriage age based on the argument that Prophet Muhammad's practice was exceptional rather than exemplary in this instance. Lynda Clarke (2003) has also remarked on the pliable nature of prophetic reports (*ahadith*) in the hands of one trained in 'skillful exegesis', asking 'why the liberals have…effectively abandoned *hadith*, leaving their opponents to harvest the field uncontested' (p. 216). Sa'diyya Shaikh (2004) has engaged with prophetic reports in the 'Book of Knowledge' in *Bukhari*, first by owning her subjectivity as a reader, and then confronting patriarchal templates of prophetic reports while also exploring alternative narratives for reading these reports.

Inspired by the work of these scholars, I shall explore two types of prophetic reports on the topic of the guardianship (*wilayah*) of women in contracting marriages. I chose to critically analyse prophetic reports on the topic of *wilayah* because, although precolonial Islamic law is characterized by patriarchy, Islamic family law provides an especially vivid case study for the institutionalization of patriarchal ideas about the sexes into legal dictates.[6]

---

[6] Mir-Hosseini (2013) writes about Tahir al-Haddad that he was 'neither apologetic nor defensive' about this point. She quotes him as saying, "'I am not oblivious to the fact that Shari'a accorded lower status to women than men in certain situations," and that the sacred texts "make us believe that in essence [Islam] favoured men over women." But he goes on to argue the need to go beyond the literal meanings of the two main sources of the Shari'a, the Qur'an and the

The case of guardianship in relation to contracting a marriage is especially important for Muslim feminists because the marriage contract sets the tone of a marriage. If a marriage contract is patriarchal, it enables a patriarchal marital structure in which the wife is disempowered in relation to her husband. It makes it all the more difficult for a wife to advocate for an egalitarian marital structure. Many Muslim women around the world today are forced into unwanted marriages by their guardians, and these marriages are justified on the basis of religious arguments. A source text that is often cited to explain that a woman need not verbally consent to her own marriage is a *hadith* in which Prophet Muhammad stated that 'a woman's silence is her consent'.

In what follows, I shall examine several prophetic reports that discuss the need – or lack thereof – of a woman's verbal consent in her own marriage. Although the prophetic reports reflect a patriarchal understanding of gender, they also problematize the straightforward application of a patriarchal vision of the genders. I shall also consider prophetic reports that combine the concerns of guardianship in marriage and polygamy. Muslim feminists have devoted a great deal of energy to tackling patriarchal interpretations of verse 4:3 of the Qur'an, which has been interpreted to condone polygamy, and I will demonstrate that the prophetic reports related to this verse lend themselves to the cause of Muslim feminists. Following Sa'diyya Shaikh's example, I shall consider both the challenges and opportunities afforded by each *hadith* to Muslim feminists who are committed to recovering Prophet Muhammad's example in promoting an egalitarian vision of marriage.

THE PROBLEM OF CONSENT

There are three prophetic reports that are immediately relevant to thinking about how a woman's consent figures into a guardian's decision to marry her off (Masud, 2013, pp. 134–5). According to the first report, Prophet Muhammad distinguished women according to two indicators – whether a woman was an orphan and whether she was a virgin – stating that in either case she should not be married against her will, but also that her silence can be taken to mean consent. A basic version of this *hadith* reads,

Prophet's Sunna: "if we look into their aims, we realize that they want to make woman equal to man in every aspect of life'" (p. 14).

Ask permission [*tusta'maru*] from the orphan girl [*yatima*] with regard to herself. If she is silent [*sakatat*] then this is her permission/consent [*fa-huwa idhnuha*], but if she refuses [*abat*] [her guardian] has no licence/authority [*jawaz*] against her. (Abu Dawud, 1998, vol. 3, p. 25)[7]

In a variation of this prophetic report, 'Aisha interchanged 'orphan girl' (*yatima*) with 'virgin' (*bikr*), telling Prophet Muhammad, 'O Prophet of God, the virgin is embarrassed/ashamed [*tastahyi*] to speak'. He responded, 'Her silence is her consent [*suktuha iqraruha*]'. In yet another version of this same report, Prophet Muhammad said that both a woman's 'silence' (*sakatat*) and her 'crying' (*bakat*) are indications of her acceptance (Abu Dawud, 1998, vol. 3, p. 25).

In the second *hadith*, under the heading 'Chapter on the divorcee/widow (*thayyib*)', Prophet Muhammad provided guidance for the previously married woman as well as the virgin. He appears to have suggested that the previously married woman does not require a guardian for marriage but that the virgin must be married off by a guardian and that her silence may be taken as her agreement to the marriage. The report reads,

The widow [*al-ayyim*] has a greater right over herself than her guardian [*waliyyuha*], and the virgin [*bikr*] should be asked permission about herself, and her silence is her permission [*wa-idhnuha samtuha*]. (Abu Dawud, 1998, vol. 3, p. 26)

The third and final *hadith* under study is not a statement of Prophet Muhammad, but a narrative about his behaviour. In this report, a woman named Khansa bt. Khidham was divorced from her husband because of her forced marriage. According to the report,

The Ansari woman, Khansa bt. Khidham, reported that her father married her when she was a divorcee/widow [*thayyib*] and she disliked this, so she went to the Messenger of God and mentioned this to him, so he nullified [*radda*] her marriage. (Abu Dawud, 1998, vol. 3, p. 27)

In a similar *hadith* report, recorded under the subheading 'Chapter concerning the virgin who is married by her father without her permission', a virgin woman complained to Prophet Muhammad about a forced marriage imposed

---

[7] All of the *hadith* translations are my own.

by her father and was similarly released from her marriage (Abu Dawud, 1998, vol. 3, p. 26).

Together these *ahadith* pose challenges and opportunities for the feminist reader. The basic assumption about gender in all three reports is patriarchal. In all three reports, men are in guardianship roles, while women are categorized by their level of economic and/or social independence and their sexual experience, and thus by their sexual value to men. All three reports discuss the boundaries of a guardian's power over his female ward, thus institutionalizing that power. In the third report, the guardian's power over the woman is restricted by another man in the community, namely Prophet Muhammad, so there is some level of social oversight. The woman's agency and power are primarily asserted through speech; she has the right to refuse a marriage (Messick, 2009). However, this is also the precise point where her agency is easily erased, since the reports state that her silence is consent. One can imagine multiple scenarios in which a woman might feel unable to reject a marriage, ranging from shyness (as mentioned by 'Aisha), a feeling of obligation, or pressure. Having her silence and perhaps even her crying (!) be indications of her consent lends itself to the institution of forced marriage. Furthermore, the reports do not specify whether others must witness the woman's silence, or how one might prove this silence.

Yet the maxim of a woman's silence being her consent, which was incorporated into the precolonial legal tradition, appears in the context of prophetic reports that break patriarchal expectations of a male guardian's authority over his female charge. The reports limit the guardian's authority and assert the agency of women, especially those who have some financial independence through marriage – such as divorcees or widows – and those with some sexual experience. In the first *hadith*, Prophet Muhammad begins by asserting that an 'orphan girl' should be consulted about herself when her marriage is being arranged. The 'orphan girl' is presumably the most unprotected of women; she is young, naive and inexperienced and has no parents protecting her interests. In a patriarchal society, this is precisely the type of woman whose agency would be denied, since she would be judged incapable of making decisions for herself. Yet, the first two reports indicate that such a woman ought to be consulted and not married against her will. But these same reports also offer a mechanism for guardians not to take the issue of consultation seriously, by turning a woman's silence and crying into consent. There are also several contextual factors that might shape the legal discourse but about which we have little or no information. For instance, how old is the 'orphan girl'? Too old and she stands to be infantilized by a guardian. Too young and she might not know that she ought to refuse the marriage, or be too intimidated by her guardian to contradict him. One might hope for greater legal protections for a young, inexperienced, orphaned woman, even against her guardian, so that she is not forced into an unwanted marriage.

It is nevertheless significant that when a woman does speak up she has the right to refuse a marriage. Her words matter; they must be taken seriously; they have legal weight. This is significant, since it disrupts a patriarchal system. This is where the final *hadith* is most pivotal, because it suggests that a woman's words regarding her marriage must be taken seriously – not just at the point of the marriage contract, but even after the marriage. Despite the emphasis on the social and legal status of a woman in the first two prophetic reports, the third report suggests that a woman cannot be married against her will, whether she is a virgin, divorcee or widow. In the report about Khansa, she herself approaches Prophet Muhammad to contest her marriage. The legal consequences of this report may be far-reaching, because this report seems to make guardianship irrelevant. If a woman can claim at any point, during or after her marriage, that she was married against her will, then she has grounds for nullifying the marriage.[8] This greatly increases a woman's access to divorce, because instead of proving that she deserves divorce for complex reasons she can simply assert that she was forced into an unwanted marriage.

Here, the fact that consent cannot be proven works in the favour of women. How would a woman argue that she was forced into marriage against her will? She might say that her silence did not mean consent, which calls into question the usefulness of this legal maxim. Or she might say that her agreement was somehow coerced, in which case she can overrule her own decision. This framework provides space for a woman to enter a marriage and then decide – after the fact – whether she would like to remain in it. Or she might argue that her guardian did not ask for her consent, so she could not provide it. In this scenario, a guardian – but especially an orphan virgin's guardian – has a great deal of power over her before marriage, but at the point of marriage some of this power is transferred to the woman herself. She can use this power to free herself of an unwanted marriage.

---

[8] Masud (2013) demonstrates that this legal opinion was absorbed into the Hanafi legal school, where 'forced marriage is, however, revocable by a minor ward on attaining adulthood, according to the Hanafis (*khiyar al-bulugh*, "option of puberty")' (p. 130).

The legal weight of a woman's word over the life of the marriage, even after the marriage has been successfully contracted, lends prophetic authority to developing legal reforms that increase women's agency in both marriage and divorce. It certainly provides a basis for eliminating the legal weight of the 'silence is consent' maxim. Still, it is important to note that these changes are in and of themselves not enough to make women equal partners in marriage. The problem of the marriage of minors (orphans and/or virgins) persists. Interpretive manoeuvring of the three *ahadith* in this section does not offer a way out of this problem. However, a critical engagement with these *ahadith* illustrates that, although these reports pose no serious challenge to the marriage of minors, they provide a basis for legal reform on prohibiting forced marriage and increasing women's agency in both marriage and divorce.

ORPHANS AND POLYGAMY

A particularly interesting prophetic report related to the discussion on *wilayah*, orphans and consent is one that discusses the responsibilities of guardians in relation to the rights of orphan girls. This *hadith* records a dialogue between Prophet Muhammad's youngest wife 'Aisha and her nephew, wherein 'Aisha offers a commentary on two Qur'anic verses. The report reads,

> 'Urwa b. al-Zubayr said that he asked 'A'isha about [verse 4:3] 'If you fear that you shall not be able to deal justly with the orphan girls, then marry those women who appeal to you...'[9] She said, 'This is about the orphan girl who lives in her guardian's home. He is attracted by her beauty [*jamaliha*] and wealth [*maliha*] and wants to marry her with less than appropriate [dower (*mahr*)] for a woman of her status. [Such men] are prohibited from marrying [such women] unless they can be equitable [*yuqsitu*] to [the women] in providing the total dower [*sadaq*]. [Otherwise] they are commanded to marry other women.

> 'A'isha said, then the people asked the Messenger of God (p.b.u.h.) for more and God revealed [verse 4:127], 'They ask you concerning

---

[9] The full text of verse 4:3 reads, 'If ye fear that ye shall not be able to deal justly with the orphans, marry women of your choice, two, or three, or four; but if ye fear that ye shall not be able to deal justly (with them), then only one, or that which your right hands possess. That will be more suitable, to prevent you from doing injustice.'

women, tell them God decrees concerning them...'[10] God explained in this [verse] that when the orphan woman is beautiful and wealthy, [her guardian] is tempted to marry her, and he will not adhere to her status appropriately by giving her complete dower. However, if she is less attractive in terms of her wealth and beauty, he is [likely] to leave her and marry another woman. He said: Just as [guardians] would leave the [orphan girl] when they are unattracted to her, they should not marry her when they are attracted to her, unless they will be equitable/just with her by completing her dower and giving her her rights. (*Sahih Bukhari*, 1979, vol. 4, p. 20)[11]

This report concerns the vulnerable status of an orphan girl in the guardianship of a man who may be inclined to take advantage of her. Like the prophetic reports encountered earlier, this *hadith* does not challenge a patriarchal social structure. The report assumes that orphan women will be under the guardianship of male relatives and also provides commentary on verse 4:3 of the Qur'an, a verse that seems to sanction polygamy. The Qur'anic text at hand has been interpreted as suggesting that Muslim men can marry up to four wives.[12] However, this point is not discussed in the prophetic report; neither 'Aisha nor her nephew seem to be troubled by the assumption of polygamy in this verse. Instead, according to 'Aisha, the verse is really not about polygamy at all, but rather about the fair treatment of orphan girls. To support this point, she

---

[10] The full text of verse 4:127 reads, 'They ask thy instruction concerning the women. Say: Allah doth instruct you about them: and [remember] what hath been rehearsed unto you in the Book, concerning the orphans of women to whom ye give not the portions prescribed and yet whom ye desire to marry, as also concerning the children who are weak and oppressed: that ye stand firm for justice to orphans. There is not a good deed which ye do, but Allah is well-acquainted therewith.'

[11] I relied on the Arabic text in this volume but provide my own translation.

[12] This position, which was widespread in the precolonial Islamic legal tradition, has been challenged by some Muslim scholars such as Tahir al-Haddad. Mir-Hosseini (2013) describes his position on this verse as follows: 'Here al-Haddad quotes verse 4:3, which says "Marry such women as seem good to you, two, three, four; but if you fear you will not be equitable, then only one." He also rejects the conventional argument that the Prophet himself was polygamous, and thus his practice should be followed: "The fact that the Prophet had many wives does not mean that he legislated for this practice or wanted the Muslim community to follow this path. Indeed he had taken these wives before the limitation had been imposed. It is worth bearing in mind that the Prophet was also a human being, and as such was subject to human tendencies as regards issues that had not been sent down to him as revelation from the heavens"'(p. 18).

connects verse 4:3 to verse 4:127, which responds to a general question about women ('they ask you concerning women') with a specific discussion on treating orphan girls (and children) in a just manner.

'Aisha's hermeneutical strategy here is especially fascinating in light of the way modern feminist scholars and activists interpret verse 4:3. For these scholars, the main focus of this verse is polygamy and the discussion of orphan girls is incidental. They bolster their argument by connecting the verse to verse 4:129.[13] So, according to Muslim feminists, verse 4:3 does not support polygamy, since verses 4:3 and 4:129 when read in conjunction clearly state that if husbands fear they will be unable to treat their wives justly then they should only marry one woman, and that husbands will never be able to treat multiple wives justly. Therefore, they argue, verse 4:129 effectively prohibits polygamy. This example illustrates that in explaining specific Qur'anic verses through the use of other Qur'anic verses (tafsir al-Qur'an bi-l-Qur'an), modern Muslim feminists emulate the methodology of 'Aisha, who used the same strategy to discuss verse 4:3. This hadith also illustrates that the particular verses that are brought to bear on the interpretation of any given verse greatly influence the meaning of that verse. So, if verse 4:3 is linked to verse 4:127, as is the case in the hadith above, the emphasis of verse 4:3 is the equitable treatment of orphan girls. However, if verse 4:3 is connected to verse 4:129, as is the case in many contemporary feminist writings, then the focus of verse 4:3 becomes polygamy.[14]

Leaving aside the question of Qur'anic interpretation, the prophetic report centres on the possibility that a guardian might abuse his authority over an orphan in his care, especially if she is beautiful and/or wealthy. The general message of the report is that a man is forbidden from marrying someone

---

[13] The full text of verse 4:129 reads, 'Ye are never able to be fair and just as between wives, even if it is your ardent desire: But turn not away [from a woman] altogether, so as to leave her [as it were] hanging [in the air]. If ye come to a friendly understanding, and practise self-restraint, Allah is Oft-forgiving, Most Merciful.'

[14] Yet another option, which was pursued by precolonial jurists, is to connect verse 4:3 and verse 65:4, which discusses the waiting period of women in instances of divorce. Masud (2013) writes, 'In order to establish the validity of the marriage of a minor and the need for a marriage guardian, the jurists refer to verses 4:2–3 and 65:4, which require guardians for orphan and minor girls respectively. Once the requirement is established, the jurists proceed to prove ijbar, as follows: since a minor has no capacity to contract a marriage, his or her consent is immaterial. As the minor's lack of capacity may give unlimited power to the guardian, the jurists feel the need to propose various restrictions on this power' (p. 133).

who is disempowered, such as an orphan girl in his care. For a woman to be married, she must first be empowered. 'Aisha pragmatically notes that the two reasons why a man might want to marry an orphan in his charge are that she is wealthy or she is beautiful. In the case of beautiful orphans, 'Aisha states, their guardians are generally forbidden from marrying them unless they treat them in an equitable manner. It is best if the orphan girls are married to someone else, so that there is some social oversight of the marriage. The role of the guardian is to advocate for his charge; if he were to marry her, then he could not advocate for her without a conflict of interest.

The temptation to marry a wealthy orphan in one's charge might arise from the guardian's desire to share in her wealth, effectively consolidating her wealth with his own. As in the case of the beautiful orphan girl, the wealthy orphan girl might well be denied a suitable *mahr* (dower) if she were to marry her guardian. Her guardian is supposed to advocate for her interest, but if he himself intends to marry her then there is a conflict of interest between her interest and his own. Hence, the wealthy orphan girl ought to be married to someone else who would give her a suitable *mahr*, thus empowering her financially. This empowerment is actual rather than merely symbolic, because through her marriage the orphan girl's status changes. When she becomes a wife, she both gains legitimate access to her husband's wealth through claims of maintenance and inheritance and secures further legal rights to her own wealth. In this way, the power of a guardian over his wealthy orphan charge is somewhat restricted.

This *hadith* is significant for the gender-egalitarian project for reasons both methodological and substantive. Methodologically, this report provides contemporary Muslim scholars with precedent to interpret Qur'anic verses with reference to other Qur'anic verses. Furthermore, this precedent is embodied in the historical figure of a woman, 'Aisha, who advocated for the rights of orphan girls. This is a powerful source of inspiration and authority for contemporary Muslims who similarly seek to protect the legal rights of the most disempowered members of society. As for substantive content, 'Aisha makes a legal point based on her reading of two Qur'anic verses. Guardians of orphan girls should not marry them, because those girls are especially disempowered and can be easily manipulated. So, although this prophetic report does not challenge patriarchal social structures per se, it does express moral concern for orphan girls which results in a legal ruling restricting the power of guardians over their charges.

FINAL THOUGHTS

The exegetical exercise above, applied to a few prophetic reports on *wilayah*, demonstrates both the challenge and utility of rooting a gender-egalitarian vision of Islam in prophetic practice (*Sunnah*). Finding an anchor for gender-egalitarian Islamic law in prophetic practice is useful for providing religious authority and legitimacy to such legal development. However, this endeavour is also challenging because of the very overt patriarchal nature of most prophetic reports that deal with issues of gender. Although progressive Muslim scholars have argued that the general ethos of *hadith* literature reflects an evolving gender egalitarianism, it is difficult to reconcile this view of *hadith* with the numerous instances in which prophetic reports confirm and institutionalize patriarchal tendencies. It is precisely the manifest patriarchal elements of prophetic reports that have led some Muslim scholars to either advocate a patriarchal vision of Islam or abandon *hadith* literature altogether in formulating a gender-egalitarian vision of Islam.

In both these instances, it is useful to acknowledge openly the patriarchal nature of prophetic reports alongside the assertion that these reports also contain counter-patriarchal influences. This approach captures the complex nature of prophetic reports and resists categorizing Prophet Muhammad's behaviour in a simplistic manner. It is also useful because it delegitimizes the position of those who use prophetic practice to argue for a patriarchal vision of Islam; just because the *hadith* literature has patriarchal elements does not mean that in all instances Prophet Muhammad advocated for patriarchy as normative. Rather, a close reading of *hadith* texts demonstrates that prophetic reports also capture a Prophet who resisted the patriarchal impulse.

In engaging with prophetic reports and applying creative hermeneutical strategies to the reading of each *hadith*, Muslim feminists may be able to recover a corpus of prophetic reports that support a reform of Islamic law with an eye to gender egalitarianism. Though this approach may be deemed selective and disingenuous, this is precisely how prophetic reports have always appeared in Muslim writings, in the pre- and postcolonial periods.

Furthermore, engaging with prophetic reports through interpretation of their texts is more effective for legal change than source criticism or historical analysis of prophetic reports. This is because historical criticism of prophetic reports is largely an academic enterprise with little bearing on the meaning-generating power of *ahadith* for living Muslim communities. Whatever the historical accuracy of a *hadith* report, living Muslims have to be able to uncover new and relevant meanings of said *hadith* for their contemporary contexts. By shifting the power of *hadith* interpretation to living communities, those communities can take responsibility and be held accountable for their interpretive choices. The exegetical exercise in this chapter demonstrates that *hadith* texts lend themselves to multiple interpretations based on the specific subjectivity of the reader and the expectations they bring to bear in their reading.

Although the prophetic reports discussed above do not subvert or displace patriarchy entirely, they do tend to provide protection and recourse to disempowered members of society, such as orphans and women.[15] The prophetic reports considered in this chapter also provide a moral and religious basis for legal reform in the direction of authorizing women to have power and agency over their bodies. Although the specific content of the reports may be ethically problematic and unsuitable for a modern, gender-egalitarian Islamic law (e.g. the marriage of minors), the normative content of the prophetic reports offers valuable guidance that is applicable and relevant to pre- and postcolonial Muslim concerns. In the case of the specific reports under study, the normative messages are that women cannot be married against their will and that those in power should not take advantage of those in their care.

In rereading Prophet Muhammad's practice to endorse a gender-egalitarian legal structure, living Muslim communities can reclaim their authority from a precolonial Islamic tradition that may be largely irrelevant to such a project. In this way, Muslim feminists can belong to and engage with Muslim communities from within, without compromising their quest for gender justice.

---

[15] This claim about *hadith* reports is somewhat similar to Mir-Hosseini's claim about what the Qur'anic text does with gender-related issues. Describing Fazlur Rahman's view of the Qur'anic text on this point, she writes, 'What the Qur'anic reforms achieved was "the removal of certain abuses to which women were subjected": female infanticide and widow-inheritance were banned; laws of marriage, divorce and inheritance were reformed. As with slavery, however, these reforms did not go as far as abolishing patriarchy. But they did expand women's rights and brought tangible improvements in their position – albeit not social equality. Women retained the rights they had to property, but they were no longer treated as property; they could not be forced into marriage against their will, and they received the marriage gift (*mahr*); they also acquired better access to divorce and were allocated shares in inheritance' (Mir-Hosseini, 2013, p. 22).

REFERENCES

Abu Dawud. 1998. *Kitab al-Sunan: Susan Abu Dawud*. Beirut: Mu'assasat al-Rayyan.

Ali, Kecia. 2004. "'A Beautiful Example": The Prophet Muhammad as a Model for Muslim Husbands'. *Islamic Studies* 43 (2): pp. 273–91.

Brown, Jonathan. 2009. *Hadith: Muhammad's Legacy in the Medieval and Modern World*. Oxford: Oneworld.

Chaudhry, Ayesha S. 2011. "'I Wanted One Thing and God Wanted Another…": The Dilemma of the Prophetic Example and the Qur'anic Injunction on Wife-Beating'. *Journal of Religious Ethics* 39 (3): pp. 416–39.

Chaudhry, Ayesha S. 2013. *Domestic Violence and the Islamic Tradition: Ethics, Law and the Muslim Discourse on Gender*. Oxford: Oxford University Press.

Clarke, Lynda. 2003. 'Hijab According to the Hadith: Text and Interpretation'. In *The Muslim Veil in North America: Issues and Debates*, edited by Sajida Sultana Alvi, Homa Hoodfar and Sheila McDonough, pp. 214–86. Toronto: Women's Press.

Goldziher, Ignác and Bernard Lewis. 1981. *Introduction to Islamic Theology and Law*. Princeton, NJ: Princeton University Press.

Masud, Muhammad Khalid. 2013. 'Gender Equality and the Doctrine of *Wilaya*'. In *Gender and Equality in Muslim Family Law: Justice and Ethics in the Islamic Legal Tradition*, edited by Ziba Mir-Hosseini, Kari Vogt, Lena Larsen and Christian Moe, pp. 127–52. London: I.B. Taurus.

Messick, Brinkley. 2009. 'Interpreting Tears: A Marriage Case from Imamic Yemen'. In *The Islamic Marriage Contract: Case Studies in Islamic Family Law*, edited by Asifa Quraishi and Frank Vogel, pp. 156–79. Cambridge, MA: Harvard University Press.

Mir-Hosseini, Ziba. 2013. 'Justice, Equality and Muslim Family Laws: New Ideas, New Prospects'. In *Gender and Equality in Muslim Family Law: Justice and Ethics in the Islamic Legal Tradition*, edited by Ziba Mir-Hosseini, Kari Vogt, Lena Larsen and Christian Moe, pp. 7–36. London: I.B. Taurus.

Sahih Bukhari. 1979. Translated by Muhammad Muhsin Khan. Chicago: Kazi.

Shaikh, Sa'diyya. 2004. 'Knowledge, Women and Gender in the Hadith: A Feminist Interpretation'. *Islam and Christian–Muslim Relations* 15 (1): pp. 99–108.

Weiss, Bernard G. 1992. *The Search for God's Law*. Salt Lake City: Utah University Press.

Islamic Law, Sufism and Gender

Rethinking the Terms of the Debate

Sa'diyya Shaikh

[In] the Muslim community... every question of law is also a matter of conscience, and jurisprudence is based on theology in the final analysis.

David Santillana (cited in Abd-Allah, 2008, p. 238)

Traditional Muslim personal law is constrained by its own underlying notions of human nature. From a contemporary Islamic feminist perspective, the limited gender understandings of human nature, as developed in different sociohistorical contexts, serve as central deficits in various iterations of classical Islamic law. The problematic may be called a shortcoming in gendered 'religious anthropology', a term that addresses questions of what it means to be a human being from a religious perspective.[1] Shifting interpretations of *qiwamah* and *wilayah* in the legal tradition suggest a fluidity of reigning religious anthropologies throughout history that are profoundly gendered in complex ways.[2]

---

[1] The term 'religious anthropology' or 'theological anthropology' is used in religious studies to refer to the study of the human being (*anthropos*) as she or he relates to God and/or a religious worldview. This specific disciplinary usage of the term is quite different from the field of study known as the 'anthropology of religion'. For a more extensive discussion on 'religious anthropology', see Shaikh (2012, pp. 6–10).

[2] This position is lucidly illustrated in Omaima Abou-Bakr's chapter in this volume.

Muslim religious anthropologies are ultimately grounded in particular understandings of the God–human relationship; that is, they necessarily draw on a theological map. In the Muslim tradition, Sufi thinkers in particular have provided detailed discussions on the human condition, the spiritual landscape of human submission to the divine will, and the ways in which the fundamental theological imperative of submission provides the ontological basis for the juridico-ethical legacy and related norms of sociability.

In this chapter, I suggest that bringing particular Sufi perspectives to debates on gender in the law offers Muslim feminists rich spaces to explore the underlying foundations of the law. Such a project directs one's inquiry to core definitions of the human being, the God–human relationship and related implications for social ethics, all of which implicitly underlie *fiqh* discussions. I argue that this level of enquiry allows Muslims to re-examine critically the formulation of the *fiqh* canon in light of the deepest existential and religious priorities in the Muslim tradition. Such an approach provides important criteria to determine whether dominant *fiqh* concepts reflect the best possible contemporary understandings of essential religious and spiritual prerogatives in Islam. Conceptually, there are traditional precedents for this approach to the law: the classical scholar Abu Hamid al-Ghazali (d. 1111) elaborated in great detail the relationship of foundational Sufi theological concepts to jurisprudence (*fiqh*).

I suggest that particular Sufi discourses present substantial resources for more relevant, enriching and benevolent interpretations of the *Shari'ah* and the related understandings of human nature reflected in the Qur'an than do the prevailing *fiqh* discourses. Drawing on central teachings of Sufism, I offer a creative re-examination of the deeper ontological and metaphysical basis for reshaping gender ethics in emerging feminist *fiqh*. In this regard I explore a key concept present in broader Muslim religious anthropology and significantly developed within Sufism, which is simple but radical in its implications: every human being has the ability and responsibility to strive towards and realize the same ultimate goals, and gender is irrelevant to the realization of such existential goals. Being a man or a woman is neither an obstacle nor a benefit in this decisive pursuit. Such a perspective potentially presents us with a central spiritual basis for resistance to the central patriarchal tenet that the male body is entitled to claim social and ontological superiority.

In addition, I explore another essential principle in Sufi psychology that presents a rigorous spiritual interrogation of all human claims to power and supremacy, since the latter are susceptible to the machinations of the lower self. This Sufi wariness against the inevitable spiritual imbalances that characterize interpersonal hierarchy presents a fruitful opportunity to critique gender discrimination.

Nonetheless, Sufism, like all other traditions of Muslim thought and practice, bears the multiple imprints of its formative history and contexts. In terms of gender, much of the influential legacy of Sufism emerged within androcentric societies and often mirrors related gender biases. However, Sufi thought concurrently offers resources on the deepest human imperatives in Islam, which are profoundly gender-inclusive and productive for feminists. I argue that the rich relationship between Sufism and Islamic law has not been sufficiently developed in terms of its possibilities for rethinking contemporary gender ethics. I critically engage what I consider a deficit in gendered religious anthropology underpinning dominant juristic views on *qiwamah* and *wilayah*. Through a feminist dialogue with particular Sufi religious anthropologies, I suggest a different premise for engaging with questions of gender relations and Muslim law.

Let me be clear: Sufis do not hold a singular position on gender nor is Sufism an ahistorical panacea of all things good and benevolent for women. Al-Ghazali, who criticized the shortcoming of a law not firmly rooted in ethical praxis, simultaneously formulated an ethics of justice saturated with male domination. Sufism as practised in a variety of historical contexts, like other areas of Muslim thought and practice, has been characterized by tensions between patriarchal inclinations and egalitarian impulses. Although negative understandings of women emerged in some strands of Sufi thought and practices from its inception, particularly during its earlier ascetic variety, Sufism in other instances has provided gender-egalitarian spaces. Textual evidence suggests that early Sufi women adopted diverse approaches to piety and practice.[3] While varying levels of asceticism and spiritual discipline formed an integral part of the religious life of these women, their lifestyles ranged from traditional gender roles as mothers and wives to non-traditional roles as independent individuals, travellers, teachers, disciples and solitary mystics. In cases where Sufi women departed from traditional gender norms, both male and female Sufis may have accepted such departures because of the greater priority most Sufis accord to the individual's inner state and the concomitantly

---

[3] For an illuminating view of early Sufi women's piety, see Abu Abd al-Rahman al-Sulami (1999).

diminished significance of gender identity for the spiritual path. In some cases, Sufi practices have subverted traditional patriarchal religious anthropology in ways that may provide contemporary Muslims with creative resources for expanding the paradigm for gender justice in their societies. In sum, this chapter suggests that a creative feminist engagement with Sufi notions of personhood may render a different set of defining terms to engage gender equality in Muslim law.

The chapter is divided into four sections. In the first section, I discuss the historical impact of patriarchal social and cultural norms on readings of the Qur'an and the formulation of the traditional legal canon. I identify the importance of developing a systematic ethical critique of *fiqh* that goes beyond a purely rights-based approach. I advocate a structural critique that identifies *fiqh* as a human-created discourse produced by a contextually responsive and historically contingent discipline that seeks to reflect a divine *Shari'ah*, but is invariably caught up in the human biases of its pre-modern male formulators. In order to overcome these androcentric biases while remaining faithful to the central theological imperatives in Islam, I propose a new reading that problematizes inherited gender constructs in *fiqh* in light of Sufi theological concepts on what it means to be a human being, to relate to God and to relate to other humans.

In the second section, I explore Sufi notions of the self and the spiritual path that facilitate a critique of gender hierarchy. I use a feminist lens to derive two important implications from Sufi teachings: firstly the Islamic view that it is not the gendered body but the human being's inner state that is the site of moral and spiritual worth; and secondly that patriarchal relations of power reflect base and unrefined human inclinations and, as such, present a spiritual obstacle that needs to be overcome.

In the third section, I focus on the works of thirteenth-century Sufi Muhyi al-Din Ibn al-Arabi. I outline his understandings of the relationship between the human and God, and of human striving for complete spiritual realization of refined divine attributes, a state known in Sufi thought as *al-Insan al-Kamal*. I foreground the processes of spiritual cultivation that demand balance between qualities of mercy and love (*jamal*) and those of power and majesty (*jalal*), such that the former take precedence.

Lastly, in the fourth section, I examine Ibn Arabi's view that all spiritual capacities are equally open to women and men alike and that such spiritual equality translates directly into the realms of social relations and the law. Here

I examine his positions on female legal testimony, women's equal capacity to set legal precedents, the *'awrah* of men and women (i.e. the private parts of their bodies which when exposed constitute nakedness and thus need to be covered according to Islamic law), and women as prophets and imams.

GENDER, LAW AND CONTEMPORARY FEMINIST READINGS

In the broader Islamic tradition, the dominant legal views on gender relations are not the only or the most benevolent ways that Muslim jurists could have interpreted sacred texts. Legal scholars selected specific terms from Qur'anic teachings and developed these into systematic foundations for gender hierarchy. In this process, the jurists took the revealed text, which already reflected some of the social hierarchies prevalent in its formative context, and superimposed additional layers of gender asymmetry that reinforced norms of male authority and female obedience.

Nonetheless, the legal tradition is not monolithic in its gendered ideology – there is evidence that some jurists at particular times, albeit ambivalently, challenged negative views of women.[4] This, however, occurred within a dominantly patriarchal conceptual world, and the resulting narrow gendered legal definitions present specific selective forms of traditional thought.[5] Today, it is imperative that Muslims seeking to live faithfully recognize that there is nothing fundamentally universal, foundational or necessary about such patriarchal conceptual frameworks.

A critical reading of pre-modern legal texts reveals the ways in which the canon reflects the subjectivities, experiences and ideas of male scholars in particular times and places. Undoubtedly, many of these men were sincere scholars with the genuine desire to faithfully interpret God's will or the *Shari'ah* to the best of their understanding. Their understandings, however, were inevitably influenced by cultural norms and pervading assumptions of male dominance and gender hierarchy. The 'naturalness' of male dominance in

---

[4] For an analysis of pre-modern Sunni legal discourses that expertly demonstrates the tensions and ruptures within the dominant gender ideology, as discussed by medieval jurists, see Fadel (1997).

[5] For an analysis of the patriarchal conceptual world of early Muslim jurisprudence, see Ali (2010).

pre-modern legal thought is unremarkable, given the androcentric sociocultural mores of most societies within which they were formulated. Scholars of hermeneutics have made us increasingly aware of the historically embedded nature of all interpretive endeavours, and how jurists and exegetes' preconceptions and situatedness impact on the meanings they derive from authoritative texts. Despite historical shifts in interpretation of gendered concepts in the legal canon, one encounters the endurance of polarized gendered binaries rendering men in positions of power and authority over women. A significant challenge to contemporary Muslims is the ways in which partial, historically and culturally conditioned interpretive legacies reflected in *fiqh* discourses have assumed universal, transhistorical, religious authority. In particular, entrenched androcentric legal notions of the human condition have enduring negative consequences for Muslim women, as reflected in the ways that legal constructs of *qiwamah* and *wilayah* continue to be derived from particular modes of reading the Qur'an.

The Qur'an provides a layered approach to the human being and gender relations. The more encompassing, generous and egalitarian visions for imagining the gender-inclusive human being in the Qur'an coexist alongside descriptions of male authority. Scholars like Amina Wadud (1999) and Asma Barlas (2002) have attended to the tensions between, on the one hand, the ways in which the Qur'an includes women as full human subjects in relationship with God and society; and, on the other, the ways in which the Qur'an describes gender roles characterizing the patriarchal seventh-century context of revelation. These scholars suggest that essential Qur'anic teachings on the God–human relationship reflecting men and women as equal subjects of its worldview have been historically neglected (Wadud, 1999; Barlas, 2002). Such teachings organically provide spaces for asserting the ontological equality of every human being and have not been fully developed for the purposes of gender equality by Muslim legal thinkers.

A central challenge to a productive Islamic feminist approach is engaging tensions between two ideas that are simultaneously articulated in the text: androcentric gender norms that reflect specific sociohistorical realities from the revelatory context and full gender-inclusive understandings of humanity. Islamic legal ethics are always grounded in primary understandings of human beings and their relationship to God; that is, in religious anthropology that presents theological imperatives for human life and spiritual transformation in accord with divine will. Rendering explicit and visible the types of religious anthropologies underpinning and sustaining our legal thinking facilitates a thorough, systematic and dynamic process of interrogating and creatively rethinking legal ethics.

Many feminist critiques of patriarchy, whether religious or secular, operate primarily within the discourse of rights. A potential shortcoming of a discourse focused solely on rights, however, is that it attends to the symptomatic effects of patriarchy without necessarily providing a thorough structural critique. As such, a rights-based discourse may unintentionally be positioned and constrained by reigning ideologies.

Within Islam, many female legal scholars operate within a rights-based discourse in their critique of gender inequality. These scholars, inter alia, highlight that traditional *fiqh* discourse offers women more rights than societies practically afford to them (Quraishi, 2002), or accentuate the variability and multivocality of traditional *fiqh* discourse in the pre-modern period which allowed Muslim women far more freedom than is currently enjoyed (Sonbol, 1996). In addition, they prioritize traditional legal positions that provide women some financial advantage, such as maintenance and dower (al-Hibri, 2000). The goal, then, is to retrieve rights for women that have been marginalized in dominant interpretations of the Qur'an and *Shari'ah*. This effectively translates into a discourse of competing equalities – that is, men and women are granted rights by traditional approaches to the *Shari'ah*; men have generally been granted their rights, but the same has not always held true for women. Hence, the goal is balance, restoring to women parallel, if not always equal, rights based on established legal traditions.

These rights-based approaches followed by many feminist Muslim scholars are strategically and pragmatically necessary. However, scholars also urgently need to engage in a comprehensive theological critique that actively interrogates the basic premises and nature of dominant *fiqh* structures.[6] A pure rights-based discourse is limited by the fact that it often deals with the symptoms of inherited structures of patriarchal discourse without necessarily or rigorously interrogating the nature, roots and assumptions of the structures – in other words, the causal factors informing such structures. A rights-based discourse often inadvertently internalizes the hegemony of inherited structures and is thus more vulnerable to reversions to patriarchal articulations in strained and conflicted social and political contexts. For example, in the current geopolitical environment, where Muslim identity in different

---

[6] Notable examples of scholarly work that problematize the premises and principles underlying *fiqh* tradition are articles by Ziba Mir-Hosseini (2003) and Kecia Ali (2003).

contexts may be perceived as under threat, reversions to patriarchal *fiqh* as the benchmark of Muslim identity and authenticity become particularly salient and charged.[7] Thus a feminist rights-based discourse needs also to be firmly wedded to a clear and strong interrogation of the central principles and values on which legal discourses are built.

Developing a more structural and theologically robust critique requires critical attention to the constructed nature of *fiqh* as a human and historically evolving interpretation of *Shari'ah*. Essential to this enterprise is to understand the *fiqh* legacy as a dynamic human interpretive process that seeks to realize particular ideals, values and perspectives of reality and that is not an end in itself. The term *Shari'ah* signifies such a vision of a moral, religious, visionary path for human fulfilment – it does not signify law in the ways we recognize Muslim law. Rather, *fiqh* represents multiple and varied human interpretive attempts to translate this vision into legal norms. A structural critique of the established *fiqh* canon would involve asking some fundamental questions relating to the nature of *Shari'ah* and its historical interpretations: What are the ideological implications of using the terms *Shari'ah* and *fiqh* interchangeably?[8] What is the continuing impact of context and historical circumstance on the formation of Islamic law? In particular, what is the notional content of the terms 'human being', 'society' and 'God' which underlies dominant positions in the *fiqh* literature? Most significantly, it is imperative to look at the nature and constitution of *fiqh* in relation to a deeper vision of ultimate reality and human purpose. Such a re-evaluation needs to ask how the inherited *fiqh* as a discourse manifests and enacts that reality and whether in fact it really does so to the best of one's contemporary understanding.

Particularly in relation to issues of gender, scholars must ask critical questions about the nature of human beings and gender differences as they are assumed to be in traditional *fiqh*. Since the established legal canon is implicitly premised on particular understandings of the nature of men and women and their relationships, it is necessary to interrogate the basis of such understandings. Doing so illustrates that many of the specific understandings of gender relationships assumed by dominant *fiqh* discourses reflect the contingent and contextual constructs of their pre-modern formulators. These discourses need to be re-examined and reformulated to be relevant and circumspect.

---

[7] An example of such implementation of law based on a politically charged interpretation of the *Shari'ah* happened in northern Nigeria in 2000.

[8] Recent research undertaken by scholars affiliated with the Musawah movement has focused on the epistemological and political significance of the distinction between *Shari'ah* and *fiqh* (Mir-Hosseini, 2009).

Any such rethinking cannot develop exclusively on the basis of contemporary social sensibilities. For Muslims, it must also be informed by metaphysical sensibilities that foreground the God–human relationship in developing ethics. Sufism organically addresses these deeper levels of meaning and human existential positioning. A comprehensive analysis and critique of social structures requires focusing on both the types of prevalent gendered practices and their supporting religious rationale. Holding the underlying issues of values, principles and human purpose – areas of detailed Sufi exploration – consistently in view enables the enquirer to arrive at different possibilities from the dominant *fiqh* discourse.

The debates on the relationship between *Shari'ah* and *Tariqah* have a long history in Islamic thought. In some groups, Sufi practitioners with advanced capacities for ethical judgement exercised their discretion in observing the law. Others insisted that religiously acceptable behaviour should always be determined by the letter of the law; in fact, in the modern period, contestations of the nature of what constitutes proper Sufi teachings and practice resulted in an intensified focus by some major Sufi groups on asserting the primacy of the *Shari'ah* in relation to Sufi practice.[9] Most of these discussions, however, generally accept the dominant *fiqh* canon, with all of its gendered assumptions, as accurate expressions of the *Shari'ah*. I question such assumptions, particularly some of the problematic presuppositions on the nature of men and women which underlie much of the inherited and socially conditioned *fiqh* canon. While for most legal scholars it is a theoretical commonplace that the *fiqh* canon represents limited human attempts to express the *Shari'ah* and that *fiqh* is the product of dynamic human processes, more ideologized and simplistic conflations of *Shari'ah* and *fiqh* often appear in popular political discourse. This phenomenon continues to have detrimental consequences for gender justice and women's rights in many Muslim societies.

SELF AND SUBJECTIVITIES IN SUFISM

The prioritization of the human being's inner state, together with the belief that people all share the same spiritual imperatives – irrespective of whether one occupies a male or female body – signifies one of the organically genderless

---

[9] For a detailed discussion of these debates in the modern world, see Sirriyeh (2003).

assumptions in Sufism.[10] In principle, Sufism presupposes that every human being can pursue and achieve the same ultimate goals and that gender does not constitute an impediment or an advantage to these existential ends. These assumptions potentially pose a direct challenge to the very basis of patriarchy, in which the male body is the signifier of social and ontological superiority. Moreover, as detailed below, Sufi psychology inherently promotes vigilance towards assertions of personal and social superiority over others. Such suspicion directed at the spiritual dynamics underpinning interpersonal hierarchy enables a productive space for a critique of gender discrimination. The following exploration of Sufi psychology allows a deeper dialogue with its gender ideology.

Personality in Sufism may be conceptualized in relation to the tripartite relationship between the soul (*nafs*), the heart (*qalb*) and the spirit (*ruh*), as identified in the Qur'an (Schimmel, 1975, p. 191). The *nafs*, identified as one's self-awareness, is a dynamic entity determined by the spiritual state of the individual (Chittick, 1989, p. 17). It can range from being dominated by base instincts and cravings to being characterized by a state of peace and submission to God, with varying intermediate possibilities. In its crudest and most unrefined state, it is described as *al-nafs al-ammara*, the commanding soul, or 'the soul that incites to evil' (Qur'an 12:53). Dominated by self-centred and egoistic tendencies, it draws a person to the realm of limited selfhood and transient desires and is responsible for separation from the original state of harmony between God and humanity. Blind to the true nature of reality, *al-nafs al-ammara* perceives worldly, ephemeral attractions such as power, fame, wealth and physical gratification as meaningful in themselves. The eleventh-century Sufi al-Hujwiri compares the *nafs* to an animal such as a wild horse or dog that needs to be trained and subdued to change its nature and teach it its place on the spiritual path (al-Hujwiri, 1976, p. 202). Refining instinctual elements of self is seen as essential to spiritual purification. Only then is it possible to attain knowledge of the complete divine imperative of agency and vicegerency that exists latently within all humanity.

The entity that represents the opposite of the lower soul is the spirit (*ruh*), which is a subtle life-giving entity blown into every human being from God's

---

[10] Cornell (2007) demonstrates how some male Sufis have ignored these basic genderless assumptions and integrated misogynist views of the self into their works.

self (Qur'an 15:29). While the *nafs* is associated with the self-centredness and blindness of the devil, the *ruh* has been associated with the angelic qualities of luminosity and discernment, drawing one towards God and the higher echelons of spiritual awareness. The opposing spiritual forces activated by the respective inclinations of *al-nafs al-ammara* and the *ruh* struggle for supremacy within the individual's heart (*qalb*) and give rise to various thoughts, ideas and impulses known as *khawatir*. Moral choice for the early masters depended on careful analysis and discernment of these forces, the resultant *khawatir* and the aspirants' responses.[11]

The third constituent, the *qalb* (heart), is the centre of human spiritual receptivity in the Sufi scheme. In a *hadith qudsi* (an extra-Qur'anic saying attributed to God), God calls the human heart God's own abode, which is not to be confused with the physical heart or the emotions. The receptivity of the heart is contingent on the spiritual state of the individual. Through succumbing to evil *khawatir* and the torpor of transient desires, most hearts become rusted or opaque. A person can only remove this rust or veil from the heart by persistent remembrance and invocation of God, abstinence from incorrect behaviour, performance of good actions, including service to other human beings, and other rigorous spiritual practices.[12] Through such spiritual discipline, the seeker's commanding soul is weakened, abandoning evil commands and transforming into a different state of being known as *al-nafs al-lawwama*, 'the blaming soul' (Qur'an 75:2). Such transformations mark the emergence of the conscience, where the striving for good has been integrated and internalized. The soul, aware of its own imperfections, reprimands the person if he or she inclines towards anything that constitutes spiritual negligence. With consistent striving and purification, the heart is cleansed and illuminated by the divine light of the spirit, and the soul of the seeker is satisfied, described as *al-nafs al-mutmainna*, 'the soul at peace' (Qur'an 89:27). This state is described in the *hadith qudsi* where God says, 'The heavens and earth contain me not, but the heart of my faithful servant contains me' (al-Ghazali, 1909, p. 12).[13] For a human being to realize fully the presence of God in the heart, it is necessary to subdue and surrender those individualistic instincts that battle to remain sovereign. Sufis suggest that it is through the complete submission of the self

---

[11] Al-Muhasibi (d. 857) developed a complex moral psychology that provided the seeker with ways to understand egoism and vigilantly monitor one's responses. For selections from his writings, see Sells (1996, pp. 171–95).

[12] For a discussion of early Sufi practices, see Sells (1996).

[13] Translations from original Arabic texts are my own.

to the Creator, through a pervasive state of *islam*, that real human potentiality can be attained.[14]

Sufi psychology provides an inherent critique of egotism which presents an opportunity to challenge notions of male superiority. Here, the commitment to a constant awareness of God's absolute sovereignty counters the human instinct to claim power, including male claims to authority over women. In this framework, any such claim demands interrogation and may be suspected as a potential trap of the lower self (*al-nafs al-ammara*). This is reflected in a number of classical Sufi narratives where interactions between women and men effectively constitute a penetrating spiritual and social critique of normative gender assumptions.

One such narrative involves the legendary and influential early Sufi Rabia al-Adawiyya (d. 801). A group of religious men apparently attempted to goad her, saying, 'All the virtues have been scattered on the heads of men. The crown of prophethood has been placed on men's heads. The belt of nobility has been fastened around men's waists. No woman has ever been a prophet.' To this Rabia serenely replied, 'All that is true, but egoism and self-worship and "I am your Lord" have never sprung from a woman's breast…All these things have been the specialty of men' (Attar, 1966, p. 48). What appears to be witty, acerbic repartee also constitutes a devastating spiritual critique of patriarchal power. Rabia rejects the men's claims to gender-based superiority by potently associating these with the Qur'anic archetype of disbelief, the Pharaoh. The latter's wilful assertion, 'I am your Lord' (Qur'an 79:24), embodies the ultimate depths of spiritual disease and desolation.

This pithy story, with its radical set of Qur'anic associations, condemns men's desire for privilege as symptomatic of a severe spiritual deficit. Rabia astutely points to the triumph of *al-nafs al-ammara* over men through chauvinism. Male subjectivities produced through patriarchy may well be spiritually compromised, since implicit assumptions of purely gender-based superiority thwart a fundamental theological imperative in Islam: the ability to discern and surrender to God as the genuine source of power is shrouded when an individual assumes arbitrary superiority over another life. Whatever distracts and misleads an individual from awareness of God's absolute sovereignty, such as social prestige premised on gender difference, is spiritually detrimental to the individual. Developing this analysis allows us to infer that patriarchy is

---

[14] In addition to the use of 'Islam' to refer to a religion, the term *islam* also refers to the process of an individual's submission to God.

reflective of a lack of spiritual discernment. In the above story, central Sufi principles concerning the prioritization of the inner state and the critique of gender-based hierarchal power are discursively implicit in traditional Sufi insights on spiritual refinement.

Elsewhere, however, misogyny is reflected in Sufi literature where, for example, womankind is associated with the destructive attractions of the commanding soul (Schimmel, 1975, p. 124). Some Sufi men linked the dangers of an overwhelming sexuality to women, relegating both to the realm of *al-nafs al-ammara*. However, their wariness towards women clearly represented an outward projection of the inner struggles that these men were having with their own desires. These reflect the partiality and limitations of a particular type of male subjectivity. Nonetheless, the above narrative about Rabia and similar Sufi stories[15] illustrate that principal assumptions in Sufism may provide resources to challenge patriarchy in so much as the latter reflects humanity's baser inclinations of *al-nafs al-ammara*. According to this interpretation, progress on the spiritual path can imply directly challenging patriarchal impulses as they arise.

GLIMPSING THE DIVINE, ENVISIONING THE HUMAN

Muhyi al-Din Ibn al-Arabi (d. 240), an extraordinary thinker and visionary who was both Sufi and jurist,[16] offered a number of radical conceptions of gender that were atypical among the thirteenth-century male scholarly elite.[17] In explaining the ontological basis of human nature, Ibn Arabi draws on the *hadith* that 'God created Adam in God's own form' and the Qur'anic verse that God 'taught Adam all of the names' (2:30).[18] The 'names' signify the attributes or qualities of God, what the Qur'an also describes as 'the beautiful names'

---

[15] For other such Sufi stories critical of male assertions of gender-based superiority, see Shaikh (2012, pp. 54–6).

[16] Although there is no evidence that Ibn Arabi was a practising jurist, Winkel (1997) and Chodkiewicz (1993) illustrate that *fiqh* is integral to his entire vision, demonstrating the extensive legal thinking and jurisprudence found in Ibn Arabi's *Al-Futuhat al-Makkiyya*.

[17] Ibn Arabi's more egalitarian gender narratives were at times interwoven seamlessly with hierarchical, androcentric elements more typical of his context, reflecting ambivalent formulations of gender that characterize the broader Muslim legacy. For a full-length exploration of the various gendered dimensions of Ibn Arabi's thought, see Shaikh (2012).

[18] In this context, Adam represents the archetypal human being; he is neither merely a prophet nor just a male human being.

(*al-asma al-husna*). Traditionally, it is held that God has ninety-nine names, qualities or attributes that reside within God's state of unity (*tawhid*). Creation occurs through a manifestation of these attributes from the original state of divine oneness.

Ibn Arabi states that among all creation humanity uniquely reflects the potential to comprehensively integrate and manifest the totality of God's attributes; in other words, a microcosm of the divine names (Ibn Arabi, 1980, p. 50). Humanity unifies and concentrates all God's attributes that are reflected in a more differentiated manner in the rest of the universe or the macrocosm. Ibn Arabi presents a particular religious anthropology through developing the Sufi archetypal human, called the *al-Insan al-Kamil* ('the Complete Human'), which represents the ideal ethical self and the exemplary standard for human beings (Ibn Arabi, 1911, vol. 1, p. 216). Those who successfully embody this archetype in their historical actualities are the prophets and the friends of God (*awliya'*), as Sufi adepts are called.

In Ibn Arabi's cosmology, all human beings embody the divine names and are rooted in God through these names, which in turn form the basis of human beings' existential identity and self-knowledge. Progressing on the spiritual path demands that a person strive to purify the self from all false deities and realize one's state of ontological dependency on God. Given this model, the question about process becomes all important in the human spiritual journey. In reality, people can embody endless variations of the divine names, accounting for the full range of human possibilities in existence, from actions that are noble to those which are blameworthy (Chittick, 1989, pp. 286–8). At various points in one's life, these names manifest themselves in different configurations with shifting intensities and complex interrelationships. Ibn Arabi reiterates that the critical enterprise of progress on the path of self-realization demands that the aspirant observes the precise limit of each attribute and does not step outside the related balance between the different names (Ibn Arabi, 1911, vol. 4, p. 3).

For many Muslim thinkers, including Ibn Arabi, the divine names can be divided into two groups that set up several sets of corresponding relationships with one another. These are broadly categorized into names of majesty (*jalal*) and those of beauty (*jamal*). Names of beauty, like the Loving, the Merciful, the Beneficent, the Gentle, the Forgiver, are closely connected to the concept of God's similarity with creation, whereas those of majesty, like the Inaccessible, the Bringer of Death, the Overwhelming, the All-High, the Great, are connected to God's incomparability with creation.

Since the human archetype, *al-Insan al-Kamil*, is comprehensive in reflect-ing the divine names, the notions of incomparability and similarity primarily aim to provide an epistemological guide to the human being. The notion that many of the majestic (*jalali*) qualities belong to the realm of incomparability implies that epistemologically the sojourner should not make any claims to these qualities at the outset. In relation to God's *jalali* qualities, human beings should adopt a relationship of receptivity and dependency. One cannot respond to God's *jalali* names with one's own ego-based *jalali* qualities, since this will only further distance one from the source and result in misguidance. Satan epitomized misplaced *jalal* when he countered God's command to prostrate himself before Adam with the claim that 'I am better than he', reflecting an arrogance born of a misplaced sense of power and majesty. This plunged him into a state of distance and expulsion from the realm of intimacy with God.

Rather, through receptivity and submission to God's *jalal*, the seeker expe-riences increasing states of nearness to God and the reality of God's beauty (*jamal*). Ibn Arabi suggests that love and submission are the ingredients that provide possibilities for assuming the divine attributes in the correct manner. This epistemological priority accorded to the *jamali* attributes for the seeker is linked to its larger ontological priority within the being of God, who says in a *hadith qudsi*, 'My mercy precedes my wrath' (Chittick, 1989, p. 23). According to Ibn Arabi, life itself is a reflection of God's all-embracing compassion and is the premise of every other relationship and name attributed to God.

For Ibn Arabi, this pervasive mercy also travels between God and human beings through the realm of human interactions, where he foregrounds the primacy of realizing God's *jamali* qualities. Reflecting on the magnitude of such *jamali* qualities, Ibn Arabi observes that God chooses the merciful ones from among his servants as special recipients of his grace (Ibn Arabi, 1911, vol. 4, p. 409). This does not imply a disregard for Allah's *jalal*, but rather that the seeker attempt to dissolve the unrefined *jalali* instincts of his or her *al-nafs al-ammara* in the ocean of God's *jamali* attributes. Through this process, the individual's *jalali* dimensions can be safely harmonized, having been puri-fied by receptivity to God and having respected the limit demanded by God's incomparability. Hence, it can be inferred that God's *jalal* in humanity emerges out of embodying God's *jamal*.

For our purposes, what is clearly illustrated in this ontological framework is that the assumption of *jamali* attributes for human beings occurs in inter-personal and social contexts. One's spiritual transformation occurs signifi-cantly through embodying certain types of behaviour in relation to other people. Character is refined through cultivating social interactions based on love, mercy, compassion and gentleness towards our fellow beings. In this framework, spiritual development demands an ethics of care that is socially engaged and not a solitary, individualistic journey.

Ibn Arabi's key understandings of God and humanity have a number of implications for gender ideology. By foregrounding the *jamali* aspects of humanity, this approach not only provides a general critique of social hierarchies and discriminatory ideologies; it also rejects social structures that prize aggression and other unrefined *jalali* qualities. In our present world, this critique is extremely pertinent, given that these unrefined *jalali* ways of engaging the world characterize the prevalent masculinist ways of being – not just amongst Muslims – and these continue to bring war, destruction, suffering and death.

Over and above providing a critique of these macho social norms, Ibn Arabi's framework directs one to the alternatives where qualities of mercy, compassion, care, justice, generosity, patience, forbearance and forgiveness are to be prioritized as qualities that human beings ought to embody. It provides a rationale for cultivating societies that value peace and justice as a necessary context for, as well as a predictable result of, the cultivation of individual character.

At this level, Ibn Arabi's teachings provide spaces for a powerful, organic and ontologically grounded critique of patriarchal power relations, in relation both to the individual and to social formations.[19] Particularly in relation to *fiqh*, Ibn Arabi's framework allows one to ask whether existing formulations of the law reflect an engagement with the foundational metaphysical principles of Islam. The theological and social prioritization of *jamali* qualities, where majesty (*jalal*) always needs to be contained within an encompassing mercy (*jamal*), offers a crucial insight for the development of a humane legal system that genuinely marries justice with mercy. Informed by ontological imperatives of mercy, a legal system would need to reflect a deep commitment to an ethics of care and justice for men and women alike. In contemporary times, it is clear that traditional Muslim laws seldom meet such conceptions of care or justice. While the Sufi theological focus on the relationship between *jamal* and *jalal* provides a way to redress the broader contours of traditional Muslim law, Ibn Arabi also presents us with a more detailed elaboration of how gendered religious anthropology impacts on sociolegal relationships.

---

[19] I differ from the approach of some contemporary scholars of Sufism, such as Sachiko Murata (1992), who presents spiritual equality between men and women as unrelated to social realities.

THE GENDERED *INSAN*: SPIRITUALITY AND SOCIALITY

Ibn Arabi's principal concept of *al-Insan al-Kamil* presents a pivotal understanding of human purpose which is significant in terms of its explicit gender
inclusivity. Ibn Arabi repeatedly says that *al-Insan al-Kamil*, the standard for
spiritual completion, is ungendered, makes identical demands on men and
women and is attainable equally by both (Ibn Arabi, 1911, vol. 3, p. 89). In
an exploration of different forms of sainthood, Ibn Arabi draws on Qur'anic
verse 33:35, which explicitly articulates spiritual virtues as gender inclusive. In
this broader discussion of human possibilities, he states, 'there is no spiritual
qualification conferred on men which is denied women' (Ibn Arabi, 1911, vol.
2, p. 35). Elsewhere he explicitly affirms women's capacity to assume the highest spiritual station in any time, namely that of the axial saint (*qutb*).[20] The
notion that virtue, vice and the whole range of human capacities and responsibilities are equally applicable to men and women is pivotal in Ibn Arabi's
teaching on human nature. This type of religious anthropology has profound
possibilities for reconfiguring the gendered legal subject, possibilities that have
been inadequately developed by dominant *fiqh* discourses.

In addition to Ibn Arabi's explicit theoretical positions on the equal capacities of men and women, his autobiography reflects his experiential knowledge
of such possibilities. Here we encounter his devotion to female spiritual teachers, his deep companionship with female Sufi peers, as well as his love for and
commitment to his numerous female disciples.[21]

Ibn Arabi's view, reflected in both his theory and practice, that the cultivation of an integrated balance between *jamal* and *jalal* makes exactly the
same demands on male and female aspirants has very significant implications
for our understanding of gender in Islam. His position provides an explicitly gender-inclusive notion of religious personhood where all possibilities of
human potential are fully available to men and women alike. Moreover, he
foregrounds the priority of *jamali* interactions between human beings as the
basis for spiritual practice and sociability.

Particularly significant for our purposes, Ibn Arabi clearly connects
women's equal spiritual capacity to agency in the social realm and, specifically,

---

[20] The *qutb* is understood to be the leader of humankind at the cosmic level, a level that saturates
every other level of being.

[21] For descriptions of his female teachers and peers, see Ibn Arabi (1988, pp. 142–6, 154–5).

in the law. For example, he invokes the case of Hajar as the initiator of the *sa'i* rites during hajj, making her the creator of a legal precedent that is applicable to the entire Muslim community (Ibn Arabi, 1911, vol. 1, p. 708). This socio-legal capacity, he argues, emerges only as a consequence of women's potential for spiritual perfection. The gendered link between spiritual capacity and the ability to set communal legal precedents reflects an explicit connection between spirituality and the law in Ibn Arabi's framework.

In another discussion, Ibn Arabi begins by informing us of a view not uncommon among other legal scholars that, despite the traditional restrictions on female legal testimony, there are situations where one woman's legal testimony is equal to that of two men:

> Usually a judge does not make a definite judgement except with the testimony of two men. Yet in some circumstances the testimony of one woman equals that of two men. For example, the judge's acceptance of her testimony about menstrual cycles as it related to the waiting period after divorce (*'iddah*), or the husband accepting her statement about his paternity of the child – despite the uncertainty pertaining to such situations. [Another example of this] is the acceptance of her testimony that she is menstruating. So she occupies in such situations, the position of two reliable male witnesses just as the man occupies the position of two women in cases of testimony about debt. (Ibn Arabi, 1911, vol. 3, p. 89)

Here Ibn Arabi is alerting us that context and experience are principal considerations when determining gender-specific legal capacity. Such an approach suggests that legal rulings appearing to favour men may simply be responsive to the realities and pragmatics of the social arena.[22] In his context, the ordinary woman's experience was limited primarily to the private realm of their bodies whereas men were active in the public arena of commerce. The weight of women's and men's respective testimonies is related to these experiential and knowledge bases. Such a reading of the law resists the notion that male testimony is inherently superior. Given the vast social and historical changes in gender relations, this approach demands a legal system that is responsive to the shifts in human gendered experiences.

---

[22] For a thorough, considered and incisive analysis of the ways in which some pre-modern jurists negotiated the gendered component of women's witness and other legal capacities, see Fadel (1997).

With this type of pragmatic reading, Ibn Arabi destabilizes some of the normative gender assumptions in traditional Muslim legal discourse: in the context of legal testimony, he subtly unsays the dominant notion of male superiority. Moreover, his examples give salience to women's agency and legal capacity contrary to more patriarchal representations of men as primary agents. The logic of this argument suggests that law is to be receptive to and informed by changes in contexts, experiences and knowledge. Ibn Arabi's approach to *fiqh* opens up ways to understand traditional legal rulings contextually and to pursue dynamic, socially engaged methods to formulate the law today.

On issues of dressing, modesty and the related covering of *'awrah*, Ibn Arabi's views are underpinned by a gender-egalitarian religious anthropology:

> Some people say that all of a woman's body, with the exception of her face and hands, constitutes the *'awrah*. Another group excludes her feet from being *'awrah*, while a third group considers all of her body without exception to constitute the *'awrah*...In our opinion, the only parts of her body that are *'awrah* are her genitals. God, the Exalted, says:'When they tasted of the tree, their shameful parts became manifest to them, and they began to sew together the leaves of the Garden over their bodies.' God put Adam and Eve on equal footing regarding the covering of their shameful parts, which are their genitals. If women are still ordered to cover their bodies, it is for the sake of modesty, and not because their bodies are shameful. (Ibn Arabi, 1911, vol. 1, p. 408)

Ibn Arabi debunks pervasive notions that women's bodies inherently and ontologically demand greater modesty than men's bodies. Drawing on the Qur'anic Adam and Eve narrative in which both are commanded to cover their genitals, Ibn Arabi infers that the genitals are the only part of the human body for both men and women that constitute the *'awrah*. His argumentation links the criterion for a firm social boundary determining women's and men's *'awrah* to the nature of the human being as depicted in the spiritual imaginary. In invoking the Qur'anic story of Adam and Eve in this manner, he foregrounds the shared, equal imperative of the human experience where action and accountability are fully and evenly shared by the archetypal man and woman from the mythic beginnings.

Moving back from the primordial into the historical, his statement, 'If women are still ordered to cover the rest of their bodies, this is for the sake of modesty,' suggests that once the boundary of covering genitals has been established, notions of modesty are then not ontologically driven but rather socially generated. The element of social contingency is also reflected in the conditional 'if' with which he begins this statement regarding the command for modesty. This logic also addresses the essential religious rationale underlying the hijab debate and offers contemporary Muslims a great deal of flexibility and dynamism to harmonize religious requirements with cultural and social sensibilities on questions of physical modesty. Islamic feminists who condemn unfair social practices that require women to take primary responsibility for containing public sexuality through their dressing can draw powerfully on Ibn Arabi's interpretation.

In another discussion on gender and social roles, Ibn Arabi presents the reader with an ambivalent and provocative position. Commenting on the equal and shared spiritual capacities of men and women as reflected in Qur'anic verse 33:35, he introduces questions of prophecy, prophetic mission and the status of an envoy. Quoting a *hadith* that states that both Maryam, the daughter of Imran, and Asiya, the wife of Pharaoh, attained complete spiritual realization or perfection (*kamal*) – in this case, in relation to the station of prophecy (*nubuwwa*) – he informs the reader that men are exclusively privy to the station of 'superlative perfection' (*akmaliyya*).

> Men and women come together at the level [*darajah*] of perfection [*kamal*]. And men are given priority with superlative perfection [*akmaliyya*], not with perfection. For indeed they are both perfected with prophethood [*nubuwwa*]. However, the men are given priority with being envoys and with prophetic missions [*risala wa batha*]. And women have not achieved the level of envoys and prophetic mission. Despite the fact that men and women share in a particular station, some in that station have priority…God has also said 'Indeed we have given priority to some of the prophets over others' (Q. 17:55)…And God has made men and women share in legal obligations. Women are obliged just as men are obliged. Even if women are specified with rulings that are not for men, then men are also specified with rulings that are not for women. (Ibn Arabi, 1911, vol. 3, p. 87)

Hence, despite basic levels of moral and spiritual correspondence between men and women, including access to prophecy, Ibn Arabi notes that serving as envoys and pursuing a prophetic mission are attainable only by men. As such, the spiritual stations of some select male prophets carry with them a divinely designated responsibility to take forth a religious message into the social and political arena to transform communities.

Ibn Arabi attributes prophecy to women in the cases of Maryam and Asiya even though the consensus among his contemporaries regarded ideas of female prophecy as heresy (Stowasser, 1994, p. 77). Ibn Arabi was thus among the minority of scholars who, like his Andalusian predecessor, Ibn Hazm, regarded prophecy as open to women. Ibn Arabi's view that women had access to this exalted level of spiritual attainment is an important assertion of female onto-logical capacity. Nonetheless, these assertions were still contained, constrained and constructed within an androcentric world in which the positions of envoy and prophetic missionary remained the exclusive purview of men. This type of gender exclusivity reflects the ways in which patriarchal forms of power exclude women from particular positions of leadership. However, it is also possible to understand the gender specificity of these two roles as functionally related to the pragmatic realities of male social power. Sending female envoys to societies where prevalent gender roles would reject them on the basis of biology would perhaps be a fruitless enterprise.

Moreover, Ibn Arabi points out that very few male prophets have been designated as messengers and envoys. Particularly interesting is the way in which he presents this priority of 'superlative perfection', informing readers that God has granted some prophets priority over other prophets. Ibn Arabi reminds his audience that although both men and women are subject to legal obligations, the particulars of such obligations may differ in varying contexts.

However, after the death of the Prophet Muhammad, who, according to Muslim tradition, has sealed the station of prophecy, there is no difference in men's and women's access to all spiritual stations. In Islam, the belief that the Prophet Muhammad was the final prophet and messenger implies that for all of his followers, and thus the entire community of Muslims with the exception of its founder, there has never effectively been a spiritual station open to men from which women have been barred. Historically, therefore, Muslim women have always held *exactly* the same capacity and access to spiritual stations as have men. For the Prophet Muhammad's followers, then, an individual's state of attainment is purely the product of spiritual refinement and grace and is never the result of gender identity.

In light of this central theological position regarding the finality of the Prophet Muhammad's mission, the assertion of men's exclusive access to superlative perfection becomes entirely theoretical or rhetorical. A feminist musing by an Ibn Arabi enthusiast might present the view that perhaps he was deliberately affirming his patriarchal audience's symbolic and psychological needs while presenting them with some unpalatable positions regarding women's actual complete spiritual equality that were almost heretically gender egalitarian. Or perhaps he was simply limited by his own subjectivity, which was always also enmeshed within a patriarchal symbolic universe. Whatever the case, Ibn Arabi accords to men only particular exclusive spiritual stations with particular social correlates that in reality are no longer applicable.

Ibn Arabi also takes a bold and daring position in terms of women's leadership of ritual prayers, an issue that has generated a great deal of debate in contemporary times:

> Some people allow the imamate of women absolutely before a congregation of men and women. I agree with this. Some forbid her imamate absolutely. Others permit her imamate in a congregation exclusively of women. How to evaluate this? The prophet has testified about the [spiritual] perfection (*kamal*) of some women just as he witnessed of some men, even though there may be more men than women in such perfection. This perfection is prophethood. And being a prophet is taking on the role of a leader. Thus women's imamate is sound. The basic principle is allowing women's imamate. Thus whoever asserts that it is forbidden without proof, he should be ignored. The one who forbids this has no explicit text. His only proof in forbidding this is a shared [negative opinion] of her. This proof is insubstantial and the basic principle remains which is allowing women's imamate. (Ibn Arabi, 1911, vol. 1, p. 447)

Here again, Ibn Arabi links a public communal role – in this case, the position of imam – with an individual's spiritual capacity, an approach described by Eric Winkel (1997, p. vii) as 'spiritual legal discourse'. Winkel observes that Ibn Arabi's spiritual legal discourse is about discerning divine guidance in ways that 'illuminate the crossover from outward ritual to inward truth' in every moment to ensure the dynamic search for divine guidance (pp. 23–4). He finds precisely this approach in Ibn Arabi's views regarding women's imamate (pp. 40–1).

Ibn Arabi explicitly connects the Prophet's affirmation of women's spiritual capacity to ritual leadership and explicitly disregards the position of scholars who reject women's imamate. In this case, complete spiritual realization implies equal and ungendered access to ritual leadership, a radically egalitarian position. Although a few scholars had taken this position on the issue of women's imamate, including the much earlier al-Tabari (d. 923), it was certainly not a popular viewpoint.[23] In fact, there are very few historically documented examples of women's imamate. Nevertheless, Ibn Arabi's discussion of this issue and his reference to other scholars' opinions prompt the question of whether women's imamate was perhaps an undocumented occurrence in certain communities. Whatever the case, discussions of these possibilities by leading Islamic intellectuals illustrate that women's imamate was never relegated to the realm of the unthinkable. The Islamic legacy contains counternarratives of gender that destabilize patriarchal norms. In addition, implicit in Ibn Arabi's argument about women's imamate is the assumption and reality that communal prayer can and should occur in gender-inclusive spaces, though this idea is still contested in many contemporary Muslim contexts.

In reviewing Ibn Arabi's various legal positions, I am not simply making the case that Muslims have a precedent for electing gender-egalitarian ways of reforming traditional law, whether it relates to questions of women's testimony, dressing, or leadership of congregational prayers. Although this might be very helpful for many, I think that particular Sufi concepts and Ibn Arabi's approach offer us resources to address deeper structural issues in the formulation of *fiqh* in more fundamental ways. In particular, Ibn Arabi urges people to grapple with the nature of religious personhood underpinning particular rulings that have evolved in Muslim legal thought.

CONCLUSION

The religious constructions of 'women' and 'men' underpinning Muslim laws should, by definition, be linked to the deepest metaphysical conceptions and the nature of human engagement with God which lie at the heart of Islam. Consequently, ethics and laws that seek to enable and inspire Muslims to embody the primary archetype of the God–human relationship need to engage explicitly with the nature of theological and anthropological categories. In all contexts, Islamic legal formulations need to be illuminated by foundational theological considerations of the nature of God and a gender-inclusive

---

[23] In *Bidayat al-Mujtahid* (1983, vol. 2, p. 289), Ibn Rushd, an Andalusian contemporary of Ibn Arabi, informs the reader that, among the various legal positions on women's leadership of congregational prayer, one such legal position permitted women to lead mixed congregations.

humanity. These insights might enable readers to approach dominant legal constructs like *qiwamah* and *wilayah* with a critical eye towards the underlying ways in which historical, cultural and theological assumptions condition their formulation.

As one attends to the limitations of gender-biased historical narratives, one can draw on the ways in which many Muslims and Sufi thinkers have asserted the complete equality of human possibility as central to defining theological visions of the God–human relationship. I argue that these are deeply productive for Islamic feminists wanting to shift the epistemological debate in Islamic law. Such religious anthropologies are part of the Muslim tradition – indeed, they are thoroughly immersed in the core theological enterprise of Islam – even if they have been neglected and marginalized in the mainstream. These perspectives beg further creative exploration by Islamic feminists, since they provide rich historical resources to develop and expand egalitarian visions of human nature within an Islamic worldview.

Islamic feminists are engaged in the important project of bringing critical feminist tools to the table of tradition and fashioning a contemporary vision of humanity which is deeply immersed in Islamic understandings of the God–human relationship and which intrinsically demands the imperative to social justice and gender equality. One of the ways in which one can effectively challenge legal and social injustice is to articulate clearly some of the fundamental understandings of human nature and ontological equality in Muslim tradition. This will facilitate the development of expansive and gender-inclusive understandings of religious anthropology as the basis of establishing alternative foundations for a gender-inclusive and egalitarian legal paradigm. Such an approach incorporates feminist theories and tools in developing dynamic Muslim perspectives of human nature as the basis for just laws that reflect the full human dignity of women and men alike.

REFERENCES

Abd-Allah, Umar F. 2008. 'Theological Dimensions of Islamic Law'. In *Cambridge Companion to Classical Islamic Theology*, edited by Tim Winters, pp. 237–57. New York: Cambridge University Press.

Al-Ghazali, Abu Hamid. 1909. *'Ihya' 'Ulum al-Din*. Cairo: Matba'at al-Amirat al-Sharafiyya.

Al-Hibri, Azizah. 2000. 'Introduction to Muslim Women's Rights'. In *Windows of Faith*, edited by Gisela Webb, pp. 51–71. Syracuse, NY: Syracuse University Press.

Al-Hujwiri, Ali bin Uthman. 1976. *The Kashf al-Mahjub: The Oldest Persian Treatise on Sufism*, translated by R.A. Nicholson. London: Luzac/Gibb.

Ali, Kecia. 2003. 'Progressive Muslims and Islamic Jurisprudence: The Necessity for Critical Engagement with Marriage and Divorce Law'. In *Progressive Muslims: On Gender, Justice, and Pluralism*, edited by Omid Safi, pp. 163–89. Oxford: Oneworld.

Ali, Kecia. 2010. *Marriage and Slavery in Early Islam*. Cambridge, MA: Harvard University Press.

Al-Sulami, Abu Abd al-Rahman. 1999. *Early Sufi Women (Dhikr al-Niswa al-Muta Abbidat al-Sufiyyat)*, translated by Rkia Cornell. Louisville: Fons Vitae.

Attar, Farid al-Din. 1966. *Muslim Saints and Mystics: Episodes from the Tadhkhirat al-Auliya (Memorial of the Saints)*, translated by A.J. Arberry. London: Routledge & Kegan Paul.

Barlas, Asma. 2002. *Believing Women in Islam: Un-reading Patriarchal Interpretations of the Qur'an*. Austin: Texas University Press.

Chittick, William. 1989. *The Sufi Path of Knowledge: Ibn Al-Arabi's Metaphysics of Imagination*. Albany: State University of New York Press.

Chodkiewicz, Michel. 1993. *An Ocean without Shore: Ibn Arabi, the Book, and the Law*, translated by David Streight. Cambridge, UK: Islamic Texts Society.

Cornell, Rkia. 2007. '"Soul of a Woman Was Created Below": Woman as the Lower Soul (*Nafs*) in Islam'. In *Probing the Depths of Evil and Good: Multireligious Views and Case Studies*, edited by Jerald D. Gort, Henry Jansen and Hendrik M. Vroom, pp. 257–80. New York: Rodopi.

Fadel, Mohammad. 1997. 'Two Women, One Man: Knowledge, Power, and Gender in Medieval Sunni Legal Thought'. *International Journal of Middle East Studies* 29 (2): pp. 185–204.

Ibn Arabi, Muhyi al-Din. 1911. *Al-Futuhat al-Makkiyya*. Cairo.

Ibn Arabi, Muhyi al-Din. 1980. *Bezels of Wisdom*, translated by R.W.J. Austin. New York: Paulist Press.

Ibn Arabi, Muhyi al-Din. 1988. *Sufis of Andalusia: The Ruh al-Quds and al-Durrat al-Fakhira*, translated by R.W.J. Austin. Roxburgh, UK: Beshara.

Ibn Rushd, Abu al-Walid Muḥammad. 1983. *Bidayat al-Mujtahidwa-Nihayat al-Muqtasid*. Cairo: Dar al-Kutub al-Islamiyya.

Mir-Hosseini, Ziba. 2003. 'The Construction of Gender in Islamic Legal Thought and Strategies for Reform'. *Hawwa* 1 (1): pp. 1–28.

Mir-Hosseini, Ziba. 2009. 'Towards Gender Equality: Muslim Family Laws and the *Shari'ah*'. In *Wanted: Equality and Justice in the Muslim Family*, edited by Zainah Anwar, pp. 23–48. Petaling Jaya: Musawah.

Murata, Sachiko. 1992. *The Tao of Islam: A Sourcebook on Gender Relationships in Islamic Thought*. Albany, NY: State University of New York Press.

Quraishi, Asifa. 2000. 'Her Honour: An Islamic Critique of the Rape Laws of Pakistan from a Woman-Sensitive Perspective'. In *Windows of Faith*, edited by Gisela Webb, pp. 102–35. Syracuse, NY: Syracuse University Press.

Schimmel, Annemarie. 1975. *Mystical Dimensions of Islam*. Chapel Hill: University of North Carolina Press.

Sells, Michael. 1996. *Early Islamic Mysticism: Sufi, Quran, Miraj, Poetic and Theological Writings*. New York: Paulist Press.

Shaikh, Sa'diyya. 2012. *Sufi Narratives of Intimacy: Ibn Arabi, Gender and Sexuality*. Chapel Hill: University of North Carolina Press.

Sirriyeh, Elizabeth. 2003. *Sufis and Anti-Sufis: The Defence, Rethinking, and Rejection of Sufism in the Modern World*. London: Curzon.

Sonbol, Amira El-Azhary. 1996. *Women, the Family, and Divorce Laws in Islamic History*. Syracuse, NY: Syracuse University Press.

Stowasser, Barbara F. 1994. *Women in the Qur'an, Traditions, and Interpretation*. New York: Oxford University Press.

Wadud, Amina. 1999. *Qur'an and Woman: Rereading the Sacred Text from a Woman's Perspective*. New York: Oxford University Press.

Winkel, Eric. 1997. *Islam and the Living Law: The Ibn Al-Arabi Approach*. New York: Oxford University Press.

Qiwamah and *Wilayah* as Legal Postulates in Muslim Family Laws*

Lynn Welchman

T his chapter discusses ways in which current Muslim family laws
have included or discarded the concepts of *qiwamah* and *wilayah* as
informing doctrines, or as legal postulates that underlie the way in
which the Muslim family is structured in these laws. Different states present
the concepts of *qiwamah* and *wilayah* as based on or drawn from classical or
dominant *fiqh*, both in explanatory memoranda to legislation and interna-
tionally, notably when they report to the Committee on the Elimination of
Discrimination against Women (CEDAW Committee) as it monitors compli-
ance with the Convention on the Elimination of All Forms of Discrimination
against Women (CEDAW). I do not here investigate those presentations with
regard to the classical sources, nor do I attempt to draw out the particular *fiqh*
distinctions between *qiwamah* and *wilayah*; I focus instead on the more obvious manifestations of the two in current legislation.

As underlying concepts, it may be possible to think of *qiwamah* and *wilayah*
as 'legal postulates' in the sense given by Masaji Chiba, a Japanese scholar of
comparative law, who added legal postulates to 'official law' and 'unofficial law'
in his attempt to analyse 'the whole structure of law of a people as a phase of

* Parts of this chapter were published in Welchman (2011). I am grateful to Reem Abu Hassan
and Nadia Shamroukh for comments when the paper was presented at a Musawah workshop
in Amman, Jordan, in November 2011. Unless otherwise noted, all translations of the original
Arabic texts, including laws and explanatory documents, are my own.

their culture and as a result of the struggles between received law and indigenous culture' (Chiba, 1986, p. 3).[1] It is worth reproducing Chiba's definition:

> A *legal postulate* is a value principle or value system specifically connected
> with a particular official or unofficial law, which acts to found, justify
> and orient the latter. It may consist of established legal ideas such as
> natural law, justice, equity and so on in model jurisprudence; sacred
> truths and precepts emanating from various gods in religious law; social
> and cultural postulates affording the structural and functional basis for
> society as embodied in clan unity, exogamy, bilineal descent, seniority,
> individual freedom, national philosophy, and so on; political ideolo-
> gies, often closely connected with economic policies, as in capitalism or
> socialism; and so on. (1986, p. 7)

In this chapter, I examine how the concepts of *qiwamah* and *wilayah* serve as
legal postulates underlying Muslim family life by first focusing on the issue of
spousal maintenance and obedience. I then look briefly at the issues of divorce
and male guardianship (*wilayah*) over children and particularly over females
in the matter of marriage. I conclude with developments related to the idea of
the 'head of the family'.

This analysis focuses on family laws in Arab states, which is my own
research focus. I use the family codes in Morocco and the United Arab Emirates (UAE) as the main examples to elaborate my arguments. I also draw on
the Musawah research paper *CEDAW and Muslim Family Laws* (2011) to
refer to other states. I include, where appropriate, relevant commentary from
the CEDAW Committee and from scholars on lived realities and the implementation of different laws.

SPOUSAL MAINTENANCE AND OBEDIENCE

Perhaps the most explicit articulation of *qiwamah* in the marital relationship
under Muslim personal status laws is the equation that sets the husband's
obligation to maintain his wife – encompassing food, clothing and shelter,

---

[1] Werner Menski has drawn on the work of Chiba to develop first a triangle (Menski, 2006) and
more recently a kite (Menski, 2012) to illustrate his theory of the constituent elements of 'living
law' in a frame of legal pluralism, which he perceives everywhere. The kite concept may be useful
in future work on the role that *qiwamah* and to some extent *wilayah* play as legal postulates in
Muslim family laws.

with no call in law on the wife's own financial means and property – against the wife's corresponding obligation to obey her husband. This is a formulation that Moors (1995) describes as the 'gender contract'. Lama Abu-Odeh (2005) refers to a 'legal structure of gendered reciprocity (husbands maintain and wives obey)' (p. 460). Judith Tucker (2008) considers the rights and duties of spouses as 'contained, in large part, in the twin doctrines of *nafaqa* (maintenance) and *nushuz* (disobedience)' (p. 50).[2]

Ziba Mir-Hosseini (2009) observes that the classical jurists held the main purpose of the contract to be 'to make sexual relations between a man and a woman licit' (p. 28). She argues that the jurists articulated the legal rights and obligations in a marriage as

> revolv[ing] around the twin themes of sexual access and compensation, embodied in the two concepts *tamkin* (obedience; also *ta'a*) and *nafaqa* (maintenance). *Tamkin*, defined in terms of sexual submission, is a man's right and thus a woman's duty; whereas *nafaqa*, defined as shelter, food and clothing, became a woman's right and a man's duty. (2009, p. 31)

Abu-Odeh (2005) similarly describes the wife in the medieval marriage as the 'provider of sexual pleasure (obedience) in return for her right to maintenance' (p. 459).

Kecia Ali (2003) has noted that this formulation is disagreeable to the sensibilities of many Muslims today (p. 170). Yet this notion is still somewhat reflected in current state codifications of Muslim personal status law in Arab states. For example, in the family codes of Morocco and the UAE, the husband's obligation begins when sexual relations commence with the consummation of the marriage, or when they are assumed to commence with the wife moving to cohabit with her husband or being willing to do so.[3] Beyond this, in the course of the twentieth and twenty-first centuries, the idea

---

[2] As an indication of how this formulation of *qiwamah* spread to other areas of law and practice, eminent Egyptian scholar Abd al-Mo'ati Bayoumi (2009) observes, 'It is strange that certain of our ancient interpreters [of the text] held that giving *qiwamah* to men over women in the family meant the preferment of man over woman absolutely, and of all men over all women' (p. 57).

[3] In Morocco, maintenance is the husband's obligation by the 'simple [fact of] consummation' (Moroccan Law of the Family, 2004, art. 194); under the UAE wording, it is when the wife delivers or 'surrenders herself' (*aslamat*) to him 'even if in theory [*hukman*]' (UAE Law of Personal Status, 2005, art. 66).

of obedience as a wider duty of the wife to her husband in return for her right to maintenance has been legislated in various Arab state Muslim family laws, to be in some cases subsequently removed. The husband's right to 'sexual access' and the wife's duty of 'sexual submission' can be seen as underlying a variety of detailed rules, even if it is not explicitly stated. For example, there is a general focus on the physical presence of the wife in the marital home, where presumably she can be sexually available to her husband; it is when she has physically left the marital home without a reason recognized by the courts and without her husband's consent that she stands to lose her right to maintenance.[4]

The codification processes that began in the nineteenth century dramatically altered the application of Muslim family law in the Arab region. In this period of its encounter with the Western imperial powers, the Ottoman Empire looked, inter alia, to the law to bolster its own declining authorities: Cuno (2009) describes it as a 'defensively reforming regime' (p. 6). Family law was not subjected to the codification process until the very end of the empire, but the Ottoman Law of Family Rights (1917) was applied to varying extents under the rule of Western powers established at the end of the 1914–18 war in Arab successor states of the empire. In Turkey, the Ottoman law was abandoned by the new Turkish state in 1926, not long after its promulgation. The state instead adapted a version of the 1912 Swiss civil code to govern family relations without formal or official reference to *Shari'ah* rules or assumptions.

In her examination of North African family law reform processes, Ann Elizabeth Mayer (1995) makes the following revealing comment:

When definitions of marriage in Maghribi laws are placed beside those in Western laws prior to the most recent modernizing reforms or those in Turkish law after Westernization, one notices striking similarities,

---

[4] There are other rules that relate to sexual relations. Most obviously, the first of the mutual rights shared by husband and wife, as specified in both the Morocco and UAE laws, is sexual relations with the spouse. There is also a connection with the wife's entitlement to full dower, which usually depends upon consummation of the marriage, at least in the assessment of financial entitlements should the marriage end (if the marriage ends before it has been consummated, only half the dower falls due). There is also the issue of withdrawal of consent to sexual relations and whether the law recognizes this within marriage; most Arab state criminal laws do not recognize marital rape as such.

such as the emphasis on the husband being the head of the family and
the wife owing him obedience. (p. 10)

Mayer emphasizes that 'the wife's duty of obedience finds support in the legal
traditions on both sides of the Mediterranean' (p. 11).[5]

Those writing on women and the law emphasize the significance of the
twentieth-century state as the key actor in the formulation of statutory family
laws. Sonbol (1998; 2003) insists that 'state patriarchy' is the critical challenge
to those seeking to better protect women's rights in the family, since it was the
key informing ideology that guided states in their 'selection' of traditional *fiqh*
doctrines to include in their new codifications of Muslim family law (see also
Moors, 2003; Tucker, 2008). Another development associated with the new
power of the centralized state, and apparently quite distinct from pre-modern
practice, was the matter of enforcement. In a number of states the courts were
empowered to instruct the police to enforce a court order holding the wife
to be disobedient and requiring her to return to the marriage home. Tucker
(2008) considers the history of such procedure to be

> an interesting instance in which a modern innovation, calling upon the
> repressive apparatus of the state to enforce wifely obedience, took on
> the aura of tradition without, in fact, enjoying backing or precedent in
> Islamic legal theory and practice. (p. 75; see also Sonbol, 2003, p. 290)

Egypt led the way in the Arab region by issuing national legislation on particular personal status issues in the 1920s and 1940s. More recently, Egypt
employed a piecemeal approach rather than producing a consolidated 'code',
as was to be the case in other Arab states.[6] In the 1950s, the first national
codifications of family law were issued in a number of newly independent
Arab states. Since then, there have been significant amendments to some
codes or – as in Morocco in 2004 and Jordan in 2010 – entirely new laws.
Others have followed with first-time codifications, including the UAE in 2005
(Welchman, 2007).

Of the codifications that occurred in the 1950s, the 1956 Tunisian Law of
Personal Status was widely regarded as the most radical in terms of protection

---

[5] Mayer (1995) includes a consideration of the Code Napoléon (1804) and its influence on the
states of the Mediterranean.
[6] Developments in Iran (which codified family law between 1928 and 1955), Pakistan and other
majority-Muslim states are reviewed in An-Na'im (2002).

of women's rights in the family, notably for its prohibition (and later criminalization) of polygamy and its unequivocal positioning of divorce as a judicial process and equalizing of the grounds on which spouses could apply. On the other hand, the text left intact the basics of the gender contract by requiring the wife to obey her husband, adding that she was to 'heed him as head of the family' and to undertake her marital duties 'in accordance with custom and usage', while recognizing that 'the wife participates in maintaining the family if she has means' (Tunisian Law of Personal Status 1956, art. 23). Jurisprudence under this law held that the husband was under an obligation to maintain his wife even if she was a salaried worker and even if she contributed to the household expenses; only his poverty excused him in this regard (al-Sharif, 1997, p. 55). Writing shortly after the original Tunisian law's promulgation, Anderson (1958) found that the text on maintenance 'corresponds closely with the parallel provisions in the Turkish Code and the code of the Turkish Cypriots, based as they both are on the Swiss Code' (p. 270). In a 1993 major amendment to the original law, Tunisia went some way in addressing the challenge of the *fiqh* maintenance–obedience formula. Reference to the wife's duty of obedience was removed, the wife was recognized as 'participating in maintaining the family if she has means', and most of the previously spouse-specific duties were made mutual under what al-Sharif (1997) terms the 'new concept of cooperation' (p. 47).[7]

Other Arab codifications also maintained the maintenance–obedience formula (Welchman, 2007, pp. 93–9; Tucker, 2008, pp. 73–4). Some summarized the obedience element as the wife's duty to obey her husband 'in lawful matters', to cohabit with him in the dwelling he has prepared and to move with him should he relocate or travel, provided the court finds no good reason for her to refuse (for example, his ill-treatment of her). Other codes (notably in North Africa but also in the first-time codification in the Gulf states more recently) addressed the relationship by way of lists, often including three separate provisions: one on mutual rights and duties of the spouses, one on the rights that the wife could demand from her husband, and one on those which the husband could demand from his wife. Scholars such as Abu-Odeh (2005) and Sonbol (1998) argue that such listings are very much a construction of the codes and constitute a take on 'the family' informed by the modern

---

[7] On the 'unusual' *fiqh* position to which a wife's financial obligations might be attributed, see Abu Zahra (1955, p. 145) and Anderson (1958, p. 276).

patriarchal state (and in some cases its historical encounter with Western colonial powers) rather than a rearticulation of classical approaches.

The issue of obedience and its relation with the wife's waged employment outside the home was addressed in subsequent decades as the laws reflected the impact of social and economic changes on family life in the region. While assuming the wife's waged work did not constitute *nushuz*, the formulations tended to require the husband's consent, or to allow him to require his wife to cease working if this was found to be against the 'interest of the family' (Welchman, 2007, p. 97).[8] At the same time, with the development of the women's rights movement, more attention was focused in civil society on the terms of the marriage contract among other family law matters. The wife's duty of obedience was challenged. Forcible execution by state enforcement agencies of obedience rulings was dropped from the laws; some now explicitly rule out such coercion. As discussed further below, state laws codified the wife's right to insert stipulations into the marriage contract which limited particular expectations of 'obedience' (Welchman, 2007, pp. 99–102). The first Arab state to drop the wife's duty of obedience from its statutory law was the then People's Democratic Republic of Yemen, which in 1974 under its socialist vision also allocated the spouses equal financial responsibilities, each according to his or her means.[9]

Over the years a major challenge for those seeking reform of the maintenance–obedience formula as articulated in the laws remained the critical importance of the 'maintenance' part of it. The husband's financial obligations continue to be extremely significant, even when the enormous impact of socioeconomic change undermines the functioning of the gendered roles as scripted in the laws (Kandiyoti, 1988). The volume of maintenance claims submitted by women to the courts, for themselves and/or their children, testifies to the continuing significance of these obligations. They may function as part of women's protective strategies, as part of a negotiating strategy (aimed ultimately at securing a divorce, for example, or at forcing the husband's hand in providing a marital home[10]) and/or as an economic necessity in family life, thus constituting a primary reason for women's recourse to the courts

---

[8] Mayer (1995) summarizes the change to such provisions after a challenge by a working woman to the Turkish Constitutional Court brought about a 'historic ruling' in 1990 (p. 444).

[9] This did not survive in the 1992 family law of unified Yemen, which reinstated the maintenance–obedience formula (Welchman, 2007, pp. 93–9).

[10] This occurs in states relying on the Hanafi tradition, where the wife's right to maintenance arises from the marriage contract, provided she is willing to go and live with her husband.

(Welchman, 2000, p. 380; Würth, 2005, pp. 292–3; Shehada, 2004; Mir-Hosseini, 1993). My own research on the Palestinian West Bank showed that maintenance claims submitted by wives for themselves and/or their children constituted the majority of all litigation cases in the *Shari'ah* courts studied (Welchman, 2000, p. 380). The 'reality of different women's lives' and the tenacity of the legal script on related areas of law (such as gendered inheritance entitlements and the law's failure to recognize women's financial contributions to the household) mean that activists do not necessarily call for the removal of the husband's legal responsibility to maintain his wife and family (Women Living Under Muslim Laws [WLUML], 2003, pp. 22, 217–21). Abu-Odeh has suggested that the goal of women's substantive (as opposed to formal) equality may require a position in statutory law where 'men maintain and women do not obey' (Abu-Odeh, 2004, p. 205).[11]

Some may consider that the 2004 Moroccan Law of the Family takes precisely the approach proposed by Abu-Odeh. Following the Tunisian precedent, the law replaces a 1957 law's lists of gender-specific rights and duties pertaining to wife and husband, which included the wife's duty to 'obey her husband in accordance with custom' (Moroccan Law of Personal Status, 1957, art. 36), with a single provision on 'mutual rights and duties of the spouses', which include jointly managing the affairs of house and children and, in an uncommon reference, sharing decisions on family planning (Moroccan Law of the Family, 2004, art. 51). Other items in the article 51 list of 'mutual rights and duties' include *shar'i* cohabitation on the basis, among other things, of good sexual relations and justice and equality in the case of the husband having another wife. Both spouses have the right of the 'mutual respect, love and affection' of the other and that the other will attend to the interests of the family. The 'respect and good treatment' of in-laws becomes a duty of both spouses, whereas under the previous law it was a right the wife owed to her husband. Finally, the spouses are provided the right to inherit from each other, though not under the basis of equality but under standard *fiqh* terms defined later in the law. Those terms entitle a Muslim wife to a fixed fractional share from her husband's estate which is half of what he is entitled from her; a non-Muslim wife is not entitled to a fixed share of her Muslim husband's estate. Article 52 states that in the

---

[11] See also Abu-Odeh (2005), who warns that a 'trade-off' whereby women forgo the husband's absolute duty of maintenance 'in return for abolishing the rule of wifely obedience' might 'prove costly for poor women' (p. 462).

event of persistent breach of these duties by one spouse, the other 'may petition for implementation of what is due', or, failing this, go through a dispute settlement process with court-appointed arbiters provided for in subsequent articles of the law.

At the same time, the law leaves the wife's maintenance as an obligation on the husband. In an article on its possible lapse as a right, the law provides that 'the wife shall be awarded maintenance from the date the husband ceased paying the maintenance that is his obligation, and it shall not lapse with the passing of time unless it has been ruled that the wife shall return to the marriage home and she has refused' (Moroccan Law of the Family, 2004, arts 194, 195). These texts are worded much the same as their equivalent in the previous law, except for the very significant absence in the current law of the term *nushuz* (disobedience), and the fact that the marital relationship is governed by different construction of spousal rights and duties. Moroccan law professor Rajaa Naji El Mekkaoui (2004) stresses that the new law makes it clear that 'marriage gives the husband no authority over the person of his wife' (p. 173).

The year that the law was promulgated, the Moroccan Ministry of Justice published a *Practical Guide to the Law of the Family* (2004a). The guide does not expand significantly on the issue of the lapse of the wife's right to maintenance, although it clarifies that the lapse of the right applies to the period following the wife's refusal to comply with a ruling for her to return to the marital home. It does, however, summarize the new definition of the family as requiring it to be under the joint care of both spouses, as a 'guarantee of its stability', and noting that the law focuses on 'having the spouses match each other in building the family and carrying its responsibilities' (Moroccan Ministry of Justice, 2004a, pp. 5–6). On the provision on the spouses' mutual rights and duties, the guide underlines 'the principle of equality (*musawah*) on which the provisions of the law are based'. This equality is shown, continues the guide, in the responsibilities spelled out in this article towards family affairs and consultation in decision-making:

> The purpose of consultation emanating from equality is arriving at a shared, consensual opinion, far away from (/rather than) obdurately holding on to personal opinion. This helps in building family affairs in a calm discussion and cooperation, shared responsibility and love. (Moroccan Ministry of Justice, 2004a, p. 46)

The insistence on equality in the official discourse is a theme repeated elsewhere. In response to questions raised in the Moroccan parliament about the draft law, the Minister of Justice was reported as confirming that 'equality is a pillar of the requirements of this law' (Moroccan Ministry of Justice, 2004b, p. 102). In the parliamentary discussion of the definition of marriage, questions were explicitly raised on the issue of *qiwamah* and 'which of the spouses bears responsibility', indicating that at least some legislators required clarifications. The following précis is given of the minister's response: 'the import of the new requirements in the definition of marriage is that each of the spouses is responsible in the family in light of shared care, even if the text does not explicitly round this out' (Moroccan Ministry of Justice, 2004b, 48). For his part, the Minister of *Waqf* and Islamic Affairs clarified,

> *Qiwamah* may come from the man or from the woman, or from both of them together. *Qiwamah* does not only mean the provision of maintenance, or being in a higher position [*al-'uluw*], which is why there is no definitive command in *fiqh* on this issue. The understanding of *qiwamah* in the new law and its role in the family relationship depends on the strongest principles, such as those of community and living together, justice, and equity. It could come under the frame of care [*ri'aya*] based on the noble hadith. It remains among general principles because of the plurality of views on interpretation of it. It is a cornerstone [in the relationship] and in practical terms it is the care of the stronger for his comrade and companion in married life. (Moroccan Ministry of Justice, 2004b, p. 49)

The minister repeated this last clarification when explaining, in relation to the basis for the duty of marital maintenance, 'qiwamah that requires the stronger one's assistance of his life companion is an element of the *shar'i* basis of this maintenance' (2004b, p. 187). Overall, the government's formulations seem to strip *qiwamah* of any notion of 'authority' and similarly deny that the husband acquires authority through his provision of support to his wife.

By contrast, the 2005 UAE Law of Personal Status – a first-time codification by this Gulf state – follows the earlier models of gender-specific rights and duties: one relating to those shared by the spouses, one relating to the rights of the wife, and one relating to the rights of the husband (UAE Law of Personal Status, 2005, arts 54–6). Rights and duties shared by the spouses include lawful sexual relations, cohabitation, mutual respect and bringing up children from the marriage. The wife's rights include maintenance and the right 'not to be prevented from completing her education', along with other rights standard in earlier Arab state codifications, such as protecting her personal property, visits to and from her relatives, and the right not to be subjected to physical or mental injury by the husband. The husband's rights include his wife's obedience 'in accordance with custom/in kindness' and her management of the marital home and its contents.[12] The list of the husband's rights also includes the wife's breastfeeding their children when she is able to do so; this is included in the Moroccan law as a child's right from the mother.

The UAE law describes in two separate articles the circumstances in which the wife's right to maintenance lapses. The first revolves around securing the wife's availability to her husband, requiring her presence in the marriage home and accompaniment of the husband if he travels, all unless there is a *shar'i* reason not to (UAE Law of Personal Status, 2005, art. 71). The second article outlines exceptions to these expectations. The first exception, familiar from earlier articulations of these rules, allows the wife to leave the marriage home 'in circumstances that allow her this according to law or custom or the exigencies of necessity' (2005, art. 72). The second exception deals with the wife's right to go out to work, considering this not to be a violation of the required obedience 'if she was working when she got married, or if [her husband] consented to her work after the marriage, or if she stipulated this in the contract of marriage' (2005, art. 72). More unusually, the marriage notary is instructed to 'enquire about' the insertion of a stipulation into the marriage contract on this matter, although it does subject even the implementation of such a stipulation to the 'interest of the family' (2005, art. 72).

The law explicitly rules out the forcible implementation of court rulings for obedience (2005, art. 158). The article-by-article Explanatory Memorandum that accompanied the law clarifies that such action would violate the wife's dignity and that coercion cannot be a basis for married life (UAE Explanatory Memorandum on the UAE Law of Personal Status, 2005, pp. 268, 100). In October 2010, however, the Federal Supreme Court of the UAE upheld a husband's right to 'discipline' (*ta'dib*) his wife.[13]

---

[12] Ali (2003) considers the use by a 'neoconservative scholar' of this phrasing in contrast to those hesitant to directly require the wife to undertake the associated tasks (p. 17).

[13] This ruling was reported by Human Rights Watch (HRW) (2010) as upholding a husband's (and father's) right to physically 'chastise' within marriage: 'The ruling, citing the UAE Penal Code, sanctions beating and other forms of punishment or coercion providing the violence

The Explanatory Memorandum provides a jurisprudential justification for the rights of the husband (in article 56), focusing on the *qiwamah* of the man in the family. This text invokes several verses of the Qur'an (including 4:34) and a set of precedents from the *hadith*, interwoven with the conclusions about the structure of the marital relationship. An example of the latter argumentation is as follows:

> Every group, no matter how small the number of its individual members, has to have one of their number with a degree of guidance and obedience, in those matters calling for obedience, to be responsible for guiding their affairs to that which brings them benefit and good. And it is known that the family is the first group in human life since Allah created human-kind and made them viceroys on earth and set some above others in degrees...And while each of the spouses is responsible for the rights of the other and for caring for their dignity and preserving [all this] in their absence, the *shari'a* sets down that *qiwamah* in the family is to the man, because of his interaction with general society, and because he is more able to be ruled by reason and to control his positions and his emotions, and because he feels the financial and other injury should matrimonial life be corrupted or cut off. (UAE Explanatory Memorandum, 2005, pp. 186–7)

This extract speaks to *qiwamah* as belonging to men in the family in general, linking it to gendered roles in society and an assumption that gender is natural or innate – a form of biological determinism that is underlined by a subsequent passage that refers to the 'different natures' of men and women and the 'distribution of tasks' required by 'their bodily formation'. Together these provide a good illustration of what Omaima Abou-Bakr in this volume identifies as the fourth stage in the 'interpretative legacy' of the concept of *qiwamah*, presented in 'the modernist development of adding the ideology of domesticity and the "scientific" justification of biological essentialism'. The last justification for the man's authority in the family refers to his financial obligations. This can be

---

leaves no physical mark.' Article 53 of the Penal Code provides that 'no crime occurs if a deed occurs in the [course of the] proper exercise of a right established by law and in the framework of that right'; the first clause (53/1) identifies as such a right 'the husband's "chastisement" [*ta'dib*] of his wife and chastisement by the father and those in his place of minor children, within the limits of what is permitted *shar'an* [by Shari'ah] and *qanunan* [by law]'. Human Rights Watch also invokes the wife's duty of obedience in relation to this ruling. The husband in this case was held to have exceeded the prescribed limits (HRW, 2010; Elsaidi, 2011).

read as invoking the arguments advanced for the husband's right of unilateral divorce and against a woman's access to 'divorce at will' through the process of judicial *khul*'.[14]

The different articulations of the husband's authority in Morocco and the UAE demonstrate the way in which articulations in law of the concept of *qiwamah* – and the paradigm of the husband's legal authority – are moving in the Arab region. Morocco may be seen to stand at one end of a spectrum: shared responsibilities and mutual consultation replace the head of the family's decision-making authority; the principle of *qiwamah* is construed as gender neutral and indicating care and support rather than hierarchy, and is a general principle rather than one entailing specific functions spelled out in other texts. The Moroccan law, which also contains an internal reference to international law, combines explicit commitments to equality with the continued obligation of the husband to maintain his wife and children – on the assumption, according to the comments from the Minister of *Waqf* and Islamic Affairs, that the husband has a 'stronger' position in this regard and is therefore obliged to assist his wife, almost as much from a practical as a jurisprudential position. This continuing obligation in law may be intended to reflect lived realities while apparently unsettling the previous jurisprudential balance or equation of maintenance–obedience. El Mekkaoui observes that accommodating the 'socio-economic changes that have affected the position of women in Moroccan society' was not easy for the drafters of the law and that some ambiguities remain in light of the fact that the wife's shared responsibilities for the household seem to include financial responsibilities (2004, p. 188). This may be a case of the legislature settling on constructive ambiguity: the possibility of withdrawal of maintenance rights from a wife who has left the marital home for no reason acceptable to the court, and has refused to return after a court ruling, means that judicial practice will need to explain the removal of the obligation of obedience and the new requirements of joint management of responsibility for the family.

Another commentator on the new law has observed that the new provision of mutual rights and duties of the spouses comes in addition to those particular to each spouse: '[T]he woman is the supervisor of her husband's house and affairs, and she must preserve him in her person and his property, and she must not in his absence cross him in something she knows would hurt him in his presence.' While not deploying the term 'obedience', this commentary

---

[14] The UAE law does not adopt Egyptian-style rules on judicial *khul*'; the Explanatory Memorandum explicitly points this out.

invokes also the earlier discourse of the husband's right to 'chastise' (*ta'dib*) his wife (Ikhraisi, 2005, pp. 183–4). Time will tell whether and to what extent dynamics inside the family are altered by the provisions of the new code, its application by the judiciary, and the substantial publicity around it, and to what extent its emerging formulation of *qiwamah* is found to reflect lived realities. In the meantime, Algeria followed the Moroccan example in amendments to its law in 2005 by removing the duty of obedience – along with other rights and duties specific to husband and wife – and substituting a set of mutual rights and duties.

At the other end of the current spectrum, the text of the UAE law and its Explanatory Memorandum present a formulation of *qiwamah* that to some extent resonates with what Kecia Ali has termed 'neoconservative' scholarly discourses of the late twentieth century (2003, pp. 172–5). The invocations of mutual compassion and affection and the emphatic rejections of coercion that appear in the UAE texts may be intended to soften or situate the specific requirement of obedience and of domestic management demanded of the wife and the potential loss of maintenance related largely to her presence in the marital home or with her husband if he travels. Other Arab Gulf states that have issued first-time laws since the UAE (Qatar in 2006 and Bahrain for its Sunni citizens in 2009) have stayed with this model of listing gendered rights and duties (Welchman, 2010). These three states all also ratified CEDAW in the first decade of the twenty-first century.

An interesting finding of the Musawah report on CEDAW and Muslim family laws is that the specific issue of a wife's duty of obedience is raised by the Committee with 'less frequency' than other issues like polygamy, child marriage and inheritance. In many states parties' reports to the Committee, the wife's duty of obedience is not mentioned; rather states may emphasize the wife's right to maintenance from her husband and his primary responsibility for maintenance of the family as a whole. As the report notes, '[t]his argument sidesteps the reciprocal aspect that a woman is required to be obedient to her husband in return for maintenance' (Musawah, 2011, p. 3).

One of the ways in which states have legislated the modification of particular aspects of the duty of obedience is through recognizing stipulations inserted in the marriage contract. Supporters of this approach argue that such stipulations have the potential to rescript parts of the marital relationship, with spouses negotiating and clarifying its parameters and the prospect of legal remedy in case of breach. Possible stipulations that are specifically presented in different Arab state laws are the wife's right to go out to work, her right to continue her education, agreement on the location of the marital home, the release of the wife from the duty of moving with her husband if he moves elsewhere, and stipulations against polygamous marriage by the husband. Scholars have observed that, before the codification of family laws, it was already a practice in different parts of the Arab world at different times among certain socioeconomic classes for spouses to outline stipulations relating to the marriage, whether in the marriage contract or in other parallel documents (Sonbol, 1998, p. 291; Shaham, 1999, p. 464; Dennerlein, 1999, p. 125). Women's rights activists have stressed the 'authenticity' of this approach within *fiqh* and historical practice (Shaham, 1999).

Egyptian activists invested years in an effort to have certain stipulations included in the marriage contract document, a campaign that eventually won the cooperation of the Ministry of Justice. The Egyptian campaign aimed at shifting the burden of initiative in the premarital negotiations from the party wishing to insert stipulations altering the terms of the established framework (usually the wife) to the party wishing to retain the more traditional parameters under the existing law (usually the husband), by obliging the latter to take the initiative of refusal (by having the preworded stipulations struck out, for example) and relieving the former of the often socially awkward burden of proposal (Zulficar and Elsadda, 1996; Shaham, 1999; Singerman, 2005). The new marriage contract document that was issued includes a list of stipulations as an annex or booklet attached to the contract, rather than in the body of the text; there are anecdotal tales of the husband-to-be removing the attachment before his wife-to-be sees it.

In Iran, the official marriage contract document includes detailed stipulations that must be signed by both parties to apply (Carroll and Kapoor, 1996, pp. 134–49). Printed stipulations also appear in the standardized form in other Muslim-majority countries such as Bangladesh and Pakistan (WLUML, 2003, p. 172). In the United Kingdom, a model Muslim marriage contract approved by a set of Muslim community institutions[15] provides a set of mutual rights and obligations to govern the marriage and then a set of duties for husband and for wife; these are identical with the exception of one additional clause obliging the husband 'not to withhold economic contribution from his wife/family'. A set of 'special conditions' that may be agreed by the spouses includes a stipulation against polygamy and the husband's delegation of his power of divorce (*tafwid al-talaq*) to his wife (Muslim Institute, 2008).

---

[15] Endorsed by the Imams and Mosques Council (UK), Muslim Law (Shariah) Council UK, Utrujj Foundation, Muslim Council of Britain, Muslim Parliament of Great Britain, City Circle, Muslim Women's Network-UK, Fatima Network, and Muslim Community Helpline.

The delegation by the husband of his general power of unilateral *talaq* to his wife is a recognized principle in *fiqh* but appears to be perceived as more unsettling to the overall narrative of the spousal relationship than when the wife's power of divorce is circumscribed to a particular eventuality or cause, such as the husband marrying another wife. In the 1990s, a survey among Egyptian university students carried out during the campaign for the new marriage contract document found that the least-favoured stipulation was that granting the wife the unconditional power to divorce (Zulficar and Elsadda, 1996). Wynn (1996) found that in Saudi Arabia such a stipulation is 'uncommon' and 'considered somewhat shameful' (p. 115). This discomfort may be linked to the challenge posed to understandings of the husband's *qiwamah*, since his authority in the marriage includes his power to end it without having to establish a reason (although this is disapproved). The wife, by contrast, is required to show cause. This leads to the issue of women's access to judicial divorce.

JUDICIAL DIVORCE

Reforms in Muslim divorce laws in Arab states have widened the grounds on which a wife can seek judicial divorce and expanded her rights on divorce. At the same time, the laws have, to different degrees, sought to constrain a husband's facility of unilateral *talaq*. But it is in the vigorous debates on judicial *khul'*, in which a woman can divorce at her own initiative and without showing fault on the part of her husband, that the *qiwamah* postulate has been invoked as under threat.

The abiding connection of *qiwamah* with divorce rights was illustrated in the public debates in Egypt that surrounded the promulgation of Personal Status Law No. 1 (Egypt Law No. 1/2000) in the year 2000 (Arabi, 2001). The law deals with a number of procedural issues in family law, but the single provision on *khul'* was hotly debated in public, press and parliament, such that the law as a whole was dubbed the 'law of *khul'*'. The relevant provision provides that where a woman's husband refuses to consent to a divorce by mutual agreement she may ask the court to rule for the divorce instead, without proving particular grounds but provided that she incorporate in her petition formal statements (drawing on particular Qur'anic phrases) as to the impossibility of the marriage continuing, return the dower that she received from her husband and waive any remaining financial rights. Senior scholars at al-Azhar articulated 'total rejection' of this provision when it appeared in draft form, inter alia because 'the right of *qiwamah*...was ignored in the provision'

(Fawzy, 2004, pp. 61–2). An opinion survey of elite professionals found that one of the reasons for objection by a 'substantial minority' (forty percent) of respondents was that '[t]he new law casts doubt on the concept of *qiwamah* in the relationship between the man and the woman' (Fawzy, 2004, p. 74). Cartoons in the press showed 'women with moustaches, women flirting with other men, men in shackles and men pushing prams' (Sonneveld, 2006, p. 51), which seem to suggest the end of the husband's *qiwamah* over his wife, linking this with a transfer of gender roles. Interviews with litigants in 2009 showed that the link between the notion of *qiwamah*, obedience and the husband's power of unilateral divorce (compared with restrictions on the wife's access to divorce) was clearly perceived by the Egyptian public, including those using the new law (Al-Sharmani, 2013).

The Egyptian National Council for Women described the 2000 provision (Egypt Law No. 1/2000, art. 20) to the CEDAW Committee as giving 'women the equal right of divorce through "*khul*", or repudiation, which is the indigenous Islamic formulation of women's right to divorce for incompatibility without need to prove damage' (Egypt Response to CEDAW Committee List of Issues and Questions, 2000, p. 4). The Committee (along with some women's rights activists) appeared unimpressed with the equality arguments. In its 2010 comments to Egypt, the Committee reiterated 'its concern that women who seek divorce by unilateral termination of their marriage contract (*khula*) under Law No. 1 of 2000 can only obtain such a divorce if they forgo alimony and return their dowry' and called on Egypt to consider revising the law 'in order to eliminate the above-mentioned financial discrimination against women' (CEDAW Committee, 2010a, paras 49, 50).

The provision on judicial *khul'* in the new Personal Status Law in Jordan (Law No. 36 of 2010) has similarly been contentious. In 2001, in the absence of parliament, an article on *khul'* had been added to the 1976 law. When parliament reconvened, the elected lower house twice rejected the amendment before it eventually passed. In 2010, the new law drafted by the Chief Islamic Justice Department, and approved by the cabinet as a temporary law in the absence of a sitting parliament, removed the references to *khul'*, instead using the pre-existing phrase that the wife 'ransoms herself by waiving all her matrimonial rights and returns the dower she has received'.[16] The remainder of the

---

[16] This phrase (*iftadat nafsaha*) uses the same language as that in Qur'an 2:229, which is cited in the draft explanatory memorandum to the Egyptian law of 2000 as a source for the provision on *khul'*. In English translations it is variously translated as 'if she gives something for her freedom' or 'if she ransoms herself' (see translations by A. Yusuf Ali and Marmaduke Pickthall).

conditions of the provision remain the same. The effect, arguably, is to invoke the Qur'anic phrasing in support of the new provision (which appears to allow for the same result as before) to the exclusion of a phrasing that added the active initiative of the wife in 'divorcing her husband'. The chief Islamic justice in Jordan was quoted as noting that the word *khul*' had been removed 'in order to protect the children of women who invoke the law from the social stigma attached to it':

> We felt that it would be hard for the daughter of a mother who divorced herself from her father via the khul law to be called the daughter of such a parent. It is socially damaging to the daughter. (Husseini, 2010)

By contrast, Jordanian activists who were involved in debates around the amended text observe that, socially, the 'shame' of a *khul*' divorce attaches to the divorced husband.

GUARDIANSHIP

The institution of guardianship (*wilayah*) may impact on women differently from men in at least two distinct aspects of their lives: in the extent of their ability to exercise financial and other authority with respect to their minor children and in their choice of spouse (or choice to marry at all).

Authority with respect to minor children turns on the distinctions between the functions of custodian (usually identified with the mother or other female relative) and the guardian (usually attributed to the father or other male guardian).[17] Some modified laws in the Arab region have transferred significant institutional prerogatives of guardianship to the mother in the event of incapacity on the part of the father; Algeria's new provision unusually allows the court, in the event of divorce, to transfer overall guardianship to the parent to whom custody has been granted. Otherwise, and in general, the guardian remains the father or other male relatives (unless the mother is appointed as legal tutor or *wasi*). Under a number of laws, if the father as guardian is unable

---

In the 2001 amendment to Jordanian law, this phrase was followed by 'and divorces [*khala'at*] her husband', *khala'at* being the verb form of *khul*'.

[17] Unless the mother be appointed guardian by her husband on the latter's death. Meriwether (1996) found that in records from late eighteenth- and early nineteenth-century Aleppo 'women were appointed as *wasi* more often than men' (p. 228).

to provide financially for his children, for example after divorce, the mother (rather than the extended agnatic family) is required to if she is able, although this does not necessarily mean that she acquires the role, authority or rights of guardianship. Furthermore, a number of Arab state laws have inserted the father after the mother but before the maternal grandmother and other female relatives in the presumptive order of custodians.[18] Under such rules, fathers stand to acquire custody rights in circumstances beyond those contemplated in the traditional rules, while maintaining the primary guardianship authority. Mothers, on the other hand, acquire particular functions of guardianship only in exceptional cases (Abu-Odeh, 2004). Such distinctions – despite the invocations of the best interest of the child in statutory instruments – would appear to contradict article 16(1)(d) of CEDAW, which provides for 'the same rights and responsibilities, as parents, irrespective of their marital status, in matters relating to their children; in all cases the interests of the children shall be paramount'.

After the end of the period of custody, the assumption in law is that the ward will transfer to the father's household if the parents are divorced or living separately. Current laws in the Arab region have generally extended the period of a Muslim mother's custody, subject to certain conditions, notably her not marrying a non-*mahram*. Most laws also set tighter limits for non-Muslim mothers. In the Explanatory Memorandum to its 2005 law, the UAE explained its identification of comparatively early ages at which the children or wards are to be transferred to their father's custody:

> Legislators have to look at what best responds to the interests of proper social upbringing and education of the child. Thus the law holds in this regard that the age for males shall be reaching 11 years, and the female 13. After this stage, the boy goes to his father to learn the bases of masculinity and men's counsel. The girl goes to her father in view of the circumstances of society that make it difficult for women to control girls. (UAE Explanatory Memorandum, 2005, commentary on art. 156)

In terms of marriage guardianship, statutory laws in Arab states now formally exclude a guardian's 'coercive' authority (*wilayah al-ijbar*) over his female ward in the matter of her marriage; elsewhere, the Musawah CEDAW report cites

---

[18] Tunisian law has no explicit statutory presumption of a mother's precedence as custodian; but when a man gets custody there must be with him in some capacity a woman to undertake the tasks involved (arts 67 and 58).

only Nigeria as retaining the power of compulsion over minor wards for the biological father in the majority-Maliki communities (Musawah, 2011, p. 33). However, many Arab states continue to require the consent (or allow the objection) of the family guardian to a woman's marriage either in general or in particular circumstances that do not apply to males. A judge can act as proxy guardian for a woman who is without a guardian, or if he finds the guardian's refusal to consent to a particular marriage is unreasonable.

The majority-Hanafi view holds that a woman of legal majority, whatever her personal status (*bikr* [virgin] or *thayyib* [previously married] in this case), can contract her own marriage without need of the prior consent of her guardian. The new Jordan Personal Status Law reproduces the text from previous laws regarding the need for the guardian's consent: 'The agreement of the *wali* is not a requirement in the marriage of a *thayyib* woman of sound mind who is above eighteen years of age' (Jordan Personal Status Law, 2010, art. 19). The new law also maintains reference to the dominant opinions of the Hanafi school as its immediate residual reference – that is, in the event of a matter not being explicitly covered in the text of the law (Jordan Personal Status Law, 2010, art. 325). Nevertheless, the law deliberately states that for a woman of full legal majority – in terms both of her age and of her mental capacity – to unequivocally *not* need her guardian's consent to her marriage, she must also have been previously married (*thayyib*). At the same time, the law does not state that a woman fulfilling all those qualities except for having previously been married needs her guardian's consent to her marriage. This is possibly another example of constructive ambiguity in the text, with this last position strongly implied in what the law *doesn't* say.

On the other hand, in some states (e.g. Kuwait, Oman, UAE, Yemen, Qatar) the laws continue to require that a woman's guardian conclude the contract on her behalf, rather than the woman doing it herself. Where this is the case, the woman's marriage is dependent upon the consent of the guardian. The process of procuring the woman's consent and her absence from the marital contract session can be and have been abused by guardians. The UAE law of 2005 maintains the requirement for the woman's guardian to conclude her contract; the 'two contracting parties' to the marriage contract are 'the husband and the *wali*' (art. 28). However, the Explanatory Memorandum stresses that the wife's consent is necessary:

The fact that the law requires the *wali*'s permission and that he carry out the contract does not mean a lack of consideration for the consent of the girl [bint]; rather the agreement of the wali and the consent of the wife and her agreement are (both) necessary, taking into consideration the consent of the bikr who has passed puberty and the thayyib all the more so – and no-one may force her into marriage, and thus it is with regard to the mature [baligha] young woman, as the law stipulates her consent and acceptance… As for the sign of consent and agreement, this is open declaration [ifsah] and announcement of consent by words or silence, and in all cases the ma'dhun must have the wife sign the contract. (UAE Explanatory Memorandum, 2005, p. 162)

The Explanatory Memorandum justifies this position on the majority *fiqh* view and in light of the 'potential hazards' of a woman contracting her own marriage. This last reference invokes the common wisdom of the protective intention behind the institution of guardianship, which may go beyond the legal constraints of *kafa'a* (determining the 'suitability' of the groom) through which statutory laws seek to regulate the authority of a guardian in controlling choice, having already forbidden him from forcing consent.

In Morocco, a guardian was previously required to represent his female ward (with her consent) (Moroccan Law of Personal Status, 1957, art. 12(2)).[19] Article 24 of the 2004 law now allows any woman of legal majority to conclude her own contract of marriage. The statutory requirements for the documentation of the contract include a record that the *ijab* and *qubul* – the formal exchanges that constitute the contract – are uttered by the two contracting parties 'enjoying capacity, discrimination/reason (*tamyiz*) and choice' (Moroccan Law of the Family, 2004, art. 67). The Ministry of Justice's guide to the new law emphasizes that 'one of the most important things that women have gained from the new law is that guardianship is her right…like the man, she exercises it according to her choice and her interests without being subjected to any supervision or consent' (Moroccan Ministry of Justice, 2004a, p. 31). The woman is entitled to conclude her own contract, continues the guide, or to delegate this function; delegation requires the physical presence of the woman[20] and the person she is delegating the function to when the contract is made and signed. In explaining the law's continuing provision for a woman to delegate this function, the guide invokes some of the same societal

---

[19] After amendments in 1993, article 12(4) allowed a woman to conclude her own contract if her father was dead.

[20] Except under certain specified conditions in which a judge has authorized delegation to a proxy (Moroccan Law of the Family, 2004, art. 17).

and familial expectations that make the removal of guardianship over an adult woman contentious in other places: 'out of consideration for what is customarily done, and in preservation of traditions that are known in the cohesion of the family' (2004a, p. 31).

In her commentary on the law, El Mekkaoui (2010) celebrates what she considers the 'resuscitation of a principle intrinsic to Islamic law…that the will of a woman is to be respected like that of a man' (p. 93). In 2005, one year after the new law came into force, the Moroccan Ministry of Justice announced statistics showing that 14.5 percent of adult women had represented themselves in their contract of marriage since the new law was passed. The minister commented that this 'demonstrates that the Moroccan woman, despite the right given her [to conclude her own contract] continues to adhere to the appropriate traditions that govern the Moroccan family; and that is also her right' (Moroccan Minister of Justice, 2005).

In Palestine, Rema Hammami (2004) reflected that the outcome of a 1995 survey that had found 'a high level of support for women's right to choose their spouse' might have been affected by how the question had been put, and that '[t]he right to choose may simply mean for many people the right of women to refuse someone imposed on them by their parents'. In support of this, she cites a 1992 survey that found that 'less than 10 percent of men and women thought that choice of spouse should be the daughter's choice alone, while the majority asserted that a decision should be made collectively with the young woman's parents'. Also relevant is the finding in a 1999 survey that forty-three percent of women and twenty-eight percent of men said 'they did not choose their spouse by themselves' (Hammami, 2004, p. 137).

In its own survey in 2000, the Birzeit Institute of Women's Studies set itself to try to 'invoke directly the contradiction between the minimum legal marriage age and the decision-making power in the marriage process'. The survey aimed to determine whether respondents felt individuals might be mature enough to get married at certain minimum ages, but not mature enough to choose whom to marry. Respondents believed that parents should continue to be involved in choosing marriage partners for their children, as neither men under eighteen nor women under seventeen 'are considered…capable of making their own decisions regarding a marriage partner' (Hammami, 2004, p. 138).[21]

---

[21] Both sexes overwhelmingly supported a minimum age of marriage of eighteen for males and females.

The issue of specific ages is significant here, but the general problem is whether a state's laws can and should accommodate or somehow make space for the family in the marriage choices of their female members – especially young ones – without reproducing the gendered authority of *wilayah*. Looking towards a future codification in Palestine, Asma Khadr proposed a text offering a limited space for the views of parents: essentially, that 'either or both parents may object to a contract of marriage' and should the judge agree with the objection the would-be spouses could 'insist on concluding' their marriage after two years had passed (Khadr, 1998, pp. 134–5). In the United Kingdom, the model Muslim contract document acknowledges the concern of parents and guardians while removing any space for their views in the actual contract. The Explanatory Note states,

> Parents are responsible for the upbringing of their children. Out of respect and courtesy, it is important that young people involve their parents or guardians throughout the process of marriage. However, parental or guardian's legal role finishes when children reach adulthood. Thereafter their role is optional and complementary. Hence the Muslim Marriage Certificate does not require the approval of the parents. (Muslim Institute, 2008, Explanatory Note, para. 7)

A final point to note here is the link between the *qiwamah* of the husband and *wilayah* of the father. Anna Würth (2005) has ably illustrated this link in an examination of a successful civil society campaign against the proposed introduction of forcible implementation of 'obedience' rulings in Yemen in 2000. The proposed amendment would have affected the ability of paternal relatives to protect the wife against forcible return to her husband. The campaign mobilized elite urban men concerned about the potential effect on their female relatives and themselves; according to Würth, the logic was that 'if a women cannot rely on her family to resolve marital disputes, but can be forced by the police to return to her husband despite her wish, then patriarchal control over women, particularly choosing a spouse for her, is intolerable' (2005, p. 301). In its 2006 report to CEDAW, after addressing the issue of forced marriage, Jordan observed that '[r]ecent research has shown that the power of the husband or the family over a woman is an unsatisfactory aspect for women in their family lives. Indeed, twenty-four percent of the women interviewed identified that as the main unsatisfactory aspect of their family lives' (Jordan Combined Third and Fourth Reports to the CEDAW Committee, 2006, para. 247).

The CEDAW Committee has raised the issue of guardianship with 'less frequency' than other specific issues such as polygamy (Musawah, 2011, p. 8). The Musawah CEDAW report considers it in light of 'the right to decide if, when, and whom to marry', although guardianship is also implicated in the matter of child marriage, which has received more explicit attention from the CEDAW Committee.

HEAD OF THE FAMILY

In some ways, the conceptualization of the husband/father as the legal 'head of the family' can be understood as the overall effect of the distinct rules aris-ing in different areas from the concepts of *qiwamah* and *wilayah* – although it was also a concept held in common with non-Muslim societies and states. In some instances this specific terminology ('head of the family'/*chef de famille*) has been incorporated into Arab family laws. Notably in Tunisia, despite the major amendments in 1993, article 23 of the law still provides that the husband is to 'maintain the wife and children in his capacity as head of the family' (al-Sharif, 1997, p. 47). Women's rights activists have been critical of this identification, which may be 'faithful to Muslim tradition' but was also 'common to all Western legislation before the sixties' (Dargouth-Medimegh, 1992, p. 54). The CEDAW Committee's 1994 criticism of laws giving the husband this status has already been noted.

In the family laws of Arab states, the matter of overall 'authority' may also be dealt with in the articles providing a definition of marriage, as we can see in the following comparison of these definitions in the laws of Morocco and the UAE:

Morocco:
Marriage is a *shar'i* agreement/contract [*mithaq*] of mutual consent and attachment between a man and a woman on the basis of permanence, its purpose chastity and modesty and the founding of a stable family under the charge/in the care of [*ri'aya*] the two spouses in accordance with the provisions of this code. (Moroccan Law of the Family, 2004, art. 4)

UAE:
Marriage is a contract that renders lawful each spouse's sexual enjoy-ment of the other, its purpose chastity and the founding of a stable

family under the charge/in the care of [ri'aya] the husband, on bases that secure for the two of them the bearing of the family's burdens in love and compassion. (UAE Law of Personal Status, 2005, art. 66)

In regard to head of the family (or *qiwamah* generally), the most pertinent point here is the assignment in Morocco of the care or charge of the family to both spouses, rather than, as in the UAE, to the husband. The UAE definition is closer to earlier *fiqh* conceptions in relating the contract's immediate effect to the lawfulness of sexual relations between the couple. In both laws the significance of 'chastity' is the marital fidelity of each spouse to the other – this is not affected, in the case of the man, by his relations with another wife under the rules on polygamy still applicable in both countries, albeit severely restricted under the new law in Morocco. It is interesting that the final phrase of the UAE text invokes the Qur'anic injunctions of 'love and compassion' (*mawaddah wa rahmah*), articulated as expectations for the conduct of the marriage on the part of both spouses. Lila Abu-Lughod has traced these phrases in Islamist discourse (specifically the women's page of the newspaper published by al-Azhar in 1990s Cairo) as invoking 'marriage as properly based on the emotions of amity (*mawaddah*) (described as a higher emotional state than love) and mercy (*rahmah*)' (1998, p. 253). The same phrase is used in the Moroccan law in its articulation of mutual rights of the spouses (Moroccan Law of the Family, 2004, art. 51), as indeed it is in the 2010 Jordanian law (Jordan Personal Status Law, 2010, art. 78).

In its 2006 report to the CEDAW Committee, Jordan addressed the issue of 'head of the family' as defined after an amendment to the civil status law; the phrase is not used in the family law. In article 55(a) of the 2001 Jordanian Civil Status Law, the 'head of the family' is the father, or 'in the event of his death or his loss or renunciation of Jordanian nationality' the wife, who in practice routinely takes this role in these circumstances (Jordan Combined Third and Fourth Reports to the CEDAW Committee, 2006, para. 63).[22] The 2006 report further commented,

According to the Act, in the event of the death of the head of the family and his wife, the eldest unmarried child (whether male or female) is deemed to be the head of the family. The available evidence, however, suggests that in practice, it is the male family members exclusively who

---

[22] I am grateful to Reem Abu Hassan for the information on standard practice.

claim the status of head of the family, even though they may be younger than their female siblings. (2006, para. 62)

This comment is interesting both for its recognition of the challenges of practice and expectations, and for *not* discussing the fact that the standard position in law is that the father is the head of the family.

CONCLUDING COMMENTS

In most of the statutory instruments considered here, the concept of *qiwamah* relates to men's financial obligations towards women (taken as normative/prescriptive rather than descriptive), including the wife's duty of obedience and the husband's of maintenance. It also involves the structure of divorce law that gives husbands the right to dissolve the marriage contract unilaterally while requiring wives – in the absence of an agreement negotiated with their husbands – to establish grounds for judicial divorce as recognized variously by the different schools of law. The institution of *wilayah* places financial obligations on the male guardian towards his wards. The link between *qiwamah* and *wilayah* in family laws remains, with many statutory instruments requiring the male guardian's consent to a marriage and giving the father primary institutional authority over his children.

In some cases, statutory modifications have been made to earlier *fiqh* positions related to wives and mothers, some codes requiring financial contributions from them in certain circumstances. Most of these laws, however, do not equitably recognize the contribution of women to the building and maintenance of the family. It is important to note that the changes in laws have not affected the distribution of estates in the laws of succession, which remain gendered in critical aspects. Gendered succession entitlements are defended against charges of discrimination at the CEDAW Committee reviews by reference to the greater financial obligations placed on men, though, as the Musawah CEDAW report (2011, p. 38) points out, this is a circular argument.

In the 2004 law of Morocco, the husband's authority of *qiwamah* has been removed and government officials have been working to explain that the ideal-type marriage is one based on consultation and consensus. Some effort has been made to address the issue of matrimonial property, or the recognition of women's participation in building the family's wealth after marriage.

In many other Arab laws the duty of obedience remains, with the postulate of *qiwamah* articulated on a spectrum stretching from a modified version to the more traditional presentation of *fiqh* positions in the UAE code. As discussed above, many women would like the husband's financial obligations to remain. Drafters may also prefer to maintain the husband's legal financial responsibilities while finding ways to recognize women's actual contribution without implicating gendered succession entitlements. Arguably, the issue of succession entitlements must be raised if men no longer legally bear the financial obligations that are used to justify their greater share of family wealth.

The different positions of the Moroccan and UAE laws considered here reveal a spectrum of approaches to *qiwamah* and *wilayah*. The contexts of promulgation of these laws are also quite distinct. Among other differences, Morocco has a long-established and active non-governmental women's movement that has invested decades of energy into family law reform. The consultative committee appointed by the King to draft the text included women, and different women's groups submitted comments and memoranda on particular provisions of the draft. Morocco ratified the International Covenants on Civil and Political Rights and on Economic, Social and Cultural Rights in 1979 and became a party to CEDAW in 1993, establishing an ongoing structured dialogue with peers in the international human rights system and opening important fora to Moroccan women's organizations.

The UAE law, on the other hand, was drawn up by an all male committee. Although other parties were consulted on the content, the Explanatory Memorandum gives no indication as to who these parties were. The UAE is still not a party to the international covenants and ratified CEDAW only in 2004. The CEDAW Committee, in its consideration of the UAE's initial report in 2010, specifically recorded that it was 'concerned about the absence of a robust civil society, including autonomous and active women's and human rights organizations, and notes the difficulties that exist for the registration of these associations' (CEDAW Committee, 2010b, para. 30).[23] This clearly impacts on the debate with the state and the penetration of CEDAW norms during these first few years of the UAE's engagement with the CEDAW Committee.

There are other economic, political and sociocultural factors that contribute to the different paths that have been taken by Morocco and the UAE towards

---

[23] On the nature of Emirati women's associations and repression by the UAE of 'independent social movements', see Hasso (2011, pp. 17–18). Hasso insists, however, that 'this should not imply that resistance to ruling elites has been or is non-existent' (p. 17).

the *qiwamah* and *wilayah* postulates. But even with the snapshot we have here, it is clear that state law and state policy in Morocco are moving towards international human rights norms and the aspirations of Morocco's women's movements, and this is clearly impacting on the legal postulates of *qiwamah* and *wilayah*. This is not yet the case in the UAE. Further research might explore to what extent lived realities are supporting these shifts in conception or contesting them; and indeed how the legal postulates of *qiwamah* and *wilayah* are understood and acted on – or not – in different sectors of the Moroccan and UAE populations today.

REFERENCES

Abu-Lughod, Lila. 1998. 'Feminism and Islamism in Egypt: Selective Repudiation as a Dynamic of Postcolonial Cultural Politics'. In *Remaking Women: Feminism and Modernity in the Middle East*, edited by Lila Abu-Lughod, pp. 243–69. Princeton, NJ: Princeton University Press.

Abu-Odeh, Lama. 2004. 'Egyptian Feminism: Trapped in the Identity Debate'. In *Islamic Law and the Challenges of Modernity*, edited by Yvonne Haddad and Barbara Stowasser, pp.183–211. Walnut Creek, CA: Altamira Press.

Abu-Odeh, Lama. 2005. 'Modern Family Law, 1800 – Present. Arab States'. In *Encyclopaedia of Women in Islamic Cultures*, vol. 2, edited by Joseph Su'ad, pp. 459–62. The Hague: Brill.

Abu Zahra, Muhammad. 1955. 'Family Law'. In *Law in the Middle East: Origin and Development of Islamic Law*, edited by Majid Khadduri and Herbert J. Liebesny, pp. 132–78. Washington: Middle East Institute.

Ali, Abdullah Yusuf. 1989. *The Meaning of the Holy Qur'an*. Beltsville, MD: Amana.

Ali, Kecia. 2003. 'Progressive Muslims and Islamic Jurisprudence: The Necessity for Critical Engagement with Marriage and Divorce Law'. In *Progressive Muslims on Justice, Gender and Pluralism*, edited by Omid Safi, pp. 163–89. Oxford: Oneworld.

Al-Sharif, Muhammad al-Habib. 1997. *Majallat al-Ahwal al-Shakhsiyya: Jam' wa Ta'liq*. Soussa, Libya: Dar al-Mizan li'l-Nashr.

Al-Sharmani, Mulki. 2013. '*Qiwamah* in Egyptian Family Laws: "Wifely Obedience" between Legal Texts, Courtroom Practices and Realities of Marriages'. In *Gender and Equality in Muslim Family Law: Justice and Ethics in the Islamic Legal Tradition*, edited by Ziba Mir-Hosseini, Kari Vogt, Lena Larsen and Christian Moe, pp. 37–56. London: I.B. Taurus.

Anderson, J.N.D. 1958. 'The Tunisian Law of Personal Status'. *International and Comparative Law Quarterly* 7 (2): pp. 263–79.

An-Na'im, Abdullahi (ed.). 2002. *Islamic Family Law in a Changing World: A Global Resource Book*. London: Zed Books.

Arabi, Oussama. 2001. 'The Dawning of the Third Millennium on Shari'a: Egypt's Law No. 1 of 2000, or Women May Divorce at Will'. *Arab Law Quarterly* 16 (1): pp. 2–21.

Bayoumi, Abd al-Mo'ati. 2009. *Min Qadaya al-Mar'a* (Women's Issues). Cairo: Center for Egyptian Women's Legal Assistance.

Carroll, Lucy and Harsh Kapoor (eds). 1996. *Talaq-i-Tafwid: Muslim Women's Contractual Access to Divorce*. Grabels, France: WLUML.

CEDAW Committee. 2010a. 'Concluding Observations of the Committee on the Elimination of Discrimination against Women. Egypt'. UN Doc. CEDAW/C/Egy/CO/7.

CEDAW Committee. 2010b. 'Concluding Observations of the Committee on the Elimination of Discrimination against Women. United Arab Emirates'. UN Doc. CEDAW/C/ARE/CO/1.

Chiba, Masaji. 1986. 'Introduction'. In *Asian Indigenous Law in Interaction with Received Law*, edited by Masaji Chiba, pp. 1–9. London: Kegan Paul International.

Cuno, Kenneth. 2009. 'Disobedient Wives and Neglectful Husbands. Marital Relations and the First Phase of Family Law Reform in Egypt'. In *Family, Gender, and Law in a Globalizing Middle East and South Asia*, edited by Kenneth Cuno and Manisha Desai, pp. 3–18. Syracuse, NY: Syracuse University Press.

Dargouth-Medimegh, Aziza. 1992. *Droits et vécu de la femme en tunisie*. Lyons: L'Hermès-Edilis.

Dennerlein, Bettina. 1999. 'Changing Conceptions of Marriage in Algerian Personal Status Law'. In *Perspectives on Islamic Law, Justice and Society*, edited by Ravindra Khare, pp. 123–41. Lanham, MD: Rowman & Littlefield.

Egypt Law No. 1/2000 Regulating Certain Litigation Procedures in Personal Status. 2000.

Egypt Response to CEDAW Committee List of Issues and Questions. 2000. UN Doc. CEDAW/PSWG/2001/I/CRP.2/Add.3. 23 October.

El Mekkaoui, Rajaa Naji. 2010. *La Moudawanah. Le Référentiel et le Conventionnel en Harmonie*, vol. 1, 4th edn. Rabat: Editions & Impressions Bouregreg.

Elsaidi, Murad H. 2011. 'A Legal Analysis Challenging the Husband's Authority to Punish "Rebellious" Wives'. *Muslim World Journal of Human Rights* 7 (2): pp. 1–25.

Fawzy, Essam. 2004. 'Muslim Personal Status Law in Egypt: The Current Situation and Possibilities of Reform through Internal Initiatives'. In *Women's Rights and Islamic Family Law: Perspectives on Reform*, edited by Lynn Welchman, pp. 17–94. London: Zed Books.

Hammami, Rema. 2004. 'Attitudes Towards Legal Reform of Personal Status Law in Palestine'. In *Women's Rights and Islamic Family Law: Perspectives on Reform*, edited by Lynn Welchman, pp. 125–43. London: Zed Books.

Hasso, Frances. 2011. *Consuming Desires: Family Crisis and the State in the Middle East*. Stanford, CA: Stanford University Press.

HRW. 2010. 'UAE: Spousal Abuse Never a "Right"'. 19 October. http://www.hrw.org/news/2010/10/19/uae-spousal-abuse-never-right

Husseini, Rana. 2010. 'New Personal Status Law Strengthens Jordanian Families – Hilayel'. *Jordan Times*, 28 September.

Ikhraisi, Su'ad. 2005. *Min Mudawwanat al-Ahwal al-Shakhsiyya 'ila Mudawwanat al-Usra* (From the Code of Personal Status to the Code of the Family). Rabat: Dar al-Salam li'l-Taba'a wa'l-Nashr wa'l-Tawzi'.

Jordan Combined Third and Fourth Reports to the CEDAW Committee. 2006. UN Doc. CEDAW/C/JOR/3-4. 10 March.

Jordan Civil Status Law. 2001. Law No. 9 of 2001.

Jordan Personal Status Law. 2010. Law No. 36 of 2010.

Kandiyoti, Deniz. 1988. 'Bargaining with Patriarchy'. *Gender and Society* 2 (3): pp. 274–90.

Khadr, Asma. 1998. *Al-Qanun wa Mustaqbil al-Mar'a al-Filastiniya*. Jerusalem: Women's Centre for Legal Aid and Counselling.

Mayer, Ann Elizabeth. 1995. 'Reform of Personal Status Laws in North Africa: A Problem of Islamic or Mediterranean Laws?' *Middle East Journal* 49 (3): pp. 432–46.

Menski, Werner F. 2006. *Comparative Law in a Global Context: The Legal Systems of Asia and Africa*. Cambridge, UK: Cambridge University Press.

Menski, Werner F. 2012. 'Plural Worlds of Law and the Search for Living Law'. In *Rechtsanalyse als Kulturforschung*, edited by Werner Gephart, pp. 71–88. Frankfurt: Vittoria Klostermann.

Meriwether, Margaret M. 1996. 'The Rights of Children and the Responsibilities of Women. Women as *Wasis* in Aleppo, 1770–1840'. In *Women, the Family and Divorce Laws in Islamic History*, edited by Amira Sonbol, pp. 219–35. Syracuse, NY: Syracuse University Press.

Mir-Hosseini, Ziba. 1993. *Marriage on Trial: A Study of Islamic Family Law*. London: I.B. Tauris.

Mir-Hosseini, Ziba. 2009. 'Towards Gender Equality: Muslim Family Laws and the *Shari'ah*'. In *Wanted: Equality and Justice in the Muslim Family*, edited by Zainah Anwar, pp. 23–63. Petaling Jaya: Musawah.

Moors, Annelies. 1995. *Women, Property and Islam. Palestinian Experiences 1920–1990*. Cambridge, UK: Cambridge University Press.

Moors, Annelies. 2003. 'Public Debates on Family Law Reform'. *Islamic Law and Society* 10 (1): pp. 1–11.

Moroccan Law of Personal Status. 1957. Ordinance No. 1-57-343. 22 November.

Moroccan Law of the Family. 2004. Law No. 70-03. Ordinance No. 1-04-22. 3 February.

Moroccan Minister of Justice. 2005. 'Opening Speech on the Passing of One Year on the Promulgation of the *Mudawwana*'. Supreme Judicial Council. 14 February. http://www.justice.gov.ma/ar/documentation/documentation.aspx?ty=0, accessed 7 November 2011.

Moroccan Ministry of Justice. 2004a. *Dalil 'Amali li-Mudawwanat al-Usra* (Practical Guide to the Law of the Family). Rabat: Jama'iyat Nashr al-Ma'luma al-Qanuniyya wa'l-Qada'iyya.

Moroccan Ministry of Justice. 2004b. *Muqtadayyat al-Jadida li-Mudawwanat al-Usra* (New Requirements of the Law of the Family). Rabat: Jama'iyat Nashr al-Ma'luma al-Qanuniyya wa'l-Qada'iyya.

Musawah. 2011. *CEDAW and Muslim Family Laws: In Search of Common Ground*. Petaling Jaya: Musawah. http://www.musawah.org/sites/default/files/CEDAW&Muslim_Family_Laws_0.pdf

Muslim Institute. 2008. 'Muslim Marriage Contract'. http://www.muslimparliament.org.uk/Documentation/Muslim%20Marriage%20Contract.pdf

Pickthall, Mohammed Marmaduke. 1938. *The Meaning of the Glorious Koran*. Hyderabad Deccan: Government Central Press.

Shaham, Ron. 1999. 'State, Feminists and Islamists: The Debate over Stipulations in Marriage Contracts in Egypt'. *Bulletin of the School of Oriental and African Studies* 63 (3): pp. 462–83.

Shehada, Nahda. 2004. 'Women's Experience in the Shari'a Court of Gaza City. The Multiple Meanings of Maintenance'. *Review of Women's Studies* 2: pp. 57–71.

Singerman, Diane. 2005. 'Rewriting Divorce in Egypt: Reclaiming Islam, Legal Activism and Coalition Politics'. In *Remaking Muslim Politics. Pluralism, Contestation, Democratization*, edited by Robert Hefner, pp. 161–88. Princeton, NJ: Princeton University Press.

Sonbol, Amira. 1998. 'Ta'a and Modern Legal Reform: A Rereading'. *Islam and Christian–Muslim Relations* 9 (3): pp. 285–94.

Sonbol, Amira. 2003. 'Women in Shari'a Courts: A Historical and Methodological Discussion'. *Fordham International Law Journal* 27 (1): pp. 225–53.

Sonneveld, Nadia. 2006. 'If Only There was Khul'...' *ISIM Review* 17: pp. 51–2.

Tucker, Judith. 2008. *Women, Family, and Gender in Islamic Law.* Cambridge, UK: Cambridge University Press.

Tunisian Law of Personal Status. 1956. Promulgated by Decree No. 229 of 13 August 1956, as amended by Law No. 74/1993.

UAE Explanatory Memorandum on the UAE Law of Personal Status. 2005. Official Gazette No. 439, 30 November, pp. 119–478.

UAE Law of Personal Status. 2005. Federal Law No. 28 2005.

Welchman, Lynn. 2000. *Beyond the Code: Muslim Family Law and the Shar'i Judiciary in the Palestinian West Bank.* The Hague: Kluwer.

Welchman, Lynn. 2007. *Women and Muslim Family Laws in Arab States: A Comparative Overview of Textual Development and Advocacy.* Amsterdam: Amsterdam University Press.

Welchman, Lynn. 2010. 'Bahrain, Qatar, UAE: First Time Family Law Codifications in Three Gulf States'. In *International Survey of Family Law,* edited by Bill Atkin, pp. 163–78. Bristol: Jordan.

Welchman, Lynn. 2011. 'A Husband's Authority: Emerging Formulations in Muslim Family Law'. *International Journal of Law, Policy and the Family* 25 (1): pp. 1–23.

WLUML. 2003. *Knowing Our Rights: Women, Family, Laws and Customs in the Muslim World.* London.

Würth, Anna. 2005. 'Mobilizing Islam and Custom against Statutory Reform: *Bayt al-Tā`a* in Yemen'. In *Le Shaykh et le procurer. Systèmes coutumiers et pratiques juridiques au Yémen et en Égypte, Égypte/Monde Arabe No. 1,* edited by Baudouin Dupret and Francois Burgat, pp. 289–308. Cairo: Centre for Economic, Judicial, and Social Study and Documentation.

Wynn, Lisa. 1996. 'Marriage Contracts and Women's Rights in Saudi Arabia'. In *Shifting Boundaries in Marriage and Divorce in Muslim Communities,* edited by Homa Hoodfar, pp. 120–41. Grabels, France: WLUML.

Zulficar, Mona and Hoda Elsadda. 1996. 'Hawl Mashru' Tatwiyr Namudhaj 'Aqd al-Zawaj' (On Modifying the Marriage Contract). *Hagar* 3–4: pp. 251–9.

Islamic Law Meets Human Rights

Reformulating *Qiwamah* and *Wilayah* for Personal Status Law Reform Advocacy in Egypt*

Marwa Sharafeldin

T his chapter explores the complexities involved when non-governmental organization (NGO) activists attempt to advocate new understandings of *qiwamah* and *wilayah* in contemporary Muslim family laws. I investigate what happens when 'Islamic law' encounters human rights norms in NGO advocacy work aiming to reform the Egyptian personal status law (PSL). I show how the encounter between the two frameworks affects NGO reform propositions on issues pertaining to *qiwamah* and *wilayah* in the PSL which are causing problems for ordinary Egyptian women today, such as maintenance, obedience, unilateral divorce by the husband, child custody and shared wealth. I highlight how the very different notions of equality and equity/complementarity found in human rights and Islamic jurisprudence may coexist in NGO reform proposals that attempt to articulate new conceptions of *qiwamah* and *wilayah*. This can create innovations and developments but also compromises and difficulties in NGOs' reform discourses. I discuss the strengths and weaknesses of such an approach.

---

* This chapter is based on my research for a doctoral degree granted by the Centre for Socio-Legal Studies, Law Faculty, Oxford University, in 2013. For extensive analysis of the issues raised in this chapter and for more details on the research findings, see Sharafeldin (2013a; 2013b). Unless otherwise noted, all translations from the original Arabic are my own.

In relation to NGOs' attempts to create new understandings of *qiwamah* and *wilayah*, I also briefly trace what seems to be the changing nature of the criteria of validity and authority that are used today to imbue a certain type of 'Islamic' knowledge with recognition and legitimacy. I argue that notions of human rights seem to be becoming part of such criteria today – albeit with problems.

The encounter between Islamic law and human rights in NGOs' work is affected by many factors, such as the political environment, the socioeconomic context, the organizational channel through which activists exercise their activism (i.e. NGOs), and also the personal beliefs of activists themselves. The NGO activists studied here find inspiration in international human rights documents such as the United Nations Convention on the Elimination of All Forms of Discrimination against Women (CEDAW). At the same time, many are devout Muslims who find similar inspiration in Islam. Others are staunch secularists who, because they operate in a highly religious context, are sometimes willing to engage with religious discourse. Therefore, the personal beliefs of the activists and the perceptions they hold of their context sometimes affect the encounter between human rights and religious law in NGOs' public PSL reform work.

My overall aim is to show that, although the exigencies of contemporary lived realities in Egypt demand the development of new conceptions of *qiwamah* and *wilayah* in contemporary Muslim family laws, the process of articulating these new conceptions through legal reform is subject to numerous factors that may encourage innovation and development, but also compromise and silence.

NOTE ON METHOD

The fieldwork discussed in this chapter was conducted through engagement with fifteen NGOs advocating for PSL reform in Egypt between 2006 and 2010, i.e. before the January 2011 revolution.[1] The fifteen NGOs are considered by most practitioners in the field to be the main organizations in Egypt

---

[1] A second cycle of interviews was conducted with most of the previous activist interviewees after the revolution in mid-2011. Because of the uncertainty of the political situation, it was very difficult for the interviewees to predict what kind of changes to the situation of women and the process of PSL reform would occur as a result of the revolution. I have therefore decided to rely mainly on the fieldwork I conducted before the revolution.

working on PSL reform from a women's rights perspective. Eleven of the fifteen NGOs are members of a network that works on women's rights within the family, which I cofounded in 2005. This network's PSL reform activities and campaigns started in 2007 and span nineteen of Egypt's twenty-seven governorates.

I conducted interviews and participant observation of the fifteen NGOs' PSL reform activities as well as discourse analysis of their written reform proposals. I focus here on the reform proposal documents of the above-mentioned NGO network, since they were the most coherent and finalized documents that I found at the time.

Because this research involves sensitive issues pertaining to religion, including critiquing traditional understandings and offering different inter-pretations of certain religious injunctions, I have withheld the names of the NGOs and activists involved. I have given each interviewee a pseudonym and briefly give relevant information on each person the first time he or she is mentioned in the text.

I explicitly mention whether a female interviewee is veiled or not, for several reasons. First, I hope to show the variety of religious opinions held by women in Egypt who decide to don the veil. Second, I want to contest two assumptions about these women: that veiled women may be grouped under a single conservative or passive label; and that activists working on women's rights are Westernized women who have no relationship with Islam and are working towards the destruction of the Muslim family. Although the veil is not the sole signifier of adherence to the Muslim faith – many of the non-veiled activists I interviewed identify themselves as observant Muslims – it does signify a public statement of a person's relationship with Islam, which in this case, contests some of the accusations made by the activists' opponents.

NOTE ON TERMS

It is important to clarify my usage of certain terms such as *Shari'ah*, *fiqh*, 'Islamic law' and '*fiqh*-based state law'. *Shari'ah* in the Arabic language means the 'path' or the 'way'. The only reference to it in the Qur'an comes in 45:18[2] to signify 'the right way of religion' (Kamali, 2008, p. 2). I use *Shari'ah* to mean

---

[2] Verse 45:18 reads, 'Thus we put you on the right way [*Shari'atan*] of religion. So follow it and follow not the whimsical desire [*hawa*] of those who have no knowledge.'

a total divine, Islamic discourse that includes spiritual, legal, moral, economic and political subdiscourses within it.[3]

However, *Shari'ah* as such requires discovery, deciphering and interpretation by human beings if it is to be lived by. This human effort is *fiqh*. Therefore, *fiqh*, or jurisprudence, is often, though not always, seen as the human understanding of this eternal divine discourse, and it changes with time and place. *Fiqh* is thus not divine, though it is sometimes conflated with 'God's law'.

Historically, 'Islamic law' was the product of the efforts of jurists in their theoretical jurisprudence (*fiqh*) to understand the legal aspects of *Shari'ah*. However, Islamic law as practised in *Shari'ah* courts was sometimes different from the Islamic law produced by jurists in their theoretical books and manuals. This is why we may have two interrelated but different manifestations of 'Islamic law'. After the advent of the nation state, Islamic law (meaning the theoretical product of Islamic legal jurisprudence rather than *Shari'ah* court practice) often became the basis of certain state laws, such as the Egyptian PSL, which also drew upon other non-religious foundations besides Islamic law.

When I refer to 'Islamic law' in this chapter, I mean the legal, theoretical, jurisprudential work of jurists attempting to understand and translate *Shari'ah* into legal rules. Therefore, 'Islamic law' here refers to positive rules of substantive content which were developed largely by pre-modern jurists (i.e. *fiqh*) and later used by the state to develop the contemporary Egyptian PSL. This definition of Islamic law presupposes the necessity of a human, fallible agency and intermediary for the laws' derivation from the Islamic sources – the Qur'an and *Sunnah*.

For the purposes of this chapter when I refer to 'human rights', I am mainly focusing on standards articulated in CEDAW. Taking the lead from most of my interviewees, I also sometimes use the term 'human rights' to mean human rights 'norms', 'law' or 'discourse', which for my informants mainly revolved around the equality of the sexes and non-discrimination as contained in CEDAW.

---

[3] My understanding of the term draws on the following works (noting the differences among the authors): Brown (1997), Mitchell (1988), Messick (1993), Sonbol (2003), Moors (1999), Cuno (2009), Tucker (1998; 2008), An-Na'im (1990), Esposito and DeLong-Bas (2001) and Kamali (2008).

NGO ADVOCACY FOR PERSONAL STATUS LAW REFORM

The Egyptian PSL, an example of *fiqh*-based state law, deals with all family issues in Egypt, including marriage, divorce, maintenance, custody, paternity and guardianship. The term PSL may be misleading, because it is used to describe not one but several laws that govern personal status, in both its substantive and procedural aspects. For instance, substantive laws in effect today include Law No. 25/1920 and Law No. 25/1929, both amended by Law No. 100/1985; the procedural law currently in force is Law No. 1/2000. The PSL is widely agreed to be based on what is perceived to be Islamic law (Law No. 1/2000, art. 3; Fawzy, 2004, pp. 32–3; Zahw, 1999, pp. 5–6; El-Ghazali and Shihata, 2005, p. 7). In many of its articles it reflects the primacy of men over women in marital affairs (Fawzy, 2004, pp. 38–9). Religious conservatives have successfully used its Islamic origins to oppose its reform (Najjar, 1988; Bernard-Maugiron, 2010, pp. 3, 5).

In line with classical *fiqh*, the underlying philosophy of the PSL is that men have *qiwamah* over women and therefore are required to provide financially for their wives and in exchange command their obedience and have authority over them. As such, the relationship between spouses is legislated as one of complementarity, not equality. This 'maintenance for obedience' equation was created through classical jurisprudence and continues today in Egypt as in many other contemporary Arab states' laws.[4] This has resulted in many legal effects such as the ease of divorce for men and its difficulty for women; husbands' obligation to maintain the family; wives' obligation of obedience to their husbands; the possibility of polygamy for men; and fathers' exclusive right of guardianship over their children. Besides causing many problems in practice today, this underlying philosophy of inequality and complementarity between the sexes also contradicts Egypt's obligations under CEDAW, which calls for equality and non-discrimination.

The primary reason that led the studied NGOs to advocate for PSL reform, as reported in my research, is the harmful effects the PSL inflicts on women and families, which the activists witness through their community work. Explaining the significance of these problems in initiating their work, Malak, a senior activist working in a Cairo-based secular feminist NGO, said

---

[4] Some family laws, such as those of Morocco and Tunisia, have been amended and no longer necessitate the wife's obedience, thus breaking this equation.

that 'the PSL contradicts the needs of real life today, so people are developing mechanisms to deal with it…to avoid the gaps in the PSL'. So the NGOs' PSL reform advocacy was not initiated because they held an ideological commitment to gender equality; neither did it come from a theoretically principled position to achieve better adherence to Islamic law or to international human rights conventions. Rather it was formulated to address the real problems they witness on the ground in their day-to-day activism and service provision to their constituents.

The network comprising eleven of the fifteen interviewed NGOs developed a joint reform proposal for the PSL, along with justifications and arguments to support their stance. They initially wrote a position paper to clarify their position on PSL reform among themselves and as an advocacy tool to the public (position paper, 2008; 2009), then developed this into a more detailed document entitled *Guiding Manual for a More Just and Comprehensive Family Law*. The manual, published in Arabic and then translated into and published in English to reach a wider audience, was printed and distributed to be tested with the public in March 2010 (*Guiding Manual*, 2010a), then revised, finalized and republished in July 2010 (*Guiding Manual*, 2010b).

The manual starts by expressing NGOs' concern for national development through the protection of the family by citing several articles in the 1971 Constitution that express this aim. This concern had also been asserted multiple times in the earlier position paper developed by the same group of NGOs. The manual then recognizes that the PSL is derived from the principles of Islamic law and its sources. However, it also indicates the current problems with the PSL that necessitate reform. It then lists the references upon which its demands are made. These, as stated in the manual, are:

+ Current lived realities of the family and society, including the problems and issues that need to be addressed in a speedy and creative way;
+ Enlightened interpretations of Islamic Law (Shari'a) that help address newly emerging issues;
+ International legal treaties and conventions ratified by Egypt which requires that Egypt ensures a decent life for all family members. (*Guiding Manual*, 2010b, p. 10)

The manual describes the developments of the Egyptian PSL across time and then outlines what it calls the 'principles' upon which a 'more just family law' should be built (*Guiding Manual*, 2010b, p. 17). In listing these principles, the manual starts with the 1971 Egyptian Constitution, highlighting the rights of equality among all citizens.

Islamic *Shari'ah* comes second, where an 'enlightened' reading of the verses of the Qur'an should bear in mind the current problems and lived realities of Egyptians. Under this section, a distinction is made between *Shari'ah* as divine and *fiqh* as the human understanding of the divine. The manual also mentions the importance of not limiting oneself to one school (*madhhab*) of Islamic thought, and that one should 'take the most facilitating of provisions within each school' (*Guiding Manual*, 2010b, p. 17). It concludes this point by stressing the importance of Islamic principles, such as that of causing no harm (*la darar wa la dirar*).

The third principle adopted by the NGO reform proposal is that of international human rights treaties, which the manual asserts to be in agreement with Islamic principles and which are recognized by the 1971 Constitution in article 151. The manual reassures the reader that ratification of these treaties in Egypt only takes place after the agreement of the Egyptian religious institutions. The manual says that the state issues a reservation to any clauses these religious institutions deem un-Islamic, meaning the state does not need to implement these provisions. The remainder of the treaties are thus considered to be both religiously and socially legitimate (*Guiding Manual*, 2010b, p. 18).

The list of 'principles' then moves to lived realities in contemporary Egyptian society, prioritizing the public interest. The manual also encourages Egyptian reformers to take into consideration and learn from other international and regional endeavours on family laws. The section on principles ends with the values that the manual aims to advance, including equality and non-discrimination, justice and equity,[5] and shared responsibility between spouses (*Guiding Manual*, 2010b, p. 19). In small text boxes throughout the manual, references are made to court cases, statistics and scientific research explaining the extent of the problems Egyptians face under this law.

The manual then outlines the NGOs' final propositions according to subjects, which include: polygamy, divorce, maintenance, obedience, financial guardianship of children, custody and shared wealth. Below, I shall summarize some of the key propositions outlined in the manual.

---

[5] Equality and equity are two different concepts, as will be elucidated below.

Polygamy

The document proposes that polygamy should only be allowed by the judge if the husband submits an application presenting the 'exceptional' reasons for which he wants to take another wife and supporting documents showing his financial and medical situation. A judge should not allow polygamy if inequality of treatment and injustice between wives is feared, or if the husband does not have sufficient resources to provide for more than one family/household and treat them equally. Also, the judge should ensure that all financial rights of the first wife are fulfilled before granting permission. If the first wife does not agree to this polygamous arrangement and asks for a divorce, she should get it without having to prove harm, in addition to receiving all of her and her children's financial rights (*Guiding Manual*, 2010b, p. 61).

The document quotes articles 40 and 41 of the 2004 Moroccan Family Code, which limit men's right to polygamy using similar conditions, as well as article 18 in the Tunisian Code, which prohibits polygamy altogether (*Guiding Manual*, 2010b, pp. 61–2).

Divorce

In this section, many propositions are put forward to make divorce easier for women. I shall focus only on one divorce-related proposition that had been problematic in earlier discussions because it attempts to limit the man's unilateral power to divorce. The manual states:

+ Divorce is an inherent husband's right, however, when he wishes to proceed with it, he should resort to court for establishing and registering the divorce. To this effect, all established entitlements of the wife and children consequent to the marriage contract and the divorce by a third party shall be ruled for.
+ Applying a penalty for the failure to register the divorce before the judge.
+ Facilitating the procedures of establishing verbal divorce by virtue of witnesses' testimony and endorsing the testimony thereof by hearing the husband. (*Guiding Manual*, 2010b, pp. 52–3)

What is understood from the first part of this proposition is that verbal utterance of the divorce formula by the husband can no longer be used to effect divorce; rather a judge's ruling is what puts the divorce into effect. However, contradictory to this, the rest of this section focuses on the necessity of *registering* the divorce in court after its verbal utterance by the husband. It demands that sanctions be placed on the husband if he does not register the divorce. It also demands that procedures required of the wife to prove the verbal divorce by her husband be significantly reformed. The NGO proposal thus seems to indicate that divorce might still take place unilaterally and verbally by the husband, and the only change would be the necessity to register it in court, which is already a legal requirement.[6]

Maintenance

The NGOs accept that the obligation of maintenance remains the husband's responsibility, not to be shared between the spouses. The manual proposes that a wife be allowed to file a maintenance case at any time without being limited by any lapse of time before filing the case. It also calls for an adjustment in the imprisonment sentence for men who cease to pay the maintenance of the wife and children (*Guiding Manual*, 2010b, p. 38). Other procedural changes are also proposed that lie outside the remit of this chapter.

Obedience

As mentioned above, the manual was printed and tested with the public in March 2010, then revised and finalized in July 2010. The only significant change in the later version was its handling of obedience. In the earlier version the document defined 'obedience' as

---

[6] Article 5 bis of Law No. 25/1929 as amended by Law No. 100/1985 states that the husband has to register the divorce with the notary within thirty days from pronouncing the divorce. A wife is considered notified if she attends the registration. If she does not, the notary is to notify her and to deliver the divorce certificate to her person or to a person representing her according to the procedures issued by the Minister of Justice. In cases where the husband does not register the divorce as stipulated in this article, article 23 bis of Law No. 25/1929 as amended by Law No. 100/1985 states that the husband will be punished by imprisonment for a period not exceeding six months and a fine not exceeding E£200, or by one of these punishments. The same punishments will apply if he provides the notary with incorrect information regarding the husband's marital status, the address of his wife, wives or divorcee.

the wife's obligation to submit to her husband and the rights he has over her based on the marriage contract, which obliges her to stay at home and to leave it only with his permission, to go to his bed when he asks her to if she does not have a legitimate excuse not to, to protect herself from all that might tarnish her and harm her husband whether in his honour or progeny, and to protect his money, this is met by the obligation of the husband to financially maintain his wife. (*Guiding Manual*, 2010a, p. 22)

The manual asserts that this understanding of obedience is problematic because women today are more educated and share the responsibility of providing for the family. It is also problematic because husbands abuse their right to the wife's obedience in court to escape their financial obligations (*Guiding Manual*, 2010a, p. 23).

The March 2010 manual then proposes that any reference to the concept of obedience be totally removed from the reformed law, because of changes in society and family relations which have caused women and men to share responsibility for the family. The document also calls for severing the link between the obedience of the wife and the financial maintenance by the husband. It explains that this link was established by classical jurists, i.e. it is not divinely ordained, and no longer suits the current context in which women shoulder the responsibility of maintaining the household either by working and earning an income, or by undertaking unpaid domestic and care work at home (*Guiding Manual*, 2010a, p. 23).

In the final July 2010 version of the manual, however, the NGOs decided to amend the section on obedience. I was not able to find out precisely why the NGOs changed their stance. Some activists stated that it was because of the heavy criticism this particular proposition received when the March 2010 version of the manual was tested with some of the NGOs' partners. Others said that it was because the entire philosophy of the law was based on maintenance in return for obedience. Removing 'obedience' would have skewed the balance in the remainder of the law regarding other rights and obligations, necessitating a complete overhaul of the law, not mere reforms. Yet others stated that it was because of the negotiation and balance of power between those NGOs wanting to remove 'obedience' altogether and others wanting to rename it. Whatever the reasons, the NGOs rephrased their position on obedience, changing the wording but not the legal effect.

Besides the aforementioned reasons necessitating the reform of this concept in the law, the July 2010 version adds that the social indignity caused by the terms *nashiz*[7] and 'obedience' could be circumvented by using other terms, such as 'mutual obligations', which fulfil the same goal without negative connotations (*Guiding Manual*, 2010b, p. 31). In this new version, the manual adopts a new definition of 'obedience':

> Obedience is a legal obligation since Islamic Shari'a has made marital rights and duties mutual and complementary. While the husband is obliged to provide for the wife within his capabilities, the wife is obliged to obey him. Obedience is manifested in the wife's dwelling in the matrimonial house made for her by the husband, provided that she feels that her person and money are safe there. The law decided that when any of the two parties fails to fulfill their duties in that respect, they shall, accordingly, lose their corresponding right. If the wife failed to dwell in the safe matrimonial house, she would lose her right to the husband's maintenance. Dwelling in the matrimonial house is called obedience (*ta'a*), and failing to do so labels her disobedient (*nashiz*). In the first case, the husband is obliged to provide for the wife, in the second, he is not. It is important to note that before the enactment of Law No. 100 of 1985, the husband could file a lawsuit against the wife who abandons the matrimonial house to force her to return to him, and the decisions would be executed by force. Such a legal stipulation is now repealed for being unjust and in contravention with religion and culture. (*Guiding Manual*, 2010b, p. 30)[8]

Instead of calling for the removal of the principle of obedience from existing laws, as in the earlier version, this new one proposes renaming relevant terms. So the manual suggests 'using the term "mutual commitments" instead of the word "*ta'a*"; and the word "failure to comply" instead of "*nushuz*", while *maintaining the effects rendered by both terms*' (*Guiding Manual*, 2010b, p. 31, emphasis mine). Through this suggestion, the NGOs are not proposing any

---

[7] *Nashiz* means a disobedient wife. However, according to the NGOs' discussions, the term in society holds very negative connotations of loose morals and rebelliousness, which usually results in social ostracization.

[8] This definition accords with article 11 of Law No. 100/1985 and most of the current jurisprudence around it (Ibrahim and Ibrahim, 2003, pp. 254–5).

substantive changes in the legal scope and effect of the obligation of obedience. The only difference the final July 2010 proposal introduces is a new name.

Other procedural changes are also proposed to make it difficult for the husband to abuse his right to his wife's obedience in court, such as fining husbands who do so and requiring that official warnings of obedience filed by the husband be received at one time instead of allowing him to file multiple warnings within short intervals before a decision on previous warnings is made.

Financial guardianship of children

In one bullet point under the NGO propositions for marriage, the manual proposes that a reform to the law be made to 'regulate the spouses' shared guardianship over the person and money (*wilaya 'ala al-nafs wa al-mal*) of the minor during marriage and after divorce' (*Guiding Manual*, 2010b, p. 28).

Custody

The document proposes that a custodial divorced mother's remarriage not deprive her of the right to child custody if that is in the best interest of the child, which is to be decided upon by the judge. This should particularly apply if the child is less than seven years old, has special needs or is ill. In the event that the mother is remarried but retains custody, the mother will not be eligible for a custodial housing fee from her divorced husband (*Guiding Manual*, 2010b, p. 41).

There is also a proposition to make the father the second in the list of family relatives who have the legal right to child custody (*Guiding Manual*, 2010b, p. 41).

The manual quotes the Bahraini family law in its advancing the best interest of the child in judgements on custody cases. It also quotes the Emirati law in putting the father second in the line of custodians for the children (*Guiding Manual*, 2010b, p. 42).[9]

---

[9] In neither of these laws is the mother put second in line for financial guardianship as an equivalent gesture; the father remains the sole guardian of a child's financial affairs.

Shared wealth

Regarding the organization of the wealth or assets acquired or shared by spouses during marriage, the manual proposes that 'the husband and wife should enjoy separate financial capacities'. However, if the spouses do not agree in their marriage contract on the division of joint marital assets, and if the wife is divorced by her husband for no fault on her part, the reformed law should enable her to acquire her rightful shares in the shared marital wealth. No details are given as to how this may be done procedurally, or the percentage of the assets that each spouse will be entitled to. These are left for the lawmakers to decide upon (*Guiding Manual*, 2010b, p. 63). NGOs largely built their proposal on the Moroccan law's article 49, which they also cited in the manual.

TWO DIFFERENT APPROACHES TO REFORM

When these NGOs began advocacy for the reform of the PSL in Egypt in 2007, they based their work on the difficult lived realities of the women they worked with, but without a clear and coherent intellectual framework. Besides using the lived realities of women as their main term of reference, the activists also drew on two discourses to justify their calls for reform: religion and human rights.

The changes proposed in the NGOs' manual represent a series of important developments, compromises and omissions. Analysed as a whole, these propositions reflect two different approaches to reform. The first is based on new, sometimes radical understandings and reforms of the PSL provisions. The second is a more cautious, gradualist and, sometimes, hesitant approach to changing the law. I shall analyse each of these approaches in turn, and then discuss some reasons why there may be tensions between them.

Several of the NGO propositions stand out as innovative: limiting polygamy; calling for the principle of shared responsibility between spouses (even if it is not linked in a meaningful way to the changes proposed on the obedience and maintenance provisions); giving mothers the right to retain child custody after their remarriage; the sharing of financial guardianship of the children by both parents; and regulating the accumulated shared wealth within a marriage.

I consider these to be important for several reasons. Some were being presented publicly by NGOs for the first time in Egypt. With the exception of limiting polygamy, which has been called for by the women's movement since the beginning of the twentieth century, the proposed reforms are novel. Calls for shared wealth, for example, despite being previously addressed in the laws of neighbouring countries such as Tunisia, Algeria and Morocco, were new in discussions of Egypt's PSL. NGOs had to coin the new term *al-tharwah al-mushtarakah* (shared wealth) and define it in their manual.

Moreover, these are changes that contradict dominant juristic provisions that have come to be equated with divine *Shari'ah*. For example, it is juristically settled that it is the man's responsibility to maintain the family financially; this is not a responsibility to be shared by spouses even if the wife is richer than the husband. NGOs accept financial maintenance as an obligation on the husband, but their call for shared responsibility and shared financial guardianship of the children thus becomes contentious, because of its incompatibility with dominant Islamic jurisprudence.

Thirdly, these propositions run against the general sensibilities and perceptions of many Egyptians, who regard women's and men's roles as fixed and complementary (Fawzy, 2004, pp. 25–9), with the husband having superiority and hence guardianship over wife and children. Calls for a remarried mother to keep custody of her children from a previous marriage could be problematic because when she remarries she is considered to come under the guardianship of another man, who is not the father of her children, and hence she may not be able to protect her children adequately should the new husband mistreat them.

All of these proposed reforms can be seen to be built around a different conception of *qiwamah*, which is understood by many of the interviewees to mean the shared responsibility between spouses over the well-being of the family, not the authority of one spouse over the rest of the family. Laila, a junior veiled lawyer working in a women's rights NGO in one of Cairo's slum areas, articulated this new understanding as follows: 'Egypt's reality today helps us to question *qiwamah* [as authority] with all these women-headed households. The Qur'anic verse says *bima 'anfaqu* [by that which they spend]; those spending here today are women.' Other activists regard the idea of maintaining a family as including more than mere financial provision. Zebeida, a veiled lawyer and senior activist located in an Egyptian coastal city, explained this as follows: 'Women now spend anyway…and even if the woman is staying at home, she is still working very hard at home, and even if she has servants, then just by being a wife' – indicating that the wife undertakes the responsibility of caring for her family.

Dina, a lawyer who founded and currently leads an NGO in one of Cairo's poorest areas, added another layer to this new understanding of *qiwamah*. She noted, 'Since women and men today have equal opportunities to pursue knowledge, with women sometimes excelling more, it would be indeed irrational to expect an illiterate man to have *qiwamah* over a female university professor, in the sense of authority.'

In some of the other propositions that the NGOs put forward, however, it is clear that they had to settle for the traditional understanding of *qiwamah* with its underlying notions of inequality, authority and superiority. The proposals that still reflect this understanding include maintaining financial provision of the family as the husband's legal obligation instead of calling for it to be a shared responsibility; renaming 'obedience' while maintaining its legal effects; the vagueness of the proposed changes on unilateral verbal divorce by the husband; refraining from calling for outright prohibition of polygamy; refraining from calling for equal shares of inheritance between women and men; and remaining silent on problems of mixed marriages, especially the inability of Muslim women to marry non-Muslim men.

Perhaps this can be partly explained by the cautious approach that the NGOs sometimes adopt in their advocacy work, which seeks to negotiate and compromise rather than shock. For example, in the final version of the manual, activists were no longer calling for any substantive changes in the principle of obedience in terms of its legal scope or effect – the definition remained the same. They simply proposed changing its name. However, what the NGOs may have wanted to achieve by renaming obedience is a shift in the general societal perception that the obedience of a wife to her husband should be comprehensive and all encompassing. A change in name without a change in legal effect would have a limited impact on the legal reality of spousal relations, since a wife would still be obliged to seek permission from her husband to leave the home. Nonetheless, language has power in the process of social change, so this may be a necessary first step towards an eventual change in the legal obligation.

The fact remains that this cautious approach towards obedience has consequences. It means that, for now, NGOs accept a wife's obligation to some level of obedience. They are not yet trying to break the historic juristic coupling of maintenance by the husband and obedience by the wife, which they previously criticized. This has its drawbacks, because conceding a wife's obligation to stay in the home will seriously limit her ability to work, attend social events, and so on. Furthermore, if wifely obedience remains intact, the proposal for shared responsibility loses much of its significance. This stance also fails to address other problems, cited in the manual, that result from the way obedience is addressed in the PSL.

The same hesitant approach can be seen in NGOs' contradictory handling of the husband's unilateral right of divorce. Whereas initial NGO discussions revolved around taking away that right from the husband and giving it to the judge when either spouse seeks divorce, the final version of the manual was not clear on the issue. It was difficult to understand whether or not the proposition was that verbal divorce should have no legal effect. It mainly focused on the necessity for the husband to register the divorce in court, which is legally required already. It seems that a negotiation process took place among the NGOs, which eventually resulted in this compromise. As with obedience, it appears that disagreement and a fear of societal resistance to this demand won over the will to pose it; hence the contradictory language in the manual.

Despite women's increasing economic contributions to their families,[10] Zebeida, one of the activists, explained, 'Maintenance should not be shared in an obligatory way by women because women in Egypt do not have the same economic power as men; they have lower skills and lower access to work. Nevertheless, there should be equality in having a shared responsibility and shared wealth. Yes, it's contradictory, I know; we still need to think it out.'[11] This particular economic situation makes it difficult for NGOs to demand equality between spouses in the obligation of maintenance. Even if this is a compromise, it also appears to be a nuanced reading of the socioeconomic context of the NGOs and the women they serve.

---

[10] A significant number of Egyptian households are female headed, meaning that a woman is the primary if not sole breadwinner. In the mid-1990s, estimates of female-headed households ranged from sixteen to twenty-two percent of total households (El-Laithy, 2001, p. 17). Practitioners in the field estimate the number to have risen to thirty percent by 2010, but no reliable figures are available.

[11] Welchman (2011, p. 12) discusses the challenge faced by activists seeking to break the maintenance for obedience equation that is reflected in several Arab family laws. Maintenance, she states, is an important need articulated by women through the volume of court cases they file seeking it from their husbands. She also states that 'the tenacity of the legal script on related areas of law (such as inheritance entitlements) means that activists do not necessarily call for the removal in law of the husband's responsibility for maintaining his wife and family'. She cites Abu-Odeh's suggestion (2004, p. 205) that a 'substantive equality' stance here might allow activists to keep the husband's obligation of maintenance while calling for the rescinding of wives' obligation to obey, thereby addressing the situation of women on the ground.

Inheritance and mixed marriage were not even put on the table for discussion among the NGOs. These topics were outside their scope of vision and attention even in the preparatory phase. There are a number of reasons for this silence. First, many activists perceive that the Qur'anic verses on inheritance are clear and definitive, rendering it above human intervention and reform. Second, activists know that calling for reforms in inheritance laws is bound to meet a lot of opposition from society at large. As for mixed marriage, NGOs' silence may arise from its carrying a strong societal taboo, which may be the reason there have rarely been disputes relating to this issue in the NGOs' legal clinics.

As can be seen, there are tensions between the different propositions. Some of the proposed changes are innovative, progressive and gender sensitive. These suggested changes – shared financial guardianship of children, child custody, shared wealth and mutual responsibility of the family – are more compatible with an egalitarian perception of spousal relationships, as is characteristic of the human rights framework. Other suggestions – regarding unilateral divorce, maintenance, obedience and polygamy – are more in accordance with notions of gender inequality, complementarity and equity, as found in the classical juristic paradigm. Some of the proposed changes are consistent neither with one another nor with the overarching guiding principles in the manual, such as equality and non-discrimination, justice, shared responsibility between the spouses, and the Islamic principle of causing no harm.

It is important to note that these NGOs are civil society organizations, meaning that they primarily focus on civil, public, activist and advocacy activities. They are neither thinktanks nor universities, where rigorous knowledge production is the primary vocation. Their activist experience on the ground prodded them to delve into knowledge-related activities, which are not their forte but which they find necessary in order to solve real-life problems created by the current PSL. Thus, it makes sense to regard the knowledge and methodologies these NGOs are producing as organic, constantly changing and evolving and very much related to the realm of practice and experience, and not necessarily theoretically consistent. Understood from this perspective, the contradictions in the advocacy strategies and goals of these NGOs are more easily understood.

But the incongruence in the reform propositions should also be understood in light of other interrelated factors. In the following section, I shall focus on only one, namely, the activists' strategy of combining Islamic law and international human rights law, two distinct discourses rooted in different worldviews.

ISLAMIC LAW AND INTERNATIONAL HUMAN RIGHTS LAW

Many interviewed activists report that the interaction between Islamic law and human rights norms has helped them develop a more egalitarian Islamic discourse to advocate reform of PSL provisions. However, analysis of their final public reform propositions shows that – despite some of the transformative and innovative aspects – this interaction is not a straightforward process with unproblematic results.

In the interaction between Islamic law and international human rights law, as Wilson (1997, pp. 12–13) states, localized laws both resist and appropriate international law. In the process, both Islamic law and human rights are reworked and transformed. Activists become selective with human rights, and their understandings of certain religious rulings relating to women undergo important transformations. Iman, an activist with a senior position in a Cairo-based NGO, explained, 'Because of human rights you start questioning things that were previously considered *thawabit* [constant] such as inheritance, guardianship…actually most issues related to women…Human rights made us look at religion in a different way, to bring out the positive in it.' But Dina, another activist, cautioned, 'Yes, human rights has helped me see things differently, but I will not accept everything in it, like homosexuality.' Ahmed stated even more strongly, 'There are total clashes with *Shariah* such as the issue of legalizing homosexuality, and here I follow *Shariah*.'

But when attempting to 'follow *Shariah*', activists like Ahmed use mixed and selective approaches that aim to negotiate with and address their complex contexts. Sometimes they follow Islamic sacred texts literally, and other times they do not. Sometimes they adopt classical jurisprudential methodologies, but at times they rebel against these methodologies and use contemporary and reformist ones. Sometimes they follow general egalitarian Islamic messages, and other times they ignore them in favour of particular discriminatory rulings. For some activists, the *Shariah* to be followed is what they perceive to be the definitive parts of source texts, such as the Qur'an, whereas for others it is the general purposes behind them. Sometimes the differences between the terms delineated previously – *Shari'ah*, *fiqh*, Islamic law and *fiqh*-based modern codes – are blurred.

For example, Nahla, a veiled lawyer who leads a Cairo-based NGO known for broaching taboo topics related to women, said, 'I have nothing called definitive verses in my dictionary; there are no limits with *Shari'ah*, we can research and interpret everything.' Hayam, a veiled junior activist, resorted to the Qur'an to justify her stance: 'All verses should be open for research and interpretation, even definitive verses. Did the Qur'an say which verses are to be definitive and closed to interpretation or not? No it didn't, so we can apply *ijtihad* on everything.'

Mariam, another veiled activist and university professor, resorted to classical jurists to explain that the Qur'an in its entirety should be subject to research, definitive and non-definitive verses alike: 'Everything will be subject and open for research and study. Classical jurists did this and we need to do this work too whilst respecting the sanctity of the text. Qur'an is the word of God and is to be researched in its entirety, but with respect.'

On the other hand, Laila, who is veiled, stated,

> I differentiate between *fiqh* and *nass* [verse]. My limits are definitive verses, I'm convinced that I shouldn't contradict them. Also if I go against the verse people will think that I'm a *kafira* [unbeliever], which I am not, it's dangerous. What *Shari'ah* says is *haram* [forbidden] is our limit…my religious faith makes me hesitant to contradict definitive verses.

On inheritance, Soraya, who is also veiled, said, 'Today both men and women maintain the household so it might make logical sense for them to inherit equally. But I still can't go against the verse, I need a Shaykh to convince me because the verse is very clear, I can't take a position myself, I need a Shaykh to tell me.' Later in the interview, when we were discussing what she thought of *maqasid al-Shari'ah* (the purposes of the *Shari'ah*), Soraya stated, 'I don't know that much about *maqasid*, but from what I got to know, it is going to be useful because it will save us from the problems of literal interpretation. It will be able to bring human rights and religion closer together.'

The lack of coherence in the approaches used by the activists when dealing with both religion and human rights may arise in part because the NGO discourse does not yet have a clear, well-defined relationship with the Qur'anic text other than adopting it in general as part of its referential system. The discourse does not address some difficult but important methodological and epistemological questions, such as: In which areas, and according to which criteria, will the activists adopt the 'spirit' or 'purpose' of a Qur'anic verse? In which other areas will they follow the verse literally? How will they respond to the criteria of the classical methodology of *usul al-fiqh*, which determines the definitive nature of some Qur'anic verses? If interpretation is open to all texts in their entirety, what measures can be taken to avoid the potential chaos, feared by classical jurists, of a plurality of opinions and an ensuing loss of consistency?

This leads to another issue that remains unclear, namely the relationship between the NGOs' discourse and the rich traditional, albeit patriarchal, jurisprudence that has accumulated over the centuries and has come to represent what 'Islam' states to be *qiwamah* and *wilayah* among lawmakers and society at large. Will the NGOs' discourse aim to effect a sharp break with this long jurisprudential tradition? Or will it continue to deconstruct elements in it selectively in order to build upon it in a slow piecemeal fashion, with all the inconsistencies involved? Abou El Fadl (2001, p. 36) informs us that classical jurisprudence gave more authority to legal knowledge and rulings that kept the same thread of thinking as their precedents, giving much less authority to those which made a sharp break with the tradition. Will this new discourse adopt the same criteria? If not, then what will be the new criteria of authority and validity for this new discourse?

If evaluated by classical juristic standards of validity, the NGO activists face a serious question of authority and recognition because of their use of international human rights as a source of law informing their PSL reform proposals. Not only is it a source external to the sacred texts of Islam, but it also implies a sharp break with established gender norms and rules and understandings of *qiwamah* and *wilayah* as developed by the schools of Islamic jurisprudence.

Despite the difficulties of referring to the human rights paradigm in Egypt, it has helped activists appropriate religious discourse in a way that clearly articulates the concept of gender equality. The unambiguous affirmation of gender equality in the human rights paradigm has helped activists to seek and focus on the principle of equality that is inherent in Islam. As Zebeida said, 'My knowledge of human rights...made me search in Islam to find these principles...These principles were already there in Islam.'

The fact remains that, although the NGOs adopt equality as a general guiding principle for their work, which they base on the discourses of both human rights and Islam, many of their reform propositions are still clearly not egalitarian. This is largely because different sources and definitions of terms inform their work. The Qur'an, the Islamic legal tradition and human rights norms all have different notions of equality and equity, which the NGOs refer to simultaneously.[12]

On the level of the Qur'an and jurisprudence, the NGOs promote equality in some cases, while favouring equity in other cases, as they attempt to deal with the complex lived realities of many Egyptian women. Today more women are the protectors and providers of their families, as well as citizens of a state that is party to human rights conventions espousing equality. Yet inequality between women and men is also socially condoned and legalized in state law, and religion is generally held in high regard. Activists have to address all these conflicting factors at once. So activists' acceptance of maintenance as the husband's responsibility, for instance, signifies their view that equality is not always the solution to some problems Egyptian women face today, whereas their call for shared responsibility is based on a notion of equality which they find inherent in both human rights norms and the Qur'anic ethical–spiritual message.

The fact that the Qur'an contains verses that sanction unequal treatment of women and men does not demean the value of the Qur'an in many of these activists' eyes, or the primacy of its overall message of equality and justice. They see this not necessarily as a contradiction within the Qur'an, but rather as God's merciful attempt to accommodate the context in which the Qur'an was revealed, which was very different from that of today. They concur that it is up to Muslims to create a new understanding of these verses based on the change in context and the overriding general Qur'anic principles of equality and justice, which they consider two of the main purposes (*maqasid*) of *Shari'ah*. This negotiation between different Qur'anic meanings and the necessities of lived experience reflects the activists' attempt to create a new understanding of spousal roles and rights – albeit with inconsistencies and contradictions.

---

[12] My research also shows that the way equality has been appropriated by the NGOs has also been affected by its relevance to sociopolitical and economic factors. Often the NGOs did not consider equality to address women's lived experiences or the NGOs' political vulnerability under Mubarak's regime. See Sharafeldin (2013a; 2013b) for more details.

This brings us back to the different sources and definitions of terms such as 'equality' informing NGOs' work. Regarding the international human rights paradigm, and particularly CEDAW, commentators have made a distinction between formal, substantive and transformative equality. Formal equality essentially treats women and men as the same and is concerned with adopting legislation that ensures a non-discriminatory legal framework. Substantive equality recognizes and aims to address differences and historic-structural discrimination between women and men and is concerned with the 'equality of results' that may be achieved through states' adoption of temporary special measures. The more recently coined concept of 'transformative equality' aims to eliminate structural inequalities in institutions and systems such as the family which hamper women's access to their rights (Chinkin, 2012, p. 114; Freeman, 2012, pp. 438–9; International Women's Rights Action Watch [IWRAW] Asia Pacific, 2009, p. 15; Raday, 2012, p. 124).

There is also an important difference between equality and equity. The CEDAW Committee in its 'General Recommendation 28' (2010) states that the concept of equity 'is used in some jurisdictions to refer to fair treatment of women and men, according to their respective needs. This may include equal treatment, or treatment that is different but considered equivalent in terms of rights, benefits, obligations and opportunities' (p. 5). But because equity is so subjective it can become 'an elusive social goal which allows government to offer all types of justifications when they fall short' (IWRAW Asia Pacific, 2009, p. 21). The CEDAW concept of equality discussed above, on the other hand, 'offers broad, objective standards for member states' (IWRAW Asia Pacific, 2009, p. 1). It 'is a human right and therefore a legal obligation which cannot legally be avoided' (IWRAW Asia Pacific, 2009, p. 21). This is why the CEDAW Committee (2010) continuously calls upon states parties 'to use exclusively the concepts of equality of women and men or gender equality and not to use the concept of gender equity in implementing their obligations under the Convention' (p. 5).

On analysing the NGOs' reform propositions, it appears that advocating for substantive equality can be more useful than working towards formal equality, as it opens up possibilities for positive discrimination in areas where women are known to be disadvantaged. This justifies propositions such as retaining the husband's responsibility of maintenance. At the same time, however, the activists are resorting to the notion of equity in regard to issues such as obedience and unilateral divorce, even though it is strongly criticized in the international human rights framework.

Merry explains that when the human rights framework meets another framework it 'adds a new dimension to the way individuals think about problems…There is not a merging and blending, but two somewhat distinct sets of ideas and meanings that coexist' (2006, pp. 180–1). These different frameworks, Islamic law – as embodied in the pre-modern jurisprudence present in the Egyptian PSL – and human rights norms, and their different notions of equity and equality, do indeed coexist in the NGOs' discourse. The outcome has been a mixed pot of propositions that may be practically appealing but are epistemologically problematic. A stark example is NGOs' call for shared spousal responsibility for the family and shared financial guardianship of the children while at the same time condoning wifely obedience. Whereas the former two propositions are compatible with a human rights notion of equality, the latter is more reflective of classical jurisprudence's notion of inequality and complementarity, as encapsulated in the juristic concepts of *qiwamah* and *wilayah*. Here, the different notions of equality and equity end up coexisting side by side in the NGOs' proposal in the form of competing demands that are not theoretically consistent with one another.

It may be useful and enriching for NGOs to draw from different frameworks that can coexist together, and it is possible to do this in a more consistent manner. If the NGOs continue in the direction of spousal equality, they can use the human rights notion of substantive equality, which allows for differences between women and men and yet preserves their overall equality. To support their arguments, they can refer to numerous works of scholarship that aim to achieve unapologetic theoretical harmonization between human rights and Islamic law.[13] This scholarship includes Mahmoud Taha's proposition of reverse-abrogation, which was adopted by An-Na'im (1990) and follows the example of classical jurists. An-Na'im suggests that the more

---

[13] Such works can also show the fictitious nature of the Egyptian state's argument that Islamic law is fixed in its different treatment of women and men, as demonstrated through Egypt's reservation to article 16 of CEDAW, which relates to equality in the family:

Reservation to the text of article 16 concerning the equality of men and women in all matters relating to marriage and family relations during the marriage and upon its dissolution, without prejudice to the Islamic Shari'a's provisions whereby women are accorded rights equivalent to those of their spouses so as to ensure a just balance between them. This is out of respect for the sacrosanct nature of the firm religious beliefs which govern marital relations in Egypt and *which may not be called in question* and in view of the fact that one of the most important bases of these relations is an equivalency of rights and duties so as to ensure complementary which guarantees true equality between the spouses. (UN Women, n.d., emphasis mine)

egalitarian Qur'anic Meccan verses, which were previously abrogated by classical jurists, should abrogate the un-egalitarian context-bound Medinan verses upon which much of the current family jurisprudence is based.

Another example is Fazlur Rahman (1966; 1979; 1982), who proposed the 'double movement theory'. This theory is premised on the difficulty of implementing the Qur'an literally and the inadequacy of classical jurists' jurisprudence in a changed context. He suggests moving from the particular to the general, then from the general to the particular: starting first with deciphering the principles and objectives of the Qur'an and taking into consideration the context of revelation; then taking these general principles and applying them in the form of legislation after studying the contemporary context.

Nasr Abu Zayd's interpretive approach to the Qur'an is also relevant and can be useful for activists. Abu Zayd (2000) proposes a linguistic and discursive analysis of the Qur'an, arguing that the language of revelation used in the Qur'an should be recognized as a human medium of communication that is affected by the different layers of context – historical, cultural and linguistic – that shape and develop its changing meanings across time. He also delineates different domains of meaning in the Qur'an (Abu Zayd, 2013). According to his delineation, the cosmological and ethical–spiritual domains of the Qur'an espouse absolute equality between all humans, while the social domain of the Qur'an, where family rulings are located, espouses inequality and complementarity between the sexes, thereby reflecting the worldly context of revelation. Abu Zayd asserts that humanity is continuously encouraged to upgrade the social domain in the direction of the equality found in the cosmological and ethical–spiritual domains.

Another example is the work of Wadud (1999; 2006), which encourages Muslims to view the Qur'an as a text that offers a starting point towards a futuristic trajectory of equality, to engage critically with the text and to say 'no' to it where it is no longer meaningful for the exigencies of contemporary times.

Finally, Abou El Fadl's (2009) theology of beauty and goodness asserts that it is imperative to reimagine the nature of the relationship between God and creation to forge a new relationship between Islam and human rights. If God is to be viewed 'as beauty and goodness', and humans are the viceroys of God on earth, then a commitment to human rights is a commitment in favour of God that aims to realize the divine in human life (p. 128).

These works, among others, can liberate women's rights activists from the literalism of the text, the sanctification of outdated classical *fiqh*, and the supposed fixity of Islamic law. They can enable activists to respond better to women's contemporary needs from within an Islamic framework. They can seriously question the juristic concept of *qiwamah* as sanctioning the mainte-nance for obedience equation, male authority, polygamy, and unilateral divorce by the husband, and provide alternative routes for different Islamic rulings on these issues.

However, taking this line of thinking not only entails a direct clash with the Egyptian state and public opinion, but also necessitates that the NGOs propose a complete overhaul of the law and its underlying un-egalitarian philosophy, rather than minor and incremental reforms. The historical devel-opment of the Egyptian PSL in the twentieth century indicates that proposing such substantive changes has often been a highly risky endeavour with little chance of success.

The direction adopted by NGOs in which the maintenance for obedi-ence equation remains largely intact and the different notions of equality and equity coexist in their proposals may be a more realistic choice for these activ-ists. It plainly has its limitations. The best it can do is to improve slightly the conditions of the classical juristic paradigm that, according to the NGOs, is at the root of the PSL's problems and its disconnect from contemporary realities. At worst, the underlying epistemological inconsistency in the activists' propo-sitions may lead to failure to solve real-life problems, as well as weaken the appeal of the NGOs' arguments. This in turn may give state institutions justi-fication not to take the NGOs' proposals seriously. In either case, the NGOs' efforts to negotiate between Muslim legal tradition and contemporary Egyp-tian reality are indeed indicative of what Mir-Hosseini (2012, p. 302) calls the 'epistemological crisis' facing Islamic legal thought today.

CHANGING STANDARDS FOR AUTHORITATIVE RELIGIOUS KNOWLEDGE IN THE MODERN NATION STATE

One of the most important burgeoning results of the meeting between human rights and religion is that the criteria for the authority and validity of particu-lar religious rulings are being questioned.[14] The context of the twenty-first-century nation state is integral here. The development of the nation state brought with it the discourse of democracy and citizenship which, in theory, entails that all citizens are equal as per their nations' constitutions. The state

---

[14] See Hallaq (2001; 2004) and Abou El Fadl (2001) for a discussion of the historical criteria for authority and validity of Islamic legal knowledge.

is premised upon this social contract with its citizens, whereby laws are made by citizen representatives elected to legislative bodies in order to manage the citizens' affairs. If these representatives fail, or make deficient laws, citizens can elect other representatives. States are also part of an international community in which treaties and conventions regulate relations among states, as well as promote human rights. Respect for such conventions normally entails inclusion and recognition in the international community.

Messick (1993) shows that in a context such as this, particularly in relation to the formation of the state and its relationship with its citizens, a significant discursive transformation in the 'form' of *Shari'ah* has taken place. Based on his study in the highlands of Yemen, he states,

> The decisive move from the old manuals to legislation, from open to closed Shari'a texts, represents the key instance of discursive transformation… As the simply organized patrimonial imamate gave way to proliferating bureaucratic segments and to the beginnings of representational government, and as a face-to-face society of witnesses and known reputations yielded to a citizenry of equivalent strangers, so individualized licenses for the transmission of specific texts were replaced by standardized state diplomas, the unitary opinion of the judge by the collective voice of members of a bench, and the stand-alone authority of the notary's hand by official registration. (1993, pp. 253–4)

A similar process has taken place in Egypt, where the advent of the nation state and its institutions has effected a discursive transformation in the form that *Shari'ah* takes. There have been several manifestations and implications of this process. These include the codification of Islamic jurisprudence into state law, contributing to its contemporary rigidity, despite its historical flexibility; and the ways in which the nineteenth- and twentieth-century reforms of the Egyptian legal system, which were based on the European legal model and included the abolishment of *Shari'ah* courts, entailed that different state institutions – government, parliament, the Supreme Constitutional Court of Egypt (SCC) and the religious establishment – became variously involved in expressing *Shari'ah* through state law. For example, after the 1980 constitutional amendment on *Shari'ah*,[15] the SCC found itself in a new position where

---

[15] In 1980, and through various political manoeuvres, Sadat pushed through an amendment to article 2 of the Constitution to state that the principles of Islamic *Shari'ah* were *the* main source

it had to reconcile constitutional guarantees of equality and human rights with the principles of *Shari'ah*. The rise of the notion of 'equal citizens' has also been used to advocate against the inequality inherent in some *fiqh*-based modern codes, both in Egypt and around the world. This is illustrated in the words of Dina, one of the interviewed activists: 'A woman today works and pays maintenance because of poverty; women today have multiple roles as a worker, a wife, a mother...She should be treated as a citizen who pays taxes, not as a sister or mother.'

The change in the form of *Shari'ah*, as Messick states, has also changed the 'nature of interpretation' (1993, p. 253). Interpretation and the production of legal rulings in the Muslim legal tradition have traditionally been conducted according to the science of *usul al-fiqh*, but early twentieth-century reformers focused on methods such as *maslaha* (public interest), *maqasid al-Shari'ah* (objectives of the *Shari'ah*) and *takhayyur* (selection of legal rules from different sources), which were not previously considered of primary importance in classical methodology (Hallaq, 2004, p. 24; An-Na'im, 1990, p. 45). In the second half of the twentieth century the SCC went further and demonstrated its ambivalence towards the sanctification of *fiqh* (Selim, 2009, p. 642) by elevating human rights as a constitutional principle that aids the court's interpretation of the constitution and its various provisions (Boyle and Sherif, 1996, pp. 89–91; Lombardi, 2006, p. 155).

In a similar vein, the researched NGOs use several other contemporary standards to query juristic rulings and legal provisions that subscribe to the criteria developed by classical jurists. The standards used by the NGOs include questioning the ability of the provisions to address the new relationship forged between nation states and their citizens, namely how the state fulfils the new needs of women citizens even in situations where this may seem to contravene 'definitive' texts. The NGOs also use 'science' as a measure to show that rigidly following Islamic texts and classical jurisprudence may have detrimental socioeconomic side effects on Muslim societies today. The NGOs produce and refer to qualitative and quantitative research that demonstrates such negative effects.[16] The NGOs also rely on the extent to which a traditional religious discourse addresses the postcolonial concern for Egypt's national development through the protection of the family, by

---

of legislation instead of, as previously, *a* source of legislation, thus giving it priority (Al-Sharmani, 2008, p. 6).

[16] Examples of this research include El-Hinnawi and Abdel Baki (2009), Zakariyya (2009), El-Sayyid (2009) and Abu Tig (2009).

arguing that the current disconnect between the PSL and reality jeopardizes national development. In addition, the NGOs use the standard of the degree of harmony between a religious discourse and 'acceptable' international norms of human rights and dignity.

Non-governmental organizations using these standards are trying to show that by addressing these issues the religious discourse that they adopt is more valid today than the traditional juristic one upon which the PSL is based. It is not yet clear whether the Egyptian state and its religious institutions, such as al-Azhar, will seriously acknowledge these standards – as opposed to the criteria developed by classical jurists – as part of the epistemological criteria of validity that imbue Islamic knowledge with authority today. So far their reaction has been governed by an apologetic and nationalist discourse. However, with the rising global power of human rights discourse, the increasing local socioeconomic problems and the advent of alternative egalitarian religious discourses that address such problems, this apologetic position may weaken, eventually inducing the Egyptian state to recognize these new standards of validity.

WHO IS DOING THE ACTIVISM?

The characteristics of the people engaging in this advocacy work is another important factor that has affected the NGOs' reform proposals and their reformulation of *qiwamah* and *wilayah*.

Because of the ways in which they engage with religious discourses, many of the interviewees can be classified as 'Muslim feminists', using a term coined by the Egyptian social scientist Azza Karam (1998). Karam defined this category of women as those who refer to the Qur'an and *Sunnah* to show that the concept of equality is supported by Islam. They try to build a bridge between religious discourse and human rights. They call for a reinterpretation of Islamic texts and sources and question the validity of classical interpretations in today's world (Karam, 1998, pp. 12–13).

In my own fieldwork, Muslim feminists also included activists who adopted a secular politics in their public work whether or not they personally observed religious injunctions in their private lives. For example, some of these feminists recounted that while in their personal lives they considered themselves observant religious believers, in their public lives, which included their PSL reform work, they identified with a secular politics that aims to take religion out of the public realm. In other words, their public activism and politics were very different from their private beliefs and practices, and they did not find any paradox in this, believing that religious faith is a private matter.

Nevertheless, the self-proclaimed 'secular feminists' I interviewed professed varying levels of willingness to work with a religious discourse, despite their overriding secular politics. Some had no problem with using a religious discourse in their PSL advocacy because they believed that the sociopolitical context dictated this, along with their feminist solidarity with the Muslim women they serve through their activism.

All of the activists had first-hand experience of the realities of the women with whom their NGOs worked. They evoked the notion of 'equal citizenship' in all of their reform advocacy documents. These characteristics, besides most of them being Muslim, empowered them to exercise their agency as activists, citizens and Muslim believers, and to critically engage with religious discourse. They invoked Islam's elevation of the use of one's own mind to decipher things for oneself without the need for intermediaries between a Muslim and her or his God. For example, Laila, one of the activists, said, 'It's my right to talk about religion; it is not anyone's monopoly. Religion used to be a monopoly for certain people, but I can myself go back to religion and work it out for myself.'

Other activists talked about how the Islamic values they grew up with greatly influenced their activism. The kind of Islam they were brought up with in their own households was one where the values of equality, justice and preservation of dignity for women were paramount. The dominant patriarchal Islam propagated by conservative religious groups in the last few decades, which was reflected in state laws, clashed with their own understanding of Islam and paved the way for their feminism. This is echoed, for instance, in Nahla's words: 'Islam is what made me believe in women's rights.'

By reclaiming their agency as autonomous Muslim believers, citizens and activists, these activists were questioning the authority of legislators and traditional religious experts and leaders to monopolize the process of determining what is Islamic and what is not in state laws. They were also challenging the traditional figures of religious authority to come up with a better deal for women. As Mariam said, 'My job is to problematize things for religious men, to show them that there is patriarchy, there is misogyny, and to ask them: How will you deal with it? My role isn't to usurp yours, mine is to problematize things for you to solve.'

Whereas for some of the activists, being observant Muslims empowered them to question the injustices of the dominant religious discourse, for many their Muslim faith seemed to constitute a ceiling to this critical process. This was because of what they sometimes perceived to be the clarity of the Qur'anic text. Whether this was because the activists themselves believed in that clarity and the need to adhere to it, or because they felt that opposing it would bring them hostility from society, even if they had no problem with it personally, this led to the same outcome: adaptation or dilution of some of their propositions for reform.

However, some of the activists questioned the assumption that Islam is the most decisive force in Muslim societies. For example, Dina criticized the 'superficial religiosity' rampant in Egyptian society, where she finds, in her experience, that religion does not necessarily have the importance claimed by fellow Egyptians. Hana pointed to the dominance of using religion as a term of reference. She recognized that in her advocacy work she could risk losing an argument or a position if she did not use religious terms and grounds to substantiate it. However, she noted that it is not only religion that counts, but also dominant societal norms, saying, 'what rules around here is what "people say/think" [kalam al-nas], not just Shari'ah'.

It is important to realize that these activists are social beings. Besides being activists, they are members of families, communities, social classes and faith groups, all of which affect their public and private actions. This may be illuminated by Suad Joseph's discussion of what she calls the 'relational' aspect of agency and rights, whereby a 'person's sense of rights flowed out of relationships that she/he had' (1994, p. 273). She writes that '[c]rucial to the construction of relational rights, as I observed in Lebanon, was that they were nested in, but not limited to, kinship relationships, idioms, and morality' (1994, pp. 274–5). This points to the important effect of one's moral beliefs on one's assessment of the rights to be sought.

What matters here is that the particular situated location of these activists affected the process of articulating their PSL reform proposals. While juggling their roles as citizens, activists and Muslims, they were also trying to address their society's problems and accommodate the particularities of their context. They were often situated in the middle and trying to negotiate a space for themselves and their discourses. Leila Ahmed's discussion of the difficult situation of Arab Muslim feminists applies here very well. According to her, they sometimes have to choose between their Muslim identity and faith and their feminist consciousness. She describes this as a distressing choice 'between betrayal and betrayal' (Ahmed, 1984, p. 122). The activists studied here were trying to bridge that divide through the discourse and reform propositions they were articulating, with all of the strengths and weaknesses that their approach involved. Whether this will successfully translate into law or not remains to be seen.

FINAL REFLECTIONS

In conclusion, the activists studied here are trying to bridge binaries such as Islamic law and international human rights law. This effort entails challenges, limitations and possibilities for positive change in understanding *qiwamah* and *wilayah*. Motivated by the goal of tackling the problems and needs of Egyptian women, arising from their complex lived experiences, these activists use advocacy strategies that resist being bound with a singular choice, approach or frame of reference. In this advocacy work, the discourses of international human rights and Islamic law interact in complex ways and with mixed outcomes. Activists negotiate between these two discourses, and, as expected from any negotiation process, innovation and compromise take place. Meanwhile, these processes of engagement and reinterpretation create spaces for contesting and reformulating the traditional standards by which religious rulings and discourses claim normative and legal authority. New standards are making their way to judge the continuing validity of traditional, religious, juristic rulings on women and their rights in the Egyptian PSL. Needless to say, this process of contestation and reformulation has been deeply affected by the socioeconomic and political context in which the process is taking place, but it has also been shaped by the characteristics of the actors engaging in this process: the activists themselves.

REFERENCES

Abou El Fadl, Khaled. 2001. *Speaking in God's Name: Islamic Law, Authority and Women.* Oxford: Oneworld.

Abou El Fadl, Khaled. 2009. 'The Human Rights Commitment in Modern Islam'. In *Wanted: Equality and Justice in the Muslim Family*, edited by Zainah Anwar, pp. 113–78. Petaling Jaya: Musawah.

Abu-Odeh, Lama. 2004. 'Egyptian Feminism: Trapped in the Identity Debate.' In *Islamic Law and the Challenge of Modernity*, edited by Yvonne Haddad and Barbara Stowasser, pp. 183–212. Oxford: Altamira Press.

Abu Tig, Mervat. 2009. *Nahwa Qanun 'Usra Jadid* (Towards a New Family Law). Alexandria: Women and Development.

Abu Zayd, Nasr. 2000. *Al-Nass wa'l-Sultah wa'l-Haqiqah* (The Text, Power and Truth). Casablanca: al-Marqaz al-Thaqafi al-Arabi.

Abu Zayd, Nasr. 2013. 'The Status of Women between the Qur'an and *Fiqh*'. In *Gender and Equality in Muslim Family Law: Justice and Ethics in the Islamic Legal Tradition*, edited by Ziba Mir-Hosseini, Kari Vogt, Lena Larsen and Christian Moe, pp. 153–68. London: I.B. Tauris.

Ahmed, Leila. 1984. 'Early Feminist Movements in the Middle East: Turkey and Egypt'. In *Muslim Women*, edited by Freda Hussain, pp. 111–23. London: Croom Helm.

Al-Sharmani, Mulki. 2008. *Recent Reforms in Personal Status Laws and Women's Empowerment: Family Courts in Egypt*. Cairo: American University in Cairo.

An-Na'im, Abdullahi. 1990. *Towards an Islamic Reformation: Civil Liberties, Human Rights, and International Law*. Syracuse, NY: University of Syracuse Press.

Bernard-Maugiron, Nathalie. 2010. *Personal Status Laws in Egypt: FAQ*. Cairo: Deutsche Gesellschaft für Technische Zusammenarbeit (GTZ).

Boyle, Kevin and Adel Sherif (eds). 1996. *Human Rights and Democracy: The Role of the Supreme Constitutional Court of Egypt*. The Hague: Kluwer Law International.

Brown, Nathan. 1997. 'Sharia and State in the Modern Muslim Middle East'. *International Journal of Middle East Studies* 29 (3): pp. 359–76.

CEDAW Committee. 2010. 'General Recommendation 28 on the Core Obligations of States Parties under Article 2 of the Convention on the Elimination of All Forms of Discrimination against Women'. CEDAW/C/GC/28.

Chinkin, Christine. 2012. 'Article 3'. In *The UN Convention on the Elimination of All Forms of Discrimination against Women: A Commentary*, edited by Marsha Freeman, Christine Chinkin and Beate Rudolf, pp. 101–22. Oxford: Oxford University Press.

Cuno, Kenneth. 2009. 'Disobedient Wives and Neglectful Husbands: Marital Relations and the First Phase of Family Law Reform in Egypt'. In *Family, Gender, and Law in a Globalizing Middle East and South Asia*, edited by Kenneth Cuno and Manisha Desai, pp. 3–18. Syracuse, NY: Syracuse University Press.

El-Ghazali, Ahmed and Rushdi Shihata. 2005. *Mushkilat wa Qadaya al-Ahwal al-Shakhsiyya li'l-Muslimin* (Problems and Cases of Personal Status for Muslims). Cairo: Maktabat al-Nahda al-Masreya.

El-Hinnawi, Hamdi and Salwa Abdel Baki. 2009. *Al-Takalif al-Iqtisadiyya wa'l-Nafsiyya li'l-Talaq fi Misr* (Economic and Psychological Costs of Divorce in Egypt). Cairo: Centre for Egyptian Women Legal Assistance.

El-Laithy, Heba. 2001. *The Gender Dimensions of Poverty in Egypt*. Cairo: Economic Reform Forum.

El-Sayyid, Hend Fouad. 2009. *Al-'Usra al-Misriyya wa Qadaya al-Ahwal al-Shakhsiyya: Dirasa Tahliliyya Ihsa'iyya* (Personal Status Law Issues and the Egyptian Family: An Analytical and Statistical Study). Cairo: Egyptian Foundation for Family Development.

Esposito, John and Natana Delong-Bas. 2001. *Women in Muslim Family Law*. Syracuse, NY: Syracuse University Press.

Fawzy, Essam. 2004. 'Muslim Personal Status Law in Egypt: The Current Situation and Possibilities of Reform through Internal Initiatives'. In *Women's Rights and Islamic Family Law: Perspectives on Reform*, edited by Lynn Welchman, pp. 17–94. London: Zed Books.

Freeman, Marsha. 2012. 'Article 16'. In *The UN Convention on the Elimination of All Forms of Discrimination against Women: A Commentary*, edited by Marsha Freeman, Christine Chinkin and Beate Rudolf, pp. 409–42. Oxford: Oxford University Press.

Guiding Manual for a More Just and Comprehensive Family Law (Dalil Irshadi li-Qanun 'Usra Mutakamil Akthar 'Adala). 2010a. Cairo: Anonymized Network for PSL Reform Advocacy.

Guiding Manual for a More Just and Comprehensive Family Law (Dalil Irshadi li-Qanun 'Usra Mutakamil Akthar 'Adala). 2010b. Cairo: Anonymized Network for PSL Reform Advocacy.

Hallaq, Wael. 2001. *Authority, Continuity, and Change in Islamic Law*. Cambridge, UK: Cambridge University Press.

Hallaq, Wael. 2004. 'Can the Shari'a Be Restored?' In *Islamic Law and the Challenges of Modernity*, edited by Yvonne Haddad and Barbara Stowasser, pp. 21–53. New York: Altamira Press.

Ibrahim, Ahmed and Wassil Ibrahim. 2003. *Ahkam al-Ahwal al Shakhsiyya f'il-Shari'a al-Islamiyya w'al-Qanun* (Personal Status Rulings in Islamic Shari'ah and Law). Cairo: al-Maktaba al-Azhareya.

IWRAW Asia Pacific. 2009. *Equity or Equality for Women? Understanding CEDAW's Equality Principles*. Kuala Lumpur.

Joseph, Suad. 1994. 'Problematizing Gender and Relational Rights: Experiences from Lebanon'. *Social Politics* 1 (3): pp. 272–85.

Kamali, Hashim. 2008. *Shari'ah Law: An Introduction*. Oxford: Oneworld.

Karam, Azza. 1998. *Women, Islamisms and the State*. London: Macmillan Press.

Lombardi, Clark. 2006. *State Law as Islamic Law in Modern Egypt*. Leiden: Brill.

Merry, Sally Engle. 2006. *Human Rights and Gender Violence: Translating International Law into Local Justice*. Chicago: University of Chicago Press.

Messick, Brinkley. 1993. *The Calligraphic State: Textual Domination and History in a Muslim Society*. Berkeley: University of California Press.

Mir-Hosseini, Ziba. 2012. 'Women in Search of Common Ground: Between Islamic and International Human Rights Law'. In *Islamic Law and International Human Rights Law: Searching for Common Ground?*, edited by Anver Emon, Mark Ellis and Benjamin Glahn, pp. 291–303. Oxford: Oxford University Press.

Mitchell, Timothy. 1988. *Colonising Egypt*. Cambridge, UK: Cambridge University Press.

Moors, Annalies. 1999. 'Debating Islamic Family Law: Legal Texts and Social Practices'. In *A Social History of Gender in the Modern Muslim Middle East*, edited by Margaret L. Meriwether and Judith E. Tucker, pp. 141–75. Boulder, CO: Westview Press.

Najjar, Fauzi. 1988. 'Egypt's Laws of Personal Status'. *Arab Studies Quarterly* 10 (3): pp. 319–44.

Position paper. 2008. Anonymized Network for PSL Reform Advocacy. Cairo, 8 July.

Position paper. 2009. Anonymized Network for PSL Reform Advocacy. Cairo, 22 February.

Raday, Frances. 2012. 'Article 4'. In *The UN Convention on the Elimination of All Forms of Discrimination against Women: A Commentary*, edited by Marsha Freeman, Christine Chinkin and Beate Rudolf, pp. 123–40. Oxford: Oxford University Press.

Rahman, Fazlur. 1966. 'The Impact of Modernity on Islam'. *Islamic Studies* 5 (2): pp. 121–2.

Rahman, Fazlur. 1979. 'Towards Reformulating the Methodology of Islamic Law'. *New York University Journal of International Law and Politics* 12 (2): pp. 219–24.

Rahman, Fazlur. 1982. *Islam and Modernity: Transformation of an Intellectual Tradition*. Chicago: University of Chicago Press.

Selim, Rajab Abdel Hakim et al. 2009. *Majmu'at al-Mabadi' Allati Qararatha al-Mahkama al-'Ulya wa al-Mahkama al-Dusturiyya al-'Ulya fi 'Arba'in 'Am 1969–2009* (The Principles Decided by the Supreme Court and the Supreme Constitutional Court in Forty Years 1969–2009). Cairo: SCC.

Sharafeldin, Marwa. 2013a. 'Personal Status Law Reform in Egypt: Women's Rights NGOs Navigating between Islamic Law and Human Rights'. PhD thesis. University of Oxford.

Sharafeldin, Marwa. 2013b. 'Egyptian Women's Rights NGOs: Personal Status Law Reform between Islamic and International Human Rights Law'. In *Gender and Equality in Muslim Family Law: Justice and Ethics in the Islamic Legal Tradition*, edited by Ziba Mir-Hosseini, Kari Vogt, Lena Larsen and Christian Moe, pp. 57–80. New York: I.B. Tauris.

Sonbol, Amira. 2003. 'Women in Shari'ah Courts: A Historical and Methodological Discussion'. *Fordham International Law Journal* 27 (1): pp. 225–53.

Tucker, Judith. 1998. *In the House of the Law: Gender and Islamic Law in Ottoman Syria and Palestine*. Berkeley: University of California Press.

Tucker, Judith. 2008. *Women, Family and Gender in Islamic Law*. Cambridge, UK: Cambridge University Press.

UN Women. n.d. 'Declarations, Reservations and Objections to CEDAW'. http://www.un.org/womenwatch/daw/cedaw/reservations-country.htm

Wadud, Amina. 1999. *Qur'an and Woman: Rereading the Sacred Text from a Woman's Perspective*. Oxford: Oxford University Press.

Wadud, Amina. 2006. *Inside the Gender Jihad: Women's Reform in Islam*. London: Oneworld.

Welchman, Lynn. 2011. 'A Husband's Authority: Emerging Formulations in Muslim Family Laws'. *International Journal of Law, Policy and the Family* 25 (1): pp. 1–23.

Wilson, Richard. 1997. 'Human Rights, Culture and Context: An Introduction'. In *Human Rights, Culture and Context: Anthropological Perspectives*, edited by Richard Wilson, pp. 1–27. London: Pluto Press.

Zahw, Ahmed. 1999. *Al-Zawaj fi'l-Shari'a al Islamiyah* (Marriage in Islamic Shari'a Law). Cairo: Law Faculty Cairo University.

Zakariyya, Hoda. 2009. *Al-Taklufah al-Ijtima'iya li'l-Talaq* (The Social Cost of Divorce in Egypt). Cairo: Center for Egyptian Women Legal Assistance.

'Men are the Protectors and Maintainers of Women…'

Three Fatwas on Spousal Roles and Rights*

Lena Larsen

D uring a conference lecture in 2000,[1] the late Dr Zaki Badawi, head of the Muslim College in London and the Muslim Law (Shariah) Council UK, exclaimed, 'I urge you women to revolt!' The suggestion was very well received by the women in the audience, but it caused a great deal of contestation among the men. They argued that such a revolt would clash with the traditional ideal of a woman fulfilling the role of the housewife and stay-at-home mother. They perceived a revolt against gender roles as a threat to the family. But the women in the room strongly objected that the traditional ideal did not accord with the lived realities of Muslim women in Europe, particularly given the fact that many women juggle taking care of their households with holding jobs.

* This chapter draws on my doctoral thesis, 'Islamic Legal Thought and the Challenges of Everyday Life: Fatwas as Proposed Solutions for Muslim Women in Western Europe' (Larsen, 2011). The focus of the dissertation was on the European Council for Fatwa and Research (ECFR) and Syed Mutawalli ad-Darsh. The dissertation drew on several sources: attendance at fatwa sessions of the ECFR from 2002–6; interviews with ECFR members; written fatwas and decisions of the ECFR; and women-related fatwas issued by ad-Darsh, most of which were published in Q-News from 1993 to 1996. Translations of Qur'anic verses are by Abdullah Yusuf Ali. All other translations from the original Arabic are my own.
[1] 'Muslims in the New Millennium: Multiculturalism, Identity and Citizenship', held in London in September 2000.

Badawi's remarks and the discussion that ensued inspired me to undertake a research project for my doctoral thesis entitled 'Islamic Legal Thought and the Challenges of Everyday Life'. While working on this project, I presented a study I conducted on Muslim women's challenges in Western Europe to the European Council for Fatwa and Research (*al-Majlis al-urubi lil-Ifta' wal-buhuth*; ECFR or 'the Council').[2] The ECFR is chaired by Yusuf al-Qaradawi, a popular and an authoritative religious scholar in Sunni Islam, an important activist and a prominent guest of al-Jazeera's religious programme *Sharia and Life* (Gräf and Skovgaard-Petersen, 2009, pp. 1–12). I argued that one challenge confronted by married women and men is that a single salary is not sufficient to support a household in Western Europe because of the high cost of living; hence women must contribute economically to their marital households. My conclusion was that traditional gender roles and norms in the Muslim family, not least rulings on inheritance, must be revisited. Al-Qaradawi, however, closed the discussion after my presentation by declaring that it is the responsibility of the husband to provide for his wife. He, just like the male listeners to Badawi's lecture, wanted to maintain the traditional juristic concept of the male husband as provider and the economically dependent and obedient wife, despite the tensions arising from the disconnect between realities on the ground and juristic norms and doctrines.

The problem is structural. There is a discrepancy between the lived realities of contemporary Muslim families in Europe, on the one hand, and the idealized notion of marital roles in Islam, on the other. This notion, at its core, is based upon men's authority over women. The idea of women assuming the role of breadwinners challenges the whole logic of male provision in exchange for wifely obedience, as encapsulated in the juristic concept of *qiwamah*. This concept is still the basis of gender relations in the thinking of modern-day jurists and Muslims who resist and denounce equality in marriage as alien to Islam.

In this chapter, I explore how practising Muslims in Europe and religious actors (exemplified by muftis) are making sense of and dealing with the discrepancy between the lived realities of Muslim families and *fiqh*-based gender norms. I focus on fatwas in order to shed light on the issue of spousal roles in marriage. A fatwa is a normative legal statement made in answer to a question (Eggen, 2001, p. 94). Fatwas, as expressions of the encounter between text and lived reality, can serve to illustrate the dilemma presented above.

---

[2] This took place in Dublin in February 2005.

I begin with a discussion of the relevance of fatwas to Muslims in Western Europe. I proceed with a description of the purpose and form of fatwas and the process of fatwa-giving in Muslim legal tradition. Next, I outline a typology of fatwa institutions in Western Europe, trends in fatwa-making in Europe, and details about two important actors involved in issuing fatwas: the mufti Syed Mutawalli ad-Darsh (d. 1997) and the transnational ECFR. I then share an analysis of two fatwas issued by ad-Darsh and one by the ECFR on spousal roles and rights in marriage. I conclude by examining a number of factors that muftis take into consideration in the process of navigating tensions arising from the gaps between the lived realities of Muslims and doctrines regulating marital roles in Islamic legal tradition. An understanding of such factors could be useful when negotiating reform on women's issues from within Islamic tradition.

MUSLIMS IN WESTERN EUROPE

The presence of Muslims in Western Europe is generally regarded as the result of the large-scale immigration from Muslim countries after the Second World War, which has led to the settlement of significant Muslim ethnic minority groups throughout Europe. Muslims in Europe are hetero-geneous groups with regard to nationality, language and religious tradition, and this is reflected in the diverse ways in which Islam is institutionalized and experienced among these different immigrant groups. That is, Islamic institutions in Western Europe are often extended branches of the corre-sponding institutions in the countries of origin, each with their distinct reli-gious authorities.

This relatively new Muslim presence in Western Europe is a challenge for Muslims themselves. How should they practise Islam in a new social context? Western Europe is like a new and open field, without a history of locally estab-lished Islamic norms. Since the 1960s, many Islamic actors and organizations have been concerned about the need for guidance for Muslims living as minor-ities in the West. This need has also been articulated through questions from Muslims themselves.[3]

---

[3] Yusuf al-Qaradawi's book *Al-Halal wal-Haram fil-Islam* (The Lawful and the Prohibited in Islam) was the result of a project initiated by Al-Azhar, based upon questions from Muslims living in the West (Larsen, 2011). For the development of *fiqh* and fatwa institutions from the 1970s onwards, see Caeiro (2011b).

Accordingly, there have been huge productions of audio and video recordings, journals, Islamic books and academic and religious conferences on and for Muslims in the continent. There has also been tremendous growth in satellite TV shows and resources on the internet targeting Muslim communities (Caeiro, 2011b). According to Caeiro, there are competing visions of 'Islam in Europe', fashioned by Muslim Brotherhood understandings of the comprehensiveness (*shumuliyya*) of Islam; Moroccan state officials' attachment to the Maliki school of jurisprudence; Saudi missionary efforts to spread Wahhabi teachings; conceptions of moderation (*wasatiyya*) and the purposes (*maqasid*) of Islamic law articulated by cosmopolitan intellectuals; and a plethora of other local and translocal constructions of European Islam (2011b, p. 256). Caeiro claims that a sense of urgency underlies debates among orthodox Muslims about the plight of Muslim minorities living in the West.

A hot topic of discussion that developed both in the West and in Muslim countries has been *fiqh* aimed at Muslim minorities in the West, called *fiqh al-aqalliyyat* (*fiqh* of minorities). The aim of those who promote this *fiqh* is to restore the role of *Shari'ah* in modern life (al-Alwani, 2003, p. 13), building upon what Caeiro (2011b) refers to as a fictional account of the legal primacy of *Shari'ah* in Muslim-majority countries (p. 109). As a result, authority lies with the recognized scholars of the Muslim community, who are entrusted with the responsibility of guiding Muslim believers. These scholars and fatwa institutions are thus among the most important Islamic institutions for Muslim minorities in the present era. A number of topics have been on the agenda of *fiqh al-aqalliyyat* discourse, such as Muslims living in non-Muslim lands, establishing a reliable prayer calendar in European countries, naturalization, Muslim political participation, buying a house with a mortgage, the Muslim family in the West, and the role of Muslim women in Europe (Caeiro, 2011b). The two latter issues, in particular, have gained a prominent position in the discourse on Muslims in the West.

FATWAS: FORM AND PURPOSE

A fatwa, in Muslim legal thought, is a normative legal statement made in answer to a question (Eggen, 2001, p. 94).[4] The practice is traditionally justified with reference to the Qur'an. The underlying formulation is 'They ask thee…Say…'

---

[4] I use the terms 'law', 'legal thought' and 'legal' in a broader sense and not exclusively to refer to the positive law of states or international legal orders.

(verse 2:189), which is a minimal definition, since it indicates only form and not substance. The Qur'an also uses various verb forms of the root *f-t-y* for question-and-answer activities: (i) asking for guidance (*istifta'*) and (ii) giving guidance (*afta*), such as in verses 4:127 and 4:176. The terminology for fatwas in Islamic legal thought is derived from the same root: *mufti*, the fatwa-giver; *mustafti*, the questioner; *futya* or *ifta'*, fatwa-giving; and *istifta'*, request for a fatwa.

A fatwa is an opinion that is neither a legally binding ruling (*hukm*) nor final. The mufti bases his fatwas on the information given by the petitioner, without investigating it further. This is unlike a court case, in which information presented is subject to scrutiny. The person who asks (*al-mustafti*) is not obliged to follow the fatwa, but can reject it and ask another mufti to see if he will give a different fatwa (and sometimes in the hope of getting a different opinion).

In spite of the non-binding nature of the fatwa, it has its own mechanisms of authority. This arises from the bond created between the petitioner and the mufti in the process of crafting the fatwa. In order to practise Islam 'correctly', Muslims provide specific information and ask specific questions to muftis about correct Islamic practice in their daily lives, in response to which they get answers or fatwas. Thus, muftis claiming authority and petitioners ascribing authority become two sides of the same coin. A mufti aims to issue a fatwa that is aligned as much as possible, to the best of his knowledge, with 'God's judgement', in regard to both this world (*al-dunya*) and the other world (*al-akhira*) (Masud et al., 1996, p. 19). A fatwa therefore plays an important role in the formation of the pious Muslim self (Larsen, 2011).

Questions submitted to individual and institutional muftis can be divided into generic questions and personal petitions. According to Caeiro (2011b), generic questions about 'what does *Shari'ah* say?' elicit informative fatwas, while petitions about one's situation result in personal fatwas that take the moral responsibility of the individual for granted. This suggests that fatwas also have therapeutic functions. In the first category, the mufti's authority is constructed by virtue of superior knowledge, while in the second category the mufti not only provides information but also takes part in a process of bettering and refining the spiritual and moral advancement of the seeker of the legal opinion (Caeiro, 2011b, p. 259–60). In other words, fatwas are complex and can serve multiple functions.

The questions of the petitioners are social data and can tell us something about the challenges that women and men face in their daily lives. For example, Jajat Burhanudin (2005) studied the spread of the reform ideas of the

notable Egyptian scholar Muhammad 'Abduh through an analysis of Southeast Asian requests for fatwas in the journal *al-Manar*, which was published
by 'Abduh. Burhanudin notes that it is the questions of these petitioners rather
than the fatwas that were enlightening, for they reflected the changing social
and intellectual circumstances of Southeast Asian Muslims at the beginning
of the twentieth century (p. 10). Amalia Zomeño (2008) also highlights the
importance of the questions: 'the question is the most interesting part of the
fatwas in terms of social data, but at the same time, it is the part of the fatwa
that has more of a translation of social facts in legal terms' (p. 32).

Fatwas can also be considered as discourses between the petitioner and
the mufti, or as the interplay between legal argument and social and cultural
reality. Fatwas can therefore provide us with insight into the dynamics of
continuity and change in the Islamic tradition. In this sense, fatwas constitute
an important aspect of Islam as a discursive tradition, defined by the anthropologist Talal Asad (1986) as follows:

> Islam is neither a distinctive social structure nor a heterogeneous collec-
> tion of beliefs, artifacts, customs, and morals. It is a tradition…A tradi-
> tion consists essentially of discourses that seek to instruct practitioners
> regarding the correct form and purpose of a given practice that, precisely
> because it is established, has a history. These discourses relate concep-
> tually to a *past* (when the practice was instituted, and from which the
> knowledge of its point and proper performance has been transmitted)
> and a *future* (how the point of that practice can best be secured in the
> short or the long term, or why it should be modified or abandoned),
> through a *present* (how it links to other practices, institutions, and social
> conditions). (p. 14)

The historical significance of fatwas and muftis in the development of the
Islamic legal tradition has been well documented (see, for example, Bogstad,
2009; Caeiro, 2002; 2004; 2011b; Heyd, 1969; Karman, 2008; Larsen, 2011;
Masud et al., 1996; Powers, 2002; Skovgaard-Petersen, 1997; Zomeño,
2008). For example, the Islamic legal expert Wael Hallaq (1994) attributes
to muftis a central role in the development and change of legal doctrines in
the law schools: 'the juridical genre of the fatwa was chiefly responsible for the
growth and change of legal doctrine in the schools, and…our current perception of Islamic law as a jurists' law must now be further defined as a *mufti's*
law' (p. 65). *Ifta*' and fatwas in Europe represent a new chapter in the history

of this discursive tradition, in this case focusing on contemporary challenges encountered by married women and men and their families while living as religious minorities in non-Muslim cultures.

FATWA INSTITUTIONS IN WESTERN EUROPE: TRENDS AND ACTORS

Futya or fatwa-giving has been one way of institutionalizing Islam in Western Europe. Since the 1980s, four categories of fatwa institutions have emerged in Western Europe. First, there is the individual learned person or mufti in the local community, who will often give religious advice to members from his or her country of origin. A notable example is Syed ad-Darsh, who will be discussed below. Second, there are *Shariʿah* councils in European countries, the best known of which is the Islamic Shariʿah Council in England. These councils were initially established to provide Muslims with *Shariʿah*-based solutions and are now playing a role in resolving marital conflicts (Badawi, 1995, p. 78; Vogt, 1995, pp. 54, 166).[5] A third category of fatwa institutions is national umbrella organizations. A clear example of this is the Union des organisations islamiques de France (UOIF), which provides answers to *fiqh*-related questions through their *Dar al-Fatwa* (the Fatwa house). Fourth, there is the transnational ECFR, discussed below, which is a category on its own.

There are several trends in the issuing of fatwas within Sunni Islam in Europe. The Salafi trend stresses an interpretation of the *Shariʿah* as unchangeable (Roald, 2001a, pp. 50–4), whereas what I shall call the *madhhab* trend stresses affiliation with a particular school of law and seeks answers to questions within the traditional teachings of the school. A third trend, the *Ikhwan* trend, is tied to Muslim Brotherhood (*al-Ikhwan al-muslimun*),[6] specifically to *Ikhwan* thought (*fikr*), as opposed to the organization (*tanzim*) (Roald, 2001a; Ternisien, 2005).

The *Ikhwan* thought is a particular development arising from the Salafi trend, which was initiated by Muhammad ʿAbduh (d. 1905). ʿAbduh, a scholar and state mufti of Egypt, was one of the architects of Islamic modernism,

---

[5] In an interview I conducted in November 1993, Syed ad-Darsh made the same point. It is noteworthy that ad-Darsh was chair of the Islamic Shariah Council until he passed away in 1997.

[6] The Muslim Brotherhood is a transnational Sunni political, social and religious movement and organization that was founded in Egypt in 1928.

which is based on renewal (*tajdid*) of Islamic thought. A line can be drawn from 'Abduh, Muhammad Rashid Rida (d. 1935), Muhammad al-Ghazali (d. 1996) to Yusuf al-Qaradawi (b. 1926). They are all recognized for their claim of taking social and cultural contexts into consideration when issuing fatwas.

Al-Qaradawi, mentioned previously as the influential chair of the ECFR, has been concerned with providing Islamic solutions to Muslims in Europe living as a relatively new minority. Al-Qaradawi has developed his own theory of *fiqh al-aqalliyyat* (*fiqh* of minorities), of which he is an advocate. The basis of *fiqh al-aqalliyyat*, according to him, is 'correct' *ijtihad*. Al-Qaradawi presents it technically as a set of Islamic norms to be eclectically reconstructed from traditional *fiqh* heritage (*ijtihad intiqa'i*) or discovered through new interpretative efforts (*ijtihad insha'i*), drawing on the concepts and methodology in the tradition which he considers most important (al-Qaradawi, 2001, p. 39). Al-Qaradawi's detailed argument for the importance of the use of certain concepts and methodology in this new *fiqh* of minorities is motivated by the desire to maintain the orthodoxy of the norms expressed in the fatwas not only through the content of the actual opinions expressed but also through the orthodoxy of the methodology and concepts used in the fatwa-giving process. This echoes Ann Elizabeth Mayer's observation that in the tradition of Islamic law it was the use of recognized juristic methods of interpretation that guaranteed the orthodoxy of results (1990, p. 194).

Research shows that Muslim women in Europe demand more fatwas than men.[7] For example, ad-Darsh published more than a hundred fatwas on women's issues in the British Muslim magazine *Q-News*, while the ECFR's two collections contain thirty-four fatwas out of eighty on these issues. Moreover, the greatest number of questions received by the ECFR relate to women's issues, as was reported to me by the secretary general of the ECFR. Al-Qaradawi, the chair of the ECFR, attributes the fact that the majority of questions come from women to the idea that women have greater concern about religion than men do (al-Qaradawi, 2000, p. 33–4). But Caeiro (2011a, p. 128) posits that this is because the discrepancies between classical *fiqh* and contemporary expectations seem to be the widest in the domain of women's issues.

According to the material I gathered for my research on fatwas, women who ask for fatwas first and foremost focus on issues related to marriage and family, education and social relations, whereas men mostly focus on economic

---

[7] See Roald (2001b). This trend was also observed in my fieldwork.

issues. Based on their questions, women's concerns could be divided into the following categories: different types of marriage; premarital stages such as engagement and rules for interaction between the sexes in this period; the marriage ceremony; marital life; the body, sexuality and reproduction; social relations; upbringing; education and work; and 'ibadat rituals.[8] In the category of 'marital life', questions centre around breadwinning, gender roles and issues relating to spouses' owning common or separate bank accounts.

FATWAS RELATED TO SPOUSAL ROLES AND RIGHTS

In what follows I discuss in some detail three fatwas that relate to spousal roles and rights, issued by two major actors: the late Syed Mutawalli ad-Darsh (d. 1997) and the ECFR. These two actors, one in England and one transnational, offer examples of the *Ikhwan* trend of thought in Europe, which is the dominant trend. They also tell us something about individual and collective styles of fatwas in Europe and the ways in which muftis respond to the concerns of Muslims in Europe. These two actors are introduced first, and then their fatwas related to women's issues are analysed.

Syed ad-Darsh

Syed Mutawalli ad-Darsh, considered to be 'the first mufti of Europe',[9] arrived in London in December 1971. Ad-Darsh had been educated at the faculty of *'usul al-din* at Al-Azhar University and studied moral philosophy at the University of Aberdeen. He was sent to the United Kingdom by Al-Azhar University in Egypt[10] and held the position of imam in the London Central Mosque until 1980. After the contract ended, he was employed by the then Ministry for Fatwa, Research, *Da'wa* and Guidance (*wizarat al-ifta' wal-buhuth al-islamiyya*

---

[8] This typology of topics differs from modern *fiqh* literature, which often has chapters on 'woman' and 'family'. Al-Qaradawi's *Al-Halal wal-Haram fil-Islam* may be the best-known example.

[9] Interview conducted by the author with Fuad Nahdi, editor of *Q-News*, Istanbul, July 2006.

[10] Interview conducted by the author with Syed ad-Darsh, Oslo, 25 November 1993.

wal-da'wa wal-irshad) in Saudi Arabia.[11] He was also a member of the Saudi fatwa institution Dar al-Ifta'.[12]

Early in the 1990s, ad-Darsh hosted a weekly programme on the London-based Arabic TV channel MBC (Vogt, 1995, p. 54) and worked as *khatib* (person who delivers the Friday sermon) at Muslim Welfare House in East London.[13] After the Friday prayer, people used to queue to ask him questions. One of these people was Fuad Nahdi, the editor of *Q-News*, who invited ad-Darsh to be in charge of a column on *fiqh* issues in the magazine. Ten to fifteen thousand people read the column every week.[14] From being an unknown, older *'alim* who meant nothing to young people, ad-Darsh became popular and influential among them. In particular, he played an important role in reinterpreting Muslim legal tradition, making it relevant for our times (Vogt, 1995, p. 124).

Ad-Darsh stressed the importance of understanding the contemporary circumstances in which Muslims live. According to him, muftis, when setting standards for Muslim behaviour, must take into account the local conditions and changing situations of Muslim lives.[15] Ad-Darsh was characterized as a grassroots mufti, available for most people. Ataullah Siddiqui, director of Markfield Institute of Higher Education (MIHE), describes the legacy of ad-Darsh as follows: 'His fatwas brought out a kind of understanding, where contextualisation began.'[16]

Ad-Darsh also cooperated with other scholars on religious-legal questions of Muslim life and conduct. This kind of cooperation led, *inter alia*, to the founding of the ECFR.

The ECFR

The ECFR was established in 1997 by the Federation of Islamic Organizations in Europe (*al-Ittihad al-munazzamat al-Islamiyya fi Uruba*) (FIOE). The

---

[11] Until the beginning of the 1980s, the ministry employed religious scholars from outside Saudi Arabia. They accepted scholars who were educated at Al-Azhar University. As Saudi Arabian universities began to produce their own scholars, these scholars were increasingly recruited to be missionaries in Europe.

[12] Author's conversation with Suhayb Hasan, secretary of the Islamic Sharia Council and a close friend of ad-Darsh, Istanbul, July 2006.

[13] Personal field notes, July 1993.

[14] Interview conducted by the author with Fuad Nahdi, editor of *Q-News*, Istanbul, July 2006.

[15] Ibid.

[16] Interview conducted by the author with Ataullah Siddiqui, Oslo, 25 November 2008.

ECFR, which has a secretariat in Ireland, claims Europe to be its Islamic legal 'jurisdiction'. Its establishment was considered to be an interim solution to solve the 'chaotic situation today of *fiqh* issues' – to fill a void until the first group of Muslim scholars graduated from another FIOE institution, L'Institut Européen de Sciences Humaines.

The Council has thirty-two members, from both Europe and Muslim-majority countries. At the inaugural Council meeting in London in 1997, Yusuf al-Qaradawi and the late Faysal Mawlawi, a Lebanese jurist, were elected as chairman and deputy chairman, respectively. The Mauritian scholar Abdullah bin Bayyah emerged as a third 'pillar' of the Council. The first two scholars are considered to have played an influential role in shaping Muslim Brotherhood *fikr* (thought), and bin Bayyah is known to be the most prominent representative of the Maliki *madhhab* today.

The objectives of the Council, according to its website (http://www.e-cfr. org), are to coordinate differences of opinion within the Islamic legal tradition, to provide collective fatwas (*fatawa*) and decisions (*qararat*) according to the needs of Muslims in Europe, to publish legal studies on new topics on the European scene and to provide guidance for Muslims in general and Muslim youth in particular by disseminating an 'authentic' Islam.

Fatwas from the ECFR are issued at its yearly meeting. Before the session, individual members or a small group of members of the Council receive the questions and prepare fatwas. In the session, the fatwas are discussed and different points of view are incorporated into the text in the process of issuing a so-called 'uniform' fatwa. If the fatwa is accepted, it becomes a fatwa of the Council. The fatwa is then included in the final declaration, which is read at the end of the session.

Publication of the fatwas is a central goal of the Council and is done through the Council's website and its journal *al-Majalla al-'Ilmiyya*. A collection of fatwas and resolutions from the Council's first session to its twentieth session, which took place in 2010, has also been published.[17] Some of the ECFR's fatwas were also published on the *Islam Online* website (http://islamonline.net), which was one of the most visited Islamic websites on the internet until a conflict between the management in Qatar and the staff in Cairo resulted in the website being frozen (Abdel-Fadil, 2012).

Although the Council claims Europe as their Islamic-legal 'jurisdiction', a claim reflecting local and geographical authority, the transnational character

---

[17] This volume is entitled *Al-Qararat wa al-Fatawa Al-Sadira 'an al-Majlis al-Urubi lil-Ifta' wa al-Buhuth* (ECFR, 2013).

of its membership and its dissemination channels makes it clearly a part of transnational Islam (Larsen, 2010).

Fatwas from Syed ad-Darsh

In a fatwa published in *Q-News*, a female petitioner asks ad-Darsh,

> What does Islam have to say about the concept of the 'house husband'? Islam obligates men to provide for their families. But what happens, as is increasingly the case in the UK, when the wife earns more than her husband? How, for example, should household duties be divided and can men just stay at home to cook, clean and look after the children? (*Q-News*, 19 February 1993)

In his response, ad-Darsh recognizes the current situation in which many women are the breadwinners in their families, but declares that this is not condoned in Islam. According to him, it is against the 'natural' state of affairs. Housebound men must never give up trying to look for work, even if it means retraining or becoming self-employed, because it is their duty to provide for their families. If socioeconomic necessities dictate, then a woman is allowed to take on the man's role if the husband has no objection. Ad-Darsh refers to a *hadith* in which Zaynab, wife of Abdullah bin Mas'ud, one of the Companions, comes to the Prophet to ask whether she is allowed to pay her *zakat* to her husband and children. Mas'ud had, according to the *hadith*, dedicated his life to the Prophet and had no income, while Zaynab used to earn a good living from spinning and weaving. The Prophet not only allowed her to support her husband and children with *zakat*, but also said she would be doubly rewarded: once on account of paying her *zakat* and twice for looking after her next of kin.

As for the last part of the question on the division of household duties, ad-Darsh expresses amazement that it could be asked. He asserts that husbands are duty bound to cook, clean, do the shopping and help out in the house in any way possible. 'We need to banish the notion of men expecting to marry hoovers and dishwashers; they are marrying partners.' But he adds that this does not extend to looking after children, which is a task for women. In his opinion, men are not equipped, emotionally or physically, to look after babies and can never be a substitute for the love, emotional attachment, care and patience that mothers offer.

Another query sent to ad-Darsh also addresses the issue of women assuming the role of breadwinner for their families:

> As a successful management consultant, my wife earns more than me. She now provides for food, children's education, clothes and pays the mortgage. This state of affairs has tilted the balance of power in the relationship towards my wife. As women are increasingly taking the role as breadwinner – or joint earner – where does that leave men? How is the man expected to fulfil his role as protector and provider when his wife controls the family purse-strings? (*Q-News*, 21–8 January 1994)

Ad-Darsh responds that men can fulfil their Islamic family duties without necessarily earning the household income. Both the husband's and the wife's ability to fulfil their Islamic roles depends almost entirely on the degree of harmony in their relationship and the extent to which they understand each other; it has very little to do with who brings in the money. He states that the norm according to Islam is that men provide for their families, but he also refers to instances in Islamic history when women were the sole breadwinners in the family. Again the *hadith* about Zaynab and Abdullah bin Mas'ud is given as an example. Ad-Darsh argues that the fact that more and more Muslim women are now carrying or sharing the burden of providing for the family should not be a reason to call for a change in the basic duties of a husband and a wife.

Ad-Darsh answered the above-mentioned questions in his column entitled 'What You Ought to Know', in *Q-News*, between 1992 and 1997. The questions are asked by individuals in specific situations and include matters outside the religious-legal realm. Ad-Darsh's answers are in turn more comprehensive and go beyond simply declaring a ruling (*hukm*). He informs readers about the sources he draws on and how he interprets them, and also provides his own personal opinions. We can also see his fatwas as means of mediation in marital conflicts that are alluded to in the questions.

One gets the impression that ad-Darsh had specific knowledge of wives who complained to him that their husbands were not working, and of husbands who were complaining about their inability to earn an income and support their families. By receiving calls and providing advice to solve people's problems, ad-Darsh clearly acquired an insight into lived experiences, not least into men's experiences and their challenges, many of which seem to be related to their financial roles in their families.[18]

In the above-mentioned fatwas, ad-Darsh reiterates that the normative model for gender roles in Muslim tradition is that men are financially responsible for their families. The undertaking of this role by women, according to him, is not in accordance with the natural state of affairs. But he also makes clear that he is aware that in the current situation in Europe many Muslim men are unemployed and unwaged. Yet he stresses that men must never cease to look for work.

It seems that ad-Darsh's suggestion that husbands seek work and earn an income not only arises from the need to maintain the traditional norms of spousal roles but is also part of an identity project to protect Muslim families and their minority communities in the 'West'. In my twenty years among Muslim communities in Norway, as both a volunteer and a researcher, I have witnessed a trend of identity politics that consists of attempts to cement 'traditional' Muslim gender roles and morality in order to 'protect' the Muslim family.

Ad-Darsh rejects the gendered notion of a 'house husband' or a 'housewife'. He sees household duties as the responsibility of both spouses, on an equal footing. This is further emphasized, but not directly expressed, in the second fatwa, where he says that a man can fulfil his duties as a husband without bringing in an income. How would that be possible? Ad-Darsh suggests that men can fulfil their role as husbands, even if they are unable to provide for their families, by undertaking household duties. This implies that there can be flexibility in marital roles and spouses can make their own arrangements regarding their roles. Perhaps this new perspective on equal spousal roles in undertaking household tasks can also be read as an attempt to resolve a potential masculinity crisis in cases where the wife earns more than the husband and has more economic power in the relationship. But though ad-Darsh makes it clear that household duties are the responsibility of both partners, he maintains that there are certain roles that should be specific to each sex, such as men serving as providers and women caring for children.

Ad-Darsh's reluctance to call for or endorse a substantive departure from the traditional gendered division of spousal roles is articulated again in the concluding sentence in his second fatwa: 'The fact that more and more women are carrying or sharing the burden of providing for the family should not be

---

[18] This was reiterated by the muftis I interviewed during my PhD research.

the reason to call for change in the basic roles of husband and wife' (*Q-News*, 21–8 January 1994).

On the whole, ad-Darsh's fatwas oscillate between suggesting a flexible model of spousal roles that allows for egalitarian gender relations, and maintaining a notion of gender complementarity and hierarchy. The latter notion echoes dominant exegetical readings of Qur'anic verse 4:34: 'Men are the protectors and maintainers of women, because Allah has given the one more [strength] than the other, and because they support them from their means. Therefore the righteous women are devoutly obedient.' Yet, by referring to the *hadith* of Zaynab and her husband, ad-Darsh affirms the importance of taking into account examples from the lived realities of Muslims in the past, rather than being guided solely by abstract juristic doctrines. Moreover, ad-Darsh opens a space for a flexible and egalitarian model of spousal roles by suggesting that the roles of a husband and wife and their abilities to fulfil these roles are to be negotiated between them in accordance with what will achieve harmony in their relationship. But he does not elaborate on this idea and how it can be used to formulate new norms for Muslim spousal roles.

In short, ad-Darsh's fatwas clearly reflect an awareness of the changing realities of spousal roles in Muslim families in Europe and the tensions arising from the disconnect between these new realities and the traditional norms of spousal roles. The fatwas also reflect ad-Darsh's grappling with his role as a mufti and religious scholar who is committed to maintaining the established model of spousal roles and gender norms yet conveys an increasing realization (though never acknowledged openly or fully) that this model is no longer adequate to address the changing needs and life situations of Muslim families. Ad-Darsh's struggle is intensified by the identity politics in which Muslim minorities in Western Europe are entangled and their strong need to maintain traditional cultural and religious norms as a way to deal with marginalization, discrimination and the 'othering' of Muslims. One can read these tensions and contestations in the contradictions, ambiguities and oscillations that are expressed in the ideas conveyed in these fatwas.

Fatwa from the EFCR

In a query sent to the EFCR, a petitioner asks,

Is it permissible for the wife to open a personal bank account with her own income, or must she place her income in one account along with her husband's income, from which he could provide for the family? (ECFR, 2002, p. 73)

The Council responds as follows. Islam has given women their full rights, without women needing to even demand these rights. Among these are financial rights, and in particular the right to ownership and private property of all kinds, in complete independence of fathers and husbands. Therefore, a woman has a full right to open a bank account in which she deposits her salary, inheritance or any sort of monetary gift from her father or otherwise. This is because provision for the household is the husband's duty alone. In answering the request, the Council makes reference to verse 4:34.

The fatwa goes on to say that a woman may, as a personal gift, assist her husband in providing for the household. But this is neither an obligation nor a duty even if she has the financial means to do so. Reference is given to the four imams, the eponyms for the four legal schools in Sunni Islam, who never obliged women to support their husbands.

The Council then presents its view regarding a woman's role in supporting the family when she is working. According to the fatwa, a woman is expected to provide for her family only if there are additional living costs that need to be covered, such as clothes for the woman because she works, a nanny for the children, a maid, etc. However, it is preferable that her contribution does not exceed one-third of the total living costs, whereas the husband should provide at least two-thirds. Because a man has the right to double a woman's share in inheritance, he must accordingly be liable for twice as much in living costs.

At the end of the fatwa the Council returns to the question of bank accounts. It recommends that each spouse has an individual bank account, so that husbands do not make claims on their wives' money. A woman must also save for the possibility of difficult times and changes in her husband's behaviour. Furthermore, the Council fatwa does not favour a woman placing all her wealth in her husband's control so that he alone officially owns everything. Finally, it declares it to be *haram* for a husband to request his wife to place her wealth under his control, since each person has a right to what he or she possesses.

Fatwas from the ECFR have a different character from Syed ad-Darsh's fatwas. This is clearly evident in the fatwa described above, where the question is more formal than the two questions in *Q-News*. It has clearly been edited to make it a more generic question, and the profile of the *mustafti* is invisible.

The language of the fatwa is also more formal, perhaps to try to enhance its authority. The choice of style and language goes naturally with the Council's self-appointment as a representative fatwa body in Europe.

With reference to verse 4:34, the fatwa establishes the norm that providing for the family is the husband's duty alone. Furthermore, the woman has the right to independent ownership. This is emphasized by declaring a husband's request for a sole account in his name to be *haram*. The woman is also urged to save money for difficult times and to protect herself from her husband's erratic behaviour. The fact that the Council regards erratic behaviour by husbands towards their wives as possible gives a glimpse of the muftis' knowledge of the Muslim communities to which they are addressing the fatwa. This differs from the mainstream religious discourse's construction of a Muslim man as strong and rational, protecting women, who are considered to be weak and emotional.

The most interesting part of the fatwa is how it deals with a wife's contribution to the household. The Council's position is that this contribution is a gift from the wife, given out of her goodwill. This does not fit with the reality in Europe, where two salaries are commonly needed to pay for the costs of the household. When the wife has the duty of provision, is it still valid to describe it as a gift? Would it not make more sense to call it what it really is: *nafaqah* (spousal maintenance)? This would produce a more egalitarian interpretation of verse 4:34, the verse that has been the basis for dominant exegetical and juristic interpretations that justify gender inequality in Muslim family laws (Mir-Hosseini et al., 2013).

The Council also declares that Islam has given the woman her full rights 'without her even demanding these rights'. But this contradicts the Council's proposal that when a Muslim woman has to work outside the home it is 'preferable' that her contribution to the household is no more than one-third, because the husband has a right to double the share of his sister in inheritance. This is the first instance in my research in which the topic of women's provision and inheritance was addressed. It is argued with caution. By using the word 'preferable' the Council does not impose a clear rule but provides advice. Clearly, no new interpretations of inheritance laws are entertained in the fatwa. Of course, the Qur'anic verses on inheritance are considered by many ulama to be among the *ayat al-muhkamat* (clear and definitive meaning), and thus unchangeable. Therefore, many religious scholars hold the position that it would be against the Qur'an to change the norm that a brother inherit twice the share of his sister. Changing the doctrines on inheritance would be a direct challenge to the patriarchal system that prevails among Muslims. Accordingly, the question of stability and change in the Muslim family is a heated topic.

It seems that there are not many petitioners asking for fatwas about inheritance issues. I did not come across any such cases in my research. When I sought an explanation for this from the late Zaki Badawi, his theory was that it is because Muslim women in the United Kingdom benefit from English state laws on inheritance, which are based on gender equality. He believed that women quietly use these laws and do not seek fatwas on inheritance-related issues. Another explanation for women not seeking fatwas that could offer new interpretations for juristic doctrines on inheritance may be that Muslim women and men have not yet made a direct connection between a wife's assuming the role of a provider for her family, on the one hand, and a sister's claiming an equal share of inheritance to her brother's, on the other.[19] Both these explanations, however, need to be substantiated by empirical studies.

The overall implication of the Council fatwa is that it acknowledges women's rights in some aspects, while it weakens their rights in other aspects. For instance, it affirms a wife's right to have her own bank account, yet it calls upon working women to provide for their families. While it does not make it obligatory for these women to undertake this financial role, it strongly encourages them to do so and even suggests the amount they are expected to provide to their families (not more than one-third of the total living costs). Importantly, the fatwa revisits neither hierarchical gender roles in marriage nor inequality in inheritance laws. This cautiousness could be explained by the fatwa's intended audience. We can infer from ECFR channels of publications that their fatwas are aimed at the ulama and lay Muslims. They are part of the transnational printed Islamic knowledge that can be accessed and read by Muslims around the world. Thus, the rules declared should not be too radical.

I posit that we are witnessing what I would call 'fatwas without borders'. The ECFR fatwa was first issued by Yusuf al-Qaradawi and published in his *Fatawa Mu'asira* (Contemporary Fatwas) under the heading *fiqh al-aqalliyyat* (*fiqh* of minorities) and the title *'Infaq al-mar'a 'ala al-bayt min maliha'* (The wife providing for the household from her money) (al-Qaradawi, 2003, p. 614). As such, it was first published as a local fatwa for Muslim minorities in a volume published in the Arab world and distributed worldwide. The ECFR then

---

[19] Interview conducted by the author with the British legal expert Prakash Shah, 30 October 2012.

adopted the fatwa and published it in its first collection of fatwas, possibly because of al-Qaradawi's prominent position as the president of the ECFR. The consequence is that a local matter became transnational, potentially of interest to Muslims both within and outside Europe.

The ECFR fatwa, like ad-Darsh's fatwas, gives us a glimpse of the changes in the circumstances of spousal roles of Muslim families in the West as well as the difficulties that both married couples and muftis are confronting in reconciling these changes on the ground with mainstream Muslim norms and juristic doctrines on spousal roles. The ECFR fatwa also contains contradictions and reflects a reluctance to provide substantive solutions. In particular, it seems to illustrate the constraints placed on muftis by the transnational field of established religious knowledge and discourses of which they are part and which delineates the boundaries of possible new solutions that the muftis are able to propose to new problems.

CONCLUSION

The framework of the fatwas presented in this chapter remains the traditional understanding of *qiwamah*. Throughout Islamic history, mainstream gendered interpretations of verse 4:34 have been used to shape a jurisprudence that links a husband's obligation to provide for his family with his wife's duty to obey him. But, as we have seen, Muslim petitioners in Europe seem to be grappling with the disconnect between the lived realities of marital roles in Muslim families and the norms dictating spousal duties and rights in Muslim legal tradition. The petitioners seek fatwas as authoritative legal and religious opinions that can help them navigate the tensions and conflicts arising from the new realities of their marriages and family lives. They are aware of the traditional norms regulating gender relations, but their daily experience of their marital roles diverges from these norms. This is the case of the husband in ad-Darsh's second fatwa who feels threatened in his sense of masculinity because his wife controls the purse, and of the woman in the first fatwa who seeks ad-Darsh's approval of her working outside the home.

The muftis are also aware that their fatwas are functioning as a tool to address challenges and marital tensions that have been created by the changing realities of Muslim marriages in Europe. In muftis' answers, we can read their attempts to balance the interest of the petitioner with the perceived interest of the other party involved. Here the muftis are also guided by an important ethical principle in Muslim legal tradition: reconciliation between disputing parties. These muftis are also seeking to fulfil one of the priorities of their role as ulama, which is, as they see it, to protect the stability of the Muslim family in the West.

Although it is not obligatory to follow a fatwa, a fatwa has its own structure of authority. There is a line of authority between the mufti and the *mustafti*, as well as a horizontal line of authority among ulama. The petitioner and the mufti are bound together in various ways in the crafting of the fatwa. The mufti's authority among other ulama worldwide is also at stake. Hence, a mufti must be cautious in crafting a fatwa to a *mustafti* in the West.

In short, these muftis' goals of working towards reconciliation, protecting the stability of the Muslim family and staying within the parameters of the dominant legal opinions in transnational Muslim fatwa discourse delineate the boundaries within which they can deliver new fatwas. Although the fatwas discussed reflect, in some aspects, a rethinking of the classical *fiqh* model of marital roles, they do not substantively diverge from or challenge classical *fiqh* doctrines on gender norms and roles.

But how relevant and important could fatwas be in the pursuit of Muslim women's rights and equality before the law? I would say they could be quite important. Recent research on Muslim-majority countries in North Africa shows that the phenomenon of Muslim women becoming the main bread-winner in the family is not limited to women in Europe (Amin, 1995; Sonbol, 2003; Bouasria, 2013). Therefore the fatwa discourses presented in this chapter could be of importance beyond Europe because the debates around issues of gender roles, equality and rights might create a wider consciousness about the matters at hand.

Furthermore, as described in other chapters of this volume, Muslim feminists have realized that promoting women's rights entails engaging meaningfully and critically with Muslim legal tradition, making use of sound religious arguments and building new egalitarian knowledge from within the tradition to counter dominant religious discourse and knowledge that condone gender inequality. Fatwas are excellent examples of how the muftis are engaging with social and cultural realities, using Islamic arguments. By analysing the fatwas and what the muftis are saying and not saying, by deconstructing their *ijtihad* and how they define and consider the different elements of the topic involved, it is possible to use fatwas to help dismantle and rebuild religious discourse on gender norms and rights. Since the fatwa and the mufti are situated at the interface between worldly dealings and the process of theorizing about them, women, drawing on both their life experiences and their knowledge of Islamic arguments, are in a position to contest fatwas and formulate new questions to promote gender equality and rights. This process of contestation and its outcomes is another chapter in the ongoing dynamic development of the discursive tradition of Islam.

REFERENCES

Abdel-Fadil, Mona. 2012. 'Living "the Message" and Empowering Muslim Selves: A Behind the Screens Study of Online Islam'. PhD thesis. University of Oslo.

Al-Alwani, Taha Jabir. 2003. *Towards a Fiqh for Minorities: Some Basic Reflections*. London: International Institute of Islamic Thought.

Al-Qaradawi, Yusuf. 2000. *Fatawa Mu'asira*, vol. 1. Beirut: al-Maktaba al-Islami.

Al-Qaradawi, Yusuf. 2001. *Fi Fiqh al-Aqalliyyat al-Muslima. Hayat al-Muslimin wast al-Mujtama'at al-Ukhra* (On Muslim Minority Jurisprudence. The Life of Muslims in Other Societies). Cairo: Dar al-Shuruq.

Al-Qaradawi, Yusuf. 2003. *Fatawa Mu'asira*, vol. 3. Beirut: al-Maktaba al-Islami.

Amin, Qasim. 1995. *The New Woman: A Document in the Early Debate on Egyptian Feminism*. Cairo: American University in Cairo Press.

Asad, Talal. 1986. *The Idea of an Anthropology of Islam*. Washington: Georgetown University, Center for Arab Studies.

Badawi, Zaki. 1995. 'Muslim Justice in a Secular State'. In *God's Law versus State Law: The Construction of an Islamic Identity in Western Europe*, edited by Michael King, pp. 73–80. London: Grey Seal.

Bogstad, Therese. 2009. 'Mellom juridisk og religiøs diskurs: Argumentasjon om islamsk skilsmisse hos Islamonline.net'. Master's thesis. University of Oslo.

Bouasria, Leila. 2013. *Les ouvrières marocaines en movement. Qui paye? Qui fait le menage? Et qui décide?* Paris: L'Harmattan.

Burhanudin, Jajat. 2005. 'Aspiring for Islamic Reform: Southeast Asian Requests for *Fatwās* in *al-Manār*'. *Islamic Law and Society* 12 (1): pp. 9–26.

Caeiro, Alexandre. 2002. *La normativité islamique à l'épreuve de l'Occident: le cas du Conseil européen de la fatwa et de la recherche*. Paris: École des hautes etudes en sciences sociales, DEA.

Caeiro, Alexandre. 2004. 'The Social Construction of Shari'a: Bank Interest, Home Purchase, and Islamic Norms in the West'. *Die Welt Des Islams* 44 (3): pp. 351–75.

Caeiro, Alexandre. 2011a. 'Transnational Ulama, European Fatwas, and Islamic Authority: A Case Study of the European Council for Fatwa and Research'. In *Producing Islamic Knowledge: Transmission and Dissemination*, edited by Martin von Bruinessen and Stefano Allievi, pp. 121–41. London: Ashgate.

Caeiro, Alexandre. 2011b. 'Fatwas for European Muslims: The Minority Fiqh Project and the Integration of Islam in Europe'. PhD thesis. University of Utrecht.

ECFR. 2013. *Al-Qararat wa al-Fatawa al-Sadira 'an al-Majlis al-Urubi lil-Ifta' wa al-Buhuth*. Beirut: Mu'assasat al-Rayyan.

Eggen, Nora. 2001. *Islamsk rettskildelære*. Oslo: Institutt for offentlig rett, Universitetet i Oslo.

Gräf, Bettina and Jakob Skovgaard-Petersen. 2009. 'Introduction'. In *Global Mufti: The Phenomenon of Yūsuf al-Qaraḍāwī*, edited by Jakob Skovgaard-Petersen and Bettina Gräf, pp. 109–48. New York: Columbia University Press.

Hallaq, Wael B. 1994. 'From *Fatwas* to *Furu*': Growth and Change in Islamic Substantive Law'. *Islamic Law and Society* 1 (1): pp. 29–65.

Heyd, Uriel. 1969. 'Some Aspects of the Ottoman Fetva'. *Bulletin of the School of Oriental and African Studies* 32 (1): pp. 35–56.

Karman, Karen-Lise Johansen. 2008. 'Rethinking Islamic Jurisprudence for Muslim Minorities: The Politics and the Work of Contemporary Fatwa Councils'. PhD thesis. Aarhus University.

Larsen, Lena. 2010. 'Islamic Jurisprudence and Transnational Flows: Exploring the European Council for *Fatwa* and Research'. In *From Transnational Relations to Transnational Laws: Northern European Laws at the Crossroads*, edited by Anne Hellum, Shaheen Sardar Ali and Anne Griffiths, pp. 139–63. London: Ashgate.

Larsen, Lena. 2011. *Islamic Legal Thought and the Challenges of Everyday Life: Fatwas as Proposed Solutions for Muslim Women in Western Europe*. PhD thesis. University of Oslo.

Masud, Muhammad Khalid, Brinkley Messick and David Powers (eds). 1996. *Islamic Legal Interpretation: Muftis and Their Fatwas*. Cambridge, MA: Harvard University Press.

Mayer, Ann Elizabeth. 1990. 'The Sharia: A Methodology or a Body of Substantive Rules'. In *Islamic Law and Jurisprudence*, edited by Nicholas Heer, pp. 177–98. Seattle: University of Washington Press.

Mir-Hosseini, Ziba, Kari Vogt, Lena Larsen and Christian Moe (eds). 2013. *Gender and Equality in Muslim Family Law: Justice and Ethics in the Islamic Legal Tradition*. London: I.B. Tauris.

Powers, David. 2002. *Law, Society, and Culture in the Maghrib, 1300–1500*. Cambridge, UK: Cambridge University Press.

Roald, Anne Sofie. 2001a. *Women in Islam: The Western Experience*. London: Routledge.

Roald, Anne Sofie. 2001b. 'The Wise Men: Democratisation and Gender Equalisation in the Islamic Message: Yusuf al-Qaradawi and Ahmad al-Kubaisi on the Air'. *Encounters* 7 (1): http://dspace.mah.se:8080/handle/2043/12617

Skovgaard-Petersen, Jakob. 1997. *Defining Islam for the Egyptian State: Muftis and Fatwas of the Dār al-Iftā*. Leiden: Brill.

Sonbol, Amira El-Azhary. 2003. *Women of Jordan. Islam, Labor and the Law*. Syracuse, NY: Syracuse University Press.

Ternisien, Xavier. 2005. *Les Frères Musulmans*. Paris: Fayard.

Vogt, Kari. 1995. *Kommet for å Bli: Islam i Vest-Europa*. Oslo: J.W. Cappelens.

Zomeño, Amalia. 2008. 'The Stories in the Fatwas and the Fatwas in History'. In *Narratives of Truth in Islamic Law*, edited by Baudouin Dupret, Barbara Drieskens and Annelies Moors, pp. 25–50. London: I.B. Tauris.

Understanding *Qiwamah* and *Wilayah* through Life Stories*

Mulki Al-Sharmani and Jana Rumminger

I n many Muslim contexts, husbands have a legal and social obligation to provide for their wives and children; wives have a responsibility of obedience in return. As a result, sexual relations are often assumed to be the right of husbands and the responsibility of wives. Men can marry up to four wives if they can provide for all of them. Husbands have a unilateral right to divorce their wives; in contexts where women can initiate divorce the process is often complicated. Men, as fathers, have privileged guardianship rights over their children, and in some contexts they also have the legal power to grant or withhold consent to the marriage contracts of their daughters.

This is how the juristic concepts of *qiwamah* and *wilayah* operate through contemporary Muslim family laws and social norms. But how do women actually

* From November 2011 to August 2013, Mulki Al-Sharmani participated in the project discussed in this chapter in her part-time role as Global Life Stories Project coordinator. Al-Sharmani's contribution to this chapter and book has been part of the collaborative research work she has been doing since September 2013 under her five-year Academy of Finland research fellowship 'Islamic Feminism: Tradition, Authority, and Hermeneutics' at the Faculty of Theology, University of Helsinki, Finland. Jana Rumminger participated in the project in her part-time role as coordinator of the Knowledge Building Initiative on *Qiwamah* and *Wilayah*, beginning in March 2011. The authors would like to thank Deena Hurwitz, Kamala Chandrakirana, Zainab Anwar, the Alimat secretariat, Isatou Touray, Samia Huq, Hoda Mobasseri, Alia Hogben and Mussurut Zia for providing feedback on early drafts.

experience these two concepts? How do the social and legal manifestations of *qiwamah* and *wilayah* influence their choices and life trajectories? How do they make sense of and deal with *qiwamah*- and *wilayah*-based norms and laws? In what ways do women's experiences depart from these norms and laws, and with what consequences?

These are the key questions investigated in Musawah's Global Life Stories Project, which documented the life stories of fifty-eight Muslim women in ten countries (Bangladesh, Canada, Egypt, Gambia, Indonesia, Iran, Malaysia, Nigeria, Philippines and the United Kingdom) over a period of three years (January 2011 to December 2013). The Musawah Knowledge Building Working Group, individual Musawah Advocates from different countries, an Indonesian pilot project team and teams from the ten countries worked collaboratively to develop the methodology used in the documentation and analysis of the life stories.

In this chapter, we provide an initial report on this process from our perspective as coordinators of the project and the larger initiative in which it was conducted. We describe the methodology that was used, including the collective process through which it was developed. We discuss the significance of this process as both a scientific enquiry that espouses feminist research principles and Islamic ethics and as part of an ongoing collective effort of building a Muslim feminist movement. We also share some of the key findings emerging from analysis of the life stories and discuss their implications. Finally, we reflect on the layered significance of the project and on challenges encountered by the project team.[1]

The first section of the chapter outlines the objectives of and process through which the Global Life Stories Project developed. The second section discusses the ethics and principles that guided our methodology, and sheds light on how we applied them. The third section explains the analytical framework that we used in making sense of the documented life stories. The fourth section examines some of the findings that have emerged from the initial analysis of the life stories. The final section presents reflections on the project and the multifaceted impact of *qiwamah* and *wilayah* in women's lives.

---

[1] The ideas and analysis put forward in this chapter draw on reports documenting four Musawah workshops held in 2011 and 2012; a 2012 report from the pilot study conducted in Indonesia; draft final reports submitted by the ten country teams in 2014; documentation of monthly Skype sessions between members of the country teams and the project coordinator; and analysis of the collected life stories conducted by the country teams and the coordinator.

BACKGROUND AND PROCESS

The Global Life Stories Project is one of three elements of a broader multi-year activity called the Musawah Knowledge Building Initiative on *Qiwamah* and *Wilayah*, which aimed to produce new feminist knowledge about the idea and realities of *qiwamah* and *wilayah*. This knowledge will in turn help Musawah Advocates[2] in their work towards egalitarian family laws and gender norms. The other two elements of the initiative involved commissioning a series of papers on different aspects of *qiwamah* and *wilayah*, which form the basis of this book, and opening spaces for scholars and activists from diverse backgrounds to forge new understandings of the concepts. Musawah's Knowledge Building Working Group[3] played the lead role in conceptualizing the initiative and coordinating the design and implementation of its activities.

The Global Life Stories Project had several objectives. The first was to understand better how women experience *qiwamah* and *wilayah* and to what degree there is a disconnect between textual (religious or legal) constructions of the concepts and lived realities. Understanding this disconnect can help problematize religious and legal understandings of *qiwamah* and *wilayah*, their underlying assumptions and the social norms that are shaped by them (ideas about male and female sexuality, sexual rights in marriage, women's economic roles, etc.). Furthermore, we hoped to understand the range and multiple ways in which this disconnect is manifested in women's lives and how it affects women's life choices and experiences.

Second, we sought to highlight the voices of Muslim women from different walks of life and diverse national contexts – both those who shared their stories and those involved in the documentation – in order to reveal insights they have gained from their life experiences, recognize the alternative knowledge they can offer and reflect their concerns and interests.

A third aim was to collectively build alternative knowledge and develop a methodology that reflected our understanding of Islamic ethics and feminism.

---

[2] Musawah Advocates share Musawah's goal of equality in the family and have a stake in and commitment to the growth of the movement. All Advocates agree with the Musawah Framework for Action (http://www.musawah.org/about-musawah/framework-action), use the framework in their activities and contribute to the achievement of Musawah's strategic goals and objectives.

[3] The Musawah Knowledge Building Working Group supports, advises and assists Musawah in developing work plans, building resources and implementing knowledge-building activities. The Working Group is currently composed of five women (including the editors of this volume) situated in different countries with various educational and research backgrounds.

We see this as one way of countering the patriarchal ethos that continues to inform Muslim family laws, practices, and methods of scholarship.

We also aimed to facilitate collective learning and capacity building for all the participants in Muslim legal tradition, and particularly in new kinds of Islamic feminist knowledge that revisit patriarchal interpretations and engage critically with the tradition (see, for example, Abou-Bakr, Lamrabet, Chaudhry, Shaikh and Wadud in this volume).

Finally, the project aimed to produce knowledge that would contribute to social change in the participating countries. Each national team tailored the methodology to their local contexts and based on their specific agendas for women's rights advocacy, public education, or other work for legal and policy reform at the country level. The knowledge developed will also contribute to Musawah's activities and advocacy at a global level.

The implementation of the Global Life Stories Project took place over several years. Musawah's Knowledge Building Initiative on *Qiwamah* and *Wilayah* originated at a conceptual workshop in Cairo in January 2010, during which scholars and activists discussed key ideas related to *qiwamah* and *wilayah* with the goal of developing a multi-year research plan. From the beginning, we wanted to include in the initiative an element that was related to women's lives, since Musawah's four-pronged holistic approach to all its work incorporates lived realities alongside Islamic teachings, universal human rights and national guarantees of equality. This is essential to capture and share women's experiences with laws and issues – as distinct from how the issues are understood in theory. The 'experts' in theology and law should be informed by and answer the challenges that arise from women's experiences.

In thinking through the Knowledge Building Initiative, we faced the challenge of how to understand and include the scope and diversity of women's lived realities in a way consistent with our principles. After some discussion, a Musawah International Advisory Group member, Kamala Chandrakirana, volunteered to explore this challenge and help with the initial conceptualization of a methodology to document women's experiences.

In early 2011, she brought together a pilot project team comprising herself and four women activists who are part of Alimat, an Indonesian coalition working on reforming religious knowledge to advance gender equality and justice. These five women activists have different skills, areas of expertise, and community backgrounds. They later recruited several others – a legal expert, a feminist journalist, an illustrator and a field researcher – to provide technical support.[4]

This team decided to focus on life stories in their entirety, rather than specific elements of *qiwamah*, recognizing that different events and experiences in women's lives are woven together and cannot be easily dissected. Together, they articulated an approach with three dimensions: it would be a collective and mutual learning experience; it would be interdisciplinary; and it would be grounded in national activism, so that all of those involved would be part of a movement-building process. The team developed a methodological framework that could be adopted and expanded by other country teams and that had two main aims: to establish women's lived realities as a foundation to Musawah's knowledge building, and to equalize the balance between academic experts and community activists in Musawah's movement building.

Over the course of a year, the Indonesian team worked carefully and deliberately to understand the issues better, decide how to undertake the process in an ethical and principled manner and document the life stories of five Muslim women from different regions of the country. With few resources and little guidance, and drawing on their practical knowledge and individual areas of expertise, the team members articulated concrete ways in which *qiwamah* and *wilayah* manifest themselves in the lives of Indonesian women, crafted research instruments with which life stories could be documented, designed tools and materials for eliciting responses during interviews and in advocacy work (e.g. visual illustrations of *qiwamah* and *wilayah* experiences) and developed materials that would be of direct use to the women taking part in the study. The project was integrated into Alimat's advocacy plans relating to the review and revision of the Indonesian marriage law. They shared their progress and insights with the larger Musawah community during three workshops and a final report. The team's approach became a cornerstone of the methodological framework that was further developed and used in the second phase of the project.

At the conclusion of the pilot project, the project coordinator recruited Musawah Advocates to take part in the global project as country teams. Given

---

[4] The Indonesian pilot project team included core members Kamala Chandrakirana, Nur Rofiah, Nani Zulminarni, Tati Krisnawaty and Dini Anitasari, with support from Sri Wiyanti, Deni Rodendo Ganjar, Ninuk Pambudi and Lailatul Fitri. We are indebted to this team for the conceptualization of the Life Stories Project and for assisting the Knowledge Building Working Group in coorganizing and cohosting the methodology workshop in Bali and in developing the framework for analysis.

limited resources and the fact that the project was a work-in-progress, we decided that the initial implementation phase should be limited to a selection of regionally representative Muslim-majority and -minority countries, with the potential for expanding to more countries later.

Musawah Advocates from twelve countries (Afghanistan, Bangladesh, Canada, Egypt, Gambia, Indonesia, Iran, Jordan, Malaysia, Nigeria, Philippines and the United Kingdom) agreed to join the Global Life Stories Project. The organizations from Jordan and Afghanistan eventually withdrew their participation because of other priorities in their national work, so the project was completed in only ten countries.[5] Ranging in size from one to seven people, the national 'teams'[6] implemented the project through the guidance of one or more coordinating members.[7] In most of the selected countries, the project was undertaken by non-governmental advocacy and research organizations that work on women's issues. The exceptions were Bangladesh and Iran, where, respectively, a team of academic researchers and an individual undertook the project.[8] In Indonesia, a new team of NGO representatives came together to implement the project in this phase, with members of the pilot team serving as mentors. Team members came from disciplines such as Islamic theology, anthropology, law, literature, agriculture, development

---

[5] We wish to extend our thanks to the organizations, institutions and individuals in the ten participating countries that completed this project. They are: BRAC University (Bangladesh); Canadian Council of Muslim Women (Canada); Women and Memory Forum, in cooperation with the Center for Egyptian Women's Legal Assistance (Egypt); Gambia Committee on Traditional Practices Affecting the Health of Women and Children (GAMCOTRAP) (Gambia); Alimat (Indonesia); Hoda Mobasseri (Iran); Sisters in Islam (Malaysia); the Nigerian coalition Musawah Global Movement, with particular contributions from Isa Wali Empowerment Initiative (IWEI) and the Centre for Women and Adolescents (CWAE) (Nigeria); Nisa Ul Haqq Fi Bangsamoro (Philippines); and Muslim Women's Network UK (United Kingdom).

[6] We use 'team' to denote the unit that worked on the project in each country, even though an individual worked alone in Iran.

[7] The contributions and insights of these coordinating members were immensely useful in further developing the initial methodology and framework for analysis. These colleagues are: Samia Huq and Sohela Nazneen (Bangladesh); Alia Hogben and Eman Ahmed (Canada); Maissan Hassan, Hoda El-Sadda and Omaima Abou-Bakr (Egypt); Isatou Touray and Amie Sissoho (Gambia); Aida Milasari, Nur Rofiah, Dini Anitasari and Tati Krisnawaty (Indonesia); Hoda Mobasseri (Iran); Rusaslina Idrus and Suriani Kempe (Malaysia); Asma'u Joda, Amina Hanga, Maryam Tauhida Ibrahim and Mariam Marwa-Abdu (Nigeria); Alpha Pontanal and Johaira Wahab (Philippines); and Mussurut Zia (United Kingdom).

[8] In Bangladesh, the approach to engaging with issues of women's lives and rights has predominantly been secular. For this reason, religion is not a central question for many organizations. In Iran, women's rights groups face security and political challenges in undertaking activist work.

studies and gender studies and worked in a range of fields such as academia, women's rights and advocacy work, international development, education, family law and human rights.

The Knowledge Building Working Group, the Indonesian pilot project team and the country teams gathered for an initial methodology workshop in Bali, Indonesia, in April 2012. Over five days, we worked together to better define our objectives, reflect on feminist principles and Islamic guiding values and understand the concepts. We then developed a methodology for the global project, building on the Indonesian framework. Participants debated how to implement different aspects of the methodology (developing instruments, selecting people to share their stories, conducting interviews, ensuring consent, etc.) in a way consistent with the agreed principles and values.

After this workshop, the country teams further elaborated the goals and work plans they would implement in their specific contexts in accordance with their own advocacy agendas. The teams spent a great deal of time in the early months trying to better understand the concepts within their own legal and social environments, and to adapt the research instruments (e.g. interview guides, illustrations, interview matrixes) to their contexts. These instruments were then used to conduct interviews and document the stories. Throughout the process of building the project at the national level, the teams collaborated through online discussions and a series of Skype meetings with the project coordinator and each other.

The ten teams eventually documented life stories from fifty-eight women. These women's stories, experiences and insights contributed valuable resources to both national and global movements for equality and justice. We thus recognize and refer to the women as 'resource persons'.

In December 2012, a mid-term review workshop was held in Kuala Lumpur, Malaysia, with representatives from the national teams and some of the scholars who drafted the background papers in the overall Knowledge Building Initiative. The workshop served as a space to explore in more depth the concepts of *qiwamah* and *wilayah* and their linkages to the documentation of stories. We discussed the teams' progress and challenges and developed a collective framework for analysis which the teams could adapt to their specific contexts as they saw fit.

After this workshop, the teams and project coordinator continued to hold individual and group Skype meetings twice a month. These sessions served multiple purposes: addressing obstacles teams encountered in implementation; sharing analysis processes; and further developing the collective

226 | MEN IN CHARGE?

framework for analysis. In addition, the group used many sessions to continue their collective learning process by discussing key articles related to *qiwamah* and *wilayah* in Muslim legal tradition and relating them to the themes revealed in the life stories.

Each of the country teams produced a final report. Musawah at the global level plans a number of outputs to highlight stories and analysis from the ten countries and share the research and advocacy instruments.

METHODOLOGICAL APPROACH: GUIDING PRINCIPLES

The Global Life Stories Project began with the question of how women experience *qiwamah* and *wilayah* in their daily lives and to what extent their experiences correlate with the theory behind the concepts. We were conscious that the project was an ongoing learning journey in which we articulated and defined our ideas and added layers of understanding as we conducted the work.

Our methodology is informed by two main principles that for us reflect Islamic and feminist values. Our approach foregrounds Islamic ethics of justice and the equal worth and dignity of all human beings, who are all God's creatures and moral agents on earth with a responsibility to do good, forbid evil and build human civilization (see Lamrabet in this volume). We undertook this project as women who believe that these Islamic ethics should have primacy in any religious knowledge that shapes Muslim legal and social norms and sensibilities. We believe that laws in Muslim countries and contexts are based on outdated and patriarchal conceptions of gender relations, but that knowledge – especially that grounded in experience – offers a path towards equality and justice. Our methodology was developed as an ethical feminist enquiry[9] characterized by a number of key elements that are consistent with Musawah's knowledge-building approach.[10]

First, such an enquiry is *appreciative of alternative forms and sources of knowledge*. This means that we recognize non-traditional forms of expertise, begin from contexts rather than texts and produce knowledge in a democratic and open manner, in which women's experiences and ways of knowing are

---

[9] For a selection of literature on feminist ethics of research, see DeVault (1999), Ramazanoğlu (2002), Guerrero (2002), Doucet and Mauthner (2008) and Ortlipp (2008).

[10] See Musawah (n.d., p. 14) for more information on Musawah's knowledge-building approach.

respected and given voice. Hence, this project was undertaken as a collective process by a diverse group of women across many countries and contexts. We value the distinct and important form of knowledge that was provided by the women – the resource persons – through the reflective sharing of their stories. In addition, the multidisciplinary experience and expertise that team members brought (as theologians, lawyers, anthropologists, activists, writers, development specialists, community workers, etc.) strengthened the methodology, documentation and analysis.

Second, we felt that a feminist enquiry must also focus on *building and valuing relationships that are based on trust, respect, care and reciprocity*. The Indonesian pilot team tried several approaches to recruiting and interacting with the resource persons. Through this process, they affirmed that when the interviewer and resource person had a relationship based on trust, care, respect and reciprocity (whether pre-existing or developed over the course of the interviews) the stories were more comprehensive and insightful and the resource persons felt valued and supported. Country teams consciously worked to ensure such strong relationships. In some cases, resource persons already had ties with the teams (as clients, volunteers, staff, or through other interactions). In other cases, teams devoted time and effort to building such relationships, for example by conducting multiple extensive interviews over the course of several months to a year.

The teams also planned for *reciprocity* with the resource persons. For example, in the Indonesian pilot project, the resource persons shared their stories with the team, and the team shared a set of materials produced during the study with the resource persons. This included theological arguments for gender equality and justice drawn from the Qur'an; different understandings of *qiwamah* and *wilayah* in Muslim legal tradition; drawings depicting the concepts; and contacts for women's rights organizations. Resource persons used these in their personal journeys and shared them in their work (e.g. as a religion teacher). The Malaysian team addressed the issue of reciprocity by ensuring that needs of resource persons that arose during the project (e.g. counselling, legal assistance) were met by either the lead or partner organizations.

Third, an ethical feminist enquiry should be *participatory on multiple levels*. This ensures ownership among all participants and allows the incorporation of diverse perspectives. In this project, resource persons played participatory roles in the interview and narration process. Introductory and follow-up questions, for example, gave space to resource persons to speak freely and spontaneously, then follow through on threads of events, thoughts and reflections without interruptions. Since resource persons told their stories over the course of several extensive meetings, there were opportunities for additions and clarifications from both sides. Resource persons' wishes were also respected when they did not want to elaborate on or talk about certain issues.

The process of producing alternative knowledge was egalitarian and participatory. All of the team members – with their diversity of skills, knowledge, experience and contexts – worked together to design collectively the methodology and analytical framework and learned from each other as work progressed. In Skype meetings devoted to analysis, for example, individual teams shared how they understood various aspects of a particular life story and related it to elements of *qiwamah* or *wilayah*, identified insights to help with analysis and found linkages between lived realities and theoretical knowledge. Our collective knowledge and expertise were broad and deep because of the diverse backgrounds of the team members.

Fourth, we felt a feminist enquiry must be *reflective* in order to improve the methodology, implementation and analysis; make visible our assumptions (discipline-based, political, personal, etc.) so that we are cognizant of how they shape the way we undertake the enquiry; and help monitor to what extent we uphold the principles we consider important. Country teams kept reflective notes while working with the resource persons to think through the dynamics of interviewing and narration, the suitability of research instruments, themes that were emerging, etc. Skype meetings included space for reflection on the process (e.g. selection of resource persons; the kinds of questions we were asking; how underlying assumptions influenced our reading and analysis of the stories).

Finally, we undertook a feminist enquiry that would be *transformative*, namely by producing knowledge that will facilitate legal reform and social changes. We are explicitly building knowledge not just for the sake of knowledge, but to be empowered, build a movement and work towards gender justice. Thus, the knowledge produced in this project was linked to national advocacy work as well as Musawah's global activities. Each country team focused on *qiwamah*- and *wilayah*-related issues that would be key points for advocacy in their national contexts. Almost every team involved different stakeholders at different stages of the project to build capacity and work towards goals (e.g. including religious scholars and family court judges in conceptual workshops; involving family law lawyers and journalists in the analysis and write-up process; working with filmmakers to make movies about the stories). Capacity building was integral to all parts of the work. Team members, for example, grappled with the concepts of *qiwamah* and *wilayah* through study circles, workshops and seminars that they organized in their countries, and also learned about the concepts through the process of conducting the interviews. Resource persons also learned about the concepts through the interviews, and in some countries were given materials on the concepts to further their understanding.

ANALYTICAL FRAMEWORK: READING LIFE STORIES

We chose to document women's life stories in their entirety both because life events and experiences are so interrelated and cannot be isolated, and in order to capture nuanced, layered knowledge about *qiwamah* and *wilayah*. This helps shed light on how the women make sense of their experiences and choices and the factors that enabled or made difficult certain choices and paths. For the resource persons, sharing a life story in its entirety also allows them to reflect on their paths and any changes in their self-understanding.

This is consistent with anthropological and sociological literature on life stories and the insights they can provide. In an article drawing on stories she collected about female Palestinian labourers in Israel, Annelies Moors (1995) points out that collecting and analysing 'topical' life stories enabled her to capture complexities and diversities in each story, and between stories, as well as to identify strategies the women used, the choices they made and the processes through which this took place. She says that the knowledge gained enables researchers to problematize 'metanarratives' and essentialized uniform 'stories'. Similarly, in our project, the life stories of women from diverse backgrounds and countries question dominant textually and legally based understandings of Muslim gender relations in the family domain, as shaped by the two concepts of *qiwamah* and *wilayah*.

Moors explains that capturing the voice of a woman through her story does not mean that the narrated story mirrors the 'truth'. Rather, Moors calls the stories 'images' that portray experiences and life trajectories as well as the meanings that women give to life. In the process of narration, the women themselves choose to talk and decide what to say or not say. While the researcher frames the narration and analysis, the narrator exercises agency and has a voice in the process and product. Somers and Gibson (1994) further argue that through the process of narration, people make sense of who they are, which contributes to their identity formation. In other words, the importance of a life story is that it provides space for the woman to give meaning to her experiences and who she is through the process of narration; and for the researcher to capture her voice and how the resource person reads this life story.

The anthropologist Edward Bruner (1984) states that narration helps shed light on the meanings of events, experiences and choices and make visible perceptions and motivations. According to Bruner, researchers and others who narrate autobiographical stories may conceive of life in three ways: 1) 'life-as lived', which focuses on events in a particular life; 2) 'life-as experienced', which entails the images, feelings, desires and thoughts of the person; 3) 'life-as told', or how the narrator gives or constructs meanings for her or his experiences and life trajectory, and how the researcher captures and explains this process and thus creates another layer of 'reading' the story.

Our goal of capturing the 'voices' of the women in this project does not mean that we equate their life experiences with 'truth' or whatever knowledge we seek. Rather, we want to depict and explain multiple layers of a life: not only significant life events, but how a woman experienced these events and explained them, the choices she made, the complexities and implications of these choices, and the changes in her self-understanding throughout her life trajectory as well as during the process of reflective narration. The analysis we produce does not simply seek to make visible particular 'lived realities'. We also hope to explain these experiences in ways that offer new insights and question assumptions and understandings about Muslim gender regimes as constructed by qiwamah and wilayah.

These points and understandings helped guide how we analysed the stories. Thus, in developing a collective framework for analysis – which country teams then applied as best suited their contexts – we wanted to identify patterns, interpretations, norms, laws and/or power structures in the stories which were traceable to the concepts of qiwamah and wilayah. We could then examine how these may have impacted on the resource persons' choices and access to rights, resources and opportunities and accordingly influenced their life trajectories.

We were also interested in capturing how those who shared their stories made sense of their experiences and in particular the changes in their sense of self and ways of knowing and relating to tradition and authority. We drew on a study relating to women's cognitive development theory entitled *Women's*

Ways of Knowing: The Development of Self, Voice, and Mind (Belenky et al., 1986). The authors explore how women from different walks of life build knowledge and acquire understanding. They identify five positions (rather than linear and sequential stages) of knowledge that women hold: 1) silence; 2) received knowledge; 3) subjective knowledge; 4) procedural knowledge; and 5) constructed knowledge.[11] In the first position, women have no voice and are silent and often silenced. At the position of received knowledge, women accept and totally rely on normative authority and dominant forms of knowledge. Subjective knowledge means women begin to question and sometimes reject this received authority and knowledge; these actions are driven and shaped by their life experiences. In the position of procedural knowledge, women seek reasoned knowledge through use of separated or connected mechanisms of external systems of knowing. In the constructed knowledge position, women integrate knowledge based on their life experiences with knowledge they learn from others. They realize that knowledge is ultimately context based and constructed. The authors refined some of these elements in a later publication (Goldberger et al., 1996).

Another guiding question in the analysis was whether the life experiences departed (e.g. with regard to gender roles, relations and rights) from the juristic *qiwamah-* and *wilayah-*based gender regimes. When such divergences were found, we wanted to identify and understand their determining factors and the consequences and implications.

We wanted to reflect on the differences between the stories within each country and between countries in terms of the resource persons' experiences, choices and views. We hoped to make sense of these differences in light of the heterogeneity of the resource persons in level of education, social class, family background, regional history, etc. Furthermore, we wanted to examine the ways in which the individual life stories might speak to a larger narrative of gender inequality and marginalization or empowerment in the national context. We explicitly recognized that one woman's experiences cannot represent other women's and that, though we can identify trends, we cannot extrapolate specific experiences in a small collection of life stories to all women in all contexts.

---

[11] Belenky et al. (1986) explain, 'We recognize that the designation of *silence* is not parallel to the terms we have chosen for the other epistemological positions; nevertheless, we selected it because the absence of voice in these women is so salient' (p. 24).

KEY FINDINGS

The ten country teams that completed the project documented a total of fifty-eight life stories from resource persons ranging in age from sixteen to seventy-eight and representing all walks of life. These women came from different regions in the countries, including both urban and rural settings. Their education levels ranged from no schooling to little schooling to university graduates. Most of them were economically active in diverse kinds of work: street vendor, farmer, domestic worker, migrant domestic worker, taxi driver, paralegal, teacher, administrator, community development worker, business-woman, village head, politician, singer, etc.

In terms of selection of resource persons, this project was not intended to undertake a statistically representative study of Muslim women's experiences of *qiwamah* and *wilayah*. Rather, our goal was to privilege the process of enquiry, the development of a new kind of methodology, and a collective effort of reflective knowledge production and movement building. This, along with the sensitive subject matter for those telling their stories, meant the research teams and resource persons needed to establish and maintain long-term relationships of trust, care, respect and reciprocity.

Given these requirements and limited time and resources, most country teams documented four to six stories over the two-year process. The Gambian team documented twelve life stories; the researcher working alone in Iran documented three life stories.

Teams selected resource persons based on a number of factors, again not concerned with statistical significance. Almost all of the teams sought people whose stories exhibited issues that were of particular concern and/or the target of advocacy campaigns in their respective countries. These issues, many of which directly or indirectly related to the concepts of *qiwamah* and *wilayah*, included: the realities and problems of the husband's role as provider; the notion of marital sex as a wife's duty and a husband's primary right; reproductive and sexual health of women; problems relating to the principle of *wilayah*; polygamy; inheritance problems; female genital mutilation; lack of legal protection for children born out of wedlock; child marriages; kidnapping of women for forced marriage; and interreligious marriages. Teams were generally interested in stories that highlighted the gaps between marriage as experienced and the normative model of gender relations and rights upheld in juristic and societal understandings of *qiwamah* and *wilayah*, as well as any tensions that resulted from such gaps.

The teams sought women who, because of personalities, temperament and/or previous trusting relationships, were capable of reflectively narrating their sometimes traumatic life experiences and describing the transformation in their sense of self and their understanding of the world around them.

We have organized the key findings from the initial analysis into six themes: 1) the myth of the male provider and women's economic roles; 2) sexual relations and rights within marriage; 3) polygamy; 4) divorce; 5) contemporary problems of male guardianship; and 6) women's self-knowledge and relationship to tradition and authority. The stories presented in this chapter are summaries written by the authors or short excerpts of life stories presented in the country teams' reports. It is not our goal here to share the full stories or extensive excerpts.[12] Nor do we claim that the stories and analysis represent the experiences of all Muslim women across all countries and contexts; this would not be possible even in much larger and more extensive studies because of the diversity of individuals, families, contexts, practices and laws. Rather, we present the stories in order to shed light on some patterns and trends of how *qiwamah* and *wilayah* function in the lived realities of these women; to show that there is a disconnect between the juristic model of gender roles and rights in the family and women's life experiences; and to explore how women negotiate and deal with this disconnect.

The myth of the male provider and women's economic roles

A core element of the juristic concept of *qiwamah* is that men have an obligation to provide for their wives and children, for which they can expect obedience in return. One common finding from the collected life stories across different national contexts is that women – whether as single daughters or as wives – are assuming active economic roles in their families. This is particularly true of the resource persons who are poor. Often fathers are unable to provide, earn insufficient incomes, or are deceased, and single daughters are the only family members undertaking the role of providing for the families. Husbands in many cases are absent, unable to earn an income or unwilling to provide.

Despite the fact that men are not actually providing for their wives and children, many families maintain the notion of a male provider/guardian who

---

[12] A larger selection of stories and more thorough analysis will be published in a separate Musawah publication presenting synthesized results from all ten countries.

has authority over his wife and/or daughters. This causes misery and injustice for women because they do not receive the maintenance or protection promised by this patriarchal structure and they continue to experience the oppression of hierarchical gender relations even when shouldering the responsibility of providing for the family. This is exemplified in the life story of Siti Nur Halimah[13] from Indonesia:

> Siti Nur Halimah is a forty-five-year-old woman who has been married and divorced three times. She has a twelve-year-old daughter whom she supports with income earned from selling traditional Indonesian clothes. Siti is also active in advocacy work with a women's rights organization in her village, where she assists other women in obtaining identity cards and provides them with information about requirements for marriage registration.
>
> Siti did not complete her education after high school because her parents decided that the family's meagre financial resources would be allocated for the university education of her brother. Siti did not question this; she was brought up to believe that her father, then her brother or her husband, would protect and take care of her, since they were her guardians.
>
> But since she was a teenager she has worked in different odd jobs to help support her extended family. In her first marriage, she worked in farming and vending and contributed her income to the support of her husband and in-laws. The marriage fell apart because of her in-laws' ill-treatment and husband's travel. In her second marriage, she was saddled with the responsibility of paying the loan that her husband took to pay for the costs of his travel to Malaysia, where he went to look for a job. The husband never came back. Her third husband, who already had another wife, abandoned her during an *Umrah*[14] trip to Mecca while she was pregnant with their daughter because his first wife found out about his marriage to Siti. After her return to Indonesia, Siti was forced to find a way to support herself and her daughter.[15]

Siti Nur Halimah never questioned the injustice of her being deprived of the opportunity to pursue higher education that was given to her brother; she

---

[13] All names are changed unless the resource person granted explicit permission for her name to be used.

[14] *Umrah* is an optional religious trip that a Muslim undertakes to Mecca to perform some of the rituals that are done in the pilgrimage.

[15] Summarized from Siti Nur Halimah's life story as told by Alimat, 'Documenting Women's Life Stories in Dealing with Practices of *Qiwamah* and *Wilayah* in the Muslim Family: Indonesian Pilot Study', January 2012.

did not question that she never received the financial support and protection that were in theory due to her from her guardian when she was single or from her husbands after marriage. For a long time, the active economic role that she played both in her extended family and her three marriages did not affect her belief in this patriarchal structure. This failure to question the disconnect between the reality of her life and the dominant normative model of gender roles is captured in Siti's reflection, 'When I was still married, I treated my husband as the leader and the head of the family even when he did not provide for us, and even when he made my life so miserable.'

But after years of struggling with poverty, working hard to support herself and her family and overcoming failed marriages, Siti became aware of the problems in the gender norms she had been raised to accept uncritically. It was during the *Umrah* trip when her husband abandoned her – while she was in a foreign country, pregnant and with no legal protection or resources – that Siti's experience of injustice, pain and hardship made her reject the patriarchal structure that she had taken for granted. Later, when Siti became involved in an advocacy organization for female-headed households, she had the opportunity to grow, acquire knowledge and skills and bring about change by imparting knowledge to other women and helping them become empowered. She also made a commitment to educate her daughter. She expressed this new sense of self as follows: 'Now I make my own decisions and am free to live my life and I am in control of my own life. Now I am actively involved in PEKKA,[16] I have a lot of friends and have become a legal cadre. As a legal cadre I help people…to get marriage licences for free so that women will not have to go through the pain I went through in my marriages.'

The myth of the male provider and the dependent daughter/wife is also reflected in the life story of Nour, an Egyptian mother of three in her late forties who was working as a taxi driver at the time of the interviews. Nour's life story indicates the problems that women suffer as result of a combination of factors such as harsh economic conditions, a failed education system, a failed state and patriarchal gender norms that promise protection to women but never deliver.

Nour, the eldest of her siblings, grew up in a poor urban neighbourhood in Greater Cairo. Since university, she had to work to help her father support

---

[16] PEKKA (Pemberdayaan Perempuan Kepala Keluarga) is an Indonesian NGO that works with and advocates for female heads of households in rural communities.

the family. After graduation, she gave up a prestigious job as a researcher and worked in a hotel to earn a larger income. Then she emigrated to a Gulf country where she worked as a wedding planner in a hotel and continued to support her family in Egypt, and even paid the marriage costs for her younger sisters and brothers.

During her many years in this Gulf country, she married twice, both times to Egyptian men, and gave birth to three children. Both marriages failed because of conflicts with her spouses about their marital roles, since Nour consistently felt that she was shouldering the financial burden of supporting the family in addition to child care and housework. She felt that both husbands took for granted her economic role while continuing to exercise control over her and withholding emotional and sexual intimacy when they had disagreements over financial issues. The marital conflicts escalated to physical violence.

After her second divorce, she returned to Egypt and tried to start a small business. These efforts failed because of problems with sexual harassment from business associates and the challenges of a precarious Egyptian market that did not really encourage investment. Therefore, she decided to pursue a very unconventional job for women: driving a taxi. The new job is not without its challenges, since her family views the role as socially stigmatizing and unsuitable for a woman, and she sometimes faces harassment from other drivers and onlookers in the street.[17]

Nour's efforts to support her family are both common and essential for poor families in her national context. On the one hand, this economic role granted Nour independence and authority in her extended family. She had the autonomy to make her own choices about marriage partners and arrange her own weddings. On the other hand, this economic empowerment forced life choices on her, such as giving up a prestigious role in order to earn more money, and created tensions in her marriages. Both husbands were dependent on her financial resources and expected her to play a major role in supporting the family. Yet both felt threatened by her role as the main provider and the partner with greater resources, ambition and success. The tension arising from this sense of threat escalated to spousal abuse and violence.

---

[17] Summarized from draft analysis conducted by the Egyptian team and the Global Life Stories Project coordinator in July and August 2013.

In short, the disconnect between the normative model of marital roles ascribed by the principle of *qiwamah* and *wilayah*, on the one hand, and the lived realities on the ground, on the other, result in marital tensions that can lead to economic exploitation of women as wives or daughters and a sense of threat and defeat on the part of husbands.

Sexual relations and rights within marriage

Although sexual relations within marriage are considered the right of both partners in dominant religious discourses (classical and contemporary), the idea that marital sex is primarily a husband's right and a wife's duty still lingers. This is traceable to classical jurists' construction of marital duties and rights as the logic of a husband providing maintenance (shelter, food and clothing) in exchange for wifely obedience, especially in the form of sexual submission (see Mir-Hosseini and Abou-Bakr in this volume). This juristic privileging of a husband's sexual rights within marriage may also be reflected in contemporary Muslim family laws, which for the most part do not recognize marital rape.

This notion of sexual relations as primarily a husband's right is reflected in several of the documented life stories. In the case of Salima from Canada, her free consent and desire were considered irrelevant:

> Salima, a forty-two-year-old Muslim Canadian woman, converted to Islam more than two decades ago. She and her husband were divorced after many years of an unhappy, abusive marriage in which he tried to exercise authority and control over her. Her husband believed that he had the right to sexual relations with her whenever he wanted regardless of how she felt, and justified these ideas on religious grounds. Salima herself shared her husband's views. She was taught that in Islam it was her duty as a wife to submit to her husband and that angels would curse her or God would curse her if she did not fulfil this role. For a long time, she thought there could be no free consent in her sexual relations with her husband. When she felt too sick or too tired and would refuse, she would feel terribly guilty and feared that God would punish her.[18]

---

[18] Summarized from Salima's story as told by Canadian Council of Muslim Women, 'Global Life Stories: Canada Country Report', January 2014.

Shahla, a thirty-one-year-old Iranian medical student, was also in a marriage where the idea of sexual relations as primarily the husband's right was taken for granted and never questioned, yet her deprivation from sexual relations remained unaddressed.

> Shahla married an Iranian who lived in the United States with his parents and brother. Because he had limited financial resources due to his father's illness and costly cancer treatment, her husband proposed that they live with his family. She agreed.
>
> The couple did not consummate their marriage. Shahla attributed this to multiple factors such as the lack of privacy in the house, since they had to sleep in a room adjacent to her in-laws; her husband's lack of affection for her and his discomfort about her wearing a hijab in public (although her father-in-law was adamant about her mother-in-law wearing a hijab); and her husband's low regard for her character, since he often told her that she was too timid and lacked confidence and knowledge.
>
> Five years after getting married, Shahla's husband entered into a temporary (mut'a) marriage[19] with an American woman and justified it on the basis of his right to lawfully fulfil his sexual needs according to Islamic religious norms.[20]

The interviewer reflected that Shahla did not talk about her sexual rights as a wife. She expressed feeling hurt by her husband's treatment, and she struggled with her sense of insecurity and lack of self-confidence because of the difficult relationship she had with her father growing up, as well as her self-consciousness about being overweight and feeling unattractive. She realized that she had not been treated well by her husband and her father-in-law. But she did not question the assumed priority given to her husband's sexual rights and needs.

The idea that a husband has an unfettered right to sexual relations with his wife in some cases results in sexual abuse against women, such as when husbands force themselves on their wives. This was the case with Rashida from Nigeria:

---

[19] Mut'a marriage is a concept recognized by Shia schools of law as a temporary contract of marriage that can be set for a certain period of time. Sexual relations are lawful within this marriage contract.

[20] Summarized from Shahla's story as told by Hoda Mobasseri, 'Global Life Stories: Iran Country Report', January 2014.

Rashida, a thirty-six-year-old Nigerian woman, was married at the age of sixteen. For twenty years, Rashida suffered abuse and lack of emotional and financial support from her husband. She had five children and struggled to provide for them. There were times when she sold her own clothes to buy school uniforms for her children. But when Rashida tried to find work, her husband refused and restricted her movement.

Rashida suffered sexual abuse throughout her marriage. Her husband was a cruel man who felt he was entitled to have marital sex with his wife any time he chose. He often forced himself on her and had very rough sexual relations with her. Once he even forced her to have sexual relations with him although she had recently given birth to one of their children and was still suffering pain and complications from the delivery.[21]

Polygamy

In countries where polygamy is prevalent, such as northern Nigeria and the Gambia, resource persons reported that the practice is justified in their communities on multiple grounds. Communities view polygamy as a religious right held by Muslim men because they believe it is sanctioned by the Qur'an and is linked to a man's *qiwamah*. The common view is that if a man can fulfil his duty to provide, then he can choose whether to take multiple wives. Polygamy is also viewed as beneficial to poor unmarried women or minor girls because such marriages can ensure they have a lawful partner and a provider.

However, the life experiences of the resource persons in polygamous marriages show that these kinds of marriages often put women more at risk of economic marginalization, spousal abandonment, lack of support for their children and lack of emotional fulfilment. In national contexts where polygamy is prevalent and accepted, most of the resource persons did not have a viable option to refuse polygamous marriages. And yet the husbands often do not support all of their wives, so the women must become the main providers for themselves and their children. This is the case of Fatou Bojang, a thirty-two-year-old finance officer in the Gambia:

Fatou Bojang is the second wife of a journalist and has two children with him. After the first few months of the marriage, he stopped supporting her. He

[21] Summarized from Rashida's story as told by IWEI, under the umbrella of Musawah Global Movement (Nigeria), 'Global Life Stories Project: Nigeria Country Report', January 2014.

refused to pay the rent and would not give her any financial provisions; he only gave her money to buy fish and cook for him when he visited. At times, the husband would abandon Fatou Bojang and their children for months. He also started hitting her. Fatou Bojang sought divorce, but her family persuaded her to give her husband and the marriage a second chance. But Fatou Bojang felt that her husband would not change and would most likely fail to support her and the children.[22]

Fatou Bojang's experience provides an example of husbands who take multiple wives, exploit them and let them fend for themselves and their children. Fatou Bojang remained the provider for not only her children but also her younger siblings, since her father was also in a polygamous marriage.

Some women manage to negotiate ways to protect themselves from the risks of polygamous marriages. Fatou Njie, also from the Gambia, initially resisted polygamy, but then found ways to remain economically secure and emotionally content in a polygamous marriage:

Fatou Njie was married at the age of fourteen to a relative of her mother who lived in Spain. Her parents and brother arranged the marriage. She joined her husband in Spain. Five years later, her husband wanted to take a second wife. Fatou Njie refused and insisted on getting divorced when her husband went ahead with the marriage arrangements. Fatou Njie returned to her home country.

Several years later, she realized that polygamy was the norm all around her and she could not avoid it unless she wished to remain unmarried. She agreed to marry a man who already had two wives. But she negotiated with her husband two stipulations. First, she would live in a separate dwelling from his other wives. Second, the income she earned from her work in farming and local politics would be entirely hers; she would not be obligated to contribute to their household expenditure. Her husband agreed. Twenty years later, Fatou Njie felt she got along well with her husband because of the independence and autonomy she had negotiated as well as her active and successful work in community development and politics.[23]

<hr>

[22] Summarized from Fatou Bojang's story as told by GAMCOTRAP, 'Global Life Stories: Gambia Country Report,' June 2014.
[23] Summarized from Fatou Njie's story as told by GAMCOTRAP, 'Global Life Stories Project: Gambia Country Report,' June 2014.

But many women cannot escape the economic marginalization and the abuse that may result from polygamous marriages. This includes Jamila from the Philippines:

> Jamila, a forty-three-year-old paralegal, suffered on multiple levels from being in a polygamous marriage. Her husband betrayed her trust by taking a second and a third wife in secret. He spent their savings on the dower of his second wife, despite the fact that Jamila had brought in some of these savings from her work and family inheritance. Her husband had not been earning an income for several years after his business had faltered. The marital conflict that ensued from the husband's polygamy escalated into emotional and physical abuse against Jamila. Though the husband eventually divorced his third wife, his marriage to Jamila had become a very unhappy and abusive one. Several years later when their three children were in their teens, they finally divorced through a mutual agreement in which Jamila had to give up her post-divorce financial rights.[24]

In short, notwithstanding that resource persons' experiences with polygamy were diverse and complex, the resource persons in such marriages, from different national contexts, suffered economic marginalization, abandonment by husbands and the burden of shouldering all the responsibilities of providing and caring for their children.

Divorce

In most Muslim family laws, men have the right to divorce their wives unilaterally. When women have options for seeking judicial divorce, however, they are often forced to opt for types of divorce that are financially costly and unjust to them. This is because such divorces are quicker to obtain and more likely to succeed than prejudicial divorce (*tatliq/tafriq*) in which female plaintiffs claim harm and are entitled to certain financial rights should they win the lawsuit.

Most of the resource persons who filed for divorce had strong claims to petition for prejudicial divorce, since they suffered spousal harm (e.g.

---

[24] Summarized from draft analysis conducted by the Philippines team and the Global Life Stories Project coordinator in July 2013.

abandonment, emotional and physical violence, non-maintenance). For instance, Jamila from the Philippines and Rashida from Nigeria, whose stories are summarized above, opted for *mubarat/ibr'a* (consensual divorce) and *khul'* (divorce initiated by the woman in which she gives up her financial rights), respectively, although they had grounds for prejudicial divorce.

Premises about marital roles that underlie family laws in most countries often exacerbate the financial marginalization of women at the time of divorce. Many laws assume that husbands provide and wives are financially taken care of by their spouses. The only financial rights that wives are owed from their husbands are *mahr* (dower) and *nafaqah* (spousal maintenance). In the case of divorce in most national contexts, wives are entitled to their dower if they have not already collected it, *'iddah* (waiting period) maintenance, child maintenance and sometimes other forms of compensation specific to the national context. But, overall, wives in most countries have no claim on assets that their husbands acquired after marriage or legally own, even if the assets were jointly purchased but are registered in his name. This model of marital financial rights, on which many Muslim family laws are based, is premised on the assumption that wives have no economic role in the family, including participating in the acquisition of joint assets and resources. This assumption is often false when it comes to women's lived realities. An example is the case of Sarah, a forty-year-old divorced teacher from Indonesia:

> When Sarah and her husband bought a house together with a loan that she secured from the bank, they wrote the deed in his name because that was the prevalent practice in her local community. But when the marriage fell apart and she sued for divorce, she could not claim the house because it was in her husband's name. Nor could she claim the money she spent over many years to support him and their children. Sarah also ended up forgoing her post-divorce financial entitlements (such as the *'iddah* and unpaid spousal maintenance) so that her husband would not derail the process. After the divorce, she continued to live in the matrimonial house with her son; she had agreed to her ex-husband's condition that she would move out if she remarried.[25]

The fact that husbands have an unfettered right to unilateral divorce in some of the countries caused harm to some of the resource persons who were in

---

[25] Summarized from Sarah's story as told by Alimat, 'Global Life Stories Report: Indonesia Country Report (Second Phase)', July 2014.

faltering marriages. For instance, Siti Nur Halimah from Indonesia spent a year trying to substantiate and register her divorce from her first husband, since he merely made a verbal pronouncement of divorce and then disappeared without registering the divorce.

The existence of multiple laws, written or unwritten, that regulate marriage and divorce rights can in theory be beneficial to Muslim women, particularly if there is a state law that guarantees equal marriage and divorce rights to both spouses and/or prohibits polygamy. However, in some cases the resource persons could not benefit from such laws. One such instance is where cultural and religious norms and laws are so dominant in the community that women cannot use the state legal system to pursue their rights and ignore the religious laws unless they are willing to be shunned by their communities. Men often benefit from this situation.

This was the case in Canada. For three of the six resource persons, the husbands used the Canadian laws to claim a fifty–fifty division of matrimonial property when their marriages broke down. In these cases, the women were the main providers and contributed the lion's share of the assets the couple had acquired during their marriage. However, when it came to the right to divorce, or to enter into polygamous marriages, some of these men did not use the state laws. They made divorce pronouncements to end the marriage or took second wives while still married to the resource persons. Although these unilateral divorces and polygamous marriages are not recognized under Canadian laws, they are still acknowledged in the communities and families of the resource persons. Therefore, laws that sanction husbands' unilateral divorces and polygamous marriages impacted on the lives of the resource persons in tangible ways, diminishing the benefits the women could gain from state codes.

The second situation in which benefits of gender-sensitive civil state codes were diminished for some resource persons was when confusion existed about whether these codes applied to Muslim women and, if so, how they would apply when the women were also married under religious laws. This was the case for Jamila in the Philippines, whose story is summarized above. Jamila filed a suit against her husband for committing polygamy because they were married under the state Civil Code, which prohibits polygamy, in addition to their religious ceremony. However, the Philippines has a Code of Muslim Personal Laws (CMPL) as well as the Civil Code, and Muslims in the country fall under its jurisdiction. The law is silent on the status of Muslims who marry under the Civil Code. Accordingly, Jamila's husband was able to take

244 MEN IN CHARGE?

a second and a third wife without any legal implications. Whether Jamila's lawsuit will proceed remains unclear.

Contemporary problems of male guardianship

Guardianship (*wilayah*) in Islamic jurisprudence and modern family laws is premised on the idea that a male guardian provides protection, financial and otherwise, to his wards and manages their affairs (Masud, 2013). This protection entails the authority of the guardian and the dependence and subordination of the ward. This power imbalance can lead to economic and social marginalization and exploitation of young women. Moreover, female wards can be deprived of the protection of their guardians when the latter are either unavailable (because they have died or are absent) or are unable to provide this protection (because of poverty or lack of social justice).

Problems relating to the failure of guardianship as a protection system emerged frequently in life stories where guardians arranged and negotiated marriages for minors. For example, the six resource persons from Nigeria were all married between the ages of fourteen and sixteen. Their marriages were arranged by male guardians (fathers or uncles) or, in one case, a senior female relative (the mother). The common rationale for marriage was to provide financial protection for the young brides and to relieve the families, who were all poor, from the burden of caring for them. But even when they were much younger these resource persons had worked to help support their families, for example as street vendors. Some of them continued working after marriage because they did not get regular financial support from their husbands.

Education of young girls was not valued or seen as a priority in their communities. Once the girls became teenagers, they were viewed as marriage-able commodities. In some cases, the guardian (*wali*) viewed the marriage of a young girl not only as providing her with security but also as an opportunity to maximize family resources, especially when the husband was well-off and would buy gifts and food for her family. After marriage, the resource persons often lived in their in-laws' households, where they came under the authority and guardianship of not only their husbands but also their in-laws. The experiences of these resource persons show that male guardianship over female wards is not functioning as a system through which young women obtain protection and security. In these examples, it has become a structure through which women are subjected to multiple forms of exploitation and marginalization.

Another problem of male guardianship arose from the tendency for state laws and/or societal norms in some contexts to be premised on the notion of male guardianship. This means that state and social institutions are more likely to deal with women only as wards of their guardians, rather than as individuals with claims to full and equal citizenship rights. Where women lack guardians, they are often unable to access important rights such as managing their economic resources, availing themselves of the protection of the state and its social welfare system, and having negotiating leverage when entering into marriage. These translate into experiences of diminished citizenship. The life story of Shukkurjan from Bangladesh illustrates some of these problems:

The father of Shukkurjan, a forty-something divorcee, died when she was six. There was no uncle or grandfather to assume the role of guardian, so her mother became the trustee of the land that her husband left. In this community, the idea of the male guardian was so dominant that people did not like negotiating with her mother regarding the management of their financial resources. Her mother had no experience in dealing with government offices, so some villagers were able to cheat her out of her land for very little money. The family's financial resources dwindled, and Shukkurjan left school to work as a domestic worker along with her sister and mother.

Shukkurjan was married at the age of thirteen to a man she had met in the market and liked. She had no male guardian, which was required in the marriage negotiations; so her employer agreed to assume the role. Shukkurjan did not pay dowry[26] to her husband because in her village, unlike other parts of Bangladesh, it was not customary to do so. However, the issue of the dowry would haunt her throughout her marriage.

After her marriage, she lived with her husband in her in-laws' household. Her in-laws ill-treated her and sometimes even subjected her to physical violence. As her husband began having problems holding a regular job and their financial problems increased, he would abuse her verbally for not paying him a dowry. The verbal abuse escalated into physical violence.

---

[26] Dowry is money and/or gifts given by the bride and her family to the groom. Dowry is not a part of a Muslim marriage contract (in which the groom must give the bride goods and/or cash called *mahr* or dower) but is common in some cultures.

Shukkurjan left her in-laws' house and went back to her mother's house. Soon after, the in-laws arranged a new marriage for the husband and he got a big dowry from his second wife. Shukkurjan realized that there was no hope for her marriage and proceeded to ask for divorce, again with the help of her employer. Her employer managed to get the husband to pay the *mahr* (dower) he owed her. However, she did not receive any post-divorce waiting-period maintenance (*'iddah nafaqah*). Shukkurjan got custody of her daughter in exchange for relinquishing all claims to child maintenance.

Her daughter has now finished university studies and is getting ready to get married. Shukkurjan does not want her ex-husband to be the daughter's guardian when it is time to draw up her marriage contract.[27]

Shukkurjan's story demonstrates how the system of male guardianship over female family relatives becomes the main structure through which women (particularly the poor) can have safety and make claim to and safeguard their financial resources. Shukkurjan's mother could not protect her claims to her husband's land because she was a woman unaccustomed to interacting with government offices and the offices made no provisions to enable such interaction. Shukkurjan and her sister could not complete their education when their father died because the state and society expected other male guardians (uncles, brothers) to provide the safety net for widows and their children, and no one did so. Shukkurjan's ability to negotiate financial rights at the time of her marriage and both financial and child custody rights at the time of her divorce required a male guardian, in this case her employer, to act on her behalf.

In other words, rather than women being guaranteed these rights as citizens, their claims to such rights are conditioned on the presence of a male guardian. The system of *wilayah* not only can give too much power to the guardian at the ward's expense, as exemplified in the problem of minor marriages, but also undermines the responsibility of the state towards women and dilutes their citizenship rights.

Women's self-knowledge and relationship to tradition and authority

Resource persons varied in how they understood the normative authority and dominant knowledge tradition that governs their world and gender rights.

---

[27] Summarized from Shukkurjan's story as told by Samia Huq and Sohela Nazneen (BRAC University), 'Global Life Stories Project: Bangladesh Country Report', September 2014.

Some were ambivalent about this tradition from childhood. This was particularly the case for some resource persons who suffered from oppressive family relations and cultural norms that were justified in religious terms, such as Nadia, a thirty-year-old British woman of Pakistani background:

> Nadia was raised by a father who was very strict and controlling of her movement and actions. Her father justified this role by invoking two notions: as the husband and father, he was the head of their household and the one responsible for their welfare (i.e. *wali* or guardian); as the daughter, Nadia was responsible for safeguarding the honour (*izzat*) of the family by behaving according to expected norms of sexual and moral modesty. But Nadia experienced her father's actions not as offering protection but rather as restricting her and as focused on him and his notion of honour. She felt alienated from her tradition and culture.[28]

Nadia's ambivalence resulted from experiences of marginalization and disempowerment in her teens and young adult years which arose from the intersection between the religious/cultural norm of male guardianship and the cultural notion of women's bodies and sexuality being the marker of their family's honour.

Other resource persons accepted their religious traditions and cultures, but used painful life experiences to reflect on the normative systems that shaped their experiences and choices. This helped them develop in their consciousness and views. The change they experienced did not lead to rejection of religious tradition but to awareness about the injustices women suffer which are justified on religious and/or cultural grounds. This subsequently led them to a different and more active engagement with the normative systems shaping their family relations and gender roles and rights. This is true of Siti Nur Halimah, whose story was presented above. The story of Elham from Iran also illustrates these points:

> Elham grew up believing that it was important for her to live her daily life according to the doctrines and norms set by Allah. She believed a good husband was a blessing from Allah. So when suitors started coming to her father, she prayed to Allah to send her a good man. Amir came from a religious and wealthy family, which made Elham happy. She kept saying *dhikr*

---

[28] Summarized from Nadia's story as told by Mussurut Zia (Muslim Women's Network UK), 'Global Life Stories Project: UK Country Report', March 2014.

and making *du'a* (supplications to God) that the marriage would go through and be successful.

At the beginning of their marriage, Elham felt thankful to God for giving her a good husband. To show her gratitude to God, she was keen to be an even more observant Muslim, which she chose to do by wearing modest clothes. But Elham ended up having a very difficult marriage because of her husband's infidelity and emotional abuse. For a long time, Elham still hoped she would be able to work things out with her husband. She agreed to her in-laws' suggestion to go on an *Umrah* trip with her husband and his family, hoping that this religious trip would bring them closer. But it did not work. After several years of unhappiness, she petitioned for divorce. Now a single parent of their nine-year-old daughter, Elham supports her child with the income she earns from teaching.

The pathway to divorce was empowering for Elham, though stressful. She eventually realized that her well-being and that of her daughter were better served by ending the marriage. She also realized that it was not a religious virtue to stay in a marriage where her partner was unfaithful and emotionally cruel. She no longer agreed with the view of her in-laws and some family members that it was her duty as a good Muslim wife to endure until her husband mended his ways.

During the difficult times in her marriage and when she finally got the divorce, Elham sometimes wondered why she was being punished in her relationship with Amir, when she had strived to be a good Muslim and wife. But five years later she saw her disappointing marriage and the divorce not as a punishment from God but as a pathway to finding inner strength, confidence and fulfilment from her work and raising her daughter on her own in a peaceful home environment where there were no marital conflicts. She no longer perceived marriage as the main way through which she could find happiness. She was now more discerning of who she might want to share her life with, and turned down many marriage proposals because they offered much less than what she wanted out of marriage, namely a monogamous relationship in which her husband was fully committed to her.[29]

---

[29] Summarized from Elham's story as told by Hoda Mobasseri, 'Global Life Stories: Iran Country Report', January 2014.

In the case of Siti Ruqoyyah Ma'shum, a forty-three-year-old Indonesian woman, her relationship to her religious tradition had always been her main source of empowerment and inner strength. But her life experiences and the gender-based abuse she suffered in her two marriages sparked in her an interest in seeking gender-sensitive religious knowledge, which led to her new mission of imparting this kind of knowledge to other women and their families in the community.

Siti Ruqoyyah's father ran a *pesantren* (Islamic boarding school) in east Java, Indonesia, that taught Islamic religious sciences to boys. Accompanying her father all day long, she became well versed in Qur'anic recitation and the religious knowledge that her father was imparting to the students. At the age of nine, Siti Ruqoyyah was engaged to be married to the son of a religious scholar who also ran a *pesantren*. She did not know the meaning of engagement, marriage, husband or in-laws because she was so young.

After her father's death when she was thirteen, she was sent to live with her uncle at his *pesantren*. Soon after, the family held a religious marriage ceremony (*nikah siri*) for her and her fiancé, though the two lived separately for another year. They were married in a religious court. When she asked why she must be married, her mother replied, 'Your father passed away when he was building a *pesantren*. And you are a woman, so there is no way you can lead the *pesantren*. Therefore you should get married so that your husband can take over the *pesantren*.' Her age was increased on the marriage certificate to sixteen; her husband was twenty-five at the time.

Impressed by her interest and outstanding learning abilities, her father-in-law tutored her extensively and relied on her in running his school. Her husband became jealous of her accomplishments and this created tensions between them. When her father-in-law died, her marital problems increased, particularly because her mother-in-law was not supportive. The marriage ended in divorce and Siti Ruqoyyah moved back to her family with her child.

A few years later, she married a divorced man with a son. One of the reasons she was attracted to her new husband was that he had a university degree in Islamic studies. She thought they had a common interest in furthering their religious education. But he turned out to be violent, controlling and unsupportive of her pursuit of education and other professional opportunities. She tried to work things out with him and even supported him in getting elected to the local government council in their hometown. But later she found out that he had taken a second wife in secret. She sued for divorce; the process was extremely acrimonious.

After her second divorce and experience of domestic violence, Siti Ruqoyyah was even more motivated than before to pursue her education. She became interested in teaching religion to girls and women and educating them about the wrongs of gender violence and injustice, particularly from the perspective of Islam. She enrolled in a university to get a degree in Islamic studies and continued to give sermons and religion lessons.[30]

Siti Ruqoyyah believed that justice and dignity for women are central to the religious tradition that was imparted to her by her father and father-in-law. So when her husbands and people in her community marginalized her or other women, it not only contravened her inner sense of what was wrong and right but also changed how she understood and experienced her religion. She learned from the experiences of abuse, violence and injustice in her marriages that she had a mission: to gain and impart enlightened and egalitarian religious knowledge to her community, particularly to women. Therefore, she set up a *pesantren* for young girls. In the *pesantren*, she discusses classical scriptures 'using a perspective of equality and gender justice'. Her goal, she says, is to 'plant the seeds of Islamic understandings that have gender justice perspective' through her teaching and public lectures.

In the context of Belenky et al.'s (1986) theory on women's ways of knowing, as discussed above, the resource persons' reflections on how they made sense of the world around them show that many were living in a position of 'received knowledge', where they accepted and relied on normative authority and dominant forms of knowledge. But, often after painful life experiences, their understandings and consciousness changed and they appeared to shift to the position of 'subjective knowledge', in which they began to question and sometimes reject the received authority and knowledge tradition on the basis of their life experiences. Siti Nur Halimah's and Elham's experiences are good examples of this shift. Siti Nur Halimah and Siti Ruqoyyah, furthermore, sought a new form of knowledge ('constructed knowledge') through reflecting on the insights gained from their experiences, engaging in community activism and learning their religious tradition anew.

---

[30] Summarized from Siti Ruqoyyah Ma'shum's story as told by Alimat, 'Documenting Women's Life Stories in Dealing with Practices of *Qiwamah* and *Wilayah* in the Muslim Family: Indonesian Pilot Study', January 2012.

REFLECTIONS: LOOKING BACK AND LOOKING AHEAD

The Global Life Stories Project is ongoing; it will be some time before the stories can be thoroughly scrutinised and a comprehensive analysis completed. Throughout this process, we have grappled with the challenges inherent in a project of this scope and nature, especially as we have tried to remain true to a set of principles. We have learned that the process necessarily involves compromises and requires honest conversations about choices we make.

A number of points are noteworthy as we contemplate the layered significance of the project, the challenges faced and the general patterns the stories reveal. First, the project was not simply about gathering data on Muslim women, but rather about engaging in a collective process towards gender equality and justice from Islamic and feminist perspectives and building a movement that combines knowledge and activism. The activities included sustained reflective discussions about the issues, our various underlying assumptions and our commonalities and differences. Through the process, we came to know one another across national borders as a group of Muslim women grappling with the question of gender in Muslim tradition, seeking nuanced understandings and multifaceted knowledge, and reflecting on the differences in our perspectives as they have been shaped by our individual trajectories and sociopolitical contexts. We all share Musawah's vision of pursuing gender equality and justice through its four-pronged approach. But there are differences in our views on how to implement this vision.

For example, one of our Skype meetings focused on the issue of child marriage, drawing on readings from Muslim legal tradition. Participants linked the issues in the readings to some of the life stories. We devoted time to reflecting on our underlying assumptions, concerns and driving issues. Three different perspectives were raised. Some felt that patriarchy is inextricable from Islam, but it is strategic to engage with religion for the sake of gender reform. Some believed in and sought the interpretation that best fulfils their aspirations for egalitarian gender norms, not for instrumental reasons, but as part of a personal quest for religious and spiritual knowledge and empowerment. Others were less concerned with the 'truth' of interpretations and more with what certain actors (*Shari'ah* court judges, community leaders, imams, women in leadership positions who perpetuate patriarchal structures of power, etc.) are actually doing with these interpretations. After identifying these perspectives, we examined linkages between our assumptions and the driving issues, on the one hand, and the kinds of arguments we were making in the discussions and our analyses, on the other. This reflective approach enabled us to scratch beneath the surface and glean noteworthy insights not only from the content of the life stories but also from the process through which different project activities were being undertaken and our own perspectives and biases in undertaking them.

Second, both the process and the knowledge outputs of this project are important to advocacy and building movements for equality and justice within each country. Each country team designed its project plan with specific activities and goals linked to advocacy and raising the awareness of different stakeholders. In the Gambia, *Shari'ah* court judges, lawyers and religious scholars were invited to workshops to inform them about the project and to disseminate findings that could improve how they approach cases involving minor marriages, polygamy and female genital mutilation. In Malaysia, capacity building was built into the research plan in the form of monthly study circles and a series of strategy and capacity-building workshops. In Nigeria, the knowledge outputs produced from the stories of women whose early marriages were all problematic will be used to advocate against child marriage.

Third, just as the resource persons changed in their self-knowledge, those developing and implementing the project also evolved intellectually and personally. This happened partly as our capacity and knowledge in the Islamic religious sciences developed. For example, many started the project thinking of *qiwamah* as a Qur'anic concept that means male authority. But, after reading and discussing certain articles (e.g. Lamrabet and Abou-Bakr in this volume), we began to understand that *qiwamah* is first and foremost a juristic concept that serves as a guiding principle for hierarchal gender relations and rights. The process of documenting and analysing the life stories added another rich layer to our new understandings. Some team members, like some of the resource persons, were able to reflect on their own life experiences and grow on an individual level and in their family relationships, drawing on the insights they gained from the project.

Fourth, the process of undertaking the project was empowering for many team members, in terms both of the knowledge gained and of the sense of solidarity that we built through our shared commitment to the goal of gender justice and our growing recognition of and respect for our differences. But though the process was in many ways enriching and fulfilling, it was also emotionally demanding for some, especially those undertaking the documentation mostly or entirely on their own (e.g. in Iran and the United Kingdom). Some project members also felt distressed by the emotional pain that some resource persons exhibited while recounting their experiences. Teams had to ensure that resource persons found adequate support to address any emotional issues raised by taking part in the study.

The multiple ways in which the project has impacted those involved mirrors the multi-layered impact of *qiwamah* and *wilayah* as experienced by the resource persons. A variety of patriarchal normative systems and structures of power intersect in the resource persons' lives, impacting on their life choices and trajectories. Religious concepts such as *qiwamah* and *wilayah* influence social and legal norms, guiding gender relations and rights. They overlap with cultural practices that discriminate against the women, such as privileging boys over girls in education, restrictions on women's movement, stigmatization of divorced women, and general acceptance of essentialist notions about men's and women's nature and capabilities. The poverty and economic hardships that many of the women confront often exacerbate the negative impacts of these intertwined patriarchal systems.

Many *qiwamah*- and *wilayah*-based marriages and family relations did not work because the gender roles constructed by this model were not or could not be fulfilled in the real worlds of the resource persons. Guardians were either absent or unwilling to provide the protection and support that was expected of and needed from them. Husbands were unable or unwilling to provide, which introduced tensions on the part of both spouses. Women as daughters and wives played central economic roles in their families yet did not necessarily gain leverage or gender parity from their contributions. State laws and social norms still sustain the ideology of the authority of the male guardian over the female ward and the husband over the wife, along with the unequal rights allocated to the two genders in these relationships.

In some marriages, men and women fulfilled their ascribed roles, but their relations were strained and conflicts arose because of the hierarchical gender relations that are enabled by the *qiwamah*- and *wilayah*-based paradigm. This frequently happened when couples were unable to negotiate their needs and aspirations successfully within this model.

Many resource persons played active economic roles in their families, thereby departing from ascribed gender roles. But this did not in itself contribute to a change in the women's consciousness or enable them to make life choices that would subvert the hierarchical gender relations of which they were part, and thus end their marginalization.

What enabled some of the resource persons to experience a shift in their situations was the process of gaining consciousness of their position in their family or community. This took place through a journey of self-knowledge and reflection on their life experiences, participation in collective efforts to educate women about their rights and advocate for them, pursuit of enlightened religious knowledge, or a combination of these factors. In addition, some of the resource persons were able to thrive because of positive, supportive family environments in which they were respected as equals and fully appreciated for their contributions or roles in the family.

The process of collecting the stories from this phase of the Global Life Stories Project has been completed; the data require more in-depth analysis and the stories will be shared more widely. As important as the stories themselves, however, is how the project developed and how it demonstrates that research can be conducted in a way consistent with Islamic and feminist values, principles and ethics. By listening, recording and amplifying the voices of the resource persons and their experiences, we multiply our own voices and our movement for equality and justice in the Muslim family.

REFERENCES

Belenky, Mary Field, Blythe McVicker Clinchy, Nancy Rule Goldberger and Jill Mattuck Tarule. 1986. *Women's Ways of Knowing: The Development of Self, Voice and Mind*. New York: Basic Books.

Bruner, Edward M. 1984. 'Introduction: The Opening Up of Anthropology'. In *Text, Play, and Story: The Construction and Reconstruction of Self and Society*, edited by Stuart Plattner and Edward M. Bruner, pp. 1–16. Washington: American Ethnological Society.

DeVault, Marjorie L. 1999. *Liberating Method: Feminism and Social Research*. Philadelphia: Temple University Press.

Doucet, Andrea and Natasha S. Mauthner. 2008. 'What Can be Known and How? Narrated Subjects and the Listening Guide'. *Qualitative Research* 8 (3): pp. 399–409.

Goldberger, Nancy Rule, Jill Mattuck Traule, Blythe McVicker Clinchy and Mary Field Belenky. 1996. *Knowledge, Difference, and Power: Essays Inspired by Women's Ways of Knowing*. New York: Basic Books.

Guerrero, Sylvia (ed.). 2002. *Gender-Sensitive and Feminist Methodologies: A Handbook for Health and Social Researchers*. Quezon City: University of Philippines Press.

Masud, Muhammad Khalid. 2013. 'Gender Equality and the Doctrine of Wilaya'. In *Gender and Equality in Muslim Family Law: Justice and Ethics in the Islamic Legal Tradition*, edited by Ziba Mir-Hosseini, Kari Vogt, Lena Larsen and Christian Moe, pp. 127–52. London: I.B. Tauris.

Moors, Annelies. 1995. 'Crossing Boundaries, Telling Stories: Palestinian Women Working in Israel and Post-structuralist Theory'. In *Changing Stories: Post Modernism and the Arab*

Islamic World, edited by Annelies Moors, Inge E. Boer and Toine Van Teefelon, pp. 17–36. Amsterdam: Editions Rodopi.

Musawah. n.d. *Musawah Strategic Direction: Setting the Foundations for a Dynamic Movement*. Petaling Jaya: Musawah. http://www.musawah.org/sites/default/files/final_0.pdf

Ortlipp, Michelle. 2008. 'Keeping and Using Reflective Journals in the Qualitative Process'. *Qualitative Report* 13 (4): pp. 695–705.

Ramazanoğlu, Caroline with Janet Holland. 2002. *Feminist Methodology: Challenges and Choices*. London: Sage.

Somers, Margaret and Gloria Gibson. 1994. 'Reclaiming the Epistemological Other: Narrative and Social Construction of Identity'. In *Social Theory and the Politics of Identity*, edited by Craig Calhoun, pp. 37–99. Oxford: Wiley Blackwell.

The Ethics of *Tawhid* over the Ethics of *Qiwamah*

Amina Wadud

The most problematic verse I have encountered in over four decades of research on the Qur'an from a gender-inclusive perspective is verse 4:34. This verse is not only used to justify domestic violence – which I have contested through numerous writings (e.g. Wadud, 1998, pp. 69–70; 2006, chapter 6) – but also provides the only textual reference for the idea of *qiwamah* as meaning male authority, protection and superiority. This concept of superiority, which permeates all aspects of society and religious practice, is closely linked to gender doctrines in jurisprudence.

The idea of male authority over women, drawn from the phrase 'al-rijal qawwamun 'ala al-nisa" (men are *qawwamun* over women) in verse 4:34, has been privileged and prioritized over the concept of reciprocity and equality in marital duties and rights as articulated in the Qur'anic phrases 'wa ja'ala baynukum muwaddatan wa rahmah' (and He has made intimate love and compassion between you) in verse 30:21, and 'hunna libasun lakum wa antum libasun lahunna' (they are [like protecting] garments one to the other) in verse 2:187.[1] This was the consequence of the pervasive and unexamined patriarchal contexts at the time of revelation and subsequently during the classical period of Islamic legal development. In other words, the meaning given to *qiwamah*

---

[1] All translations from the original Arabic are my own.

and its subsequent legal applications are constructs built within patriarchal contexts. But patriarchy itself – no matter how benevolently conceived – is neither eternal nor universal. It is subject to radical reconsideration in light of our current understanding of human beings and human relationships with each other and with the divine.

At the onset, I acknowledge that once any such construct is built into a system it is not possible to deconstruct all the ways in which it is manifest and practised nor to disentangle its full impact on explicit aspects of family law and Muslim cultures without seeming to destroy the whole of the law, the culture or the society in which these have become customary. The goal, however, is not mere deconstruction, but rather building a more just society that fulfils the higher objectives of Islam and Islamic ethics.

In this chapter, I share my personal and intellectual trajectory of grappling with the concept of male authority and gender inequality socially, textually and legally, based on my understandings and perspectives on the issues and events that I describe. I also reflect on how my thinking about the issues has developed.

In the first part of the chapter, I look at the context of Islam in America among African-Americans and the impact this context had on my theology, spirituality, ethics and activism. I then outline my engagement with other Muslim women around the world and our struggles to overcome binaries within feminism and religion. At several important junctures in my journey, I realized that the patriarchal family standard in *fiqh* was projected as a given or ideal across time and geography. I had to either accept it, thus rendering my various roles – mother, sister, daughter, in my family and in my life's work – as deviant, or I had to search for a new construct. I opted for developing a new construct.

In the second part of this chapter, I outline the new construct I developed, which is built upon the fundamental Islamic principle of *tawhid*, or monotheism. The tawhidic paradigm offers a way to reach the goal of a society that is built on Islamic ethics and that overcomes the injustice that *qiwamah* entails in our time and in many Muslim contexts. Reaching this goal can only be successful with a paradigm shift; it is not possible to adjust a little here and there without bringing down the whole house of cards. I propose that the ultimate objective of Islam is equanimity and reciprocity, not hegemony, and that this ethic can be applied to gender relations in the family and indeed to all human relations. The paradigm shift is based on rethinking Islam *through* Islam itself, but without the confines of patriarchal interpretations and the cultures they spawned. There is no Islam without *tawhid*. This theological principle can and must be applied to social interactions, particularly to gender relations.

THE HISTORICAL LEGACY OF AFRICAN-AMERICAN MUSLIMS

My interest in developing a new notion of gender relations based on *tawhid* rather than *qiwamah* proceeds from my own free and equal legal agency as a Muslim by choice from the United States. The American Muslim population is a small minority that is extremely complex and diverse.[2] The largest ethnic group of Muslims in America is of African descent, although African-Americans have no unbroken historical or cultural links to any current Muslim nation state. Although a large percentage of those forced into slavery in the Americas came from African Muslim backgrounds, Islam did not survive the brutal North American institution of slavery.

At the end of the nineteenth century, the same century in which slavery was outlawed, African-Americans began to turn voluntarily to Islam. Although substantial numbers of converts come from all ethnic groups in America, including the white majority, African-Americans by far outnumber any other ethnic group or immigrant composite in the numbers of Muslims in America.

The concept of *qiwamah* entails men providing protection and maintenance for women in exchange for those women's obedience. For African-Americans, be they Muslims or not, slavery is the common historical bond. As an institution, slavery precluded the idea of men serving as protectors and maintainers. As slaves, African-American men had no means to protect themselves, let alone their wives, the women of their community, or their children. All were equally subject to the whims of the slaveholder as personal property, no less than a field animal. Any attempt to exert protection was viewed as a threat to white power and would be severely punished – even to death.

Furthermore, every man, woman and child had to work and no one was paid. Therefore, no one could provide for another. There are some cases, rare and often romanticized, when a freed black man – or woman – endeavoured to earn enough to pay the purchase price for members of their biological family who were still enslaved. This did not occur often enough to bring about a systemic change. Thus the situation of slavery did not allow African-

---

[2] For recent statistics, see *Huffington Post* (2014).

American men to assume the role of either 'protectors' or 'providers' for women (and children).

After slavery, during the Postbellum period, any ideal of men as 'protectors and maintainers' was further diminished simply because black women were more likely than men to be given even meagrely paid employment. Furthermore, the perceived threat of African-American men led to the establishment of violent vigilante white supremacy groups, like the Ku Klux Klan, and to treacherous conditions for the security of both black women and men. Black masculinity was deemed a threat to white patriarchy, such that discrimination against black men and boys was standard and violence against black men and boys was rampant. The disparity of employing women over men led to the necessity of reconstructing the black family; some would even call this a kind of matriarchy.

Although African-American women were more likely to be permitted paid employment, they were routinely subjected to white racist and sexist violence, rape and abuse, with little or no means to access anything remotely resembling protection from their men, let alone maintenance. The overwhelming majority of killings resulted from assaults on black men, who were tortured and mutilated with no recourse before the law.

This legacy frames a radically alternative perception and experience of *qiwamah* in the Muslim community from which I come (Wadud, 2006, chapter 4). Ironically, this legacy also led that community to hold a tenacious romantic attachment to the illusion of male power and privilege presumed to be a part of the *qiwamah* construct. African-American Muslims, both women and men, held on to this romantic ideal, despite its conflict with the survival mechanisms for black families in America.

African-American Muslims have used Islamic patriarchy as a construct to counter the burden of the historical legacy of assault on black masculinity and exposure of black women to white patriarchy. The idea of *qiwamah* was an illusion used to support patriarchal constructions of family like those promoted in classical *fiqh* and reflected in many Muslim cultures worldwide, despite the reality of women's greater access to paid employment under racism in America. Even if an African-American Muslim male did not provide sufficiently to support a wife (or wives) and children – let alone extended family members – the family would hold on tenaciously to the *idea* that he was the *qa'im* (head) of the family. As *qa'im* he was due unquestioned obedience and authority. It was not difficult to find cases where the man in the family wanted all the authority even while unable or unwilling to fulfil any financial responsibility.

The tenacious tendency to hold on to the idea that men have authority increased the occurrence of domestic violence. Although domestic violence cuts across race, class and religion, it manifests in the black community in direct relationship to the history of racism. However, in the African-American Muslim context, it was given (false) justification, such that classical interpretations of verse 4:34 became an 'Islamic' right to beat recalcitrant women.

To compensate for the manifest contradictions between an ideal of men as protectors and providers and the circumstances that made it impossible to fulfil this ideal, African-American Muslims would hold onto *qiwamah* as an ideal despite their inability to routinely experience men as the providers and maintainers. This is the dilemma of intersectionality when history, spirituality, political circumstance and economic opportunities collide. The male superiority foundational to Islamic *fiqh* was an idea that was not lived (or experienced) in the realities of black men and women when they began to turn back to Islam in large numbers at the end of the nineteenth century.

To be sure, the path to overcoming systemic racism and its corollary, poverty, meant that black women and men needed paid employment and to further their education while raising their families. This created a dilemma in the growing convert Muslim communities: either men actually did provide for and protect their families, or women compensated in order for their families to survive in racist America. African-American Muslim women also asserted their allegiance to the ideal of the patriarchal, despite the actual realities. If they sought a different model – or addressed the lived realities – it would have been taken as a rejection of Islam because the *qiwamah* of men over women had become synonymous with Islam. In practice, however, African-American Muslim families thrived through a variety of economic arrangements, the most successful being the dual-career household.

The irony is that the notion of a man as the sole provider would be linked to his unquestionable authority and then be projected as an inherent characteristic of all good men – just for being male and Muslim – no matter if he provided little or nothing to the actual maintenance needed by the family. In dual-career households, where both the mother and the father had paid employment, it was not uncommon for African-American Muslim women to downplay their financial contributions while overemphasizing their domestic and childcaring roles. They would subsume their independent earning into domestic upkeep, rendering it invisible under the projection of the 'male-only provider' mirage.

I cannot believe how often I heard the refrain, 'In Islam, a Muslim woman's money belongs to her; she does not even have to pay towards her family.' Meanwhile, I never knew a single family where the woman did not also contribute to the family upkeep.

This is also my story in my various roles as an African-American daughter, sister, wife, mother, divorcee and Muslim scholar-activist. Given this personal context, it is no surprise that my research and textual analysis primarily focused on the ethical values and spiritual worldview of the Qur'an. In part, I was looking to uncover the greater flexibility of a Qur'anic worldview that could support family models used for survival even if these were not encoded in classical *fiqh*, practised by Muslim cultures or apparently even perceived by Muslim modernists. If the family is the primary unit of human survival and African-American families had survived slavery and racism in America, I believed we needed a new notion of an 'ideal' family beyond the *qiwamah* model.

OVERCOMING BINARIES

After completing my doctoral studies, which focused on reading for gender in the Qur'an, I joined the International Islamic University in Malaysia. Within one month, I began meeting with women who were confronting widespread gender inequalities that were often being justified in the name of Islam. At first, the method they used in such confrontations was moral outrage. I recommended a different approach: reading the Qur'an as a way to become better equipped to meet the false justifications. Slowly we began to read the Qur'an together and use our understanding to raise public awareness of the incongruence between the sacred text and certain cultural practices. Through this process, we founded the organization Sisters in Islam and promoted the perspective that there are multiple meanings to interpreting Islam. For us, an egalitarian Islam was primary.

While in Malaysia, I published the first edition of *Qur'an and Woman*, my seminal book on rereading the sacred text from a woman's perspective. More than twenty years later and in new editions, *Qur'an and Woman* has become a major source for the facilitation of women's reading the Qur'an and understanding Islam, which is being used to challenge the fundamental patriarchy that historically and culturally limits women's full agency in Muslim contexts.

As a member of Sisters in Islam, I travelled to the Fourth World Conference on Women in Beijing in 1995, after I had returned to the United States from Malaysia. It was there I first became aware of a tension between various perspectives on gender among Muslim women.

More Muslim women were present at this United Nations meeting than at any previous efforts, so the Muslim participants decided to come together and form a caucus. Each night, however, the caucus meetings descended into chaos. It was not a surprise to anyone that there was great diversity among us – our experiences, perspectives and objectives across countries and cultures obviously varied greatly – but it was disappointing that we were unable to mediate across our differences and that the differences seemed irreconcilable.

In the caucus, two main polarized perspectives emerged that had dominated academic research, political action and international interventions on Muslim women for decades. One side believed that Islam was irretrievably patriarchal, always had been and could never change. Religion, and Islam in particular, could not be accepted as a source for women's liberation and must be kept out of any discussion or discourse regarding women's human rights. Belief, culture or identity are personal matters and should remain out of public space. For the most part, these activists simply articulated their position as wholesale acceptance of international instruments for human rights, including the Convention on the Elimination of All Forms of Discrimination against Women (CEDAW). Underlying this perspective was the adage 'Islam oppresses women'. No effort was made to define Islam, and the global acceptance of this adage would go relatively unchallenged, especially during the rise of Islamism.

The other dominant group took an Islamist stance, projecting itself as authentic, indigenous and authoritarian. The main voices argued that there could be no position for Muslim women without the faith, and, taking the high road of religious elitism, they projected this stance as the most viable opposition to Western hegemony. Islam was presented as a powerful challenge to wholesale acceptance of the 'West' and its history of colonialism and exploitation of third world peoples, including Muslims. Because Islam is a complete way of life and has its own ethical framework and notions of human rights, supported by the primary sources of Qur'an, *Sunnah*, *hadith* and *fiqh*, Islam is the better alternative for establishing the roles of Muslim women in society. However, Islam had to be accepted without question as a mark of faith and identity.

'Islam', whether situated in the time and circumstances of the Prophet and his Companions or after several centuries of Islamic legal theory, was seen as an idyllic proposition or pristine period that could be championed as without error. The solution of our current problems was simply to return and live *that* Islam, unfettered by the historical consequences of the end of empire, the establishment of the nation state, and the formation of the UN.

With 'Islam' primarily defined along these oppositional terms, anyone who questioned this proposition was identified as anti-Islam and accused of being pro-Western. This accusation alone was sufficient to make all conversation moot. Thus all research, activism, policies and politics advocated by anyone who questioned the Islamist agenda and its effects on women's roles were also marked as anti-Islamic.

The caucus of Muslim women during the Beijing conference typified the either/or decision faced by Muslim women's rights activists. How does one proceed when forced to choose between Islam and human rights? The strategy of uncritically using the term 'Islam' while simultaneously critiquing any opposition as un-Islamic was highly effective in gaining support for the Islamist agenda and deterring many Muslim women from clarifying their location between secular feminism and Islamism.

But most Muslim women actually fall somewhere between these two perspectives and perhaps share more in their views with groups, such as Sisters in Islam, who were voicing a third way. For the next decade, this third and more nuanced perspective would get pushed to the side by one or the other of the two dominant agendas. If we accepted human rights standards, Islamists accused us of being Western agents or secular feminists. Meanwhile, many secular feminists and international human rights organizations criticized us for not abandoning our faith perspective, or accused us of being Islamists. Rather than concede to either side, I chose to describe myself as 'pro-faith and pro-feminism'.

The binary between Islam and human rights provided more effective support for a patriarchal Islamist agenda than we find today. Many aligned themselves against Western hegemony in the name of Islam by referring to a shared Muslim heritage ('my grandfather was a *shaykh*') or to their current Muslim culture as a priority over any Western ties. This was done, however, without examining or questioning what 'Islam' is. The 'Islam' that was referred to was generally consistent with classical *fiqh* understandings, thus supporting a patriarchal idea of the family. Men are 'maintainers and protectors' of women, who must defer to men in all things domestic and public. Women need men's protection and provision. To reject any aspect of this proposed ideal was the same as being anti-Islamic, or a feminist, and thus also to be depicted as anti-family and anti-culture.

On the other side, the logic was that the classical *fiqh* perspective on gender relations is patriarchal because it is based on the idea that men are superior to women and that women need men's approval and support for their agency, faith and identity. Thus, Islam itself is patriarchal.[3] The wholesale acceptance of patriarchy as inscribed into Islam means that for anyone to adhere to Islam is the same as to adhere to patriarchy. This was the underlying objection of many Western feminists and human rights advocates, which allowed them to challenge any Muslim woman who still identified as a believer.

What was evident from this period in the gender struggle is that the two dominant voices agreed that 'Islam' had to be patriarchal, had to support female subjugation and male superiority; and that 'feminism' and 'human rights' had to be secular, even, in many cases, aggressively closing out religion (and most specifically Islam) in their construction. Many Muslim women were forced to choose: either Islam without full and equal rights, or human rights and feminism without Islam. This binary can be traced back to the early twentieth century and remained the state of affairs when Muslim women activists tried to come together at the Beijing World Conference on Women.

The rise of Islamic feminism beginning in the late 1980s and continuing through and after Beijing was a reaction to this binary choice. Musawah is one voice among several that have emerged to develop, promote and give evidence for ways of mediating between the two sides of the road to gender reform.[4] This type of effort starts by recognizing the history of and the necessity for believing women and men's active participation in the construction of unifying ideas like 'Islam', 'Islamic ethics' and Islamic law or *fiqh*. It also asserts the need for an active construction and understanding of key terms or ideas like 'democracy', 'human rights' and 'feminism' before they can be applied to the diverse realities of human communities. Gender-inclusive theology and textual analysis are used to demonstrate an inclusive Islam as fundamental and that Islam's major ethical principles, including justice, dignity, honour and agency, are an essential part of the faith. In addition, the lived realities of Muslim women today need to be understood to show

---

[3] One male scholar who considers himself progressive even told me that he believed the 'God of the Qur'an is patriarchal'!
[4] See Anwar (2009).

the disconnect between what is promoted as an Islamic ideal and what is experienced in reality.

Although women's subjugation to men is a common aspect of gender relations in classical *fiqh*, it is not something that must continue to have priority over other constructs of gender relations in Muslim family laws, especially given current lived experiences. The basis for a theological reconstruction of *qiwamah* is the tawhidic paradigm, which can move us beyond centuries of patriarchal theology.

TAWHID: THE ULTIMATE REALITY OF ALLAH AS THE INSPIRATION FOR GENDER EQUALITY

The starting principle and ethical imperative of Islam is *tawhid*. How is this theology of unity applied to living communities and to all aspects of human social interaction, including to constructs of family? Furthermore, how does one move beyond *tawhid* as a utopian abstraction? With these questions facing me, the tawhidic paradigm was an inevitable next step. That step would bring the highest principle of Islamic thought into practical terms for the ways we relate to each other as human beings.

When we look at Islam, it is important everywhere and in every circumstance to distinguish between universal principles and the anthropology of Muslims in diverse communities across history. Reading Islam through its ethical principles has extensive intellectual precedent historically. Human communities, however, live according to standards established through the very process of living, including the frailties and shortcomings that are part of the human experience. When Islam proposes an ethical vision of the world, it is meant for application in real communities, no matter how fragile their practical circumstances. Here I return to the Islamic ethical principles, which have always been part of Islam's intellectual history, to assess the ways in which they have been successfully implemented or thwarted by people who identify as Muslim.

Islam is based upon the ultimate reality of *tawhid*, monotheism, or the unicity of Allah. There are several dimensions to Islamic monotheism. First of all, God is one: '*Qul huwa Allahu ahad*' ('Say: He is Allah the One,' or, 'Say: Allah is One') (Qur'an 112:1). Second, all attributes of Allah and their essences are in absolute harmony and unity. What may seem like contradictions adhere equally to Allah: the One Who Has Wrath is also the One of

Infinite Mercy; the One Who Punishes also has Unlimited Forgiveness; the

Infinite Mercy; the One Who Punishes also has Unlimited Forgiveness; the One Who Gives Life also causes Death. Third, *tawhid* also means Allah is unique: *'laysa ka mithlihi shay'un'* (There is no thing like It) (42:11); *'wa lam yakun lahu kufuwan ahad'* (And there is not one thing like It) (112:4). It is thus impossible for Allah to have gender. He is not male. She is not female. Gender is a social construct often ascribed to the biological sex of animals, plants and women and men. In uniqueness, Allah, the Creator, cannot be subjected to any such created ascription. Furthermore, the Qur'an also describes created things in dualist form: *'wa min kulli shayin khalaqna zawjayni'* (From all created things we made the two-pair) (51:49). Thus female and male are part of the paired system in the created world while Allah, the Creator, is not subject to the conditions and limitations of creation and thus cannot have gender.

Because Arabic is a human language, it functions to reconfirm its own etymological context. The context of Arabic is the patriarchal culture of pre-Islam. This context had an impact not only on the language but also on its usage as the spoken word of Allah through revelation. Sometimes a reader will confuse what can be applied to the Ultimate Transcendent Being because of the words that are used to designate meaning (Wadud, 1998, p. 6). By the very nature of language, all words used to discuss or describe God are limited by their linguistic context. Yet, God is not limited.

Language is inherently unsuitable for discussing the ineffable, but it is the only means we have to engage in discussion. Thus it is not uncommon for certain inherent characteristics adhering to God in Its essence to be misconstrued because of the language used to describe or discuss Allah. 'Language is intrinsically unfitted to discuss the "supernatural" literally' (Burke, 1961, p. 15).[5] For example, in Arabic the word *huwa* is used both as a designation of the male (and of maleness) as well as merely a grammatical term that functions or operates linguistically as a pronoun. It is difficult for some readers to see past the designation for maleness when a term is also used in the Qur'an with regard to Allah, who is unique in *tawhid* and not limited by language – even the language of revelation from Allah.

Interestingly enough, it is easiest for speakers of languages that do not have distinct male and female forms of pronouns to understand a pronoun's potential both to reify gender and to defy it. Because languages like Bahasa Indonesia, Turkish and Persian have only one pronoun form, they understand it as

---

[5] Burke (1961) also says that 'all words for "God" must be used analogically' because these matters 'transcend all symbols-systems' (p. 15).

a grammatical construct and do not tend to make it an essence of gendered meaning. Arabic has two pronouns and these are used for all things sentient, inanimate and even transcendent. English has three pronouns, used to distinguish male and female sentient from non-sentient beings and sometimes with the transcendent. Because English is my first language, I use He/She/It to refer to Allah. This is done intentionally to break the preoccupation that gendered language *must* imply gendered meaning when used in discussions about the transcendent. By avoiding the use of any one particular pronoun I intend to stimulate awareness of the false associations that flow from using only the male pronoun all the time. This is further supported when the Qur'an uses the plural form of the first person pronoun 'We' in reference to Allah, the One. All exegetes interpret the plural pronoun for Allah as allegorical, making the metaphysical reality of oneness take precedent over the literal of grammar.

The theological aspects of *tawhid* described above stem from the oneness and uniqueness of Allah as prescribed under monotheism. However, the word *tawhid* has one other dimension of great importance to social interaction. *Tawhid* also means 'Allah unites'. That is, Allah in Her ultimate sense causes other aspects of atomic, subatomic cellular and stellar reality to *come together over seemingly irreconcilable differences*. This is significant for the differences perceived between people in all social interactions. Thus *tawhid* can serve as the operating principle of unity above hegemony, the latter resulting in dominance and oppression, while the former requires reciprocity, equality and harmony in all human relationships. The tawhidic paradigm is the counter-construct used to overcome the hierarchical terms of *qiwamah* as the basis for social interactions in intimate family relations. It is also an aspect of spirituality that enables integration of the self over psychological and spiritual chaos, with the result that a person becomes unified in wholeness and well-being.

A Muslim is a believer in Islam based on the theology of *tawhid*. This belief has social consequences, since Islam is a way of life and not mere theology. As a worldview, this theological construct has certain practical implications for those who profess to believe in Islam. The tawhidic paradigm also has universal dimensions that I shall discuss below in relation to human rights. The point here is that, from an Islamic perspective, social interactions must unquestionably be grounded in *tawhid*. Belief in *tawhid* precludes anyone who identifies as Muslim from developing 'special exemptions' in the social and political applications of *tawhid*, since a core principle of this paradigm is that just and egalitarian relationships among humans are an integral part of seeking a relationship of 'engaged surrender' to God and affirming God's unity (Wadud, 2006, p. 22).

Qiwamah not only requires unequal relations; it also requires men exclusively to be the providers and protectors for women (and children). This implies that women are incapable of providing for or protecting themselves, or men, or children. The factual evidence is against this in the sheer numbers of female heads of households. Women around the world provide for themselves, for men and for children. Women also protect themselves, men and children. My goal here is to articulate the significance of an egalitarian perspective on gender relations based upon Qur'anic principles and Islamic ethical mandates.

Too much has been said about verse 4:34 and its unequivocal statement that men are qawwamun over women. The Qur'an contains both descriptive and prescriptive passages. Sometimes, a description has been further elaborated by the development of culture, history and law so that it has turned into a prescription. Omaima Abou-Bakr's chapter in this volume discusses how the Qur'an's descriptive reference to qawwamun turned into a prescription. During the classical period, Muslim societies operated with near total female dependence and qiwamah needed to be enforced for their protection. However, human communities, including Muslim families, no longer live in exclusively patriarchal contexts. The verse in question represents a description of one way of organizing families during pre-modern times, but that way is no longer efficient and ethical in our current social and cultural realities.

While some may propose that we simply go back to such pre-modern circumstances, such a proposal is untenable given the plurality and complexity of today's world. It is my contention that verse 4:34 may describe a scenario popular at the time of revelation, but that it does not prescribe it as an irrefutable and irreplaceable commandment that must be encoded in the law and practised by all who adhere to Islam as their way of life. It was of great consequence that classical fuqaha gave so much emphasis to this term when the Qur'an expresses also the rudiments of equitable, reciprocal relations between women and men in the family. These egalitarian postulates were ignored or seen as tangential. The reasons for now making the egalitarian verses more prominent are both circumstantial and textual.

I propose a way forward in which primary Islamic theology can support policies, and these policies can be used to fulfil our ethical vision as Muslims. The tawhidic paradigm links us to the core and fundamental values of Islam while propelling us out of the quagmire of patriarchy that threatens the life, well-being and continuity of our communities. The social application of *tawhid* leads to egalitarian families in egalitarian societies.

Understanding the contexts for such a hegemonic structure allows us to move forward with the Qur'an and not go against Islam. Irrespective of how benevolent it was for men to hold an exclusive right to authority over women at some point in history, Muslim communities are not constructed that way now. A positive view of this historical reality does not support a negative view of contemporary reality. More importantly, Muslims need to look coherently for a way forward. Fortunately, that way has already been presented in the Qur'an. It is clear that it is mandatory for us to embrace its full implication and practical implementations under an ethic of *tawhid*.

THE WAY FORWARD

My experience as an African-American Muslim woman shows that even in a culture where Muslim women were supporting the men and children in their families, they were forced to promote the false *qiwamah* construct that says that Muslim men are authority figures, protectors and providers, or else be seen to be against Islam. Needless to say, the *qiwamah* 'ideal' is even more strongly defended in other Muslim cultures. When Muslim women have questioned the construct or talked about gender equality, they have repeatedly been presented with two opposing views: either promote human rights, which include gender equality, and give up Islam, or give up these 'Western constructs' and stick with Islam. As a unifying principle, *tawhid* moves us beyond these unnecessary binaries towards greater harmony and becomes the foundation for arriving at a perspective that promotes gender equality and embraces both Islam and human rights.

'Human rights' can quite simply be seen as constructs based upon fundamental ideas about what it means to be human. We can draw on Muslim sources to understand such rights and uphold them. The basic Islamic construction of what it means to be human starts with Qur'anic verse 2:30: '*inni jaa'ilun fi al-'ard khalifah*' (I will surely create on the earth a *khalifah*). The basic teleology, or divine purpose, for human creation on the earth is to be a *khalifah*.[6] A *khalifah* is an agent of the divine will. While Islamic law seems to reduce the divine will to a set of precepts and practices, *khilafah* as

---

[6] For further discussion of this idea, see Lamrabet in this volume.

agency is really an ethical term. It means one who is free to choose, namely right from wrong, but also one who is competent to control the choices he or she makes. This free will is essential to the idea of the human being in Islam. Free will cannot be limited to male persons and then made contingent upon family for female persons – even though this is how many aspects of classical *fiqh* operate and how many Muslim patriarchal cultures developed and still practise.

Islamic ethics is more than a set of dos and don'ts, or rules and postulates. The divine will extends beyond the historical constructs of human communities. It affects the entire universe. Key to the order of the universe is, of course, *tawhid*, because the whole universe is unified, orderly and harmonious. Using this Qur'anic construction, the human being is an agent of *tawhid*. The moral responsibility of all humans is to support and maintain harmony and reciprocity between self and other.

Throughout my years of studying Islamic ethics and spirituality, I have been struck by the way the dominant discourse has constructed human relations in a vertical line. Allah, the highest metaphysical essence, was at the top. Man, or the male person, was in the middle. This position was not only in direct relationship below Allah, but also above woman, or the female person, who was at the bottom:

Sometimes this was made colourful by metaphorical analogies with other essential pairs in the creation. For example, Sachiko Murata explains in the introduction to *The Tao of Islam* that the Qur'an says everything is created in pairs and 'several of the pairs…take on special importance', including the Pen and the Tablet, and the Heavens and the Earth (1992, pp. 12–13). These were then put into a necessary contingent relationship: 'Without the Tablet the Pen could not write' (p. 13). So whatever the Pen wrote required the Tablet in order to be manifest. Likewise the analogy of the Heavens and the Earth: whatever the Heavens brought down had to be taken up by the Earth. '[T]he term *heaven* refers to everything that stands above something else, while the term *earth* refers to everything that stands below something else...[T]here is always a heaven and an earth, an aboveness and a belowness, in creation' (1992, p. 13).

There is no problem with these models with regard to the metaphysics of Allah's supremacy, but the impact is profound when they become parallel to human relations: some one(s) has to be above and some one(s) has to be below. Following the vertical direction down from Allah to the man, we note there is a direct relationship to the Creator. Yet the underlying principle of Islamic theology also holds an unconditional, direct and unmediated relationship between Allah and *every* human being. In this vertical model this *only* applies to the man. The model does not provide direct access between the female, the Tablet or the Earth (at the bottom) and Allah – except as mediated by the male, the Pen or the Heavens in the position between her and Allah. It seems simple enough: the model is flawed and the consequence of the flaw is also evident in the way patriarchy functions in Muslim communities.

As I struggled to imagine another model to replace the female in full and free agency directly connected to Allah, I came up with the tawhidic paradigm (Wadud, 2009, pp. 107–9).

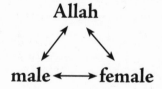

The tawhidic paradigm maintains the metaphysics of Allah's supremacy, located at the top. However, it reconstructs the diagram so that male intervention between the female and Allah is replaced. It removes the female's dependency on the male and returns her to a direct line with the divine. As a result of placing the female as well as the male – human agents before Allah – in a direct line with the divine, the human-to-human relationship can only be constructed horizontally, as one of mutual support and reciprocity.

So, as the Qur'an says in verse 2:187, '*hunna libasun lakum wa antum libasun lahunna*' (they are [like protecting] garments one to the other). By virtue of *tawhid*, a horizontal line of equality and reciprocity operates between each and the other; the same construction of human rights and substantive justice. From this Islamic perspective, justice can only be reciprocal and equal. No human being, no group of human beings, no class, race, gender or other aspects of orientation and ability can be in a location that disrupts the direct relationship of other beings, other groups, gender, races or orientations from direct interaction with Allah.

Qur'anic cosmology gives an interesting version of the vertical model, where one intervenes between Allah and the full agency or *khilafah* of another. It is the story of Iblis with the primordial parents in the garden before earthly existence. As the story goes, upon the completion of the human creation, all unseen beings were asked to bow down to Adam to indicate both their obedience to Allah and their acceptance of the superiority of this agent created by Allah: the human being. Satan refused to bow. When asked why, Satan said, 'I am better than him. I am made from an atom of fire and that being is made from an atom of dirt.'

Throughout the Qur'an, this becomes a kind of satanic logic that prevails when one group (or gender) proposes to *be better* than another group (or gender). I call this the logic of *istikbar* (from the root form of the word *kabura*), which means 'to make oneself better than another'. It was demonstrated primordially by Satan and became a moral lesson for all humans to avoid this sort of thinking. Patriarchy is not only satanic logic; it also constructs entire systems based on that logic. This is the way *qiwamah* is used to limit women's potential – by affirming their deference to men. At the same time, the *qiwamah* model of gender relations implies that men are better just because they are men. The logic is nonsensical because women are actually human beings too. It makes men more than merely human, or justifies oppression of women as deviant or deficient humans. Women become less than men and in need of men for protection or maintenance.

Then the protection is constructed as a kind of generosity and benevolence. Women need men in order to be whole; a woman must only defer to a man to gain the much deserved honour of being cared for by him, the superior being. Eventually other reasons are contrived to give further credence to this skewed logic, like biological differences, intellect and even the difference in prayer performance arising from jurisprudence on menstruation. It is when these are falsely reflected back onto Allah that the logic reaches the epitome of corruption. Allah is blamed for this construction, and there is nothing a believer can do but surrender. The Qur'an is emphatic: Allah does not do *zulm* (oppression). Thus, *zulm* is human-made and must be alleviated by human beings. Allah, on the other hand, operates on the basis of *tawhid* universally manifest as unity, harmony and justice.

Although consideration of the tawhidic paradigm began with specific concerns over unequal gender relationships as encoded in Islamic jurisprudence and practised in patriarchal cultures worldwide – including among Muslims – its implications are more widespread. It was like unravelling the Islamic equivalent of the Martin Buber (1958) ethics of reciprocity in the 'I–Thou' formula. Whenever another human being is made a utility for the full moral agency and practical function of another human being, that person becomes an 'it' to the 'I' of the first person. That is exploitation, corruption and inequality. Not only was this an important personal discovery for me when it was applied to rereading Islamic ethics, but it also shed light on the basic paradigmatic flaw that undergirds so much of jurisprudence, patriarchal ethics and philosophy in the Islamic intellectual legacy. It was then necessary to consider how a tawhidic paradigm of equality and justice could be applied to social contracts, including marriage. For, though I did find traces of this discourse about *tawhid* and social justice (Lakhani, 2006), it was limited to relationships between males: ruler to ruled, teacher to student, etc. Nowhere was its application to gender ever considered.

Clearly it was necessary to come to the understanding that gender is a category of thought. We have to ask time and again whether our constructs and our postulates are meant to privilege one human being over another and in particular one gender over the other. Although human systems often prefer one group over another, such a construct cannot be assigned divine sanction because it not only removes us from the full responsibility and consequence of our actions, but also reduces the divine to a projection of our whims.

Every person, male or female, is a *khalifah* before Allah, responsible not only in a patriarchal system but beyond patriarchy in egalitarian systems. Any construct of the divine–human relation that reduces another person to a subcategory is doomed to fail. This has to be applied to gender. No matter how long patriarchy has been the bulwark of human communities, it is unsustainable, untenable and un-Islamic. Islamic personal status laws are up against their own error of unequal relations. It is futile to ignore the realities of diverse family constructs by continually resorting back to a system that is no longer tenable today. Women are full agents in the family, in society, in Islam and as human beings. We have the capacity and responsibility to fulfil roles according to our diverse circumstances and ecological arrangements – public, private and spiritual.

REFERENCES

Anwar, Zainah. 2009. 'Introduction: Why Equality and Justice Now'. In *Wanted: Equality and Justice in the Muslim Family*, edited by Zainah Anwar, pp. 1–9. Petaling Jaya: Musawah.

Buber, Martin. 1958. *I and Thou*, translated by Ronald Gregor Smith. New York: Charles Scribner's Sons.

Burke, Kenneth. 1961. *The Rhetoric of Religion*. Boston: Beacon Press.

Huffington Post. 2014. 'Muslim-American Demographics Reveal a Diverse Group that Rejects Categorization'. 26 March. http://huff.to/1h9Jbfa

Lakhani, M. Ali (ed.). 2006. *The Sacred Foundations of Justice in Islam: The Teachings of 'Ali ibn Abi Talib*. Bloomington, IN: World Wisdom.

Murata, Sachiko. 1992. *The Tao of Islam: A Sourcebook on Gender Relationships in Islamic Thought*. Albany: State University of New York Press.

Wadud, Amina. 1998. *Qur'an and Woman: Re-reading the Sacred Text from a Woman's Perspective*. Oxford: Oxford University Press.

Wadud, Amina. 2006. *Inside the Gender Jihad: Women's Reform in Islam*. Oxford: Oneworld.

Wadud, Amina. 2009. 'Islam Beyond Patriarchy through Gender Inclusive Qur'anic Analysis'. In *Wanted: Equality and Justice in the Muslim Family*, edited by Zainah Anwar, pp. 95–112. Petaling Jaya: Musawah.

About the Contributors

Omaima Abou-Bakr is a professor of English and comparative literature at Cairo University, Egypt. She specializes in medieval Sufi poetry and comparative topics in medieval English and Arabic literature. Her scholarly interests also include women's mysticism and female spirituality in Christianity and Islam, feminist theology, Muslim women's history, and gender issues in Islamic discourse. She has published a number of articles in both English and Arabic on poetry and medieval literary texts, historical representations of women in pre-modern Muslim societies, women and gender issues in religious texts, and Islamic feminism. Her most recent publications are two edited volumes of collected articles: *Feminist and Islamic Perspectives: New Horizons of Knowledge and Reform* (2013) and *al-Niswiyyah wa al-Manzur al-Islami* (2013). Omaima is also a cofounder and board member of the Egyptian NGO Women and Memory Forum.

Mulki Al-Sharmani holds a doctorate in cultural anthropology from Johns Hopkins University, United States. Since September 2013, she has been a lecturer and a research fellow at the Faculty of Theology, Study of Religion Unit, University of Helsinki, Finland, working on two research projects: 'Islamic Feminism: Tradition, Authority, and Hermeneutics' and 'Transnational Muslim Marriages in Finland: Law, Gender, and Wellbeing'. From 2010 to 2011, Mulki was a research fellow at Helsinki Collegium for Advanced Studies, University of Helsinki. From 2005 to 2010, she was a joint research–teaching faculty member at the American University in Cairo. Mulki is a member of the Musawah Knowledge Building Working Group and coordinated the Global Life Stories Project focusing on *qiwamah* and *wilayah*. She is the editor of *Feminist Activism, Women's Rights, and Legal Reform* (2013).

Ayesha S. Chaudhry is an assistant professor of Islamic studies and gender studies in the Department of Classical, Near Eastern and Religious Studies and the Institute for Gender, Race, Sexuality and Social Justice at the University of British Columbia, Canada. Her research interests include Islamic law, Qur'anic exegesis and feminist hermeneutics. She is the author of *Domestic Violence and the Islamic Tradition: Ethics, Law and the Muslim Discourse on Gender* (2014). This book explores the relationship of modern Muslims to the inherited Islamic tradition through a study of legal and exegetical discussions of wife-beating in the pre-and postcolonial periods. Currently, she is working on a collaborative project on interfaith feminist hermeneutics entitled 'Difficult Texts or Difficult Women? The Challenge of Scripture to Feminist Readings', which explores and challenges the limits of feminist interpretations of patriarchal religious texts in the three Abrahamic faiths. She is an Early Career Scholar at the Peter Wall Institute for Advanced Studies and the recipient of the Research Mentorship award for an interdisciplinary project on domestic violence. Ayesha is also developing methods of bridging the academic–community divide by translating her research interests into performance art. This project, entitled 'Cover Story', explores the meanings of multiple intersecting political discourses surrounding Muslim women's sartorial choices.

Asma Lamrabet has been the director of the Research Center on Women's Studies in Islam of Rabita Mohammadia des Oulémas in Morocco since its founding in 2010. She is also a haematologist at Avicenna Hospital in Rabat, Morocco. She has studied women's issues in Islam for many years and has delivered lectures on this topic at various conferences around the world. From 2004 to 2007, she was the coordinator of a research and reflection group on Muslim women and intercultural dialogue in Rabat. She was the president of GIERFI (International Group of Studies and Reflection on Women and Islam) and is currently a member of its board of directors. She is also the author of many articles tackling Islam and women's issues, as well as numerous books, such as *Musulmane tout simplement* (2002); *Aïcha, épouse du prophète ou l'islam au féminin* (2004); and *Femmes et hommes dans le Coran: quelle égalité?* (2012), for which she received the Arab Woman Organization award in social sciences in 2013.

Lena Larsen has been the director of the Oslo Coalition at the Norwegian Centre for Human Rights, University of Oslo, Norway, since 1999. She obtained her PhD with a thesis on 'Islamic Legal Thought and the Challenges of Everyday Life: Fatwas as Proposed Solutions for Muslim Women in Western Europe' (in Norwegian, 2011). She coedited *Gender and Equality in Muslim Family Law: Justice and Ethics in the Islamic Legal Tradition* (with Ziba Mir-Hosseini, Kari Vogt and Christian Moe, 2013) and *New Directions in Islamic Thought: Exploring Reform and Muslim Tradition* (with Kari Vogt and Christian Moe, 2009) and was an associate editor of *Facilitating Freedom of Religion or Belief: A Deskbook* (with Tore Lindholm, W. Cole Durham, Jr, Bahia Tahzib-Lie and Elizabeth Sewell, 2004). These publications are a result of projects of the Oslo Coalition on Freedom of Religion or Belief.

Ziba Mir-Hosseini is a legal anthropologist specializing in Islamic law, gender and development. She has a BA in sociology (1974) from Tehran University, Iran, and a PhD in social anthropology (1980) from the University of Cambridge, United Kingdom. A professional research associate at the Centre for Middle Eastern and Islamic Law, University of London, United Kingdom, she has held numerous research fellowships and visiting professorships, including fellow of the Wissenschaftskolleg zu Berlin, Germany (2004–5), and visiting professor at the Hauser Global Law School, New York University, United States (2002–8). She is a founding member of Musawah. Ziba's publications include *Marriage on Trial: A Study of Islamic Family Law in Iran and Morocco* (1993, 2002); *Islam and Gender: The Religious Debate in Contemporary Iran* (1999); *Islam and Democracy in Iran: Eshkevari and the Quest for Reform* (with Richard Tapper, 2006); and *Control and Sexuality: The Revival of Zina Laws in Muslim Contexts* (with Vanja Hamzic, 2010). She coedited *Gender and Equality in Muslim Family Law: Justice and Ethics in the Islamic Legal Tradition* (with Kari Vogt, Lena Larsen and Christian Moe, 2013). She has also codirected two award-winning feature-length documentary films on Iran: *Divorce Iranian Style* (1998) and *Runaway* (2001).

Jana Rumminger is a human rights lawyer who has been based in Southeast Asia since 2004. Her scholarship and activism have focused on human rights issues at the intersection of gender, race/ethnicity and religion. She has worked with Musawah in a variety of roles since 2007, including coordinating the project in the lead-up to the 2009 launch and coordinating the Knowledge Building Initiative on *Qiwamah* and *Wilayah* since 2011. She has also worked with a number of women's rights organizations in South and Southeast Asia, such as International Women's Rights Action Watch Asia Pacific, Sisters in

Islam, Women's Aid Organisation and South Asia Women's Fund, as well as several non-profit organizations in the United States.

Sa'diyya Shaikh is an associate professor in the Department of Religious Studies at the University of Cape Town, South Africa. Working at the intersection of Islamic studies and gender studies, she has a special interest in Sufism and its implications for Islamic feminism and feminist theory. Her areas of research include gender-sensitive readings of *hadith* and Qur'an; theoretical debates on Islam and feminism; religion and gender-based violence; and an empirical project entitled 'South African Muslim Women, Marriage, Gender and Sexuality'. Her published books include *Sufi Narratives of Intimacy: Ibn Arabi, Gender and Sexuality* (2012) and *Violence against Women in Contemporary World Religion* (coedited with Dan Maguire, 2007). Sa'diyya is married, a mother of two, and a student of Bawa Muhaiyaddeen.

Marwa Sharafeldin is a women's rights activist based in Cairo, Egypt. She has a PhD in law from the University of Oxford, United Kingdom. Her research covers Islamic law, international human rights law, civil society and women's rights. She is a campaigner for the reform of personal status laws in Egypt, a member of Musawah's International Advisory Group, and has been actively involved with Musawah's Knowledge Building Working Group. She is also the cofounder of an Egyptian network for women's rights organizations and of the Young Arab Feminist Network, as well as the NGOs Fat'het Kheir and Nahdet El-Mahrousa in Egypt. Since the beginning of the Egyptian revolution, she has been involved in several women's groups and activities to advocate for better women's rights in the transitional process and the ensuing constitutional-drafting processes. Marwa is also a story collector and a writer. Her writings, which focus on women's issues, have been published in widely circulated Egyptian publications such as the newspapers *Al-Masry Al-Youm* and *Al-Shorouk*.

Amina Wadud is Professor Emeritus of Islamic Studies and a visiting scholar at the Starr King School for the Ministry, part of the Graduate Theological Union, in Berkeley, California. She is author of the groundbreaking *Qur'an and Woman: Re-reading the Sacred Text from a Woman's Perspective* (1992), now translated into over a dozen languages. Her follow-up publication, *Inside the Gender Jihad: Women's Reform in Islam* (2006), traces the route of gender-inclusive theology into social action and policy reform. Since her retirement she has been an independent scholar, having previously taught at International Islamic University, Malaysia; Gadjah Mada University, Yogyakarta, Indonesia; University of Melbourne, Australia; and in the United States at Harvard Divinity School, California Institute for Integral Studies and Virginia Commonwealth University, among others. She is currently an international consultant on Islam, gender and human rights. One of the founders of Sisters in Islam, Amina frequently serves as a resource person for Musawah knowledge-building and capacity-building activities. She is known as the Lady Imam for her efforts to live justice and equality for Muslim women in all aspects of her life: intellectual, spiritual, moral and political. She is also a proud mother and grandmother.

Lynn Welchman, a professor at the SOAS School of Law, University of London, United Kingdom, specializes in law and society, Muslim family laws, women's rights and human rights in the Middle East and North Africa. She has published widely in her research areas, including the book *Women and Muslim Family Laws in Arab States: A Comparative Overview of Textual Development and Advocacy* (2007). Her edited volumes include *'Honour': Crimes, Paradigms and Violence against Women* (with Sara Hossain, 2005) and *Women's Rights and Islamic Family Law: Perspectives on Reform* (2004). Before joining the SOAS staff in 1997, she worked in human rights, primarily with Palestinian human rights NGOs on the West Bank, but also with international human rights organizations, mostly in the Middle East. She is a board member of the Euro-Mediterranean Foundation for the Support of Human Rights Defenders and a founding coeditor of the *Muslim World Journal of Human Rights* and the Oxford Islamic Legal Studies Series. In 2007 she established the International Human Rights Clinic in the SOAS School of Law.

Index

Shaltut, Mohammed 83
Sharafeldin, Marwa 8, 163–96, 278
shar'i 48n6, 139, 141–2, 155
Shari'ah
  'return to', slogan 18, 24, 36
  and *fiqh* 29, 36, 38, 107, 109,
    112–4, 165–6, 169, 181, 189,
    200
  Shari'ah councils 146n15, 197–8,
    203
  Shari'ah courts 139, 166, 188,
    251–2
Sisters in Islam 261–3
slavery
  in Muslim contexts 15, 21, 26, 68,
    79, 81, 104n15
  in North America 258–9, 261
Sonbol, Amira 136–7
stipulations in marriage contract, *see*
  marriage contract
Sufi 5, 31, 45, 57, 106–31
  thought 108–9, 114, 118
  psychology 107, 115, 117
Sunnah 20, 25, 89, 94–9, 103, 166,
  190, 262

ta'a, see obedience
ta'dib 16, 47, 142, 144–5
tafsir, 'ilm al-tafsir 44–64, 80, *see also*
  hermeneutics
talaq, see divorce
tamkin, see obedience
tawhid 67, 81, 119, 257–8, 265–73
tawhidic paradigm 257–8, 265,
  267–9, 271–3
Taymur, A'isha 57–8
testimony, women's 110, 123–4
thayyib 96–8, 151–2
theological imperatives 107, 109, 111,
  117
Tucker, Judith 134, 136
Tunisia 19–20, 23, 38, *see also* family
  laws, Muslim

ulama (sing.*'alim*) 25, 30, 47, 49,
  93–4, 102, 206–7, 213–4, 216
United Arab Emirates, *see* family laws,
  Muslim
United Kingdom 146, 154, 205–6,
  208–11, 247
usul al-fiqh, see Islamic jurisprudence

veil, veiling, *see* hijab
vicegerency, *see* khilafah
virgin 95–9, 151–2

Wadud, Amina 9–10, 29, 48, 52, 58,
  60–1, 256–74, 278–9
Welchman, Lynn 7–8, 15, 132–62,
  178n11, 279
wilayah 2, 34, 57–8, 72, 75, 80, 86, 88,
  95–100, 102, 149–55, 157, 167,
  180, 219, 233–5, 244–7, 253
  financial 59, 149–50, 157, 167,
    169, 174–6, 179, 185, 235,
    244, 246
  in marriage 1, 2, 94–102, 133,
    150–5, 157, 174–5, 219,
    244–6
  over children 1, 4, 101, 133,
    149–50, 154, 157, 167, 169,
    174–6, 179, 185, 219, 233, 246
wali 2n2, 72–2, 151–2, 244, 247
women's rights 4, 16, 24, 26, 28–30,
  38, 104n15, 114, 136–8, 146, 148,
  155–6, 186, 191, 214, 216, 222,
  234, 263
women's self-knowledge 233, 246,
  252, 254
Women's Ways of Knowing 230–1,
  250
Würth, Anna 154

Zaytouna 19
zulm 272–3, *see also* justice